ISRAELI–SOVIET RELATIONS
1953–67

ISRAELI–SOVIET RELATIONS
1953–1967

From Confrontation to Disruption

YOSEF GOVRIN

FRANK CASS
LONDON • PORTLAND, OR

First Published in Hebrew in 1990 by the Magnes Press,
Hebrew University of Jerusalem, Jerusalem

First English edition published in 1998 in Great Britain by
FRANK CASS PUBLISHERS
Newbury House, 900 Eastern Avenue
London IG2 7HH

and in the United States of America by
FRANK CASS PUBLISHERS
c/o ISBS, 5804 N.E. Hassalo Street
Portland, Oregon 97213-3644

Website http://www.frankcass.com

Transferred to Digital Printing 2004

Copyright © 1998 Yosef Govrin

British Library Cataloguing in Publication Data:

Govrin, Yosef
Israeli–Soviet relations, 1953–67 : from confrontation to
disruption
1. Israel – Foreign relations – Soviet Union 2. Soviet Union
– Foreign relations – Israel – 1953–1975
I. Title
327.5'694'047

ISBN 0-7146-4872-8 (cloth)
ISBN 0-7146-4427-7 (paper)

Library of Congress Cataloging-in-Publication Data:

Govrin, Yosef.
  [Yaḥase Yiśra'el Berit-ha-Mo'atsot. English]
  Israeli–Soviet relations, 1953–67 : from confrontation to
disruption / Yosef Govrin. – 1st English ed.
    p.   cm.
  Includes bibliographical references and index.
  ISBN 0-7146-4872-8 (cloth). – ISBN 0-7146-4427-7 (pbk.)
  1. Israel–Foreign relations–Soviet Union. 2. Soviet Union–
Foreign relations–Israel. 3. Soviet Union–Foreign
relations–1953–1975. I. Title.
DS119.8.S65G6813   1998
327.5694047–dc21   97-45497
                                                             CIP

Typeset by Vitaset, Paddock Wood, Kent

To my wife Hanna and our children Leora and David
with love

Contents

List of Illustrations

Abbreviations

CPSU	Communist Party of the Soviet Union
ECOSOC	Economic and Social Council of the United Nations
GA	General Assembly of the United Nations
Maki	Miflagah Komunistit Israelit, Israeli Communist Party
Mapai	Mifleget Po'alei Erez Israsel, Israeli Labor Party
Mapam	Mifleget ha-Po'alim ha-Me'uhedet, United Workers Party
MFA Arch.	Ministry of Foreign Affairs Archive
MK	Member of Knesset (Israel Parliament)
PLO	Palestine Liberation Organization

Letter to the Reader

Dear Reader,

I was First Secretary of the Israeli Embassy in Moscow when the Soviet government informed the government of Israel, on Saturday 10 June 1967, of its decision to sever diplomatic and consular relations with Israel following the results of the Six Day War. This announcement was the culmination of Soviet political support – in addition to massive military support – for the Arab countries in their fight against Israel.

That day at noontime I was walking from our residence at the Sadovo-Samotechnaya to the Embassy of Israel on Bolshaya Ordinka Street. It was a lovely sunny day. My heart was torn in two. On the one hand, I felt extremely happy to know that my country – Israel – had been able to defeat the Arab countries who had threatened, in so many declarations, to destroy us. On the other, I could only assume – at that stage – that the victory of Israel's Defense Forces had been achieved at the very heavy price of many dear lives of young soldiers and officers, who were dreaming of living in their Homeland in peace and security, like any other normal people on this earth, their futures awaiting them, and now they had left behind deep pain and profound grief in the hearts of family and friends.

Walking through the central streets of Moscow I encountered many cars with loudspeakers informing the public of the Soviet breach of relations with Israel. For a moment it seemed as if the Soviet Union was declaring war against Israel. Indeed, from that moment on the Soviet Union stood completely at the side of Israel's enemies, on bilateral and international levels. In fact until then, between Israel and the USSR, there had never been a conflict, either territorial or military. On the contrary, historic social and cultural ties connected both nations. True, there were ideological differences – the Soviet Union fought against Zionism, with no reason, and rejected, categorically, Israel's pleas to let Jews living in the USSR emigrate to Israel. Yet, from that to the breach of diplomatic relations was a long distance. Moreover, the breach constituted an act which weakened the international system of relations rather than strengthening it.

Upon reaching the street where the Embassy stood, I could hardly make my way through. Hundreds, if not thousands, of workers, brought in from all the different enterprises in Moscow, blocked the entrance to the Embassy. They were carrying anti-Israeli slogans, shouting every few minutes 'Doloy [Down] with Israel'; the most humiliating slogan was the one comparing Israel to Nazi Germany.

I went up to the second floor of the building and, together with the rest of our staff, looked through the wide windows at the outrageous mob outside the gate. It was a frightful scene, as if they were going at any moment to penetrate into the courtyard and then into the building itself. It was hours before they left, but not before we were instructed several times by the Protocol of the Soviet Ministry of Foreign Affairs to pull down our flag. And we did so, at sun set, singing our national anthem, 'Hatikvah' ('The Hope').

On 18 June 1967 we locked the building (handing over the keys to the Dutch Embassy which represented our interests in the Soviet Union during the entire period of the breach in relations, 1967–1989) and left Moscow for home.

From then until now, nearly 30 years have passed. I served at various posts in the Foreign Ministry in Jerusalem and in our Foreign Service abroad. The last positions I held abroad were as Israel's Ambassador to Bucharest, during the Ceausescu era (Romania was the single country in the Communist bloc not to have severed its relations with Israel following the Six Day War), and lately as Israel's Ambassador to Austria and to the UN organizations in Vienna as well as non-resident Ambassador to Slovakia and Slovenia.

After my return from Bucharest, I was appointed Deputy Director General of the Ministry for East Europe. We were then engaged in the process of renewing our diplomatic relations with the east European countries. It was in this capacity that I returned for the first time to Moscow, in September 1990, as head of the Ministry's delegation, for talks held with officials of the Soviet Foreign Ministry in preparation for the renewal of Israeli–Soviet relations.

It was only natural that I returned to the premises of our Embassy building, where an Israeli consular delegation had been operating from 1989. Excitedly, I went up to the second floor to the same window looking out over Bolshaya Ordinka, where I had stood watching the mob outside who shouted humiliating slogans against Israel when the Six Day War ended. Now I saw through the window hundreds of men and women all along the street – just as then – but lining up quietly, waiting to get an entry visa to Israel, mostly for permanent residence.

A year later, I revisited Moscow along with my colleague and friend (we had served together as First Secretaries in Moscow until 1967) Judge David Bartov to participate at a reception given by A. Levin, Consul General (later Ambassador) of Israel in the USSR on the occasion of the renewal of Israeli–Soviet relations. The invited Soviet guests, hundreds of them, were joyful over the resumption of contacts, as if 23 years had not separated us.

On 13 December 1991, the Soviet Ambassador to Israel, A. Bovin, presented his credentials to the President of Israel, H. Herzog, at a very solemn and exciting ceremony, since it was the first time after more than 24 years that a Soviet Ambassador had done so in Jerusalem. A fortnight later, the Soviet Union dismembered itself into 15 independent republics, the red flag was taken off the Kremlin and the Ambassador automatically became the Representative of Russia. It so happened that he was the last Soviet Ambassador to have presented his credentials and that this was the last time the Soviet anthem was played at such an occasion anywhere in the world. And so, it seems that the last ceremonial requiem to the USSR was held in Jerusalem, between the hoisted flags of Israel and the USSR.

Fortunately, Israel's relations with Russia and the other republics of the former Soviet Union are speedily developing both in volume and content. We are building together relations of friendship and co-operation between our nations toward a common future of peace and security free of interbloc confrontations.

This process began during the Gorbachev era and continues to this day.

Israeli–Soviet relations constitute a most dramatic chapter in the history of Israel's foreign policy. I also dare to think that they constitute no less a turbulent chapter in Soviet policy in the Middle East, directly and indirectly related to British policy as well, particularly from 1948, starting with Israel's independence up to the 'Suez Campaign' and later.

This study fills a gap, which had not thus far been extensively or academically treated in the historiography of Israeli–Soviet relations. It was first published in Hebrew by the Magnes Press of the Hebrew University of Jerusalem in 1990, and in 1994 it appeared in Russian translation in Moscow through 'Progress' Press. Thanks to the publishers Frank Cass & Co. English readers the world over will be able to become acquainted with the subject until additional studies will appear.

I do hope that readers and researchers will find this book interesting, not only because it constitutes a source of abundant information and references related to Israeli–Soviet relations but also as a basis for political conclusions to be drawn from this chapter of history which left a very strong imprint on the mutual relations between the two countries for over 40 years.

One day, when the Russian Ministry of Foreign Affairs will open the Soviet Archives of Foreign Policy to the period dealt with in this book, the reader no doubt will have access to additional material reflecting this dramatic chapter (though I believe that the basic picture will remain basically unchanged). Until then, and well afterwards, this book will fulfill its mission in eliminating the 'blank spots' in the history of Israeli–Soviet relations.

Respectfully,
Yosef Govrin, Ph.D.

Preface

THIS BOOK deals with the period ranging from the first severance of Israeli–Soviet relations in the last stage of Stalin's rule through their renewal, shortly after his death in 1953, to their being severed again under Brezhnev's rule, in 1967. This period – the longest in the annals of Israeli–Soviet relations – is extensively examined with regard to two parallel processes:

1. Development of trade and cultural relations accompanied by a harsh political dialogue and limitation of the number of Jewish emigrants permitted to leave the USSR for Israel.
2. Confrontation areas that led gradually to the severance of diplomatic relations following the Six Day War in 1967: on the one hand, Soviet policy in the Middle East aimed at forming a united Arab anti-Western front against Israel's wish to entrench its security and independence with Western assistance, in face of Arab threats to Israel's existence and, on the other hand, Israel's struggle for Soviet Jews to have the right to emigrate to Israel and the right to preserve their cultural and national heritage – thus clashing with Soviet ideological interests.

The subject of Israeli–Soviet relations has always been in the forefront of public interest in Israel: first, owing to the significant USSR support extended to Israel during the early stages of its independent existence and the drastic shift in this stance, from the beginning of the 1950s, to siding with Israel's enemies – a change then fateful for Israel's survival; secondly, because of Israel's growing concern for the fate of Soviet Jews; thirdly, because of the hope that Israeli–Soviet relations would be restored to their former splendor.

This book is the first academic attempt to research this chapter in Israeli–Soviet mutual relations between 1953 and 1967 and to assess the roots of the confrontation between the two countries against the background of the political and ideological motivations of each *vis-à-vis* the other. This work is based on a doctoral thesis carried out under the supervision of the late Prof. Shmuel Ettinger and Prof. Yaacov Ro'i.

This work was preceded by Dr A. Dagan's book *Moscow and Jerusalem* (English; 1970) which contains a wide, varied selection of important historical documents on the period of Israeli–Soviet relations from their inception in 1948 until their rupture in 1967, and by Yaakov Ro'i's doctoral thesis, 'Israeli–Soviet Relations, 1947–1954' (in Hebrew). Taking up the historical narrative after the period covered by Dr Ro'i and carrying it through to the June 1967 break in relations, this present study offers the first survey of:

(a) the whole ensemble of problems as they manifested themselves in relations between the two countries on the bilateral plane;
(b) the role of Israeli foreign policy alongside that of the Soviet Union in the formation of the system of mutual relations and then in its breakdown;
(c) the inception and development of the campaign fought on behalf of Soviet Jews;
(d) the degree to which the Jewish factor alongside the Middle Eastern one influenced the course of the development of mutual relations.

THE BILATERAL PLANE

On the bilateral plane a detailed account is given of the scale of commercial and cultural relations, and the issue of emigration from the Soviet Union and eastern European countries is examined. A distinction is made between situations in which the Soviet Union supported emigration from the eastern European countries to Israel as a function of its readiness to strengthen Israel's demographic potential and those in which it refrained from doing so as a result of Arab pressure.

Also scrutinized is the Soviet Union's double standard of conduct in its relations with Israel as compared to its conduct towards other countries with which its relations were tense. The Soviet Union, it is well known, upheld the principle of universality of relations (having been itself the target of blockades and sundered relations in the early years of its existence), while it cut off relations with Israel twice. No other country the size of Israel received as much attention from the Soviet communications media in the form of criticism bordering on vilification, or was subject to such gross attacks as those voiced against Israel during the period under review. The Soviet Union questioned no other country's legitimate right to exist as it did Israel's.

THE MIDDLE EAST PLANE

I analyze the confrontation of Soviet policy in the Middle East (defined in the Soviet political vocabulary as 'a region situated in proximity to the southern borders of the USSR'), aimed at getting Western influence out of the Middle East by forming a united Arab anti-Western front, and Israel's wish to entrench its security and independence with Western assistance in face of the Arab countries' growing strength with Soviet assistance and their threat to Israel's existence. From the point of view of Soviet policy, Israel had a double role: it stood as an obstacle in the way of eliminating Western influence in the Middle East, but it was also an instrument for strengthening the Soviet foothold in the Arab countries by exploiting the Israeli–Arab conflict in order to further the USSR's aims in the Middle East.

From the point of view of Israel, the Soviet Union was on the side of enemies bent on its destruction (although the USSR never went back on its recognition of the State) and was therefore seen not only as a factor strengthening the Arab countries' aspirations to wipe out Israel but also as the main obstacle to the promotion of peace in the region.

THE JEWISH PLANE

I discuss the gap between the theoretical approach and the pragmatic one in Soviet policy towards the Jewish minority in the USSR. Israel's activity among Soviet Jews is reviewed and its influence on the process of national revival among them is assessed. This assessment embraces the beginning of the struggle for the cause of Soviet Jews, its defined goals and the way it was led, its institutionalization in Israel and abroad, and the expansion of its activities.

Israel's fight for the cause of Soviet Jews, fostered by the Jewish national awakening in the Soviet Union itself, was seen by the Soviets as a campaign to blacken the name of the Soviet Union internationally, as part of the East–West confrontation. In Soviet eyes, Israel was putting itself at the head of the Jewish world in an attempt to drag it into acting on behalf of Israeli political, national and social interests, and not only at the head of a Jewish Diaspora in the west but also of the Jews in the Soviet zone of influence. Israel for its part saw defending persecuted Jews in the world as a national obligation, neglect of which would rob the State of its *raison d'être*. As one of the few countries in the world that do not belong to any bloc in the international arena, it was 'the natural thing' for Israel to turn to its Jewish allies to help buttress its independence. This aspect of the relations between the two countries is also treated here in historical perspective.

A certain difficulty in carrying out this research has been the impossibility of studying documents in the Soviet archives which might throw additional light on motives for Soviet decisions in shaping policy regarding Israel. As there was no prospect of the Soviet Foreign Policy archives being opened to foreign researchers in the foreseeable future – even at present (1996), access to Soviet Foreign Policy Documents is quite restricted, and in the best case quite selective – I had no choice but to base research on open Soviet sources, which do in fact afford faithful enough sources on Soviet policy, whether openly stated or not. These open sources are the Soviet press, official statements and the concurrent political commentaries, interviews with Soviet leaders by Soviet and foreign journalists, and verbal communications to Israeli and Western leaders and diplomats by Soviet leaders. This study is supplemented by an analysis of the Soviet government's Notes to Israel and by the reports of Israeli diplomats in the Soviet Union on their conversations with Soviet representatives as well as their interpretation of developments in Israeli–Soviet relations. Use has also been made of documents of the Israeli Foreign Ministry. Interviews with Israeli personalities who were active during the period under review were also an important source of information, as were Knesset debates, discussions in the Israeli press, and statements and memoirs of Israeli statesmen who shaped Israel's foreign policy as a whole and policy with regard to the Soviet Union in particular.

Finally, I would like to express my gratitude to: the late Prof. Shmuel Ettinger and to Prof. Yaacov Ro'i who encouraged me to publish the Hebrew edition of this book; to the late Katriel Katz, Israel's last Ambassador to the USSR before the 1967 severance of relations, with whom I served harmoniously as First Secretary of the Embassy during 1964–67, for his genuine support in publishing this book in Hebrew; to my colleague and friend David Bartov, one of the prime movers in the struggle for Soviet Jewry and who has been engaged for many years in their cause, whose invaluable support and untiring encouragement contributed to the publication of this work (in Hebrew and Russian). My appreciation is also given to the director general of the Hebrew University's Magnes Press, D. Benovici, under whose auspices this book appeared in Hebrew.

My very profound gratitude goes to my late mother Zadcanit Hurvitz (*née* Lerner), who spread the Zionist idea and the teaching of Hebrew in the Diaspora and later taught in Israel and who trudged alongside me on a long road of hardship in our struggle for survival and redemption, and to my late father, David Hurvitz, who shaped my early childhood but fell as a victim of Nazi executioners during the Holocaust, while still a young man, and who did not live to see the Day of Victory over Nazi Germany nor Israel's independence. It is from both of them that I acquired Hebrew as my mother tongue and my deep attachment to the Jewish people in Israel and in the Diaspora.

Yosef Govrin

Introduction

WHEN THE Palestine Question was brought up before the UN General Assembly in May 1947, the USSR made a surprising move by departing from its hostile attitude towards Zionism, a stance well known from the 1920s in the USSR itself as well as in the communist world. Andrei Gromyko, head of the USSR mission to the UN, in his address delivered in the plenary meeting of the Assembly, on 14 May 1947, proposed to establish an independent, democratic Jewish-Arab state in Palestine. Should that prove impossible to implement, owing to deteriorating relations and irreconcilable differences between the Jews and the Arabs, he then suggested that the territory of Palestine be partitioned into two independent states: one Jewish, the other Arab.[1]

The position of the USSR regarding the right of the Jews to their own state in Palestine – as expressed by its representatives in the UN debates during 1947 – was based on the following arguments:

1. The aspirations of a considerable part of the Jewish people are linked with Palestine and its future, as well as to the administration which will govern it. The Jewish people, like the Arab people, have historical roots in Palestine – the Homeland of these two peoples.
2. The suffering and sorrow which were the lot of the Jewish people in the Nazi-occupied areas, having been subjected to almost complete physical annihilation, cannot possibly be described. The fate of the Jewish people continues to be tragic since hundreds of thousands of Jews are wandering about in various countries of Europe, searching for a means of existence and for shelter.
3. The fact that the countries of Western Europe were unable to ensure the defense of the basic rights of the Jewish people and to

safeguard it against the violence of the fascist executioners explains the aspirations of the Jews to establish their own state. It would be unjust to deny them this right.

4. The partition of Palestine into two separate states will be of deep historical significance, since this decision will satisfy the legal claims of the Jewish people, hundreds of thousands of whom remain without a land and without a home.

5. The decision to partition Palestine is not aimed against either of the two peoples living in Palestine. On the contrary, the decision is congruent with the national interest of both peoples – the Jews and the Arabs.

This forcefully expressed position of the USSR had a decisive influence on the crystallization of the UN General Assembly resolution on 29 November 1947 regarding the Partition of Palestine – a decision which brought about the end of the British Mandate in Palestine and the declaration of the establishment of the State of Israel on 15 May 1948.

The Soviet position revealed no identification with the Zionist vision. Two new principles, however, could be discerned in the USSR's position at that time:

(a) the recognition of the Jewish people's historic connection with Palestine – the Land of Israel, as called by Jews the world over throughout the centuries;
(b) the right of the Jewish people to establish their own independent state, which would absorb tens of thousands of Jewish refugees, survivors of the Holocaust.

Thus, two national interests coincided here: the Soviet interest in pushing the British out of the region – one of its main reasons for supporting the partition of Palestine – and the Jewish interest in establishing an independent Jewish state in the Land of Israel.

MAIN LANDMARKS IN ISRAELI–SOVIET RELATIONS FROM THEIR ESTABLISHMENT IN 1948 TO THEIR BREAK IN 1953

The USSR recognized the State of Israel, *de jure*, on 18 May 1948, and was the first to accord full recognition to the newly born state. Recognition was accorded following a note addressed by Israel's

Minister of Foreign Affairs, Moshe Shertok (later Sharett) to V. Molotov, USSR Minister of Foreign Affairs, on 16 May, in which he requested the Soviet government's official recognition of the State of Israel and its provisional government. Shertok expressed his hope that this recognition would 'strengthen the friendly relations between the Soviet Union and its peoples' and 'the State of Israel and the Jewish people of Palestine'. On this occasion, Shertok also expressed the 'deep gratitude of the Jewish people of Palestine shared by the Jews throughout the world, for the firm position adopted by the Soviet delegation to the UN which advocated the establishment of a sovereign and independent Jewish State in Palestine, and for its unfailing support of this position, in the face of all the difficulties, for the expression of sincere sympathy to the Jewish people who suffered in Europe at the hands of the fascist butchers and for the support of the principle which stipulates that the Jews of Palestine are a nation which has the right to sovereignty and independence'.[2]

In according official recognition by the USSR government of the State of Israel and its provisional government on 18 May 1948, V. Molotov expressed the hope that the 'creation of their own sovereign State by the Jewish people will promote the strengthening of peace and security in Palestine and in the Middle East' and the Soviet government's 'confidence in the successful development of friendly relations between the USSR and the State of Israel.'

18 May 1948

Kol Haam ('Voice of the People'), the Israeli Communist Party organ, notes in its editorial that in view of the USSR's recognition of Israel, relations between the USSR and Israel should rest 'on the basis of friendly relations, cooperation and mutual assistance'. The paper also called upon Israel to create an alliance with the USSR which should secure Israel's independence against the imperialists' attempts at subjugation of Israel and the opening of possibilities to receive practical support in our war (meaning the war imposed then on Israel following its Independence Declaration, when seven Arab armies invaded its territory aiming to conquer it and negate the existence of Israel). *Kol Haam* concluded the article by saying that in order to consolidate peace in the world 'Israel should not demonstrate the same attitude toward warmongers as to peace lovers'.[3]

In those fateful days the USSR stood by Israel's side both in the UN – where it sharply condemned the Arab armies' invasion into Israel's territory and called for their immediate withdrawal (27–28 May, during the Security Council's debates) – and in the granting of military assistance, through Czechoslovakia, that was of utmost importance in rebuffing the invading armies. In exchange for its political and military assistance, the USSR expected that Israel would side with the USSR in its confrontation with the west.

30 May 1948

The greetings sent by the Moscow Jewish Anti-Fascist Committee to the President of Israel, Dr Chaim Weizmann, stated:

> The Jewish Anti-Fascist Committee in the USSR is sending you, and through you to the Jews of the State of Israel, ardent congratulations on the occasion of the Jewish State's establishment. Reactionary forces that serve imperialism continue their dark activities, trying to suppress the people's aspiration for freedom and independence. But we believe in the victory of progress and democracy. We hope that only this way the young Jewish State will succeed to overcome all the disturbances and will thus occupy its worthy place among nations who fight for real democracy and peace throughout the world ... The Jewish people acquired for the first time in its entire history of suffering, a truthful defender for its rights, its interests, the USSR, a friend and defender of all nations.[4]

27 June 1948

Tel Aviv and Moscow officially announced the exchange of official Envoys between their respective states. Mr P. Yershov was appointed the USSR's Envoy Extraordinary and Minister Plenipotentiary to Israel (the USSR Legation opened in Tel Aviv on 10 August 1948) and Mrs Golda Meyerson (later Meir) was nominated Israel's Envoy Extraordinary and Minister Plenipotentiary to the USSR (the Israeli Legation in Moscow was opened on 6 September 1948).

15 July 1948

The Ukrainian Representative at the UN Security Council sharply condemned Count Folke Bernadotte's program (which recommended transferring territories in the Negev and Galilee to the Kingdom of Jordan), defining it as a program aimed at the liquidation of Israel.

26 August 1948

At a farewell reception held in Tel Aviv by the Friendship League with the USSR, in honor of Mrs Golda Meyerson on the eve of her departure to Moscow as Israel's plenipotentiary Minister, Mrs Meyerson declared:

> We have to develop understanding and mutual friendship with the USSR. I wish to set up a direct and close relationship with Soviet Jewry. I would like to work with them in a friendly manner and receive in turn friendship from them. I would have liked that out of this direct connection, we should get also to a good relationship with the USSR Jews.[5]

15 September 1948

Deputy Minister of Foreign Affairs Zorin told Mrs Meir:

> A Jewish question exists and will exist only in those States which do not advance towards Socialism. From there Jews will emigrate to Israel and it is Israel's role to absorb them ... Even after a large immigration, many Jews will still remain in the capitalist countries and for their well being it is essential to fight not only for the State but also for democratization all over. In each state there are active progressive forces and the very creation of Israel is none other than an expression of these forces' influence. It is not by chance that the democratic states were the first to recognize Israel. It is our hope that Israel will follow the road of progress.[6]

21 September 1948

An article in *Pravda*, the organ of the Communist Party of the Soviet Union (CPSU), signed by the Jewish-Soviet writer Ilya Ehrenburg – member of the Jewish Anti-Fascist Committee directorate in

Moscow and one of the most important spokesmen of the Soviet press during World War II against the Nazi invaders – sums it up as: Israel, yes! To Jews' emigration from the USSR to Israel, no!

Here are its main points:

> The Soviet Union stood by Israel's side in its war against the Arab invaders. Now, however, Israel is facing another invasion, less alarming, less dangerous – that is the invasion of American capital. US programs of military bases and installations are the danger threatening Israel. Israel is a capitalist state. Its leaders are not representatives of the working class. 'The Jewish Question' will be resolved in each place as a result of social and spiritual progress. The solution of the Jewish question doesn't depend upon Israel's military successes but upon the victory of socialism over capitalism. The interconnection among Jews is anti-Semitism. 'This is solidarity of the offenders and embittered.' It isn't to the credit of Zionism that more Jews are flowing to Israel, but as a result of anti-Semitic persecution ... These Jews didn't come to Israel to find wealth but a right to human dignity. The Soviet Jews are proud of their country and regard it as their homeland. Neither do they want the Jews of eastern European countries to emigrate to Israel. They sympathize with the struggle of Israeli workers, but every Soviet citizen realizes that the problem isn't related only to the national character of the State but also to its social regime.[7]

This article marked the beginning of the USSR's turn in its attitude towards Israel. (In days to come Ehrenburg will argue in his memoirs that this article was dictated to him.) Its publication was intended to warn Israel that it should not allow itself to be influenced by American capital, which could lead to the loss of its independence, and that it should not encourage Soviet Jews to emigrate to Israel, which would result in political confrontation between Israel and the Soviet authorities and among Soviet Jews themselves.

5 October 1948

The military attaché of the Israeli Legation in Moscow discussed with Soviet military authorities the subject of military co-operation with Israel with regard to: (a) short- and long-training of commanders; (b) supply of arms from German loot; and (c) air and sea delivery bases.

After a month, Mrs G. Meir (Meyerson) and Mr M. Namir, Counselor of the Legation, submitted a detailed list of military equipment – required by Israel – to the Head of the Middle East Department of the Soviet Ministry of Foreign Affairs. His reaction was somehow reserved. He was said to be afraid that the matter would become publicly known, 'whilst the UN prohibits the supply of arms to the conflicting sides.' He added, 'This matter will not only be inconvenient for us, but will also make your situation more difficult. My Arab friends have an advantage, geographically speaking: they have depots in their vicinity and they would be able to act publicly and extensively, whilst they are compelled now to act clandestinely and in a limited manner.'[8]

24 November 1948

The Soviet Union presented a draft resolution, in the third (political) committee of the UN General Assembly, demanding the immediate withdrawal of the Arab armies which had invaded Palestine.[9] The USSR representative, Kisselev, declared that Israel was born as a result of an armed fight for freedom and independence.[10]

29 November 1948

Comment made by I. Ehrenburg to M. Namir in Moscow:

> Soviet Jews fought against Hitler, not only because of his anti-Semitism, they shed their blood in defense of this country and this regime to which they are wholeheartedly devoted and will never give up their Soviet citizenship.
>
> The State of Israel should understand that in the USSR there is no Jewish problem and that the Soviet Jews should not be bothered and that all attempts at attract them to Zionism and emigration should cease. Otherwise, it will encounter sharp resentment, both on the part of the Soviet authorities and amidst Jews themselves. The State of Israel will then be the loser – this he said 'is my friendly advice'. You

are stuck in a region of pure Anglo-Saxon influence. Your situation will never permit you to be in complete solidarity with the Soviet Union! Who knows? The notion should not be discounted that in a time of crisis we shall find ourselves on both sides of the front as enemy camps.[11]

16 December 1948

The Soviet weekly *Novoye Vremya* complained that Israel was ungrateful to the Soviet Union, that it had adopted an anti-Soviet attitude in her policies, 'in spite of the constant support extended by the USSR to the Jewish State'.

19 December 1948

The Soviet Union voted in favor of Israel's admission to UN membership. The proposal was rejected in the absence of a sufficient majority.

7 February 1949

The first Soviet protest note to Israel's Legation in Moscow on account of two allegations.[12]

1. The Legation is engaging itself in sending letters to Soviet citizens of Jewish nationality, encouraging them to leave the Soviet Union, abandon their Soviet citizenship, and emigrate to Israel. Since this act is illegal and does not correspond to the status of a diplomatic Legation, the Soviet Ministry of Foreign Affairs is proposing that the Israeli Legation cease this activity.
2. The Legation is distributing an informative bulletin contrary to the existing regulations in the Soviet Union. The Legation is being requested to stop doing so.

13 February 1949

The Soviet Ambassador to the USA, Panyushkin, commented to Israel's Ambassador in Washington, Elath, that Israel might join the Marshall Plan:

The Soviet Union has no intention of asking Israel to join the bloc of countries that it is heading, but it does ask Israel to remain independent in its foreign policy and free from foreign influence and rule.[13]

20 March 1949

TASS, the Soviet news agency, quoted the General Secretary of the Israeli Communist Party, Mr Shmuel Mikunis, as having said that the American loan given to Israel would fortify imperialist positions and would permit the Anglo-Saxon superpowers to control Israel's economic sovereignty.[14]

20 March 1949

The Knesset's Declaration of Basic Principles stated that Israel would be loyal to the UN Charter and to friendship with all peace-loving nations, in particular the USA and the USSR.

14 April 1949

Mrs G. Meir commented to Soviet Minister of Foreign Affairs Vishinsky in Moscow upon her visit to bid farewell at the conclusion of her mission as Israeli Minister to the USSR:

We are determined to lead a neutral foreign policy, to not be driven by any bloc nor to join any group of countries aimed against this or any other world factor, nor against the Soviet Union, especially ... We decided to maintain neutrality, this is the will and aim of all responsible factors who are leading our State ... We have taken a firm decision to safeguard our independence and not to allow any military bases on our territory to England or any other party ... We shall not deviate from our Foreign Policy principles, which are: the non-adherence to any organisation oriented against the Soviet Union whose friendship with us is in our basic interest ... We have a coalitionary government, and although there are workers' parties outside this coalition, the majority of workers are represented in the government whose aim is to build Israel as a Socialist State.

In this conversation, Mrs G. Meir requested (a) trade credit from the USSR; (b) expeditious treatment of Israel's application for arms from the Soviet Union; and (c) the exertion of Soviet influence upon Romania and Hungary to permit Jews from those countries to emigrate to Israel.

Vishinsky reacted very positively to these assurances of Israel's neutrality; responded encouragingly to the idea of increased trade with Israel; refrained from supplying Soviet arms to Israel; and argued that permission for emigration from neither the Soviet Union nor the eastern European countries would be granted because Jews were an element faithful to the communist regime and were therefore important to the process of its consolidation.[15]

5 May 1949

The Soviet representative to the UN demanded Israel's admission as a member of the UNO without any further delay and condemned the foot-dragging demonstrated by certain countries in this regard.

11 May 1949

Israel was admitted as a member of the UNO thanks to vigorous Soviet support. After the vote the Ambassador of Poland noted,

> The period of sentimental interest in the fate of Israel has come to an end. An era of cooperation based on mutual interest is beginning. The Jewish people advancing along peaceful and progressive lines can rely on the assistance of Poland, the Soviet Republics and the People's Democracies of Europe. Israel will doubtless remember that those countries have been its true friends at the troubled time of its emergence ... neither should [it] be forgotten that Israel is deeply indebted to the working classes. Poland will watch the future of Israel with sympathetic interest.[16]

7 July 1949

M. Namir presented his credentials as Minister Plenipotentiary of the State of Israel to the President of Supreme Soviet.

9 August 1949

The USSR representative to the UN, Tsarapkin, demanded the liquidation of the UN staff control over Palestine, the dissolution of the Conciliation Commission, and facilitation of direct negotiations between the conflicting parties – Jews and Arabs – without UN interference, or outside pressure.[17]

5 December 1949

Israel's Minister of Foreign Affairs, M. Shertok (later Sharett), declared, 'Israel's foreign policy is "a non-aligned" policy in distinction to "neutral". Permanent ties with Soviet Jewry are impossible at present, because of the Russian authorities' rejection for reasons which I don't want to judge.' He stressed the fact 'that Israel will refrain from identifying itself with any of the sides involved in the cold war between the blocs'. He also added that Israel would not participate in any imperialistic program.[18]

19 April 1950

The Permanent Representative of the USSR to the UN, J. Malik, presented to the General Secretary of the UN, a Note, stating:

> It has become clear now that the General Assembly's resolution of December 1948, determining an international regime in Jerusalem satisfies neither the Jewish nor the Arab population in Jerusalem itself and in Palestine as a whole. In such circumstances the USSR government sees no possibility for continuing to support the said resolution. The USSR government is confident that the UNO will succeed in finding a solution to the problem of Jerusalem that will be acceptable to the Arab and Jewish residents.[19]

23 May 1950

Prime Minister David Ben Gurion made the following statement at a Mapai (Labor party) convention in kibbutz Afikim:

> The Soviet Union has promised national equality to all nations inhabiting its territory and has kept her promise. But

the Jewish people in the Soviet Union do not have a school of
their own, nor a newspaper, neither in Hebrew nor in Yiddish.
There is no anti-Jewish discrimination in the Soviet Union,
and anti-Semitism is prohibited, but the Soviet regime has
not succeeded in understanding the uniqueness of the Jewish
problem. The Jewish people who have succeeded to build their
independence will not give up the right of any Jew to immigrate to Israel and join the builders of the Homeland. We
demand from the Soviet Union that the right be given to Jews
who inhabit the USSR to join with us and participate in the
building of our independence. Let us send from here our
greetings to the Jews of Russia and let us tell them: Our/Your
hope has not been lost, and to the Soviet Union we shall appeal
with the call that the opportunity be given to every Jew in the
USSR – who so desires – to take part with us in our creativity.
Let us not despair and let us live with the knowledge that
there are still many Jews in the world who are with us in spite
of all the misfortunes. Let us hope that the day will come
when they will, with total freedom, be able to join us in our
enterprise.[20]

25 May 1950

Israel welcomed the 'Tripartite Declaration' (American-British-
French) concerning the supply of arms and security guarantees to
Israel and the Arab states (in the face of very sharp Soviet criticism).

3 July 1950

Israel condemned the North Korean aggression towards South
Korea (for which it was sharply criticized by the USSR).

20 August 1950

Prime Minister D. Ben Gurion made the following statement at the
Labor Party (Mapai) convention:

> The [Israeli] government always objected to having its foreign
> policy defined as neutral. We are not neutral regarding the

supreme question of mankind in our days. Peace and war. No people is so eager to safeguard peace as the Jewish people, and we therefore cannot be neutral towards those deeds that determine peace or war.[21]

4 October 1950

Korean War. Foreign Minister M. Shertok opposed the Soviet draft resolution at the UN calling for the withdrawal of American troops from South Korea. Israel announced that it was dispatching medicines to South Korea.[22]

30 October 1950

Israel's representative at the UN joined those opposing a Soviet draft resolution concerning a peace treaty and the prohibition against the use of atomic weapons.

9 January 1951

At the UN the Soviet Union rejected the proposal of Israel's mission on the question of Korea (a seven point program presented by Israel's head of Mission at the UN, Mr A. Eban) demanding the immediate withdrawal of all foreign troops from Korea.

20 May 1951

The USSR abstained on a draft resolution presented by the Western bloc at the UN calling for condemnation of Israel for having bombed El-Hama and for an order demanding the cessation of the draining of the Hula Sea.

21 November 1951

In a note addressed by the Soviet Union to all the Middle East countries, including Israel, the USSR Minister of Foreign Affairs, A. Gromyko, denounced the US plan to set up an Allied Middle East Command. He warned that any country which would join the Command would bring about a deterioration in its relations with the USSR.[23]

8 December 1951

In its reply to the government of the USSR, concerning the Middle East Command, the government of Israel noted that Israel was not invited to join the Command. It was informed, however, about the plan to set it up, but was at the time assured that there was no aggressive intention behind its establishment. It also mentioned that there were no foreign military bases on its territory (as the Soviet press claimed at that time) and that Israel aspired for peace to prevail with its neighbors.

On this occasion Israel called upon the USSR to permit Soviet Jewish emigration to Israel.[24]

9 December 1951

Israeli–Soviet trade negotiations were concluded concerning the exportation of 5,000 tons of citrus fruit from Israel to the USSR.

1 March 1952

An agreement was signed regarding the exportation of 50 tons of bananas and 30,000 boxes of oranges from Israel to the USSR.

6–12 April 1952

Israel participated at the International Economic Conference held in Moscow and negotiated on the exportation of citrus fruit from Israel to the USSR in exchange for importing agricultural machinery from the USSR.

19 May 1952

An Israeli–Soviet agreement was signed on the exportation of 50,000 boxes of citrus fruit from Israel to the USSR, in exchange for which Israel would import oil products from the USSR. Negotiations were also held regarding the purchase of crude oil and grain from the USSR.

8 December 1952

Pravda denounced the 'incitement campaign of the Zionist leaders' against the Slansky Trials in Prague, whereupon the Secretary of the Czechoslovak Communist Party was accused of weaving a plot with Israel as well as Zionist and Jewish organizations to overthrow the communist regimes in Czechoslovakia and its neighboring countries. (Slansky, of Jewish origin, was executed. With the passage of time, the Czechoslovak post-communist government rehabilitated him and exonerated him from the charge of treason.)

13 January 1953

The 'Doctors' Plot' was announced in the Soviet media. A large group of Jewish doctors were accused of attempting to poison Stalin, according to instructions they had, allegedly, received from Jewish and Zionist organizations. (The group was expected to be sentenced to death; after Stalin's death, the charges were dropped.)

19 January 1953

In his Knesset speech, Israeli Foreign Minister M. Sharett made the following statement concerning the 'Doctors' Plot' and the Soviet media's claim that they were Jews:

> The State of Israel will not remain silent in the face of an attempt made by any power to defame the name of the Jewish people and of a danger threatening masses of the Jews wherever they may be.
>
> The government of Israel has always regarded friendship with the USSR as one of the pillars of its international position and as a precious asset for the entire Jewish people. It views with deep sorrow and grave anxiety the malignant course of hatred against Jews officially adopted in the USSR, which must arouse most vehement indignation and condemnation on the part of Israel and the Jewish masses throughout the world ...
>
> The government of Israel will denounce in the UN and on every other platform the campaign of incitement conducted in the communist countries against the Jewish people, and the abomination directed at its authoritative organizations and will warn of the dangers threatening the well being of millions of Jews in these countries. The government of Israel

will continue to demand even more vigorously, the right of all Jews who aspire to Zion to be permitted to emigrate to Israel.'[25]

9 February 1953

A small bomb was hurled at the Soviet Legation in Tel Aviv. Three Legation employees were slightly injured by the explosion.

The President and the Prime Minister of Israel, in fact the whole government and Knesset, expressed their deep regret at the incident, condemned it and promised to catch the criminals and bring them to court.

13 February 1953

The government of the USSR informed the government of Israel of its decision to break off diplomatic relations with Israel.

17 February 1953

Prime Minister D. Ben Gurion expressed in the Knesset his amazement and deep concern in view of the Soviet decision to sunder diplomatic relations with Israel.

NOTES

1 Speech by Andrei Gromyko, 14 May 1947, in the United Nations General Assembly, First Special Session 77 Plenary Meeting, Vol. 1, pp. 127–35.
2 *Kol Haam*, 18 May 1948.
3 Ibid.
4 Ibid., 30 May 1948.
5 Ibid., 27 Aug. 1948.
6 M. Namir, *Mission to Moscow* (in Hebrew) (Tel Aviv: Am Oved, 1971) p. 52.
7 *Pravda*, 28 Sept. 1948
8 M. Namir, op. cit., pp. 63–73.
9 General Assembly, Official Rec. 3rd Year, 1 Community. Doc. A/c 1/401, 25 Nov. 1948.
10 General Assembly, Official Rec. 3rd Session, Gen. Comm. 211 Meeting, 24 Nov. 1948, p. 741.
11 M. Namir, op. cit., pp. 90–91.
12 Ibid., p.109.
13 A. Dagan, *Moscow and Jerusalem* (London: Abelard and Schuman, 1970) p. 40.

14 Ibid., p. 41.
15 M. Namir, op. cit., p. 116–18.
16 A. Dagan, op. cit., p. 44
17 Sec. Council, Official Rec. 4th Year, No. 37, p. 5, 9 Aug. 1949.
18 *Davar* (Heb. daily), 5 Dec. 1949.
19 Gen. Assembly Official Rec. 5th Session Suppl. No. 1, 8, 6, 19 April 1950.
20 *Davar*, 23 May 1950.
21 Ibid., 20 Aug. 1950.
22 Ibid., 4 Oct. 1950.
23 A. Dagan, op. cit., p. 59–60.
24 Ibid., p. 59–60.
25 *Divrei HaKnesset* (Knesset Verbatim), Vol. 13, p. 493.

Part 1

From severance of diplomatic relations in February 1953 to their renewal in July 1953

1 · Ideological and psychological aspects of the USSR's decision to sever its relations with Israel

THE CAUSE AND BACKGROUND OF THE BREACH

ON 9 February 1953 a small bomb was thrown on the Soviet Legation in Tel Aviv. The ensuing explosion damaged the building and wounded three Legation employees. This event was used by the Soviet government as a pretext for informing the Israeli government of its decision to sever Soviet–Israeli diplomatic relations.[1] The USSR regarded the blow to its Legation in Israel as a by-product of the angry manifestations against it at that time in Israel, both among the public and in the government, in consequence of anti-Semitic and anti-Zionist accusations which were manifested at the Prague Trials and in the case of the 'Doctors' Plot' in Moscow.

In the notification transmitted to Israel's Legation in Moscow on 11 February 1953, the Soviet government placed the responsibility for the criminal act on the government of Israel basing its argument 'on the well known and indisputable facts concerning the engagement of Israel's government representatives in hostile acts of systematic incitement against the USSR'.

The USSR also stated in its notification[2] that

> the apologies expressed by the President of Israel and the Minister of Foreign Affairs, the condemnation of the act and the promise they made to find the criminals and punish them, 'are in contradiction to the acts of incitement' against the

3

USSR. All is simply 'a fraudulent show' aimed at evading the assumption of responsibility for the attack.

The 'provocative'[3] policy of the government in Israel towards the USSR, was characteristic not only in the press siding with the ruling parties in Israel, but also of the statements made by their representatives in the Knesset as well as those of government ministers, in particular those of the Minister of Foreign Affairs, M. Sharett, on 19 January 1953, 'who openly incited hostile acts against the USSR'.

Elementary conditions are lacking in Israel for carrying out normal diplomatic activity by Soviet representatives. Therefore, and in view of what was stated above, the USSR government has decided to call back its Minister and the diplomatic staff of the Legation and to sever its relations with Israel.

No warning was given to Israel prior to the notification of the breach of relations, either on the diplomatic plane or in the Soviet media. The actual notice did not include any reference to the defamation of Israel in the Soviet press following the Prague Trials and the 'Doctors' Plot' in Moscow. In Israel itself the announcement of the break in relations was received as a grave and unexpected political development, with serious implications of concern for the situation of the Jews in the USSR and for Israel's position in the international arena.

THE REACTION IN ISRAEL

In the Knesset debate on the Soviet announcement on the severance of relations with Israel, Prime Minister D. Ben Gurion said that the government of Israel had received it 'with astonishment and concern'.[4]

Zalman Aran, Member of the Knesset (MK) for the Labor Party, when speaking of this said, 'Since the day Israel was established the sky has never been so clouded as at this time,' and that for him the breach was a 'Soviet political bomb' thrown at Israel 'which was struck by a mighty political blow'.[5]

MK Y. Ben Aharon of Mapam (the United Workers Party), then in the opposition, described the event as 'one of the gravest incidents to occur to our young country during its short existence' and as 'a bitter day for our country and a terrible notice to the masses of our people all over the world'.

The 'astonishment' with which the government received the announcement probably derived from the fact that Israel, as a Jewish state with Zionist objectives, was hurt by the defamation aimed – directly and indirectly – at Israel itself and at the Jewish and Zionist organizations, at the Prague Trials and through the 'Doctors' Plot' in Moscow. Bearing in mind the anti-Soviet spirit that then prevailed in Israel in face of these defamations, people were asking whether Israel would have intended to sever its diplomatic relations with the USSR. To this Foreign Minister M. Sharett replied that the government of Israel had had no such intention, since 'breach of diplomatic relations is not a way that leads to peace'.[6] The leadership of the country had probably not realized that a break in relations could ever have been initiated by the USSR. Perhaps the government of Israel was impressed by the fact that the USSR never broke its relations with Yugoslavia in spite of the bitter and persistent ideological confrontation between them. Moreover, the USSR was engaged, at the time, in a sharp political clash with the USA and a number of European countries, without any break in diplomatic relations between them; there was not even any Soviet threat of potential severance. Breaking off diplomatic relations was considered a very unusual phenomenon in the system of international relations. Thus it was apparently felt after the breach that the USSR regarded Israel differently from the way it regarded the rest of the world.

The 'grave concern' stemmed, apparently, *firstly* from fear for the fate of Soviet Jews – who in many cases faced oppression and persecution – whose situation would possibly worsen in view of the breaking up of diplomatic relations with Israel. *Secondly*, there was concern for the wide gap then created between the Soviet Union's former position of extending unlimited support to the establishment of Israel, strengthening it politically and militarily, and its new position, aimed at humiliating Israel and weakening it in the international arena. And last, but not least, it was the first breach of diplomatic relations Israel had ever experienced – and with a superpower.

In the Knesset debate, following announcement of the severance of relations, Foreign Minister Sharett somehow avoided making any comment on the political significance to Israel of this act.[7] A fortnight after the debate, he belittled the value of its importance by saying that 'from the practical point of view, we have lost nothing from the break in relations, while we have never enjoyed anything from them'.[8] He adopted the same attitude in his instructions to Israeli diplomatic representations abroad. In this he differed from his fellow party members, including Prime Minister D. Ben Gurion.

A statement issued by the Spokesman of the Ministry of Foreign Affairs in Jerusalem on 12 February 1953 synthesized, on the governmental plane, the various reactions expressed by government spokesmen, representatives of the coalition parties in the Knesset, in shifting the weight of all explanations to the traditional hatred of the USSR for Zionism, Judaism and Israel. Here is the full text:

> The official reason given for this act is nothing but a pretext. The decision taken (regarding the breach of relations) is the climax of open hostility and a poisonous defamation campaign against the State of Israel, the Zionist movement, Jewish organizations, and Jews as such – a campaign conducted for a long time in the USSR, one which in recent months has increased to a threatening state. The true aim of this campaign is to completely isolate and intimidate Soviet Jewry, whose fate arouses profound fear.[9]

In the guidelines M. Sharett addressed to Israel's Diplomatic Mission abroad on 9 March 1953 he stressed that in explaining the break in Israeli–Soviet diplomatic relations, 'we ought to contradict their assumptions: *firstly*, that the breach constitutes a catastrophe for Israel; *secondly*, that it brings us to an impotent dependence on the good graces of the USA, without any countersupport; *thirdly*, that it raises the status of Arabs over us'.[10] Clarification of these three assumptions constitutes a kind of summary of Israeli–Soviet relations, as follows:

The USSR always regarded Zionism as an adversary. Its turnabout in 1947 was more for the purpose of expelling the British from Palestine than for the love of Zionism. The retreat from a position of advocacy for the establishment of the Jewish State began shortly afterwards when the USSR became aware of:

6

(a) the necessary link of Israel with the West, and

(b) the connection between the Soviet Jews and Israel.

Things came full circle and the USSR returned to its position prior to Israel's independence. The historic balance sheet shows that we have not lost anything by the rupture of relations, but we have gained our independence. The USSR never served us as a counter-support against the US and the West, it never extended us any aid and never opened any door for us to allow us to become closer to it.

Our dependence on the West, prior to the breach, was not weaker than it is at present, nor did it become stronger because of the rupture. If the breach caused any change in the situation, it is rather in the direction of increased sympathy in the world towards Israel. The breach and the hostility preceding it plugged a hole in the wall of isolation in the world separating the Soviet Jews and Israel. Gaining sympathy towards the Soviet bloc among the Arab countries was not the aim, but at most an attempt to gain secondary benefit. But the Arab leaders hostile to Israel knew full well that they would not gain from Communist aid, but that they must be wary of it, and the Western leaders know that the Arabs know this and the Arabs know that the West knows that they know that it is an imaginary benefit.

In neither the official reaction nor the information guidelines is there mention of Israel's policy of estrangement from the USSR or of its drawing closer to it – except for the Jewish aspect – as a factor in the Soviet–Israeli relationship.

According to this concept, the nature of Soviet policy towards Israel was deterministic. Namely, it was not Israeli policy towards the USSR – in the internal, bilateral, regional, or international arenas – that set the tone. No matter what Israel's policy would be, it would not have any influence on Soviet policy towards Israel, owing to the traditional Soviet hostility to Zionism, Judaism and Israel. Israeli government spokesmen unhesitatingly rejected the assumption that their angry reaction – no matter how justified from the Jewish national point of view – contributed to the deterioration of relations with the USSR, to the point of severance. Moreover, there was an increasing tendency to obscure this opinion as much as possible and to adopt in its stead the idea that the breach in relations was merely a continuation of the series of events that had

7

begun with I. Ehrenburg's article in *Pravda* on 21 September 1948 and culminated in the 'Doctors' Plot'.[11]

The left-wing opposition parties held an opinion completely opposed to the official line. It ignored the significance of the anti-Zionist and anti-Semitic elements in Soviet policy towards Israel while linking the reasons for the breach with Israel's policy towards the USSR in the internal and international arena. MK M. Sneh was the spokesman for this approach. When he referred to the Soviet reasons for taking such a step against Israel, he said,[12] 'The true chain of events as it has become clear to us is: the break in diplomatic relations was preceded by an attack on the Soviet Legation; the anti-Soviet attack was preceded by anti-Soviet incitement; the anti-Soviet incitement was preceded by an anti-Soviet policy ...'

After enumerating the various aspects of Soviet support for Israel in 1947–49, he continued with:

> This was advance payment for Soviet friendship towards Israel. And in this same UN arena, how did the Israeli delegation stand *vis à vis* the USSR? How did the delegation act when the USSR presented basic proposals at the UN for securing world peace? What stand did you take in the Korean conflict? What was the matter with you when you identified yourself with McArthur and Syngman Rhee? Why did the Israeli Foreign Minister give his blessing to the American invader to cross the 38th parallel north? ... And when the idea of a Middle East Alliance came up – an idea which has not yet been realized – you were the first in the region to express in a thousand ways your readiness to join it. And when the Prime Minister was in America, didn't he promise that Israel – side by side with Turkey – would fight alongside the West? Didn't Abba Eban [head of Israel's Delegation to the UN] state at the UN forum that granting military bases to foreign powers did not contradict the concept of state sovereignty? And when A. Eban visited Israel didn't he state that the Israeli Defense Forces had an international duty 'to defend the whole region'? Defend against whom? Against the USSR? ... In view of these facts, which occurred a long time before the Prague Trials, can one accept the theory of 'an anti-Jewish attack' as the reason for your anti-Soviet stance?

In putting these questions, MK Sneh took Israeli policy makers to serious task for switching from supporting neutrality between the two blocs to siding gradually with the USA in its confrontation with the USSR.

The Mapam party spokesman, as distinguished from the leftist party headed by Sneh, declared that his group would never accept the putative connection between Zionism and the world Jewish organizations with Soviet civil crimes. As to the remaining accusations, the Mapam approach differed only slightly from the statements by MK Sneh.

A draft resolution presented by Mapam at the end of Knesset debate on this subject stated:[13]

> The Knesset regards the rupture of diplomatic relations on the part of the USSR with Israel as a grave political blow to the Jewish people, to Zionism, and to the State of Israel. Without ignoring the background of the USSR's anti-Zionist attitude towards us, as was expressed in the Prague Trials and in the Moscow publications, the Knesset cannot acquit the government from its responsibility for the development of events that led to the breach of diplomatic relations. After having abandoned the policy of non-alignment and neutrality, the government undertook a policy of increasing subjection to the West, encouraged incitement against the USSR by official bodies, turned the justified defense against the constantly increasing attacks on Zionism and Israel into an anti-Soviet defamation campaign in contradiction to Zionist and Jewish responsibility and did not know how to prevent the malicious assault on the Soviet Legation, perpetrated by fascist elements ...'

The draft resolution was rejected by a majority of votes. The proposals submitted by Maki (the Israel Communist Party) and MK M. Sneh were not even brought to a vote. The Knesset accepted the draft resolution presented by the coalition parties, saying that the Knesset aligned itself with the Prime Minister's statement in which he appealed to the Soviet authorities: (a) to permit Soviet Jews to emigrate to Israel, and (b) to behave towards Israel according to the principle which the USSR professes of 'fraternity and peace between nations'.

To sum up, opinions differed in Israel as to the Soviet motivation for breaking off its relations with Israel. The coalition and rightist parties regarded the ideological aspect (namely, Soviet hostility to Zionism) as the decisive factor leading to the breach. The leftist parties ascribed the reason for the break to political motives (such as, Israel's siding with the USA in its confrontation with the USSR, while at the same time carrying on public and official incitement against the very basis of the Soviet regime). Factions of the leftist oppositions, however, differed among themselves over the question of whether they should react at all, and if so, how they should respond to the USSR for having connected Zionism and Jewish organizations with Soviet internal affairs. The majority of the opposition parties believed that the Israeli government's response to the 'Doctors' Plot' should have been more controlled and restrained, in such a way as to not endanger the fate of mutual relations between the two countries. The minority, including Maki and the leftist faction of MK M. Sneh, ignored this issue altogether.[14]

THE USSR'S CONSIDERATIONS IN DECIDING ON THE SEVERANCE OF RELATIONS

We do not know whether the USSR's decision to break off relations with Israel was the result of a planned anti-Israel and anti-Zionist campaign, as MKs of the coalition parties assumed in the Knesset debate held following the announcement on the severance of relations,[15] or was, perhaps, a reaction to the turn taken in Israel's foreign policy moving from declared neutrality to increasing alignment with the USA in its confrontation with the USSR.

The Soviet government in its note informing Israel of the decision to break off relations explained its decision as deriving from the assault on the Soviet Legation in Tel Aviv as well as from the statements made by spokesmen of the Israeli government, headed by the Minister of Foreign Affairs himself – following the 'Doctors' Plot' – which openly incited, as stated above, hostility to the USSR.

On what was the Soviet reasoning based? Were the reasons given what actually prompted its decision?

The political aspect

It might be assumed that the response by the coalition parties' Knesset representatives, and particularly the reaction of the Foreign

Minister, considering its scope, sharpness, and main objective[16] – the mobilization of world public opinion and that of Western countries and the UN in the struggle for the annulment of the charges in the 'Doctors' Plot' and for the improvement of the lot of the Soviet Jews – was probably regarded by the Soviets as the decisive factor behind the rupture. All other factors referred to by the Soviet commentators after the break in relations – although the Soviet note did not mention them – displayed no new argument. The accusation that Zionism was serving American imperialism and was acting on behalf of its intelligence, or that Israel was leading an anti-Soviet policy according to the directives of the USA, aimed at inflaming a new war[17] – all these accusations had been repeatedly made in the past without causing the rupture of relations between the USSR and Israel. They never disappeared from the Soviet media frame and were never brought up on official Soviet Notes. On the contrary, the majority of the MK reactions created a new dimension in the history of Israeli–Soviet relations. Representatives of the ruling party (Mapai) and its official spokesmen criticized the USSR in a systematic and broad manner which they had previously avoided during any Knesset debate or similar platform. This fresh criticism comprised:

1. Condemning the Soviet regime as 'a regime of spiritual annihilation and national oppression', condemning its anti-Semitic policy and accusing it of making mass preparations to strike the Jews (pogroms).
2. Exposing the tragic situation of the Soviet Jews, facing spiritual and physical annihilation; challenging the Soviet authorities to account for it; energetically demanding the restoration of the rights of Soviet Jews and permission for them to leave for Israel.
3. Condemning the legal and judiciary system in the USSR, 'based on threats and forgery'.
4. Appealing to public opinion in the free world with the aim of shattering its indifference, urging the free world to take immediate steps to avoid a holocaust.
5. Determination to urgently bring their problem onto the UN agenda.
6. Warning that appropriate steps would be taken in Israel against the supporters of the USSR incitements and libel policy against the Jews.

11

The condemnations, criticism, appeals, demands, and all these warnings were expressed for the *first* time publicly, not only within the framework of a Knesset debate but as a demonstration of Jewish solidarity and as a government operational program for the fight against the USSR's anti-Jewish policy. For the first time, Israel's leaders referred in very critical terms to the USSR's policy in internal affairs and regarding the Jews who live within its borders. The State of Israel, in fact, appeared to the USSR as the spokesman of Soviet Jews and of world Jewry and as one who would openly station itself in the camp of the 'instigators'. This dimension might have been decisive in the USSR's determination to break its relations with the Israeli government, against the background of ideological and psychological enmity that the USSR projected towards Israel.[18]

The ideological aspect

The Prague Trial – and immediately afterwards the 'Doctors' Plot'[19] – provoked Israel's leaders, for the first time, to take a route leading to an open ideological conflict with the USSR.

Anti-Semitic expressions and the proof, as it were, of a conspiracy between Zionist Organizations, Israel with the Prague defendants and the accused doctors (the majority of whom were Jewish) in Moscow (against whom it was alleged that it had been their mission to poison the Soviet leadership on behalf of Zionist and world Jewish organizations) increased the level of 'negation' to that of dangerous hostility. The Prague Trials and the 'Doctors' Plot' constituted to a great extent the background to Israel's change of attitude, influenced by the enmity these two events fomented against Soviet Jews, world Jewry, and Israel.

Israel's leaders not only rejected the putative accusations against Zionism and Israel, but also revealed the evils of the Communist regime in the USSR and the 'satellite' countries in eastern Europe, exposing them as a danger to mankind as well as to Jewish existence. Prime Minister Ben Gurion addressed this in particular in his public speeches and in the polemical articles he signed with the pseudonym 'Saba shel Yariv' ('Yariv's grandfather'), an allusion undoubtedly understood by the Soviet Legation in Tel Aviv.[20]

During the Knesset debate on the Prague Trials, on 22 November

1952, Foreign Minister Sharett defined the trials as a 'deceiving show' and as a 'vision of moral suicide and self-degradation shattering the heart of anyone who believes in the holiness and spiritual strength of a human being's personality'.[21] As for the nature of the trials, the Foreign Minister's evaluation was that it was permeated with a malignant anti-Semitic spirit and replete with 'bombastic propaganda and anti-Semitic incitement in line with pure Nazi tradition'.[22]

In that debate Prime Minster Ben Gurion enumerated four aspects characterizing the trials:

(a) the human essence of the Prague tragedy;
(b) its terrible international significance (without commenting on it);
(c) the expected fate of the Jews under the Communist regime (spiritual and physical annihilation);
(d) the implications for Israel itself: the need to draw proper conclusions while coming to terms with Mapam through moral self-examination.[23]

'Communism', he noted, 'is based on two dicta: (1) loyalty to the policy-line, whatever it may be, "even if today is the opposite of tomorrow, and tomorrow the opposite of today"; (2) the end justifies the means – all means, without exception, including alleging of libels, falsifications of history and truth, deceiving slogans, and the murder of innocent people when necessary to increase the rulers' power or to cover up their failures.'[24]

The debate in the Knesset, in which cabinet ministers participated actively, spilled over into criticizing the judicial system and the terror methods of the Communist regime, but the contents of the draft resolution submitted for Knesset approval by the Committee for Foreign and Security Affairs – and which was accepted by a majority vote – attested to the delicate care being taken to not deviate from the defensive nature of the debate, while intentionally overlooking its offensive character.[25] The aim was probably to not overtly aggravate the ideological conflict with the USSR. The debate was not subject to clarification at the diplomatic level, so one may perhaps conclude that the Soviets were ready to accept it as it was, at that stage.

The 'Doctors' Plot', which aroused great fury in Israel and in the Knesset, broke the bonds of restraint that had characterized Israel's leaders since the establishment of Israeli–Soviet diplomatic relations and gave them a free hand in revealing the nature of the Communist regime and its leader, Stalin. The criticism leveled was sharp, penetrating, and daring. We may assume that its forcefulness must have shocked the Soviet personalities who read it.

In January and the beginning of February 1953 articles appeared in the daily *Davar* written by Prime Minister Ben Gurion signing himself as S. Sh. Yariv. Presumably, they significantly influenced the USSR's decision to break off relations with Israel. Though the series of articles 'on the Communism and Zionism of Ha-Shomer ha-Za'ir' was intended for local consumption, it was clear to all that its barbs were simultaneously aimed at the USSR.[26]

There was nothing new in the ideological and critical attitude of Ben Gurion, Sharett, and their associates, within the party as well as outside of it, regarding the methods of terror customarily applied by Communist regimes of eastern Europe and their hostile attitude to Jews, Zionism and the State of Israel. The innovation, however, lay in their determination to open an ideological struggle, alongside the political one, against the Communist enmity embodied in Stalin's character. It cannot be discounted that factors prompting Israel's leaders to enter the fray were, on the one hand, the lessons of the Holocaust, and on the other, reports by Israel's representatives in Moscow about the tragic distress of Soviet Jews and their expectations of redemption by Israel – as the official representative of the Jewish people – and this over and above their feeling that the Jews in the USSR stood on the threshold of spiritual and physical annihilation.[27] They saw it as their national and moral duty to rush in to rescue the Soviet Jews with the help of the only weapon they could employ against a superpower: enlightened public opinion in the West.

The conclusions which could be drawn, from the USSR's point of view, were as follows:

1. Israel's government supported the Jews of the USSR as strongly as if they were its nationals. This contradicted not only the Leninist theory that there is no Jewish nation, but also justified the communist accusation that Zionism considers all Jews of the world

to be one nation and that from the national aspect political borders separating them are irrelevant.

2. Israel as a Jewish–Zionist state was setting itself up as the spokesman and defender of Jewish communities the world over, and in particular of those subjected to Communist rule in eastern Europe.

3. The government of Israel was not deterred from criticizing, in the sharpest terms, the Communist regime in eastern Europe, despite its political and military support of the establishment of Israel. This criticism put Israel in the Western enemy camp against the USSR – by uncovering its reign of terror and its trampling of human rights, and by denigrating Stalin publicly.

The USSR's battle against Zionism began long before the Prague Trials and the 'Doctors' Plot'. Both Lenin and Stalin rejected every aspect of Zionism, claiming that it was a reactionary movement aimed at diverting the Jewish masses from the entire proletarian struggle and leading it towards national and petit-bourgeois isolationism. But unlike Lenin, who knew how to appreciate Jewish intellect and recognized its important contribution to the development of civilization, science, and medicine, Stalin viewed the Jews with great hostility and tried as early as the 1930s to remove Jews from high positions in the Soviet administration and the Communist Party in the USSR. After the establishment of the State of Israel, when he realized that there was strong attachment to the newborn state among the Soviet Jews, his enmity towards them deepened. This antagonism was mixed with the fear that their influence would, perhaps, be detrimental to the crystallization process of Soviet society, since he regarded them as a foreign element, the bearers of Western and Zionist ideas, particularly those Jews in highly influential posts in administration and training. The result was the policy of oppression and deportation initiated by him on the eve of 'the black years' in the USSR.

The Prague Trials and the 'Doctors' Plot', which were accompanied by a large-scale anti-Semitic campaign in the USSR and eastern European media, moved Israel's leaders to deviate from their previous line of restraint and to rise up to defend the Soviet Jews and Jewish national honor.

Opening a fight against Soviet policy on the Jewish plane while exposing the evils of the Communist regime was likely to have shocked the Kremlin. The decision to sever relations with Israel was probably a response reciprocating the new dimension of the Israeli reaction. From Israel's point of view it was, probably, the price it was compelled to pay for its fight on behalf of the Soviet Jews, a struggle that started with the 'Doctors' Plot' and which continued, uninterruptedly, until the dissolution of the USSR. The 'Doctors' Plot' shocked Israel more than any previous event on the Israeli–Soviet plane – and from then on the subject of the Jews in the USSR became a dominant factor in the relationship between the two countries.

The psychological factor

Three types of psychological residue can be discerned in the USSR's political consciousness of the Soviet Jews and of Israel.

1. The anti-Semitic residue, whose roots are to be found in the historic, cultural and social heritage of Russia and in the assumption that in case of an East–West confrontation the Jews all over the world would stand by the West. Hence, the perception of the Jew as a 'cosmopolitan' who should be isolated.
2. The residue of enmity towards the State of Israel, whose very existence stirred national feelings among Soviet Jews to an extent that the USSR had not anticipated. This phenomenon contradicted the 'Soviet theory' about 'eternal fraternity among nations' in the USSR. No doubt that explains the Soviet aspiration to break the links between the Jews living in its territory and the other Jewish communities in the world, and particularly to prevent the Jews from having any contact with Israel, for fear that they would become a sort of fifth column within the USSR in case of an East–West bloc confrontation. (During World War II, the USSR could rely upon the patriotism of Jews, because of their resentment of Nazi Germany. This was not the case regarding the West.)
3. The residue of disappointment at Israel's pro-Western orientation. From the Korean crisis onwards, Israel was intensively identified as a servant of Western interests. To this one must add Israeli efforts, as the Soviets saw it, to join a Middle East defense

alliance, whose main aim was anti-Soviet, as well as the declarations by Israel's leaders that in the event of a third world war, Israel would side with the West. All this was set against the background of consistent Soviet support for the establishment of the State of Israel, its military strengthening of Israel during the War for Independence, and its reinforcement of Israel's international status. MK M. Sneh referred to this element of disappointment when he noted in the Knesset debate on 16 February 1953 that it was impossible to compare the Soviet attitude towards other countries with its attitude to Israel. Thus, the State of Israel was fortunate to receive from the USSR political and military assistance from its very beginning, something no other country was graced with.[28]

The element of disappointment in the USSR's political consciousness in its approach to Israel, thus, did not derive solely from the change in Israel's policy – from neutrality to a pro-Western orientation – but also from a feeling of Israel's having betrayed the bloc of countries that had assisted it in the hours so fateful for its existence. Little evidence of this can be found in writing[29] – not because such a feeling did not exist, but because it was probably more convenient for the USSR to conceal its support for Israel while it was oppressing manifestations of Jewish national aspiration in its own country.

At a later time – after the renewal of Soviet–Israeli diplomatic relations – the USSR probably did not consider it necessary to emphasize this assistance, since it was intent on gaining the sympathy of the Arab world, which negated Israel's existence.

It may therefore be presumed that the psychological aspect, with all the above-mentioned implications, had been taken into account in all the USSR's considerations, along with the political and ideological aspects, which were decisive in the severance of relations with Israel.

Israel found itself, unexpectedly, in a confrontation with the USSR the result of which was the Soviet decision to break off relations. Without Israel's fiercely angry response – which reached its high point over the 'Doctors' Plot' – it is doubtful that the USSR would have taken its decision to sever those relations.

ISRAEL'S POLITICAL BATTLE AGAINST THE 'DOCTORS' PLOT' AND THE USSR'S ANTI-ZIONIST AND ANTI-SEMITIC CAMPAIGN

The rupture of diplomatic relations between Israel and the Soviet Union did not deter Israel from planning a battle to annul the anti-Zionist and anti-Semitic accusations of the Soviet Union and to improve the situation of the Jews in the Communist bloc. Following the break, Israel did not refrain from standing up against Soviet representatives in the international arena and stating its claim. Public opinion in the Western world sided with Israel's position. Initial steps were taken to raise the issue at a World Jewish Conference, in the US Congress, and at the UN.

When explaining the intention of the World Jewish Conference to discuss the 'lack of security in the life and existence of the Jews in the USSR', MK M. Argov (Mapai), head of the Knesset Committee for Foreign and Security Affairs, noted on 25 February 1953:

> World Jewish solidarity exists, and this should be drummed, day and night, into the ears of the Soviet rulers, who make use of the radio, press and propaganda channels in every country under their control – to defame the Jewish people and Zionism. And Zionism is the Jewish people.
>
> At this conference, there should not be any incitement against the USSR, but rather an attempt at fending off the libels spread regarding Israel and the Jewish people. The State of Israel will not formally participate in it. The question as to whether the Knesset should or should not send a delegation [to the conference] was raised in the Committee for Foreign and Security Affairs. The majority felt that Israel should participate in this conference as part of the Zionist Organization ... This conference has a pressing need to defend the honor of the Jewish people, the Zionist Organization, and the State of Israel.[30]

Thus the foundation was laid for the institutionalization of the future struggle for Soviet Jews.

The US Senate Foreign Relations Committee voted unanimously on 25 February 1953 for a resolution 'condemning the persecution of Jews in the USSR'. The resolution appealed to US president

Dwight Eisenhower to undertake the appropriate steps in order to protest in the UN and on other platforms against the libels. At the same time the US Ambassador to the UN condemned the persecution of 'Christians, Moslems and Jews in the USSR', adding that peace depended not only on collective security, but also on the 'equal treatment of human beings'.[31]

The government of Israel decided to send Mrs Golda Meyerson (later Meir), Minister of Labor and formerly Israel's Envoy to the USSR, to lead the struggle in the UN. Her status as cabinet minister and her former mission to the USSR, added a great deal of authenticity and importance to raising the subject in two stages: stage one, when the First (Political) Committee discussed the Soviet-Chinese-Czechoslovak draft resolution on 'US interference in internal affairs of other countries';[32] stage two, when the same committee discussed the Polish proposal on 'Means to prevent threats of a new war'.[33]

During the first stage, on 25 March 1953,[34] Mrs Meyerson stated that as a result of the debate in the committee, Israel's government was expecting two developments:

1. That the Communist governments, particularly the Soviet government, would take into account the international condemnation regarding their anti-Jewish policy and would abandon it.
2. That the governments of the USSR and other Communist countries would respond favorably to the request to permit Jews from their countries to emigrate to Israel.

During the second stage, Mrs Meyerson spoke at length in the debate on the Polish proposal.[35] The main points of her address, given after the cancellation of the 'Doctors' Plot' trial had become public knowledge, follow.

The groundless accusations and libels alleged in the Prague and Moscow trials of a world Jewish conspiracy were irreconcilable with the course of peace and friendship amongst the nations. Israel regarded with deep anxiety the anti-Jewish agitation that accompanied the trials. The revival of anti-Semitism by east European governments as an instrument of political aims should be of concern to the UN. Israel welcomed the USSR's announcement that the accusations against the doctors were found to be groundless and derived satisfaction from the Soviet criticism that condemned the libel in stronger terms than those of Israel's Foreign Minister on 19 January 1953, whose statements now had the endorsement of the Soviet government. It was to be hoped that after the repudiation of the 'Doctors' Plot', all other anti-Jewish manifestations would be condemned, discrimination against Jews prohibited, and propaganda against them ended. Israel would continue to watch the situation of the Jewish communities in eastern Europe. The best guarantee for the prevention of difficulties would be the granting of self-determination rights for cultural and communal life to the Jewish communities in eastern Europe and free choice on emigration to Israel. The problem should be debated as part of the broad spectrum of international relations, peace amongst nations, and respect for human rights.

The address delivered at the UN by the Israeli Minister of Labor was accompanied by similar statements given by representatives of delegations from Panama, the Netherlands, the Dominican Republic, China, Cuba, the USA, and Uruguay.[36]

Israel's first battle in the international arena was successful. For the first time the issue gained an international dimension. The lessons drawn by Israel from this battle was that it was possible to find assistance among Western public opinion in the struggle against Soviet anti-Semitism and for the improvement of the status of Soviet Jews. As for the USSR, it learned that this dimension must have a place in its future considerations.

NOTES

1 *Izvestia*, 12 Feb. 1996.
2 This notification was cited by the Prime Minister, when giving a statement on the attack to the Knesset, *Divrei HaKnesset*, Vol. 13, p. 682.
3 Provocation has two meanings in the USSR's lexicon: (a) treachery-slander; (b) inciting masses to damaging acts. In this case (a) applies.
4 *Divrei HaKnesset*, Vol. 13, p. 720, 16 Feb. 1953.
5 Ibid., p. 722–3, 16 Feb. 1953.
6 *Davar*, 19 Jan. 1953.
7 *Divrei HaKnesset*, Vol. 13, pp. 745–7, 17 Feb. 1953.
8 *Kol Haam*, 27 Feb. 1953.
9 *Davar*, 13 Feb. 1953.
10 *Yediot Lenetziguyot Bechul*, No. 37.
11 G. Meir's statement in the Knesset, *Divrei Haknesset*, Vol. 13, p. 747, 17 Feb. 1953.

12 Ibid., pp. 737–8, 16 Feb. 1953.
13 Ibid., p. 474.
14 Representatives of the left – Mapam and Maki – stated in face of the forceful reaction that 'the best we could do now for the sake of the Jewish people is to wipe out this debate in the Knesset from the pages of our life. In my opinion never has the highest institution and the one most responsible for the fate of our people, ever wreaked such havoc, worsening the situation of a people scattered all over the globe, as in this debate' (MK Y. Hazan, *Divrei HaKnesset*, Vol. 13, p. 489). 'I regard this choir as one black incitement of the whole reaction of this parliament' (MK Y. Yaari, ibid., p. 490). These two spokesmen noted that their party would not reconcile itself to the connection made between the Zionist movement and the Jewish world institutions with criminal acts of Soviet citizens. While MK Sh. Mikunis of Maki held fast to accusing Israel of leading anti-Soviet incitement and anti-communist hysteria, the sources of which were not in the exposure of 'the doctors' terrorist group in Moscow', but rather in the decision by 'our country's rulers' to hasten preparations for war and the attachment of Israel to the 'anti-Soviet aggressive bloc following Washington's order' (*Divrei HaKnesset*, Vol. 13, pp. 492–3). Maki's representatives were the only ones in the Knesset who aligned themselves unreservedly with the Soviet authorities' charges against the doctors. To be sure, there was a certain link between their stand and Foreign Minister Sharett's warning that should parties in Israel justify the Soviet incitement, the government of Israel would draw its conclusions about them (meaning to outlaw them).
15 Ibid., pp. 720–49.
16 Ibid., p. 481–94.
17 *Pravda*, 14 Feb. 1953; *Literaturnaya Gazetta*, 17 Feb. 1953; Izvestia, 14 Feb. 1953; *Novoe Vremya*, No. 6, 1953.
18 Though already during the Prague trials there were Knesset Members who drew attention to the existence of a Jewish problem in the USSR, this did not include cabinet ministers, who avoided making any public statement on this subject. For instance, in the Knesset debate on 4 Nov. 1952 on the status of the Zionist organization (*Divrei HaKnesset*, Vol. 13, p. 24), D. Ben Gurion declared: 'Even if Israel were to determine that the Zionist organisation represents the two million Jews of the USSR, it would be entirely senseless, baseless, and unreal. It would encounter justified opposition on the part of those who speak on behalf of Russian Jews who would claim, "Who authorized you?".'
19 Y. Ro'i, 'Israeli–Soviet Relations 1947–1954'. The dissertation deals broadly with these two events, the background, accusations and assessment of Soviet and east European commentary on them.
20 MK Y. Ben Aharon (Mapam) commented in the Knesset debate on the severed relations,

> In the coming days people will ask: 'What did the Prime Minister and his Foreign Minister do in those dangerously fateful days for Israel, why did that change take place?' Then they will reveal that in their articles – whether published under their own name or a pseudonym – there was an effort at expanding the conflict, deepening the abyss, bringing upon us by their own hands not a reduction in tension, not the prevention of a disaster, but its advancement and acceleration. Thus this government carries full responsibility for this development. (*Divrei HaKnesset*, Vol. 13, p. 721)

MK. M. Sneh stated in that debate:

> Where is the reciprocity to the Soviet Union that, according to all opinions and even to the Prime Minister's cable – but not according to the S. Sh. Yariv articles – saved Jewish refugees from the Nazi claws and extended a hand to us in the establishment of the State? Is this how you reciprocated? And all that was prior to the Prague Trials ... (*Divrei HaKnesset*, Vol. 13, p. 738)

Hence, it could be assumed that the true identity of S. Sh. Yariv was also known to the Soviet Legation in Tel Aviv which maintained close contacts with the leftist opposition. The articles were written against the background of the polemical exchanges between D. Ben Gurion and Mapam. According to Ben Gurion, Mapam's position on the Prague Trials was ambivalent. On the one hand, Mapam claimed that Mordekhai Oren, who acted on behalf of the party in Eastern Europe – and was then arrested by the Czechoslovak authorities – was entirely innocent and was compelled to confess to crimes charged against him. On the other hand, Mapam demonstrated complete identification with the course of the trials and with the accusations made by the Czechoslovak prosecution against leaders of the Czechoslovak Communist Party and its activists on the bench of the accused, whilst Oren was forced to serve as a witness to the prosecution's charges. Ben Gurion also commented critically on the contradiction in the resolution adopted at Mapam's congress on 24–25 Dec. 1952 which declared, 'Mapam regards itself as a Zionist-pioneering-revolutionary-socialist party and as an inseparable part of the camp and world headed by the USSR.'

21 *Divrei HaKnesset*, Vol. 13, pp. 130–31, 156–78.
22 Ibid., pp. 130–31.
23 Ibid., pp. 130–31.
24 Ibid., pp. 165–6.
25 Ibid., p. 178.
26 The three-article series appeared in a booklet, S. Sh. Yariv, *On Communism and Zionism of Ha-Shomer ha-Za'ir* (Tel Aviv: Mapai Publishing, 1953).
27 *Davar*, S. Sh. Yariv, 30.1.1953.
28 *Divrei HaKnesset*, Vol. 13, p. 738.
29 When Israel was admitted to UN membership on 11 May 1949, thanks to the vigorous support of the Soviet bloc, Poland's representative stated:

> Israel will doubtless remember that those countries [the USSR and the People's Republics] were its true friends in the troubled times of its emergence ... It was not long since the British Foreign Office had tried and failed to prevent the creation of Israel. United Kingdom and United States diplomacy had been ready to betray the new state before its birth. The US government's change of policy with regard to Israel had occurred for reasons of political expediency divorced from any sense of justice or faith in Israel's future. That should not be forgotten ... (A. Dagan, *Moscow and Jerusalem*, p. 44)

> In an article on his visit to Israel, Hazov wrote in the Soviet weekly *Novoe Vremya*, 5 July 1951, *inter alia*: 'Three years of Israel's existence cannot but disappoint those who had expected that the appearance of a new independent state in the Middle East would assist in strengthening the peace forces and democracy ...

Likewise in the *Great Soviet Encyclopedia* (1952), p. 512, the entry on Israel notes, 'In May 1948, according to the UN General Assembly resolution of 29 Nov. 1947, the State of Israel was established on a portion of Palestinian territory, but this was not a democratic and independent state, such as had been proposed by the delegation of the USSR in the UN.'

30 *Divrei HaKnesset*, Vol. 13, pp. 820–21. In response to a question put by MK M. Sneh as to the nature of the conference about which he had learned from the *Jerusalem Post*, 24 Feb. 1953, which seemed to him to be 'a tool for anti-Soviet incitement'.
31 *New York Times*, 26 Feb. 1953.
32 GA, 7th Session, First Committee, 587 Meeting, 25 March 1953.
33 GA, 7th Session, First Committee, 596 Meeting, 10 April 1953.
34 *Davar*, 26 March 1953.
35 GA, 7th Session, First Committee, 597 Meeting, 13 April 1953.
36 GA, 7th Session, First Committee, 597, 598, 600, 601, 602, Meetings, 13–15 April 1953.

2 · *Changes in Soviet internal and foreign policy after Stalin's death and the resumption of Israeli–Soviet diplomatic relations*

THE DEFAMATION campaign against Zionism, Jewry and Israel – which reached its climax in the 'Doctors' Plot' – was an integral part of the policy of incitement and terror that characterized the Communist regime in the USSR and the Soviet bloc towards the end of Stalin's era. The 'Doctors' Plot' itself was an obvious ploy and would have been only the first of a string of such libels had Stalin not died on 5 March 1953.[1]

The USSR's decision to sever relations with Israel was not an exceptional phenomenon in its foreign policy. West European countries frequently received serious warning notes because of their connections with NATO, hinting broadly at invasion of their territories should the American military bases not be removed from them. Moscow Radio used to broadcast appeals daily to the citizens of Yugoslavia to revolt against Tito and remove him from power. Anti-Tito incitement was not limited to propaganda. Yugoslavia was threatened with a stranglehold economic boycott and by border clashes staged by the neighboring Soviet bloc countries. Turkey and Greece were under constant political pressure. In the Far East, the Soviet Union blocked progress towards a settlement of the Korean conflict. In the UN arena the voice of the Soviet Foreign Minister, Vyshinsky, was heard aggressively threatening the USA. The East–West confrontation stood at the threshold of 'a hot war' for which Stalin himself was responsible. Three years elapsed before his successors revealed some of his crimes.[2] Allusions hinted that the number of crimes yet unrevealed exceeded those that had been made public.

Shortly after Stalin's death, tension abated in relations between the USSR and the outside world as a 'thaw' set in; a way opened for initiatives on East–West co-operation on crisis resolution and for peaceful co-existence.

INTERNAL POLICY

On the first morning after Stalin's death, significant changes were introduced into the structure of the high party institutions, so designated at the 19th Congress of the CPSU (5–14 October 1952). The presidency of the party was reduced to 10 members (instead of 25) and to 4 candidates (instead of 11). On 14 March 1953 the functions of the Prime Minister were separated from those of the First Secretary General of the party, and the Secret Police was included among the competences of the Ministry of the Interior.[3] On the one hand, there was a tendency to divide power within the ruling circle while on the other hand entrusting the function of the party's First Secretary General to a person outside the party leadership, to avoid the repetition of a one-man dictatorship and to return to the party the authority lost during Stalin's era, and thereby reinforcing its status with the assistance of a 'collective leadership'. Even if it was learned afterwards that there had been a struggle over succession, the party's authority in the administration, security services and army was not undermined at all.

The masses were promised lower prices on consumer goods and their speedier supply. An amnesty for prisoners was declared. There were signs of 'thaw' in cultural fields. But above all stood the annulment of the 'Doctors' Plot' and the release of the accused 'as the result of an investigation that proved that the doctors were unjustly arrested and without any legal basis', on 4 April 1953. The official announcement on the annulment as well as in a lead article in *Pravda* published one day later contained elements important for understanding the upheaval in post-Stalin Soviet internal policy, namely:

1. The doctors were accused on the basis of false accusations. The proofs cited against them were absolutely baseless.

2. The confessions of guilt were obtained by methods of investigation interdicted by Soviet law.

3. Those responsible for the Plot had lost their links with the people and the party, forgetting that they are their servants and that it is their duty to implement strictly the law they grossly violated. They forced the facts 'and dared to mock' the inviolable right of the Soviet citizen.

4. In the course of the investigation those responsible for the Plot were inciting national hatred, an element extraneous to Socialist ideology.

And with a look towards the future:

.1. No one will be arrested except by court decision.

2. The Socialist law 'that defends civil rights in the USSR, according to the constitution' is the most important basis for the continuous development and strengthening of the Soviet Union and nobody will be allowed to violate Soviet law.

Just as the Plot beamed as a clear signal of the political and moral deterioration in the USSR towards the end of Stalin's era, so did its annulment after his death stand out as a clear sign of the new era in the USSR. The removal in June 1953 of L. Beria from his posts as Deputy in Chief of the Council of Ministers, Minister of the Interior and his notoriously-held position as Head of the Secret Security Services along with the appointment of Marshal Zhukov, known as the Hero of the Nation, to the post of Deputy Defense Minister were intended, no doubt, to strengthen people's confidence in the new 'collective leadership' that aimed (*inter alia* by revealing the truth about the Plot) at eliminating from the Socialist regime and the CPSU the residue of negative events. The irony of fate is that the condemnation of the 'Doctors' Plot' by Stalin's successors endorsed the assessments of the Communist regime in the USSR made by Israel's Prime Minister D. Ben Gurion as published under the pseudonym S. Sh. Yariv two months earlier. Not only that, the Soviet condemnation gave validity to Ben Gurion's idea that human justice is impossible without giving justice to Jews. The same applied to the statement made by Foreign Minister Sharett in the Knesset on 19 January 1953 that had served as the pretext for the Soviets severing their relations with Israel. The annulment of the Plot, the acquittal of the defendants from all accusations, the confession to the fabrications and gross falsifications in the judiciary system, and the national campaign of incitement to hatred that had characterized the course of the 'Doctors' Plot', all paved the way for the renewal of diplomatic relations between the USSR and Israel.

FOREIGN POLICY

The new composition of the Soviet Government immediately after Stalin's death included V. Molotov who returned to the posts of Minister of Foreign Affairs and Deputy Prime Minister from which he had been dismissed in 1949. Foreign Minister Vyshinsky was deposed from the position of Deputy Foreign Minister and appointed Head of the Soviet delegation to the UN. By having entrusted Molotov with the leadership of Foreign Policy and Vyshinsky with the representation in the UN, there was a certain continuation of Stalinist policy without Stalin, but with a difference in emphasis.

Upon presenting the composition of the new Government in the Supreme Soviet on 15 March 1953, the new Prime Minister Malenkov outlined the guidelines of the USSR's foreign policy:[4]

1. The strengthening of peace, ensuring the USSR's security and defense, conducting a policy of co-operation with all countries, developing trade relations with them on the basis of mutual interest.
2. Close co-operation politically and economically with China and the Soviet bloc countries.
3. Respecting the rights of all nations and countries, large and small.
4. Underscoring that there is no controversial or unsolved issue that cannot be settled by peaceful means on the basis of mutual agreement between the countries in question. 'This refers to our relations with all countries including the USA.'
5. 'Countries interested in preservation of peace can be sure in the present and in the future of the uninterrupted peace policy of the Soviet Union.'

These guidelines contained nothing new other than the tone in which they were presented, highlighting the fact that the Soviet

Union aspired to settle controversial problems by peaceful means. This tone attested to a certain openness previously unknown, and raised hope in the Western camp for enhanced possibilities in the search to reduce East–West tension. Hence, both sides undertook initiatives which led to agreements paving the way to broader possibilities for settling 'controversial problems', as for instance, an agreement to exchange prisoners, the sick and wounded, in Korea. The Soviet Union supported China's proposal for the return of the remaining prisoners – steps that led in July 1953 to an armistice agreement in Korea. The stalemate in the election of the UN Secretary General was broken with the selection of Dag Hammerskold on 31 March 1953. Concrete progress was made in settling the problem of Austria; willingness was expressed to negotiate the reduction of strategic weapons and the introduction of international control on atomic energy including the signing of a treaty to forbid the use of atomic weapons. An extensive correspondence was conducted with the USA and west European countries on these subjects and on a Western proposal to convene a summit conference.

Malenkov's emphasis on the USSR's readiness to strengthen peace with 'all countries' and to respect the rights of all countries as well as its aim to disengage itself from the 'Cold War' atmosphere also contributed to the removal of obstacles – as in the field of internal policy – blocking the path to the renewal of Israeli–Soviet relations. Indeed, the first official sign was given by Israel's Foreign Ministry spokesman, who reacted satisfactorily, on behalf of Israel's Government on the acquittal and release of those accused of the 'Doctors' Plot'. In his reply the spokesman stressed that the Israeli Government 'was hoping that the amendment of the distortion would be completed by the cessation of the anti-Jewish campaign' and that 'it would welcome the restoration of normal relations between the USSR and the State of Israel'. *Kol Haam*'s correspondent, who reported this response 5 April 1953, added that according to the UP news agency, Israeli sources had revealed that in Israel's statement there was 'a clear attempt at probing the issue of the renewal of diplomatic relations with the Soviet Union, and that a formal proposal in this instance should come from Moscow since it was the Soviet Union that severed the relations'. Also, the political correspondent of *Davar* reported on 7 April 1953 that Israel was prepared to renew its relations with the Soviet Union, 'but as long as there is no hint from the Soviet side in this direction, it could not be presumed that a concrete step would be made towards a Soviet–Israeli contact'.

This seemed to be the opinion held by Foreign Minister Sharett[5] and by Prime Minister Ben Gurion.[6] Yet, nothing ever really happened. The Soviet Union did not take any step in the direction hoped for by Israel. The personal initiative of Dr Ben Zion Razin, former Chargé d'Affaires of Israel's Legation in Sofia, did lead to negotiations towards working out the conditions for the resumption of relations,[7] whilst Israel's Government and the Committee for External and Security Affairs thought that the initiative came from the Soviet Union. Later on, Sharett revealed in his diaries, that he himself was misled and misled others when he presented the subject as a Soviet initiative and not as an Israeli one.[8] Publicly Sharett did not admit this mistake, leaving the erroneous impression to prevail until Dr Razin published his evidence in *Maariv* on 10 March 1972.

The question of which of the two sides initiated the renewal of relations does not seem to be relevant, since an agreement was reached. Yet, it was of significance to the process of negotiation over the conditions of the renewal, since the initiator (Israel) was compelled to accept conditions dictated by the opposite side who consented to accept the initiative (USSR).

THE AGREED CONDITIONS FOR THE RENEWAL OF RELATIONS

On 18 May 1953 – about six weeks after Israel's hint to the Soviet Union – the Chargé d'Affaires of Israel in Sofia was instructed to inform the Soviet Ambassador officially (following some unofficial contacts that they maintained between them) of Israel's proposal to renew diplomatic relations with the USSR. On 28 May 1953 the Chargé d'Affaires and Israel's Plenipotentiary Minister to Bulgaria were received by the Soviet Ambassador, M. Bodrov (later Soviet Ambassador to Israel). After hearing the proposal, Bodrov replied that he would inform the Soviet Ministry of Foreign Affairs. On 2 June 1953 the Soviet Ambassador communicated the answer he had received from his Ministry, saying, 'The Government of the USSR is prepared to consider (that is, without any prior commitment), the Israeli Government request regarding the renewal of relations.'

Towards that end the Soviet Ambassador asked for a commitment in the name of Israel's Government to carry out three guarantees: (1) that Israel would apprehend the three perpetrators who had thrown the explosive on the Soviet Legation in Tel Aviv – which was the source of the rupture in relations with Israel; (2) that Israel would aspire to 'always [maintain] good relations with the Soviet Union'; (3) that 'Israel should not conclude a military alliance or pact directed against the Soviet Union'. Bodrov added that 'the Soviet Union, which had taken an active role during the establishment of Israel, declares its willingness to maintain friendly relations with Israel'. It was concluded, upon the suggestion of the Soviet Ambassador, that Israel's Minister of Foreign Affairs, M. Sharett, would officially apply to the Soviet Minister of Foreign Affairs to propose the renewal of relations, including the three guarantees. It was made clear to Israel's Chargé d'Affaires that Molotov would give a positive reply to his Israeli colleague, in writing, and would include in his response the reference made by the Soviet Ambassador regarding the USSR's role in the establishment of Israel and its intention to maintain friendly relations with Israel.[9]

The Government of Israel, which might have perhaps feared letting the opportunity for the renewal of relations with the Soviet Union slip away, consented to the Soviet demands in a note addressed by Israel's Minister of Foreign Affairs to the Soviet Minister of Foreign Affairs on 6 July 1953.[10] On the surface, it seemed that there was no objection to offering the proposed guarantees for the following reasons. As to the first condition, in any event judicial procedures were being conducted against the perpetrators and the Government of Israel had promised the Government of the Soviet Union immediately after the bombing that it would search for those responsible and bring them to justice. Regarding the second guarantee, the Government of Israel had already declared in its Note of 8 December 1951 to the Government of the Soviet Union that '[it] is most anxious to maintain friendly relations with the Soviet Union'.[11] As to the third condition, it had already been declared in the above-mentioned note that 'Israel had never agreed and would never agree to support any aggressive activities aimed against the USSR or against any other peace-loving country'.[12]

The positive response to the three Soviet demands – as formulated in Sharett's note to Molotov – could not, in any case, be regarded as a deviation or change in Israel's foreign policy towards the Soviet Union and all that was needed now was to reinvest a prior declaration with vigor. Indeed, this was exemplified when Sharett gave Molotov an additional promise that 'this policy is still in force' and that 'Israel has no hostile feelings towards the Soviet Union but, to the contrary, being anxious to establish and maintain friendly relations with the USSR, Israel will not be party to any alliance or pact intended to be aggressive towards the USSR'.

Molotov's positive response in his 15 July 1953 note to Sharett stated that the Government of the Soviet Union 'had taken into account the assurances given by Israel's Government and that for its part the Soviet Union would aspire to maintain friendly relations with Israel', and therefore 'considered it possible to re-establish diplomatic relations with the Government of Israel'.[13] (The expected reference to the USSR's role in the establishment of Israel was not included in Molotov's reply.)

The announcement of the resumption of diplomatic relations was published simultaneously in Moscow and Jerusalem on 1 June 1953. (The letters of accreditation of the designate Ambassadors were presented to the respective Presidents – in Moscow and Jerusalem – only in December 1953.) The Soviet press reported the resumption of relations extensively, publishing in full the exchange of notes between Sharett and Molotov, but without any commentary.[14]

ASSESSMENT

Israel apparently was compelled to pay a political price in exchange for the Soviet Union's consent to renew its diplomatic relations with it. It is to be presumed that the price of Israel's having given the required assurances to the Soviet Union, meant from the Soviet point of view:

On the bilateral level, Israel's abstention from hostile acts toward the Soviet Union, whether from attacking it in the press or from criticizing it publicly, mainly regarding the subject of Soviet Jews and the nature of the Soviet regime.

On the regional level, stopping Israel from being integrated in British-American programs to establish military pacts in the Middle

East, about which the Soviet Union had warned the countries in the region, including Israel, since it considered these pacts to be, above all, anti-Soviet pacts.

Indeed, in the course of time, Maki MKs referred more than once to Israel's assurances to the Soviet Union when they were attacking its policy towards the Soviet Union against the background of Israel's struggle on behalf of Soviet Jews, and its probing towards integration in whatever form into a regional defense alliance.

Along with Molotov's note to Sharett of 15 July 1953 in which Israel's assurances to the Soviet Union were quoted, Malenkov, the new Soviet Prime Minister, referred to them when he presented on 8 August 1953 the new guidelines of the USSR's foreign policy, stating:[15]

> In its efforts to bring about a general relaxation, the Soviet Government agreed to re-establish diplomatic relations with the State of Israel. It took into consideration the Israeli Government's undertaking that 'Israel will not be a party to any alliance or pact aiming at aggression against the Soviet Union'. We assume that the re-establishment of diplomatic relations will contribute to co-operation between the two States.

and with a look towards the Arab states:

> views expressed by part of the foreign press, according to which the re-establishing of diplomatic relations with Israel will result in a weakening of the relations between the Soviet Union and the Arab states are groundless. The activities of the Soviet Government will be directed also in the future to the strengthening of friendly co-operation with the Arab states.

That co-operation with Israel was not mentioned in the company of the adjective 'friendly' was not an inadvertent oversight, nor was it happenstance that when it was Arab States that were referred to, the co-operation was crowned with the modifier 'friendly'.

Molotov's and Malenkov's references to Israel's commitments may demonstrate that Israel's acceptance of the Soviet conditions paved the way to the resumption of diplomatic relations in a time characterized by Soviet slogans calling for 'peaceful co-existence', 'relaxation of international tension', 'co-operation among nations', etc. The era of 'thaw' by itself without Israel's commitment would not have been of decisive weight in the USSR's decision to renew its relations with Israel. This special treatment received from the Soviet Union would accompany Israel until the relations between both states will be again severed (1967) and even well afterwards.

NOTES

1   Krushchev in his speech before the participants in the 20th Congress of the CPSU, on 24 Feb. 1956, noted that Molotov, Voroshilov and Mikoyan were purge candidates.
2   Ibid.
3   *Pravda*, 16 March 1953.
4   Ibid.
5   Concluding his statement in the Knesset on 17 Feb. 1953 on Israeli–Soviet relations (*Divrei Haknesset*, Vol. 13, p. 747), Foreign Minister Sharett said: 'Renewal of relations depends only on the other side and, if they are to be renewed, what their content and nature will be.' It seems that Sharett adhered to the approach that the one who severed relations should initiate their renewal, should he wish to do so.
6   M. Bar Zohar, *David Ben Gurion*, Vol. 2, p. 961, cites Ben Gurion's diary saying 'on 30 April 1953 Ben Gurion concluded a consultation in the MFA regarding the Soviet bloc: "I concluded: no harassment now, no appeal for the renewal of relations ... friendly talks with Soviet representatives in the satellite countries. If they wouldn't be advantageous – they would not harm".'
7   B. Z. Razin, 'I negotiated the renewal of diplomatic relations with the Soviet Union', *Maariv*, 10 March 1972. Compare this with what is written on this by A. Dagan in *Moscow and Jerusalem*, pp. 72–3.
8   M. Sharett, *Yoman Ishi* (Heb., 'Private Diary') Vol. 1, pp. 64, 79.
9   B. Z. Razin, *Maariv*, 10 March 1953.
10 *Davar, Kol Haam*, 21 July 1953.
11 The contents of this note were quoted by the Prime Minister in the Knesset when he replied to Maki MK M. Wilner's interpellation (*Divrei Haknesset*, Vol. 11, p. 1465, 27 Feb. 1952).
12 Ibid.
13 *Davar, Kol Haam*, 21 July 1953.
14 *Izvestia*, 21 July 1953.
15 *Izvestia*, 9 Aug. 1953.

Part 2

Bilateral relations – from their resumption to their severance

3 · *Israel between East and West*

ISRAEL'S POLICY towards the Soviet Union from the early 1950s was shaped by pragmatic, ideological and national considerations. Those who conducted Israel's foreign policy had kept in mind the needs most vital to the State and to its existence, the linchpins being security and immigration.

To achieve the first – the security of the State – it was necessary: (1) to secure sources for the purchase of defensive and offensive arms in sufficient quantities and to a quality that was as advanced as possible, in view of the Arab states' arms race and their frequently declared intentions to annihilate Israel; (2) to locate military colleges abroad that could assist officers of the Israeli Defense Forces in absorbing the military equipment and train them in the use and application of modern military know-how; (3) to have the opportunity to be integrated within a Western regional security system as a guarantee of security in face of the Arab danger.

To achieve the second goal – immigration to Israel – it was necessary to secure free access to the Jewish communities in the Diaspora for the encouragement of immigration, and Israel had to receive economic aid. It was also necessary to obtain loans and financial credits for the development of agriculture, industry, and housing, for the building of roads, and for the expansion of its educational, cultural, and scientific network.[1]

To achieve these goals it was important to negotiate with state organizations and banking institutions in the Western countries and to activate personalities and those who shaped public opinion. Israel anticipated no assistance from the Soviet Union for any of these endeavors. The borders of the USSR were closed to Jewish emigrants; numerous appeals to the Soviet Union requesting aid were rebuffed.

Moreover, the Soviet Union was engaged in its own rehabilitation and recuperation from the ravages of World War II, and had not yet developed programs of economic aid to newly independent states. Israeli leaders were, therefore, inclined to consider the West as Israel's source for economic and security-related support. The military and political assistance which the Soviet Union extended to Israel in the first phases of its independence were taken by the country's leaders as a phenomenon of the past that had played itself out.[2] Yet, Ben Gurion did not belittle the strength of the Soviet Union as a 'great Superpower' which could be helpful or harmful. 'Only a stupid politician whose antagonism to communism has driven him to distraction could relate with equanimity to the Soviet Union's positive or negative attitude on the international plane.'[3] This stance, however, did not divert Israel from looking to the West for its primary support.

In addition to their pragmatic approach, Israel's leaders – Ben Gurion, Sharett, Meir, Eshkol, and their Mapai party colleagues – had a national and ideological grounding that deeply influenced the country's policy towards the Soviet Union: their negative attitude to the Soviet regime and the Soviet Union's enmity towards Zionism, Israel and the Jewish people. As for Israel's place between East and West, Ben Gurion set out the main lines of his approach before the members of Mapai's political committee in March 1953 as follows:[4]

> In time of war, Israel can't remain neutral. The parties which will be involved in war will take into account Israel's neutrality, and should the Soviets conquer Israel, even temporarily, the Jewish State and Zionism will come to an end. Israel is the West's bastion in the Middle East. Because of its military might, Israel's value during a war will be more important than that of the Arab states during peace. Israel should concentrate its main efforts on convincing the USA that it should turn Israel into 'the base, workshop and granary' of the Middle East. Israel has no interest in 'a regional set-up' but rather 'in an arrangement between us and America or with all of NATO'.

This view, presenting the prime importance of Israel to the West in time of war, was presented to US Secretary of State John Foster

Dulles when he visited Israel in May 1953. By then, however, a significant turn had already taken place in the East–West atmosphere. The new Soviet leadership was making efforts to relax the Cold War tension that had characterized the Stalin era after World War II, and Ben Gurion's principles no longer coincided with the new reality. It was, therefore, not surprising that Dulles rejected them on the spot. Nevertheless, for a long time, Ben Gurion's principles continued to guide Israel's foreign policy.

At that time, the Soviet Union had not yet become a political factor in the Middle East, so the advantages and disadvantages of a pro-Western orientation were not taken into consideration by Israel. Neither did it consider the possibilities of political support which the Soviet Union could have extended to Israel in its conflict with the Arab states. Foreign Minister Sharett believed that Soviet policy towards the Arab states had not changed, whilst the Arab states would not look for salvation from the USSR.[5] The possibility that Soviet policy in the Middle East would change from a passive stance to an active one was noted only after the USSR used a veto in the UN Security Council and – moreover – after the Soviet–Egyptian arms deal became known.[6]

The renewal of Israeli–Soviet relations in July 1953 had not yielded a real *rapprochement* between the two countries. In spite of the fact that the mutual representation was raised to ambassadorial level[7] and despite the declarations given by both parties about their aspirations to open a new chapter in their relationship, the gap between their positions grew constantly wider against the background of two parallel processes. They were: (1) Israel's struggle for the cause of Soviet Jews; (2) the USSR's active alignment with the Arab states in the Israeli–Arab conflict. Both processes gradually crystallized into determining factors in the relationship. As for the first process, Israel had the offensive role and the USSR the defensive one. Regarding the second, the roles were reversed. Both were linked to East–West relations: Israel – aiming to forge supportive public opinion in the West for the cause of Soviet Jews; the USSR – aiming, on its part, at exploiting the Israeli–Arab conflict for its own confrontation with the West.

Israel's policy-makers faced a difficult dilemma: on the one hand, Israel aspired to narrow the gap yawning ever-wider between the two positions – Israeli and Soviet – over the Middle East arena. On the other hand, Israel wished to tighten security and economic links with the West in view of the growing strength of the Arab states with the USSR's help and their threats to annihilate Israel. Israel also aspired to obtain the assistance of the West in its struggle for the cause of Soviet Jewry, a battle which turned into a permanent clash with the USSR.

What follows is a characterization of the phases of Israel's policy towards the USSR from the renewal of relations in 1953 until their rupture in 1967.

Clarifying Israel's assurances to the USSR

Answering questions put by Israeli journalists as to the significance of the assurances given by Israel to the USSR in exchange for the renewal of diplomatic relations with it, the spokesman of the Foreign Ministry in Jerusalem said:

1. There is no change in Israel's policy – following its renewal of relations with the USSR – neither towards the USSR nor to the West. [The intention of this declaration presumably was to dispel the suspicion that Israel's links with the West would become weaker following the assurances given by Israel to the USSR.] (*Haaretz*, 11 August 1953)
2. Should the Middle East Pact be established and Israel invited to participate in it, and should Israel's assessment be that this pact is of a defensive and not aggressive nature, then Israel's assurances towards the USSR would not be relevant. (*Kol Haam*, 22 July 1953)
3. Israeli–Soviet friendly relations could be based only on the principle of mutuality. This principle includes, according to Israel's understanding, granting permission to Soviet Jews to immigrate to Israel. The solution to this problem will be a touchstone 'to the mutuality of friendly relations between both states'. (*Haaretz*, 11 August 1953)
4. Israel's foreign policy would not be able to overlook the fact that millions of Jews live in the USSR and be forced to insist that a way be found to enable those Jews who so desire to leave for Israel. (*Haaretz*, 11 August 1953)

Israel's clarification campaign continued on other occasions. On two of them Foreign Minister Sharett himself commented:

1. During the Knesset debate on 7 December 1953, M. Sharett clarified that Israel was interested in a friendly relationship with the USSR, without having been required to renounce its regime and 'its historic aspirations'. He also made the friendship with the USSR conditional upon its permitting Soviet Jews to emigrate to Israel, on enabling them to maintain free contacts with Israel, on making it possible for Israel to address them and provide informative and cultural material (on Israel and Judaism). He also demanded from the Soviet authorities that they accord Israeli diplomats in Moscow the same freedom that Soviet diplomats enjoyed in Israel.

In fact Sharett demanded from the Soviet authorities that they should treat Israel in a special way such as had not been granted to any other foreign representative in their country. Inherent in his demands was a certain deviation from the USSR's norms in its relations with foreign countries. It is doubtful whether the conditions laid down by Israel's leaders – contrary to Soviet procedures – could have gained much sympathy in Soviet eyes. Moreover, Israel's demands, no matter how justified they might have appeared in the eyes of Israel's leaders, could only have aroused doubts among the Soviet authorities as to Israel's keen aspirations for establishing friendly relations with the USSR.

2. In concluding the political debate in the Knesset on 1 September 1953, Sharett (then Prime Minister as well as Minister of Foreign Affairs) repeated this thesis in a pessimistic tone adding to it a dimension of currency linked to Soviet policy in the Middle East,

> We are interested in friendship with the USSR if it is possible to reach a reciprocal friendship on her part; reciprocal friendship as we understand it ... but what are the chances of such a policy on a reciprocal basis? Could we have full friendship with a superpower when this friendship is hanging over a yawning abyss separating us from the Jews in the USSR? Is it possible to reach a total and sincere and true friendship by continuous attempts to gain the hearts of our enemies, on our account? We are unable to free the Soviet Union from the responsibility for accelerating the appeasement race rushing now towards the Arab states, in view of its statements made in the Security Council.[8]

In retrospect it seems that each party made its own comments on the mutual assurances, particularly on the subject of the 'Pact' and the 'friendly relations' that were presented as a condition for renewal of diplomatic relations.

Here is a brief comparison of the two parties' perception of these assurances.

The Middle East Pact

The Soviet authorities regarded this pact – inspired and encouraged by the USA and perhaps with its direct participation – as a strategic challenge to the USSR's security. Hence, they applied their efforts to deterring Middle Eastern countries – including Israel – from becoming integrated in it, under the pretext that it was an anti-Soviet pact. The USSR's demand from Israel that it should commit itself not to join such a pact as a condition for the renewal of relations was presumably intended not only to deter Israel from participating in the establishment of such a pact, but also to prevent the offering of military reinforcement to Israel through such a pact, if established.[9]

On the other hand, the leaders of Israel thought that Israel's security and its very existence would be seriously threatened if it were not an integral part of such a pact when it was set up since the Arab states that were invited to become members of this union would wish to exploit it with the aim of annihilating Israel. For this reason they thought the 'omission of Israel from membership in such a pact would signify, politically, the abandoning of Israel, as if it had no place amongst the Middle East states, or that nobody would care what its fate would be in days of calamity'.[10]

In arguing with Israel's leftist parties – which protested vehemently against the government's intention to join the pact – Sharett stated that at issue was a defense pact defending Israel 'and not an aggressive conspiracy aimed against someone'.[11] At a later time Sharett would argue before the USSR's Minister of Foreign Affairs, Molotov, that 'a defense treaty between Israel and the USA is intended to defend Israel and not to "defend the region"'.[12]

Friendly relations

Soviet representatives used to indicate in their talks with Israeli representatives that they expected Israel to prevent manifestations of acts, declarations, articles, and votes in the international arena displaying negative attitudes towards the Soviet Union. It could be understood from what they said that, generally speaking, the principle of friendly relations obliged, in their opinion, the opposite partner more than the Soviet Union itself, unless it concerned a country, which in the Soviet Union's estimation, 'has chosen the non-capitalist road of development', or neutrality, or resented USA policy. Israel was not included in any of those three categories.

The leaders of Israel presumed that the USSR's assurance that it would 'maintain friendly relations with Israel' gave them the authority to demand:

(a) a solution to the Jewish problem in the USSR, including permission to emigrate to Israel;
(b) application of the principle of mutuality by the dissemination of information between both partners;
(c) the non-alignment of the USSR with the cause of the Arab states that were threatening Israel's security and existence.

At a later time, Sharett confessed to US Secretary of State Dulles that Israel had lost its world to the Soviets without gaining a defense treaty with the USA and that the Soviets did not find it necessary to permit Jewish emigration to Israel as long as Israel's leaders declared their willingness to conclude a defense treaty with the USA, 'which meant – as far as the Soviets were concerned – enslavement, military bases, and all other abominations'.[13] Molotov noted in his conversation with Sharett that the USSR was interested in maintaining friendly relations with Israel and with Egypt, and if Israel had been truly willing it could have already achieved them (according to Sharett's version 'then the relations would have been entirely different').[14]

The gap between the positions of Israel and the USSR was not created owing to opposing interests (as Israel had no intention of opening a war against Soviet penetration into the Middle East, exactly as the USSR did not intend to annihilate Israel), but from clashing interests. (Soviet penetration into the Middle East was exploited by Israel's enemies for the undermining of Israel's security.) Thus, relations between the two states gradually deteriorated (with short intervals that aroused Israel's hopes for an improvement). However, when Sharett realized the Soviet turn-about after the Soviet–Egyptian arms deal, he stated:

> We have to declare, time and again, that no matter what the reasons and considerations are – whether national or universal – that determine the policy of one superpower or another, as far as we are concerned, the decisive and deter-mining factor in our approach to any world factor, is to what extent its policy and acts endanger, strengthen or weaken Israel's existence and security.[15]

Over time, this attitude became a criterion by which Israel judged the USSR's policy towards it. There was a certain risk of slipping into predetermined notions, namely, that Israel's policy course towards the USSR had no importance, since it was the USSR who dictated the course of the mutual relations system, whilst Israel had no influence on it.

ISRAEL'S POLICY TOWARDS THE USSR AFTER THE SOVIET–EGYPTIAN ARMS DEAL

The arms deal created a new focus of tension in Israeli–Soviet relations. Israel's leaders condemned it from the Knesset forum and defined it 'as an alliance which might cause a disastrous revo-lutionary turnabout in Israel's security posture'.[16] At the same time, the USA and Britain were sharply criticized for their policy of appeasement towards Egypt. Thus, Israel's policy-makers attempted to avoid giving the impression that they were mobilizing world opinion against the deal, either out of enmity to communism or out of eagerness to integrate in the Western anti-Soviet alignment.[17]

The arms deal became a subject of diplomatic talks between Israel and the USSR, in which Israeli representatives attempted to persuade the USSR to recognize the fact that a danger was looming over Israel's existence from the large arms arsenal accumulated in Egyptian hands. The reference was to Nasser's declarations and the Fedayeen penetrations into Israel from Egyptian territory, with Nasser's open encouragement, in the frame of his declared aim of destroying Israel with the help of Soviet arms.[18] A further escalation

of tension in the relations between both countries was due to the
Sinai Campaign. On 5 November 1956 Soviet Prime Minister
Bulganin sent a sharp and threatening note to Israel's Prime
Minister Ben Gurion, in which he noted:

> In acting according to the will of others by instructions from
> abroad, the government of Israel is playing with the fate of
> peace, with the fate of its own people. It is sowing hatred for
> the State of Israel among the Middle Eastern nations such as
> cannot but make itself felt with regard to the future of Israel
> and which is putting in jeopardy the very existence of Israel
> as a state.[19]

and the note included a threatening sentence directed at Israel:

> The government of the USSR, vitally interested in the
> maintenance of peace and the safeguarding of tranquillity in
> the Middle East, is undertaking measures now to put an end
> to the war and curb the aggressors.[20]

This was the first time, since the establishment of diplomatic
relations between Israel and the USSR, that such a threat had been
sent by the Soviet Union to Israel. The leaders of Israel, and with
them the leaders of France and Britain, interpreted the Soviet
threat as a serious intention to carry it out if Israel would not retreat
to the Israeli–Egyptian armistice line border. In his reply on 8
November 1956 to Bulganin, Ben Gurion expressed his surprise and
regret 'at the threat to the integrity and very existence of Israel',
contained in Bulganin's note. 'Our foreign policy,' added Ben Gurion
'is dictated by our vital interest and by our desire to live in peace,
and no foreign factor determines it or will determine it.'[21] And
although the Soviet threat was firmly rejected, in a restrained
manner, there was still profound fear that the Soviets might carry
out their threat. This happened to carry decisive weight in Ben
Gurion's consideration in favor of a retreat.[22] The Israeli government itself – should we accept G. Meir's evidence – had not
anticipated that the USSR's reaction to the campaign would be so
vehement and dangerous as expressed in its notes to Israel.[23]

After the retreat from Sinai and the Gaza Strip, Israeli–Soviet
relations returned to their normal situation (except that mutual

trade had not been renewed). The shadow of the campaign, however, interpreted by the Soviets as an attempt to return Britain and France to domination of the Middle East, would cast its shadow on the system of mutual relations as long as they existed (until June 1967).

ISRAEL'S POLICY TOWARDS THE USSR IN THE AFTERMATH OF THE SINAI CAMPAIGN

On 29 November 1956 *Izvestia* published an article under the heading, 'The road to suicide which the adventurous policy of Israel's ruling circles is leading to'. In vehemently condemning Israel for the campaign and its Prime Minister Ben Gurion, the article argued: 'In challenging the Arab nations and all the nations of the East who struggle against colonialism, Israel is digging a grave for itself' and under the circumstances that 'the ruling circles in Israel are obliged to reach the appropriate conclusions from the lessons derived from recent events: Israel's existence as a state is being placed in the balance'. This was part of a delegitimization campaign against Israel's right to exist as a state. A team of experts in the Ministry of Foreign Affairs analyzed this campaign and among their conclusions were the following:[24]

The Soviet Union had decided to adopt a long-range anti-Israel policy.
Izvestia's article is a declaration of political war against Israel whilst aligning itself completely with the Arabs.
This policy would not pass even after the Sinai Campaign crisis was over, but would continue as long as the USSR and the USA continued to fight to gain footholds in the Middle East.

The team felt that one of the reasons for the deterioration in the USSR's attitude towards Israel was the damage Israel had caused to the USSR in the region (following Israel's military victory) and the Soviet fear of additional damage to its status (in the Middle East). The team also considered that despite the fact that Israel had come to be seen as 'a factor capable of action' in the Middle East, the USSR was still far from drawing the conclusion that it should come to terms with Israel on the basis of its power. The team believed that in planning Israel's information activities in the international arena with the aim of proving to the USSR that Israel was insisting upon its right to defend itself, it would be necessary to take into account 'that the situation of Soviet Jewry is directly influenced by the nature of Israeli–Soviet relations'.

Two conclusions could be drawn from this analysis:

1. There was no chance that Israel would be able to change the anti-Israel policy of the Soviet Union as long as the East–West confrontation continued in the Middle East. This approach had been acceptable to the Mapai leaders, including Foreign Minister G. Meir, a long time before the Sinai Campaign, therefore there was nothing new about it.[25] This view, however, contradicted the team's assessment that one of the reasons for the deterioration in Israeli–Soviet relations was the damage that Israel caused to the Soviet Union's status in the Middle East. For Israel's participation with France and Britain in the Sinai Campaign – whatever Israel's national motives were – had made it in effect an integral part of the East–West confrontation and proved that it was in Israel's power to influence the conflict and not just to be influenced.
2. There was an interrelationship between the situation of Soviet Jews on one hand and the state of Israeli–Soviet relations, on the other. Taking this interconnection into account should have alerted Israel's policy-makers. They should have been aware that if the situation of the Soviet Jews required the maintenance of normal or even friendly relations between the USSR and Israel the struggle might lead to a severe clash with the USSR and consequently to worsening of relations with it.

In both situations Israel was placed in the camp of those opposed to the USSR. The military and political assistance extended to the Arab states by the USSR was encouraging them not to accept Israel's existence and not to relinquish their desire to destroy it. The common denominator of both countries (Israel and the USSR) was the growing gap between their declared aspirations for an improvement in relations between them, and their actual policies.

In the course of the debate held in the Knesset at the end of October 1957, Foreign Minister G. Meir responded to the 'various sides' regarding their proposal that Israel should completely change its foreign policy towards the Soviet Union by saying:

> It is not Israel's fault that there are countries which, because of their political considerations, don't wish to maintain friendly relations with Israel. Friendship with any country should not be acquired at the price of Israel's renouncing its means for safeguarding its security and the existence of its independence and its territorial integrity.

She also expressed her confidence that there was no sense in searching for an explanation for the USSR's attitude towards Israel 'according to Israel's stance or acts' but rather 'according to entirely different considerations'.[26] Though the Foreign Minister did not pinpoint those considerations, it could be presumed that she was referring to Soviet interests in gaining footholds in the Arab world.

In her reaction, the Foreign Minister probably referred to the proposal by Dr N. Goldmann (then the President of the World Zionist Organization) that Israel should conduct a policy of neutrality between the Eastern and Western blocs, based on two principles:[27]

(a) calling for a meeting of leaders from the USA and the USSR to establish a comprehensive settlement in the Middle East between Israel and the Arab countries;
(b) demanding that a total arms embargo be imposed on the Middle East, agreed upon between the USA and the USSR.

Goldmann's views were to a great extent influenced by the stance of the USSR, which initiated extensive diplomatic activity towards integration with the other three superpowers, particularly the USA, in the process of establishing peace in the Middle East, by being neutral and out of the arms race.[28] The Soviets praised Goldmann's proposals in their conversations with Israeli personages, remarking that if accepted, they would help to improve mutual relations by urging the Americans with the help of Israel and world Jewry, particularly USA Jewry, to sit around one table with the Soviets and settle the problems in order to prevent the outbreak of a third world war.[29]

48

The Israeli government rejected these proposals for two main reasons.

1. Because of fear that co-operation between East and West concerning the Israeli–Arab conflict would be carried out to the detriment of Israel's vital interests. This apprehension was based on the USSR's and the USA's tendency to court the Arabs and appease them. It seemed that the success of the proposals depended upon the extent of the pressure applied to Israel in order to extract concessions, either in territory or by getting Israel's acceptance to absorb tens of thousands of Arab refugees within the geographical borders to be agreed upon by the Great Powers. For this reason, Israel's leaders tended to prefer the status quo in spite of its disadvantage in the absence of peace.

2. Because of fear that the embargo on arms deliveries to the Middle East would first of all cause damage to Israel's defense capability, whilst the Arab states would continue to receive arms from the USSR. This one-sidedness could have placed Israel in an inferior position and put an end to its military force as a deterring factor.

Even if Israel had accepted these principles and could have thus improved its relations with the USSR and its image in the West – even then it seemed that the disadvantages outweighed the advantages.

The professional level in the Foreign Ministry, which did not appeal against these principles when they were extensively discussed, believed that between the complete rejection of the idea and its total acceptance, there was still a certain amount of room which Israel's foreign policy could and should exploit for the improvement of mutual relations, even in a limited way.[30] Indeed, here and there one could discern a noticeable improvement in the style and substance of the relations, mainly in the bilateral field. As for the Middle East aspect: in the second half of the 1950s Prime Minister Ben Gurion, and afterwards Prime Minister Eshkol, conceived the idea that without the USSR's guarantees regarding the integrity and independence of all States in the Middle East – in co-operation with the USA – peace would not prevail. This conception continued to exist until the Six Day War, but received no positive response from the USSR, though the USSR itself had believed it in the past.

ISRAEL'S ATTEMPTS AT CO-OPERATION WITH THE USSR

In the political review delivered by Ben Gurion to the Mapai Political Committee on 4 March 1958, he also referred to the Israeli–Soviet aspect.

> There are people who believe that Russia is Israel's sworn enemy. There are two reasons for that:
>
> (a) *The Arabs.* For the Russians friendship with the Arabs is more important than friendship with Israel. Dominating the Middle East means domination over oil and passage to Europe.
> (b) *The Jews of Russia.* The same factor that is of assistance to Israel in America operates in Russia in the opposite direction ... But what is helping us in America is working against us in Russia, because Israel is a great disturber; this makes the Jews in Russia an unreliable element. Israel – as the Russian rulers understand it – is a force for disloyalty among the Jews in Russia. To a certain degree, this is true.
>
> There are two reasons for Russia's enmity. Despite that, I did not come to the final conclusion that Russia, for her part, will do all she can to destroy Israel. I don't know if there is a basis for such a conclusion. Just because Russia has global interests, interests aiming at world domination, she knows that striking Israel may cause her damage.
>
> In any case, Russia's hostile stance is one of the factors explaining why there is no chance that the Arabs would like to reconcile with us in the near future. They feel that there is an immense power siding with them ... There is no hope – this could be said in almost full confidence – that Russia will be amongst those assisting us in the near future, such that we would get help from the Russians to strengthen our position, and thus reach a better understanding with the Arabs. Help will not come from there. We shall be satisfied if no great and harsh disturbance comes from there.
>
> We should strive at getting guarantees for a status quo in the Middle East. Should it be possible to involve Russia in such guarantees, it would be a great achievement. I would not

say that this is 100 per cent impossible. But, I would say that it is about 95 per cent impossible. It would be difficult to presume that Russia would accept now a status quo in the Middle East ...[31]

In presenting the reasons for Soviet hostility towards Israel not much was new. Actually, in the majority of cases, assessments were similar (Ben Gurion himself also mentioned this). Two innovations, however, were remarkable: (1) the readiness to admit the fact that Jews in the USSR were not loyal to the Soviet regime because of Israel (the source of their national awakening, their defender and fighter on their behalf); (2) the concept that without the USSR's involvement in the peace process between Israel and the Arab states, peace between them would not be achieved. Therefore, his conclusion was that Israel should strive at getting guarantees from the USA and the USSR for its existence within the armistice lines 1949–67 as a long-range policy.

Ben Gurion, in the conversation he initiated with the Soviet Ambassador in Israel, M. Bodrov (who was instrumental in the resumption of Israeli–Soviet relations from his post in Sofia in 1953), on 17 July 1958, brought up the subject of guarantees with the purpose of testing them in reality. He proposed[32] to the Ambassador three ways to advance co-operation between Israel and the USSR.

1. *Friendship with Israel.* Ben Gurion did not specify what he exactly meant other than creating a friendly atmosphere between both states. The Ambassador's reaction was that it depended upon Israel. Ben Gurion insisted that it depended upon the USSR as a great power. Finally, the Ambassador concluded that it was up to both sides.

2. *Sale of Soviet arms to Israel.* Ben Gurion detailed the categories: tanks, Ilyushin and MiG aircraft.

3. *An International conference to conclude a peace agreement between Israel and the Arab states.* Ben Gurion suggested that the conference be called at the USSR's initiative. It demonstrated Israel's willingness to involve the Soviets in the peacemaking process in the Middle East.

With regard to the second proposal, the Ambassador did not react. This was the first time that Israel's Prime Minister had put such a request to a Soviet Ambassador in Israel. Even before, when

Sharett was Prime Minister and Minister of Foreign Affairs, Ben Gurion had formulated the idea that the Soviet Union should be approached with the request to sell Israel arms, but Sharett thought that 'it will be a rash step as long as there is hope [getting them] from the USA'.[33] Sharett admitted that he realized (apparently later) that he was not always right in this respect and when the subject came up in the Knesset Committee of Foreign Affairs and Security (in early 1956), he based his reservations upon the following arguments. (1) Israel will not be able to pay for the arms except with US dollars received from Jews in the USA 'and they will distance themselves from Israel and the Jewish Appeal', when they learn the purpose for which their money is destined. (2) All the possibilities for getting arms from the West had not yet been exhausted. (3) There was no assurance that the Soviets would respond positively.

Two unofficial attempts were made to clarify the possibility of buying Soviet arms by the (then) Minister of Internal Affairs, Bar Yehuda, and the (then) Chairman of the Knesset Committee of Foreign Affairs and Security, M. Argov, who met with representatives of the USSR and Bulgaria. The answer was negative.[34]

The main difference in the attitudes between Ben Gurion and Sharett, in this respect, was that Sharett was completely reluctant to co-operate with the USSR while Ben Gurion was interested in the benefit which might have been gained, both from acquiring arms for its own sake and from the cessation of Soviet hostility towards Israel. (Perhaps this is what he had in mind in his talk with the Soviet Ambassador about Israeli–Soviet friendship).[35]

In addition to the above three proposals Ben Gurion requested of the Ambassador that the Soviet Union and the USA together give security guarantees to the Middle East states and that the USSR permit Soviet Jews to immigrate freely to Israel. To these two requests Ben Gurion added: 'If possible'. The Ambassador promised to pass on these proposals to his superiors in Moscow. Whenever Ben Gurion met the Ambassador and asked him whether he had received a reply, the Ambassador answered, 'Not yet'.

We learn from all this that the USSR regarded these proposals doubtfully and negatively. Hence, the assessment in Mapai circles was strengthened, namely, that the USSR was not interested in co-operating with Israel.

SOVIET–AMERICAN SECURITY GUARANTEES

In April–May 1963 Ben Gurion returned to his wishful ideas regarding Soviet–American security guarantees.[36]

This came about when Egypt, Iraq and Syria declared, on 17 April 1953, the establishment of a common Federation, one of its proclaimed aims being the destruction of Israel. It seemed that Israel was dangerously encircled. Being deeply concerned about a new situation, Ben Gurion sent urgent Notes to the heads of the USSR, the USA and France, asking for their urgent support to remove the Arab threat from Israel. He asked France 'to base the great friendship between both states on a treaty which should secure military aid for Israel, in case of an Egyptian attack on Israel'. The USSR and the USA were requested to guarantee together the borders of all states in the region. The leaders of France and the USA answered negatively. They did not share Ben Gurion's concerns. After a short time it became known that the idea of the Federation was an abortive one. The USSR did not reply.

This call by Ben Gurion, also aired in the Knesset and supported by various parties, constituted a change in the consciousness of Israel's leaders who shifted from complete reservation, like that of Sharett in 1955,[37] to a striving for – first in 1958 and now publicly – Soviet involvement in regional security arrangements, under the assumption that without the USSR the status quo and peace in the region would not be guaranteed.

When Israel's Prime Minister and Foreign Minister changed in 1963, Israel made a special effort to improve its relations with the USSR. Hopes were raised in Israel by cultural relations begun in the early 1960s; the nature of the improved Soviet attitude toward Israel; and the Soviet dynamics in developing connections with foreign countries in the economic, scientific and technological fields. Prime Minister Eshkol, presenting the new government's policies in the Knesset on 12 January 1966, referred to Israel's expectations of the USSR. A selection from his statement (in translation) follows:[38]

> Israel appreciates the friendship and understanding displayed by many nations of the world ... Some nations openly declare their support of Israel's independence and integrity and help, to a certain degree, in strengthening its defense and

economy. There are nations with far from balanced policies towards Israel and Arab countries. There is no doubt that the prospects for peace and stability would increase if the USSR and the Western powers would agree upon a policy which both theoretically and practically supports the independence and integrity of all the states in the Middle East. This perspective was in my mind, when two years ago I expressed the hope that greater understanding would prevail between Israel and the USSR, parallel to our close ties with the US, France, and England. Although there has been no great progress in this direction, we must not become discouraged or abandon hope. The policies of the United States and the Soviet Union coincided in 1947, at the momentous hour when the *yishuv* (Jewish population of Palestine until Israel's independence) broke the political blockade, relieved itself of the yoke of foreign rule and emerged into national independence. If the USSR and the Western powers would join forces today, adopting a positive, unified and steadfast policy, this could have the crucial effect of introducing peace into our area. And so, Gentlemen, logic decrees that greater understanding should prevail between Moscow and Jerusalem.

Israel does not participate in what is called the Cold War. On the contrary, it strives for its conclusion or eradication. Israel supports the principle of avoiding the use of force as a solution to territorial disputes, as set out by the USSR at the beginning of 1964. The Soviet representatives declared then that this principle should be applied universally, therefore, it also applies to the situation in our area.

On many occasions we have demanded that this principle be applied not only to the Near East, but also to national frontiers in central and eastern Europe and the entire world. We could, therefore, expect a more positive atmosphere in relations between the two states, extending beyond the partial achievements which have been accomplished in some areas and which themselves require greater expansion.

These were the friendliest words that had ever been expressed towards the USSR by any Prime Minister or Foreign Minister of Israel.

Eshkol's statement included a number of new elements: *on the global level* – the expression of Israeli support for the territorial status quo in Europe; *on the Middle East level* – the demand for a Soviet–American *rapprochement* in order to ensure the independence and peace of all the countries in the area, which constituted an attempt at designating the USSR as the decisive factor – not just an equal – in the Middle East, without which peace could not be achieved in the area; *on the bilateral level* – the call for improved relations, beyond what had already been accomplished.

The declaration of Israel's support for the territorial status quo in Europe, which was undoubtedly welcome to the Russians, included an indication of Israel's expectations in return, namely, the USSR's recognition of the cease-fire lines as the final borders between Israel and its neighbors. Whilst the reference to the USSR's part in the establishment of the State of Israel was directed primarily towards the Arab nations rather than to the Soviet Union, as regarded both the past and the future, it was also intended to deter the Arabs from their aspiration of totally annihilating Israel. Up to this point Eshkol's statement seemed reasonably acceptable to the USSR. Eshkol continued, however, in sharp contrast to the first part of his speech by introducing the situation of the Soviet Jews in a harsh tone, such as never had been used before towards the USSR. This angered the Soviets and was the subject of official talks between them and the Israelis, both in Jerusalem and Moscow.[39] The Israeli government was accused of crude interference in the USSR's internal affairs and of undermining the grounds which were supposed to serve as the basis for improved relations between the two states. The USSR's furious reaction to the 'Jewish' part of Eshkol's policy speech heavily overshadowed the 'political' part which paradoxically leaned much more towards the USSR than any speech given by his predecessors. Hence, it seems that the speech's severe statement on Soviet Jews damaged relations between both states more than its political section had helped them.

THE JEWISH FACTOR IN ISRAELI–SOVIET RELATIONS

On 5 February 1960, the Director General of Israel's Ministry of Foreign Affairs clarified his view on Israeli–Soviet relations following a series of debates which took place in the Ministry at the end of

55

1959. His approach reflected that of the debaters; the salient points of the discussion follow.

There was no chance for improvement in Israeli–Soviet relations in the near future. The problem of Soviet Jews was one of the greatest obstacles on the road to understanding between Israel and the Soviet Union. There was no viable alternative here. It was inconceivable that Israel would abandon its interest in Jews of the USSR merely for a vague chance of improved relations.

Being conscious of the difficulties did not mean that Israel would slacken its search for possibilities to widen the scope of dialogue. Any occasion would have to be exploited to make general declarations sympathetic to USSR plans – as for instance on issues of disarmament, world peace, and so forth – without damaging Israel's relations with other states. Israel's aim was to attenuate as much as possible any collisions with the USSR. In this respect, Israel was to be more flexible than in the past – but without illusions.

Despite skepticism as to the results, attempts to enhance the dialogue should continue with: contacts with Soviet Ambassadors wherever they may be; clarification of fundamental problems; and attempts at maintaining talks in Moscow as far as possible.

All of the above would not change the situation immediately, but would yield increased revelation of Soviet intentions and perhaps serve in due course as a motivating factor for a policy change, something in the spirit of 'Cast thy bread upon the waters'.[40]

One group among the debaters pointed out the anti-Semitic and anti-Israel campaign increasingly waged at that time in the Soviet media, out of all proportion to the USSR's relations with conflicting states. In fact, they admitted to not being able to formulate any broad-based explanation for this campaign other than: (a) the enmity of the Soviet regime towards the Jewish minority which, through its national awakening, had became an oppressive annoyance impossible to eliminate, either by expulsions, or by emigration or granting it cultural autonomy; and (b) anti-Semitic motives carried over from the past to the present.

The majority of the discussion's participants was of the opinion that the Jewish factor and Israel's interest in it was detrimental to the relations. Yet, despite that, it was decided, following the Foreign Minister's proposal, to continue with the activities among the Jews in the USSR and on their behalf.[41]

The Foreign Minister G. Meir believed that the presence of Israel's Embassy in Moscow was a vital necessity for the encouragement of the Jews there. In this respect she did not differ from her predecessor, M. Sharett, who also believed that Israel needed 'a foothold in Moscow for the encouragement of and fraternal alliance with that Jewry itself by our presence there'.[42]

This view was based on the assumption that there was at any rate no possibility of influencing the Kremlin's leaders to improve relations with Israel. The debaters on their part attached great importance to demonstrating the Israeli presence and enlarging the circle of contacts as much as possible with the local Jews.

The improvement in the atmosphere between East and West, since the 20th Congress of the CPSU, and the exposure of the Soviet population to the outside world most probably made it easier to maintain contacts with local Jews. But the expectations in Israel for such contacts were seldom greater than the possibilities for materializing them. Hence the importance Israel's leaders attached to the spreading of information amongst Soviet Jews. Even Israel's cultural, scientific and technological events in the USSR, which gradually increased over 1962–66, were considered to be Israeli information activities amongst the Jews more than just cultural relations between the peoples of both states.[43]

Israel's leaders had a profound sentiment for the Jews in the USSR. The information about them, which was streaming in to them, reinforced even more their determination to carry on the struggle on their behalf. Beside the human tragedy of the Jews in the USSR, Israel's leaders regarded it as their national duty – as leaders of the free sovereign Jewish people in its homeland – to invest maximum effort towards redeeming them from their national and human distress and bringing them in large numbers to Israel. They saw this Jewry as the greatest immigration reservoir of the Jewish people which, if allowed, could help in the development of Israel and in the strengthening of its security. This task was taken by them to be supremely vital for Israel's future, and they were therefore ready to risk paying a heavy political price in return for carrying it out.

This political line, which became predominant in all its force during the 'Doctor's Plot', declined in the years following, and came to the fore once more at the end of the 1950s, creating high tension in the mutual relations. At the Soviet end, a great deal of enmity accumulated – because of Israel's part in the increased national awakening of the Jews in the USSR and because of Israel's contribution to the creation of a negative image of the USSR in the Western world through the revelation of the tragedy of Soviet Jewry.

This high tension combined with Israel's blow to the USSR's prestige in the Six Day War led to the Soviet Union's decision to break off its relations with Israel in June 1967.

NOTES

1 D. Ben Gurion, *Our Foreign Policy: Vision and Way* (Hebrew), Vol. 3, 3rd edition, 1957, pp. 241–54.
2 Ibid., p. 245, as well as Sharett's statement in Eilat, *Kol Haam*, 27 Feb. 1953: 'Communism was from its very inception an enemy of Zionism. The support which we received in the UN also served communism, when imperialist power was removed from here. When Israel – which is basically Zionist – was established, communism returned to its previous lines of open enmity towards Zionism and Israel.'
3 S. Sh. Yariv, *On Communism and Zionism of Hashomer Hatzair*, p. 57.
4 M. Zohar, *David Ben Gurion* (Tel Aviv: Am Oved, 1977) Vol. 2, p. 912.
5 Sharett's guiding lines to Israel's Diplomatic Missions abroad. See note 10 in chapter 1.
6 Following the Soviet veto in the Security Council in March 1954 on a Western draft resolution calling on Egypt to enable Israel to transfer maritime goods through the Suez Canal and the Gulf of Aqaba, Foreign Minister Sharett reacted in the Knesset in May 1954, saying: 'The line taken by the USSR in the Security Council of employing a veto on every proposal undesirable to the Arab states and of supporting at each phase – be it in content or in procedural questions – the Arab position causes serious problems which might lead to far-reaching results. This system could paralyze the Security Council as a debating and decision-making institution on questions related to the Middle East and to Israeli–Arab relations, or turn it into a one-sided mechanism only able to operate against Israel. In the long run this line could be ever more harmful to Israel's vital interests and to the interests of peace and stability in the entire region. The change in the USSR's stance reinforces the marked tendency in this policy to plead the Arab states' cause and to worsen Israel's cause' (*Divrei Haknesset*, Vol. 15, p. 1596).
7 Following the proposal from Israel's Ministry of Foreign Affairs to the USSR of 29 April 1954.
8 *Divrei Haknesset*, Vol. 16, p. 2564, 1 Sept. 1954.
9 A. Eban, Pirkei Haim ('Chapters of Life'), (Tel Aviv: Sifriyat Maariv, 1978) Part 1, p. 180. Eban is quoting Molotov saying during their meeting in San Francisco in April 1955 that, according to his information, the USA was about to sign a defense treaty with Israel. 'This will be a tragic development. The central aim of Soviet policy is to prevent a situation in which the USSR would

be encircled by American [military] bases and other imperialist bases. In the past the Soviet Union helped Israel to be born, in the hope that Israel would never become a base for hostile activities of one superpower against another.'

10 *Divrei Haknesset*, Vol. 16, p. 2549, 30 Aug. 1954.
11 *Divrei Haknesset*, Vol. 17, pp. 106–7, 16 Nov. 1954.
12 M. Sharett, *Yoman Ishi*, Vol. 5, pp. 1273–4, Sharett's meeting with Molotov, Geneva, 31 Oct. 1955.
13 Ibid., p. 1266.
14 Ibid., p. 1274–5.
15 *Divrei Haknesset*, Vol. 19, p. 86, 18 Oct. 1955.
16 Ibid.
17 MFA Arch. File 103.1 SSR.
18 Conversations held by Sharett and Abba Eban with Molotov; see notes 9 and 12 above.
19 Bulganin's Note to Ben Gurion, *Izvestia*, 6 Nov. 1956, also quoted in *Divrei Haknesset*, Vol. 21, p. 259, 14 Nov. 1956.
20 Ibid.
21 Ibid.
22 M. Bar Zohar, *David Ben Gurion*, Vol. 3, pp. 1271–3, 1283, 1287, 1292. A considerable role in the increase of the Soviet threats was due to the French, British, and Americans, who emphasized in their talks with Israeli representatives that the Soviets intended indeed to carry out their threats.
23 M. Brecher, *Decisions in Israel's Foreign Policy*, p. 283, quoting G. Meir saying: 'I think Ben Gurion believed that we could remain in Sinai and Gaza. Neither he nor anyone of us considered that the Soviet Union would react as it did.'
24 G. Rafael, *Besod Leumin* ('Destination Peace'), pp. 110–11 as well as private sources.
25 *Divrei Haknesset*, Vol. 13, pp. 730–32 (Mrs G. Meir's speech in the Knesset debate on Israeli–Soviet relations).
26 *Divrei Haknesset*, Vol. 23, p. 2853, 28 Oct. 1957.
27 A. Dagan, *Moscow and Jerusalem*, p. 128, *Al Hamishmar*, 25 Oct. 1957.
28 On 11 Feb. 1957 the Soviet Union appealed to the USA, Britain and France with a proposal to sign a joint declaration (together with the USSR) consisting of six central paragraphs: (a) the settlement of the Middle East problems by peaceful means alone and through negotiations; (b) non-interference in the internal affairs of Middle East countries, respecting their sovereignty and independence; (c) the renunciation of all attempts to involve these countries in military blocs in which great powers participate; (d) the liquidation of foreign bases and the withdrawal of foreign troops from their territories of the Middle East countries; (e) reciprocal refusal to deliver arms to Middle East countries; (f) the promotion of economic development in the Middle East countries, without any attachment of military, political or other terms to this with the dignity and sovereignty of these states (*The USSR and the Middle East, Problems of Peace and Security 1947–1971*, Moscow: Novosti Press Agency Publishing House, 1972). In the course of 1957 the Soviet Union repeated its proposals with minor changes addressed separately to the three superpowers mainly to the USA. The last one was submitted on 3 Sept. 1957. On 21 Sept. 1957 USSR Foreign Minister Gromyko presented them in the UN, and on 24 Sept. 1957 they were rejected by the three superpowers.
29 A Soviet diplomat who served in Moscow told this to Ben Zion Razin, Secretary of the Israeli–Soviet Friendship League, during a reception held at the Soviet

Embassy in Israel, on 7 Nov. 1957 (MFA Arch. File 103.1 SSR).

30 12 Nov., 26 Nov., 26 Dec., 31 Dec. 1957. MFA Arch. File 103.1 SSR.

31 From D. Ben Gurion's diary, quoted in *Yediot Ahronot*, 4 Dec. 1961 and in M. Bar Zohar, op. cit., Vol. 3, pp. 1360–61.

32 M. Bar Zohar, op. cit., Vol. 3, p. 1336, and in a more detailed form in MFA Arch. File 103.1 SSR.

33 M. Sharett, op. cit., Vol. 5, p. 1348, 14 Feb. 1956.

34 MFA Arch. File 103.1 SSR.

35 In the Foreign Affairs Committee meeting of 28 Dec. 1955, D. Ben Gurion suggested asking the USSR to sell arms to Israel. He estimated the chances of receiving a positive reply were 10 per cent, or less. The proposal was based on two arguments. (1) Should the USSR respond positively, then it could be presumed that no war would break out between Israel and Egypt. Nasser would not dare to attack Israel knowing that the USSR was supplying Israel with the same sort of arms as Egypt was receiving. (2) Should the USSR answer negatively, at least 'we shall not have a bad conscience all our life that we remained without arms, or with sufficient weapons, just because we did not apply to the USSR' (Mapai Archive, Beit Berl, File 26/55, Protocol of the meeting of 28 Dec. 1955, p. 6).

36 M. Bar Zohar, op. cit., Vol. 3, p. 1551; also *Divrei Haknesset*, Vol. 37, p. 1769.

37 M. Sharett, op. cit., Vol. 3, p. 727, 15 Feb. 1955. 'I rejected the unusual thoughts of Livneh on Soviet guarantees together with American guarantees' – stated in the Knesset Committee of Foreign Affairs and Security.

38 *Divrei HaKnesset*, Vol. 44, p. 345, 12 Jan. 1966.

39 A. Dagan, op. cit., pp. 168–9.

40 MFA Arch. File 103.1 SSR.

41 Ibid.

42 M. Sharett, op. cit., Vol. 4, p. 1139, 18 Aug. 1955.

43 Interview by Mrs G. Meir to *Maariv*, 16 April 1956.

4 · Phases in the USSR's attitude towards Israel, 1953–1967

S OVIET ASSESSMENT of Israel's policy was first published in
October 1949 by a Soviet expert on Middle East affairs.[1] This
evaluation stated that Israel's leaders had opened the gates
of their state to American economic influence; that they were
prepared to join an aggressive Mediterranean bloc together with
England and the USA; that Mapai leaders were siding with the West
in its confrontation with the USSR; and that they were serving as
agents of American imperialism. As a result, this analysis concluded,
the State of Israel could not be considered independent and
democratic as had been expected when it had been established with
the USSR's support.

A similar evaluation but even more extreme in its formulation
was published in the second edition of the *Great Soviet Encyclopedia*
in 1952.[2] The article noted that from the very beginning of its state-
hood, Israel had been leading a chauvinistic policy with Western
orientation, that American imperialism had turned it into its colony,
into a strategic military base and into a bridgehead to an aggressive
war. As for Israel's internal policy, it claimed that Israel's leaders
were leading a policy of oppressing the progressive and democratic
forces and negating the rights of the Arab minority by creating
a nationalistic atmosphere amongst the various strata of the
population.

This was the fundamental assessment before the severance of
relations with Israel in 1953 and it underwent no basic change after
their renewal. Moreover, over time additional negative facets were
added in consequence of the worsening of the Israeli–Arab conflict:

Israel's aim to integrate in a defense pact with the USA and the broadening of its connections with West Germany and Africa.

Thus the USSR's assessment regarding Israel's foreign policy based itself on three major criteria:

(a) the extent of Israel's economic and security dependence on the USA;
(b) Israel's inclinations towards military alliances in the Middle East with US inspiration;
(c) Israel's position on subjects connected to the Soviet–American confrontation.

On all three criteria, Israel was found to be siding with the Western powers.

Israel's diplomatic relations with the USSR, from their renewal (1953) to their severance (1967), were at different times stable, tense, calm, and critical. We now survey the main characteristics of these relations over the period 1953–1967 by stages of development.

FIRST STAGE: THE STABILIZATION OF RELATIONS FROM
THE END OF 1953 TO JUNE 1955

This period is characterized by the USSR's giving political credit to Israel by demonstrating restraint and at times a balanced policy. Some of its milestones follow.

Malenkov expressed a positive attitude towards Israel when he made his political presentation on 15 August 1953. Israel was included among a restricted group of states he mentioned and with whom the USSR wished to maintain normal relations.

The USSR abstained from voting in the UN Security Council in November 1953[3] on a draft resolution presented by the three Western powers condemning Israel following its military retaliation in Quibia (even if the USSR did not want to vote in alignment with the Western powers).

On 15 December 1953 the USSR gave wide publicity on *Izvestia*'s front page to the speeches by Israel's newly appointed Envoy, Elyashiv, and the USSR's President, Voroshilov, on the occasion of the Minister's presentation of his letters of accreditation to the

President. Included in the quote from Elyashiv's speech was the sentence indicating that Israel remembered the support extended to it by the Soviet Union at the time Israel emerged as a state, as well as the fact that the USSR recognized *de jure* the newborn state immediately after it proclaimed its independence. In Voroshilov's response, as quoted in the paper, he expressed his hope that relations between the two states would develop according to 'the understandings reached between them', upon the renewal of relations. Also included was his statement that the Minister's activity aimed at 'strengthening and developing the cordial relations between Israel and the USSR will enjoy the support of the Soviet government'. Finally the paper cited the greetings of President Voroshilov to the 'Jewish people in Israel and its government'. Giving publicity to this event was considered an unusual gesture as well as a reminder of the conditions agreed upon for renewal of relations.

The USSR's newly appointed Minister to Israel was the first diplomat to present his letters of accreditation to Israel's President in Jerusalem, thus establishing an important precedent in diplomatic procedures.

A trade agreement between Israel and the USSR was signed at the beginning of 1954.

A long article in *Novoe Vremya* on 9 January 1954 under the heading 'Hypocritical Friends of the Arabs' on US activities in the Middle East did not mention US support for Israel and did not aim at gaining sympathy for the Arabs at Israel's expense. (On the Israeli–Syrian conflict over the use of water from the river Jordan, presented as an American plan aimed at securing an economic foothold in the region, the article hinted that any regional plan – however constructive – would be considered invalid because of its links with the USA.)

The first Soviet veto wielded against Western draft resolutions at the UN Security Council (regarding Israel's attempts at diverting a channel from the river Jordan from the Israeli–Syrian demilitarized zone into Israel's territory, and on the free transit of Israel's goods through the Suez Canal) in January–March 1954 damaged Israel. From the USSR's point of view the veto was directed against the strengthening of the Western powers' standing in the Middle East, demonstrating at the same time Soviet political support for the Arab states.

In both cases the Soviet Union presumably feared the Western initiatives: in the first instance, lest the American plan for regional water diversion (Johnston's Plan) lead to American economic domination in the area;[4] in the second case, lest the resolution interfere with Egyptian plans to nationalize the Suez Canal.[5] The USSR's Deputy Foreign Minister Vishinsky gave no hint of any attack on Israel in his explanatory speech before the Security Council prior to the voting. What was clear was his effort to be seen as adopting a balanced approach to the conflicting parties, particularly in his call to both of them to settle their dispute through direct negotiations, with the help of the head of the UN Observers.[6] In both cases, the Soviets tried to keep the local issues away from the involvement of the Western powers, while recognizing the need to achieve an agreed solution to the problems by direct negotiations between the conflicting sides.[7]

In May 1954, by mutual agreement, the representation between the USSR and Israel was raised from Legational to Ambassadorial level.

On 16 April 1954 the Soviet government published a statement (the first of its kind) on the situation in the Middle East, in which the USSR warned the Arab states not to integrate into Western military alliances. Israel was not mentioned there.

To the Agricultural Exhibition of July 1954, the Soviet Union invited – for the first time – an official delegation from Israel to be headed by the Deputy Minister of Agriculture. The group was warmly received.

In September 1954 the editor of Israel's daily *Davar* (organ of the Trade Unions) paid an official visit to the USSR.

SECOND STAGE: 1955–1956 – FROM A RESTRAINED TO AN ANTI-ISRAEL POSITION

This period is characterized by the USSR's transition from a restrained attitude towards Israel, concerning the Arab–Israeli dispute, to a pro-Arab stand, which held the inherent promise of weakening the influence of Western powers among the Arab states. In the USSR itself Molotov's position declined with the beginning of Krushchev's rise towards the head of Soviet leadership and the crystallization of a foreign policy with a strong emphasis on extending massive military assistance to Third World countries of anti-Western inclination. The first half of 1955 was characterized by the formation of Western alliances in the Middle East[8] and Israel stepped up its activities aimed at obtaining defense commitments from the USA. From the Soviet point of view these pacts, and Israel's activity towards becoming an integral part of them, bore an anti-Soviet character.

Some of the facts concerning that period are presented below.

On 11 June 1955 *Izvestia* published an article firmly warning Israel of the danger of its being integrated into Western pacts and emphasizing that such a step contradicted the assurances Israel had given the USSR when their relations were renewed.

In consequence of the Soviet–Egyptian arms deal Israel protested to the USSR, complaining of the danger threatening it from Egypt and initiated extensive political activity to gain arms from the USA, Britain, and France. Israel's leaders repeatedly called upon the USA to conclude a defense treaty with Israel. The American President confirmed on 15 November 1955[9] that the USA would be prepared to conclude a formal pact with Israel and other countries in the Middle East. Israel's sharply intense reaction on the diplomatic and public planes coincided with the Western powers' apprehensions about their standing in the Middle East. As a result of these circumstances Israel found itself once again in one camp with the Western powers *vis-à-vis* the USSR. The USSR's reaction was at first of a defensive, calming nature: Israel need not fear; Egypt will not attack Israel; the Arabs won't be able to destroy Israel; Israel is stronger than the Arab states; 'The world will not let …'; 'Should there really be a threat to security, there are means to deal with such a situation – we shall be ready' (Molotov's statement to Sharett at their meeting in Geneva on 31 October 1955).[10] Sharett interpreted it as a hint 'that the USSR is prepared for a comprehensive settlement' between Israel and the Arab states, 'in which the USSR will also participate'.[11] This course came only to a dead end.

With the intensification of American activities in the region and after Israel's complaint about the Soviet–Egyptian deal, official Soviet verbal attacks against Israel began to be aired. When surveying the political events of 1955 in the Supreme Soviet, Krushchev, First Secretary of the CPSU, referred to Israel saying:

> Deserving of condemnation are the activities of the State of Israel which from the first days of its existence began to threaten its neighbors and to conduct an unfriendly policy towards them. It is clear that such a policy does not suit the national interests of the State of Israel. Behind the backs of those who had such a policy, stand the well-known imperialist states. They aspire to exploit Israel, with their arms, against the Arab nations with the aim of crudely ravaging the natural treasures of this region.[12]

This was the first time that a Soviet leader had described Israel as threatening her neighbors 'from the first days of its existence', not only in contrast to historical reality, but in contradiction of the many expressions of Soviet representatives in the international arena, during 1948, condemning the Arab states for invading the territory of Israel, with the aim of destroying it. Krushchev's words were expressed with reference to the Baghdad Pact, spreading praise to those Arab states who did not join it. And, despite the fact that Israel condemned the establishment of the pact, the Soviets avoided referring to it publicly. To them, Israel's desire to conclude a military treaty with the USA seemed like the Baghdad Pact itself. From their point of view, they were the same thing. Israel attempted to show that the Baghdad Pact was a hostile one, while an alliance between Israel and the USA – if established – should be regarded as a deterrent factor against an Arab attack.

On 1 February 1956 Foreign Minister Molotov presented an overview of his perceptions about Soviet–Israeli relations to Israel's Ambassador to Moscow, Y. Avidar, by drawing up a balance sheet on them up to that time.

Molotov opened his survey by saying that it should be remembered that the USSR helped the emergence of Israel and encouraged its independence. The USSR had hoped that friendly relations would develop between it and Israel. But, a foreign and 'aggressive' influence began to make itself felt in Israel – in official and non-official circles – and Israeli leaders began 'to conduct an extremely anti-Soviet policy towards the Soviet Union, similar to that of the most reactionary and aggressive circles in the world'. This position, stressed Molotov, and the public speeches accompanying it, caused the 'incident in Tel Aviv' and a break in relations. With the healing of the rupture, normal relations began to develop between the two countries, until 'certain countries' started to blow up the 'modest arms deal' between Czechoslovakia and Egypt, accusing the Soviet Union of various negative intentions and initiating a new anti-Soviet campaign. Israel on its part joined the strong and aggressive foreign influence in blowing up the deal. The pronouncements heard in Israel against the Soviet Union, in this respect, were much harsher 'than those expressed by the extremists among those of selfish interest in the region who were trying to maintain their status'.

As for Krushchev's pronouncement about a month earlier, Molotov noted that it was indeed the only time that critical comments had been made about Israel. But, he believed that more severe pronouncements against the USSR were heard in Israel. In his opinion, Krushchev analyzed the situation fairly. His conclusion about Israel's behavior was that 'strong anti-Soviet influences' were present there. Therefore, it was not the Soviet Union that was to be blamed if Israeli–Soviet relations were not developing. The USSR was prepared to maintain close and friendly relations, and that depended only upon Israel.

Molotov summed up by saying that the Soviet Union had no territorial claims against Israel. And if Israel had not been harnessed to the 'anti-Soviet wagon', which did not serve her interests, relations most certainly would have been developing further. No doubt this would have been in favor of Israel 'and it is worthwhile for Israel to take it into consideration'.[13]

Reading Molotov's survey it seems that the main Soviet claims against Israel – and its main disappointments – were not because of economic, political and cultural attachments of Israel to the West, but because of Israel's policy that made it possible for the Western powers to increase their presence in the Middle East, assisting them in creating an anti-Soviet atmosphere in the world with the aid of propaganda. This was the main factor which, according to Soviet assessment, was an obstacle on the road to improved relations between both states.

On 2 April 1956 Israel's Ambassador in Moscow, Y. Avidar, in his talk with the USSR's Foreign Minister, Molotov, reviewed the following international subjects on which Israel and the USSR held identical views:

Israel's objection to the establishment of aggressive military pacts in the Middle East (as, for example, the Baghdad Pact and the pact between Egypt, Syria and Saudi Arabia).

Israel's objection to the arms race, in particular in the Middle East.

Israel's objection to the existence of foreign bases on its territory.

Israel's interest in the advancement of peace in the world and in the Middle East, which Israel is in need of no less than any other peace loving country.

Israel is in favor of a creative peace competition for building and development in the world and in the Middle East. Israel is in need of technical aid and is ready to receive it from any country willing to extend it. On the other hand, Israel is ready to extend aid to those who may be in need of it.

Israel is in favor of settling conflicting problems in the Middle East through direct negotiations between the concerned parties and without foreign factors dictating solutions.

Israel's Ambassador added that his country's attitude to the Soviet Union was cordial. True, there were objections against the USSR's policies in the Middle East exactly as there were against other super-powers. Yet, the criteria for determining Israel's stance towards them were based on the actions of those super-powers and not on those performing them. In its response Israel took into consideration its independence and security interests, and in this respect regarded the military reinforcement of the Arab states as an act threatening its security, thus endangering its very existence. It referred, in particular, to those Arab states which rejected the negotiation of peace with Israel and prepared themselves openly for a war against Israel with the arms they received. Since the arms supplied them, with Soviet support, had determined the superiority of the Arabs over Israel, Israel's sympathy towards the USSR was not increased.[14]

Molotov repeated the arguments he had previously expressed in his talk with Foreign Minister Sharett (in Geneva at the end of October) and his talk with the Ambassador himself two months earlier, whilst adding that Israel's war preparations were of concern to its neighbors.[15] Thus, he focused the conversation on the future instead of analyzing the past.

The importance of this talk, like the previous one between them, was: *first* the mere fact that it took place – evidence that both sides were interested in the continuation of the dialogue – despite the gap between them; and *second*, its evidence that the USSR attached no importance to the degree of Israel's convergence with Soviet political principles as long as Israel backed the main thrust of the Soviet point of view: ousting the Western powers from the Middle East.

Israel's Ambassador to Moscow analyzed Israeli–Soviet relations in mid-November 1955 with the conclusion that the Soviet Union viewed Israel as an American satellite because of its repeated turning to the US State Department concerning the Security Agreement. In the Ambassador's opinion no Israeli propaganda would have convinced the Soviets that it would be possible to reach a security treaty with the USA without committing Israel, openly or secretly, to the granting of bases to the USA in Israeli territory, and without such a treaty being directed against the USSR.[16] The mutual relationship was overshadowed by Soviet fears of an Israeli–American connection by a security treaty that would assist the USA to deepen its penetration in the Middle East, by a formal agreement or by another means.[17] From the chronological point of view Israel's activity to secure an alliance with the USA preceded the Czech–Egyptian arms deal of September 1955.[18] Hence, Israel's public or concealed drive to secure this treaty played a certain role in the deterioration of its relations with the USSR. And as the Soviet Union accused Israel of serving as an instrument of Western imperialism in its aims to dominate the Middle East, so it served the Soviet Union as a political propagandistic means in facilitating its penetration into the region. And, as the chances for an Israeli–American alliance increased, in Soviet eyes, in the security field, so did the Soviet anti-Israeli propaganda. This was accompanied by hostile declarations against Israel, which in their extreme and poisonous nature, were far stronger than those directed by the USSR against members of Western military alliances in the Middle East that were explicitly anti-Soviet inclined.

The first half of 1956 was characterized by a cessation of Israeli activity towards reaching an alliance or security guarantee with the USA. It seems that Israel's leaders were simply skeptical about achieving it. We do not know if this was the determining factor in the Soviet Union's decision to shift its policy and undertake a more balanced stance towards Israel, as evident in the USSR's Foreign Ministry statement on 17 April 1956, or perhaps this shift was due to Israel's clarification as argued by Foreign Minister Sharett.[19] Its main components were positive for Israel, since they emphasized the USSR's support for Israel's independence, the USSR's objection to changing by force the armistice lines (between Israel and its neighbors) and the USSR's call for a peaceful settlement of the Arab–Israeli conflict.

The same applies to Soviet Prime Minister Bulganin's statement on 18 May 1956 during his visit to London in which he not only called for the settlement of the Arab–Israeli conflict by peaceful means but also stressed that the source of tension in the Middle East was not the conflict but the military pacts that were being established there. In this respect he differed from his host's view.

This was an important and positive change from Israel's point of view. At that time Soviet Ministers participated in the Independence Day reception held by the Israeli Embassy in Moscow – apparently a demonstration of good will in improving the atmosphere of the mutual relationship. But this shift did not last long. The defense measures undertaken by Israel, in case of a possible confrontation with Egypt, were not hidden from Soviet eyes.[20]

The second half of 1956 was characterized by the Sinai Campaign, which caused the USSR to wage a harsh struggle against Israel which – as already noted – attempted to place a question mark on Israel's right to exist as a state. *Izvestia* on 29 November 1956 took the State of Israel and its leaders to task which bears witness to the USSR's unique attitude towards Israel as to its political, ideological and strategic components.

The USSR's assumptions and hopes that Israel would choose a pro-Soviet orientation turned out to be wrong. Israel put itself at the disposal of the 'imperialist forces' and was prepared 'to carry out blindly any order of its patrons', even if it did not join the military pacts in the region. When Israel was established 'a handful of irresponsible adventurers', headed by Ben Gurion, took control of the state and were playing with the fate of world peace and the fate of its people ... Ben Gurion alienated the sober politicians (hinting at Sharett's removal) and initiated an 'activist policy' towards the Arab states, meaning 'Peace from a position of Power'.

The article concludes by noting:

Drunken from the 'Position of Force' policy, and in jumping in haste into an aggressive adventure, the ruling circles in Israel destroyed Israel's international position, stirred deep enmity of other nations in the East against Israel, and led to deterioration of relations with other states. So great is this hostility of the nations of the East towards Israel, in consequence of the robbery attack on Egypt, that it will not be so easy to uproot it. The hostility will be felt for several generations. All this cannot but leave its imprint on Israel's future, putting a question mark on the mere existence of the state.

The discreditation of Israel theme was repeated time and again in the second half of 1957, against the background of Israel's support for the Eisenhower Doctrine.

The USSR's Foreign Minister Gromyko ascribed to Israel aspirations for war against Syria, in concert with Turkey and the USA, stating in the UN General Assembly on 22 October 1957 that 'Israel pays little heed to the course of its future development or to its very existence as a state ... Israel appears to be hacking away at the branch on which it is sitting ...'.[21]

The Sinai Campaign and Israel's announcement of its support for the Eisenhower Doctrine[22] – after many debates and hesitations – were the climax of tension that ruled Israeli–Soviet relations from July 1953. Soviet print media and the political periodicals set out on a wide-ranging campaign of criticism against Israel's leaders' policy, headed by Ben Gurion. *Pravda*, at the vanguard of the campaign, announced that there was in Israel a forceful objection to the decision taken in support of the Eisenhower Doctrine, and reminded readers that the support for the Doctrine was in complete contradiction to Israel's assurance given to the USSR 'that it would not join in any pact or agreement that bears aggressive intentions against the USSR'. In this respect, *Pravda* noted that 'Israel's government's official announcement was ever-visible to the Soviet government when it decided to renew diplomatic relations between our two States'. This 'ought to be considered by those responsible for Israel's policy'.[23]

In January 1958 Israel's Ambassador in Moscow visited the Soviet Deputy Foreign Minister. The Ambassador opened his talk in an optimistic, hopeful tone with regard to the improvement of Israeli–Soviet relations, but he got the impression that his interlocutor rejected it on the spot. The Deputy Foreign Minister said that Israel's position had not changed and therefore the USSR's policy towards Israel had 'not changed either'. 'Israel's policy,' said the Deputy Minister, 'continues to be harnessed to the forces of yesterday and doesn't integrate with the interests of the states of the liberating East'. As an example he brought up the Sinai Campaign and Israel's identification with the interests of the Western powers in the region. The Soviet press articles reflected, in his opinion, the feelings of the USSR towards Israel, and 'it would be worth it if Israel gave some thought to it, what the Soviet public is saying and the way it assessed Israel'. The USSR, he said, would not have supported the establishment of Israel, had it foreseen its development. The Soviet Union, he said, regretted the difficulties which Israel might be experiencing, because of its policy, but it was Israel who should decide to correct its way.

According to the Ambassador's assessment in view of the Deputy Foreign Minister's comments, the Soviet Union regarded Israel as one of its greatest opponents, repeatedly threatened Israel's existence, regretted its support for Israel's establishment and expressed discontent at its existence, as it was.[24]

Noteworthy is the fact that despite the expressions of disappointment at Israel's policy, despite the hostile criticism of Israel and the discreditation of the state, the political dialogue did not stop between the two states. True, the USSR called its Ambassador in Israel to return to Moscow a short time after the start of the Sinai Campaign, but in comparison to its threatening expressions against Israel, it was rather a routine act that bore evidence of the desire to continue with formal relations with Israel, more than to bring them to the breaking point. The threats, however, had considerable influence on the Israeli government's decision to withdraw its troops from Sinai and the Gaza Strip. The threats were taken seriously in Ben Gurion's considerations and in his decision to commit himself publicly to withdraw Israeli troops from Sinai and the Gaza Strip, according to the conditions worked out by Israel's government in co-ordination with the US government (not exactly according to Soviet will).

THIRD STAGE: 1957–1958 – RESTORING THE RELATIONS

When the Soviet Ambassador returned to Israel to resume his duties, and Israel committed itself to retreat to the Israeli–Egyptian-armistice line, attempts were made to restore bilateral relations. Israel's representatives continued with the political dialogue with the Soviet Union that gradually improved the style and essence of mutual relations. The Soviet print media abandoned the threatening tone on Israel, but the basic Soviet assessment towards Israel's policy remained in force, and at times this assessment contradicted the improvement which was felt in the tone of political talks that were conducted in Moscow and Jerusalem and in several capitals of the world. Out of tens of anti-Israel publications during 1958–1961 we shall look at the more characteristic ones on the Soviet attitude towards Israel's policy and its social and political development.

FOURTH STAGE: 1959–1961, ISRAEL IN THE MIRROR OF THE USSR

1. The article 'Israel and American Imperialism' by G. S. Nikitina[25] in the scientific periodical *Sovietskoe Vostokovedeniye*, September–October 1958, was the most significant publication of its category out of scientific articles written to that date about Israel. Its main argument was that Israel was established by the USA for its imperialist aims in the Middle East. Expression of this already appears in the article's historical preface reviewing the period from the Balfour Declaration to the establishment of the State of Israel in 1948. From the very outset of Israel's existence, American leaders attempted to put the new(born) state at their disposal.

They regarded Israel as a strategic position and their stronghold in the Middle East, a tool for pushing the British competitors out of the region, a means for pressuring the Arab states and a 'bridgehead of their expansion in the area'. The history of Israel's ten years of existence had proved, according to Nikitina, that these intentions had been implemented. the author enumerates the volume of American aid to Israel and notes that 'American billionaires did not hesitate to exploit the vast possibilities that were opened before them'. Economic domination brought in its wake

73

political domination. The American penetration caused an Americanization in cultural, scientific and spiritual life. Also, the Israeli press was under US control and received directly from the US Embassy information for their readers. The American control dominated even the army and foreign policy. Israel was obliged, according to its agreement with the USA, to defend the region. For this reason Israel put at the USA's disposal 'equipment, services, and other aid', including the exploiting of Israel's territory for war purposes. Israel was pursuing a provocative and aggressive foreign policy towards the Arab states with US inspiration, aiming to expand in the Middle East. A close relationship had been formed between American interests in the Middle East and the top level leadership ruling Israel, through Zionism, 'the reactionary nationalistic ideology of the Jewish bourgeoisie, preaching for social peace between rich and poor people'. Israel's leaders used Zionism as a plan for maximum expansion of Israel's frontiers at the expense of Arab nations. Because of this the Arab peoples justly regarded Zionism as a direct threat against them. In contrast to these leaders there were elements in all political parties – with the exception of Herut – who strove for peace with the Arab states and to pursue a neutral policy. To conclude, the author stated that 'Israel's dragging after the adventurous and dangerous policy of the USA in the Middle East is severely complicating the situation of Israel – endangering the security and life of its people.'

The conclusion one draws from reading this work (which became a textbook in Soviet universities) is that Israel determined its destiny from the very beginning (of its existence) when it bound itself in a non-written alliance with the USA. And although the question of Israel's right to existence does not appear in the book, it becomes quite clear from reading it that Israel was destined to doom from the moment it took up the role of 'imperialism's servant', and its aims at expansion were but one of the functions of this service to imperialism.

2. The book, *The State of Israel: its Situation and Policy* by Ivanov and Scheniss,[26] is the first Soviet attempt (since Genin's book *The Palestine Problem* (Russian), Moscow, December 1948) to present a comprehensive description on Israel: its establishment, political development; analyses of Zionism, the Jewish question and its

solution, and, at its end, an ideological explanation of the USSR's policy in the Middle East and its attitude to peoples gaining liberation and Israel's place among them.

The Soviet critics praised the book,[27] which for a long time was considered a basic text on Israel.

The book does in fact repeat the truths reviewed by Nikitina but in greater detail and more comprehensively. Its innovation is in describing the economic situation of Israel, which was 'extremely bad' and completely under the control of the capitalist monopolies of the USA. Half of the population did not have the required minimum for a living. There was no common denominator between Jewish newcomers from various countries, and there was no equality between them. Oppression and racial discrimination held sway [in the state].

Another innovation is the attempt to settle the contradiction in the Soviet stance towards the emerging liberated peoples in the Middle East on the one hand and towards Israel on the other hand. In the authors' opinion, Marxism does not consider the 'national question' as a goal in itself, but that it should be considered in relation to the general liberation movement. There are liberation movements whose aim is to liberate peoples from enslavement – and the Arabs are included in this category – and there are national liberation movements which are bases and positions of power for imperialism – and it was clear to all that Israel belonged to this category. The conclusion runs thus: 'If a particle contradicts the rule, it should be negated.' Israel found its place in the bitter camp of the enemies of peoples' freedom in the East – along with American, British and French imperialism.

And what is the solution to the Jewish question according to the authors of the book? 'It is possible to dismiss the hostility to foreign strata of the population [meaning the Jews] by making the strata of foreign population cease to be alien and making them amalgamate with the general population (meaning the assimilation of the Jews into the general population). This is the only solution to the Jewish question, and we have to support all those who assist the removal of Jewish seclusion.' The inevitable collapse of world imperialism is the guarantee for the final solution of the Jewish question on a world scale, meaning that as long as 'world imperialism' is in existence, there will always exist a 'Jewish question' as the Jews are not assimilated in the general population.

The book was presumably intended for readers interested in the Jewish question and Israel and in the USSR's attitude towards them, and for the Communist party propagandists and researchers. It may be possible that by denigrating Israel the authors aimed at justifying the one-sided Soviet policy towards the Arab states. But, it may not be impossible that the book was intended to depress national consciousness amongst the Jews of the Soviet Union even more than it was aimed at the Jews in the West. In general, the book is saturated with anti-Semitic spirit and its conclusions incite anti-Semitism and anti-Israelism.

3. The article 'The Line to Abnegation of Israel's Rulers' by Nicolayev[28] has a title which speaks for itself. The article tends in a visible manner to rewrite historical facts, making them fit the Soviet stance concerning the Arab–Israeli conflict. the following is a summary of it.

Israel emerged according to the UN resolution regarding the establishment of two sovereign states in the territory of Palestine. The resolution was not fully implemented, since only Israel was established. In the course of the Israeli–Arab War 'which broke out not without the incitement of the ruling circles in Israel that exploited the split amongst the Arab states and their military and economic weakness', Israel conquered 6,000 square kilometers of the territory designated to the Arab state that was supposed to emerge. The 1948–49 events (referring to Israel's War of Independence in face of seven Arab armies' invasion into the territory designated for the Jewish state) gave birth to the Arab–Israeli conflict 'which continues to deepen for reason not dependent upon the Arabs'. The Sinai Campaign aggravated the conflict even more 'and makes it more difficult to settle it'. Israel rejected, despite UN resolutions, 'satisfying the legal demands of the Palestinian refugees'. Israel's leaders aroused military provocations 'in an attempt to compel the Arab states to concede in accepting Israel's conditions for a settlement between them'. One of these attempts was the Sinai Campaign. Despite the defeat of their policy Israel's leaders continued to act from a position of force towards the Arab states. This course was supported by the Western powers who assisted Israel through money and arms.

The Ben Gurion government was sacrificing Israel's sovereignty by concluding an alliance with the USA, in joining the Eisenhower Doctrine and by striving to join NATO. This policy was convenient to the Western powers who were exploiting the Arab–Israeli conflict for their penetration and foothold in the Middle East and the Afro-Asian continent. Israel's government was strictly obeying the Western powers in the international arena on different issues, such as the Peoples' Republic of China. Its political standpoint was completely identical to that of the Western powers.

In Asia and in Africa Israel's government took upon itself the role of the 'Trojan Horse' of Western imperialism. In extending technical aid to the Asian and African states with American finance, Israel was trying to divert them from the road to independence by duplicating Israel's methods there, in the guise of progress. The Israeli government was conducting pure anti-Communist propaganda there. As for West Germany, Israel was pursuing a policy of military co-operation. In fact, the government was acting to strengthen 'the revanchist forces' in the country, pushing the Nazi crimes into oblivion. True, the Eichmann trial was destined to prove that the government of Israel was not accepting the Nazis' rehabilitation. But, during its course attempts were made to not reveal former Nazis. Ben Gurion announced that he would not permit the trial to damage relations between Israel and West Germany.

Israel's leaders were constantly 'waging an unrestrained campaign of slander and defamation' against the USSR with the aim of condemning the Socialist system 'and to undermine the sympathy and respect for [the USSR] amongst the masses of Israel's people'. They conducted their anti-Soviet activity 'from the stand of Zionism, by submitting provocative demands in respect to the question which they invented called the "Jewish Question". In such activity they imitate their patrons across the sea.'

In the domestic field Ben Gurion's government always pursued a social and economic policy of an 'anti-national nature contrary to the interests of the people', in enabling the USA to drag Israel into an arms race 'for the preparation of a war and subversive activities against socialist and neutral states'. In the Israeli economy American monopolists occupied the key posts before whom 'the Ben Gurion government opened up broadly the whole country'. The main burden fell on the workers' shoulders. The trade deficit was increasing from year to year. The main budget was devoted to military targets. The military leaders, who waved the banner of deterrence as the only factor that insured peace for Israel, moved the country into a permanent military psychosis. The military policy influenced the state's economy destructively. Israel's government was trying to complete the financing of armament by imposing harsh taxes, raising prices and 'by the impoverishing of workers'. The Mapai leadership was pursuing a policy of racial discrimination. The Arabs were not the only ones who were badly discriminated against. They were joined by immigrants from Africa. The Mapai leadership was trying to introduce in the country a personal dictatorship by Ben Gurion.

The article presumes that this dictatorship will arouse amongst the people vigorous objection, which had already been expressed in demonstrations and strikes, and in the weakening of its power in the Knesset. At the end, the article notes that 'today the people's masses not only condemn the anti-national policy of their government, but also firmly demand a change in policy towards neutrality, peace and democracy'.

To sum up, the assessment of the Soviet media (reflecting the official attitude towards Israel) showed the following ideas:

The external and internal policy of Israel was enslaved in the hands of the USA. At the root of the evil lay the economic, military, political, ideological and cultural dragging of Israel after the Western powers.
Israel's clash with the USSR was taking place on four planes: (1) the strategic Israeli–American co-operation in the Middle East; (2) the strengthening of West Germany and the assistance extended to it (moral, security) by Israel to become once again a European power (anti-Soviet); (3) penetrating the Western anti-communist ideology into Africa; and (4) defaming the USSR in the world because of its policy towards the Jewish minority in its territory.

In conclusion, Israel would have the right to existence if it pursued a neutral policy (in the East–West confrontation), a democratic policy (in weakening its links with the USA) and peace: meaning, the abandonment of the principle of force deterrence towards the Arabs and acceptance of the Arab conditions for peace (the return of territory to the Arabs and the absorption of the returning refugees).

FIFTH STAGE: 1961–1965, ISRAEL'S EFFORT TO IMPROVE
ITS RELATIONS WITH THE USSR

In their talks with their Soviet colleagues during 1961–1966 Israel's leaders and its ambassadors used to reiterate their wish to improve mutual relations in the political, economic and cultural fields. The Soviet responses were somehow vague and evasive.[29]

They could be classified into three categories.

1. It is not the Soviet Union's task to advise Israel how to improve its relations with the USSR. Israel alone should know what it should do; it depends on Israel itself.[30]
2. Three negative factors have a detrimental influence on Israeli–Soviet relations. (a) Israel's policy constituting a stronghold against Communism in the Middle East. The USSR cannot change its policy towards Israel just because Israel wishes to improve them. First, there should be a change in Israel's policy towards the USSR. (b) The USSR's policy towards the Arab world in connection with the East–West confrontation. Israeli policy harms Soviet interests. Hence, 'under present circumstances' there is no room for a change in the relations.[31] (c) Israel's involvement in the struggle for the sake of the Jews in the USSR.[32]
3. There is no controversy between Israel and the Soviet Union; and there are no conflicts between them. Relations are normal and properly correct, 'even if not so warm'. The USSR supported the establishment of Israel and there is no reason why Israel should hold a grudge against the USSR because of its Socialist-Communist regime. Soviet policy wishes to aim at maintaining fitting relations and peaceful co-existence with every country, including Israel, despite the differences in social administration.[33]

The Non-Official Level

On the non-official level, Israel's representatives heard the following assessments from Soviet representatives:

It is not the aim of the Soviet Union to lead to the annihilation of Israel; the opposite is the truth. The USSR understands the reasons for the economic and material dependence of Israel on the West, particularly the USA. But, in Soviet opinion, from the institution of Israel's policy of non-alignment and up to this day (October 1958), Israel has leaned over towards the West to an excessive degree and become a tool assisting imperialist plots. Had Israel abandoned this course, an opportunity would have been created for the USSR – in view of its status in the Arab world – to act as a mediator and assist in achieving a settlement of the Israeli–Arab conflict. (In clarifying this position the Soviet representative noted that since the Soviet–Arab *rapprochement*, not a single joint declaration had ever been published protesting at Israel's very existence).[34]

At the end of January 1962, MK M. Sneh (Maki) told MK Abramov (Liberals) that in January 1955 a Maki representative in Moscow was told that Soviet policy towards Israel was aimed at developing friendly political relations to be expressed, in practice, mainly in the development of cultural and economic relations. The Sinai Campaign, however, had 'damaged the entire fabric of the relations'. Maki asked Moscow in 1957 if it would be possible to return to the principle set down in 1955. The answer was that 'the time has not yet come' but 'if Israel would be friendly towards the USSR, it would be possible to presume that the situation of the 1955 principle would return'. Sneh also told Abramov that in the second half of 1961 three members of Maki's leadership visited Moscow and once again tried to clarify 'in the appropriate Party department' the course of Soviet policy towards Israel. They were told that there was a Soviet readiness to return to the principle of 1955 'if only Israel would act on a few matters that did not seem to the Soviets to be difficult to implement from Israel's point of view'. It was clear to the Soviets that Israel was living on American political and economic support and that Israel could not, therefore, clash with the USA. It seemed, however, to the Soviets that Israel was going too far in its close devotion to America. Therefore, they would ask that along with Israel's adherence to the USA on matters which it deemed vital, Israel should adopt an increasing tendency not to vote in the UN against the USSR 'on all those disputed issues'.

MK Sneh added that according to the Soviets' assessment there was a matter of greater importance than Israel's voting in the UN, namely, Israel's open and public relations with West Germany. According to the Soviets, it was not correct to say that the whole Western world had accepted the complete rehabilitation of West Germany as a *fait accompli*. In this regard, Israel carried, according to the Soviets, much weight and unique influence in the world. The Soviet Union demanded from Israel that it should not co-operate with the USA in an effort to convince the world that the West German government and its policy towards the Nazi past and their aspiration for expansion and revenge were acceptable. The Soviets did not expect Israel to shout that 'Bonn is wrong.' It was clear that Israel should continue to receive reparations from West Germany. But, Israel should refuse to help in the attempts at the moral purification of West Germany. Israel could refrain from doing so from a purely Jewish stance, with no harm coming to it from the USA for adopting such a position. The USSR's request of Israel, according to Sneh, was not that Israel should defame West Germany, but just 'not praise West Germany'. Sneh added that he had gained the impression from his conversations with the Soviets that for them this matter was very important and that they believed 'that Israel and the Jews in the world carried much weight in this matter'.

As for the Arab–Israeli conflict, Sneh remarked, the Soviet leadership knew that the arms deliveries to Egypt constituted a security problem for Israel. The Soviet leaders, however, did not leave any doubts in the minds of the Arab rulers that Israel was an existing fact. They also exerted a restraining influence on the Arabs when they talked about their wish to attack Israel. According to the Soviets, the key to progress in Israeli–Arab relations lay in Moscow no less than in Washington, and it could be that at a more appropriate moment – from the point of view of the end of the cold war – when better opportunities opened up in the Arab–Israeli dispute, the Soviets would use the key in their hands to advance the settlement of the conflict.

As for Jewish emigration from the USSR to Israel – Sneh said at that meeting – the Maki delegates explained to the Soviets that this problem disturbed their activities in Israel. The Soviets answered that this problem too was connected to the cold war, though it was not the only consideration in their policy in this matter. 'If the

81

previous matters were to be settled in a satisfactory manner, it would be possible to advance also in this matter.'[35]

These impressions of MK Sneh were brought to the knowledge of Foreign Minister Mrs G. Meir, who also read them. MK Z. Abramov was then Chairman of the Israeli–American Friendship Association, and it could be presumed that MK M. Sneh believed that he could pass on his assessments via Abramov to Israel's Foreign Minister and to limited circles in the USA.

In April 1962 MK Abramov met with the Counselor of the USSR's Embassy in Israel at the latter's initiative. Reporting the contents of his conversation MK Abramov noted the main points made by the Counselor who remarked:

Israel is not a small country, because it maintains connections with various parts of the world and exercises its influence on various sectors of world public [opinion]. In order to establish peaceful co-existence it is necessary to create a suitable atmosphere in the world. Israel could assist in the creation of such an atmosphere, but does not act in this direction. The Jewish public in America, who helped in creating a favorable atmosphere for the renewal of Soviet–American relations in Roosevelt's days, now refrains from assisting and this may be 'because of Israel's direct or indirect inspiration'. Regrettably, though Israeli–Soviet relations are normal, they are still far from what they could have been. Israel should remember that the USSR and the USA will finally co-exist peacefully. It is only a matter of time. From this point of view alone, Israel's assistance, rather than indifference, would be worthwhile.

To think that it is not in Israel's power to do anything towards the advancement of its relations with the USSR is fundamentally mistaken. 'If this kind of thinking continues, no good will come out to it.' To think that improvement in Israeli–Soviet relations must be achieved at the expense of Israel's relations with the USA is also a mistake. The Soviets understand that it is in Israel's national interest to maintain friendly relations with the USA, and Israel should continue with that. It is in Israel's power to improve its relations with the Soviet Union without causing any harm to its relations with the USA. The scope for possible improvement of relations is wide and this too will become part of the relaxation of international tension. The USSR supported the establishment of

Israel. It supports all those who fight against colonialism everywhere in the world. Soviet policy in the Middle East is based on one principle: to prevent, directly or indirectly, any opportunity for the colonialists returning to the Middle East. The USSR's reaction towards Israel for her part in the Sinai Campaign was as it was because Israel helped colonialism to come again to the Middle East, even if that was not Israel's intention. Had the campaign been successful, 'the colonialists would have been seated on the Suez Canal'. Israel's policy is built on two assumptions: *one*, that the return of the colonialists to the Middle East might help Israel's security; *second*, that a war with the Arabs is inevitable, since there is no chance of reaching a peace settlement with them. Both assumptions are wrong from the USSR's point of view. There is reason to believe that the USA agrees with this view. Israel is not interested in an improvement of relations with the USSR. Israel's reaction to anti-Semitic phenomena in the USSR causes much harm to its image and this is why there is so much resentment in the USSR, since the inflating of events is comparatively out of proportion with similar phenomena in the USA. Because of that a suitable atmosphere for the improvement of relations is not being created. Had the Israeli government been interested, it would have restrained the Israeli press, or would have guided it, to show a lesser degree of enmity towards the USSR.

To Mr Abramov's question, why did the Counselor initiate this talk with him, the Counselor answered: 'I want to prove that friendship with the USA does not contradict friendship with Russia and the striving for peaceful co-existence between both blocs.'

As in the case of the Abramov-Sneh conversation at the end of January 1962, so in this case Foreign Minister G. Meir and the Directorate of the Ministry read this report.[36]

On the Party Level

In November 1965 Maki representatives submitted to the representatives of the CPSU a memorandum of 10 questions aimed at clarifying the Soviet position concerning the political and ideological course of Maki. The memorandum was submitted after the split in the Israeli party. Representatives of both factions – Maki (Israeli Communist Party) and Rakach (New Communist List) –

visited Moscow in the hope that each faction would gain – separately – USSR recognition. Some of the questions were relevant to the basic truths of the Arab–Israeli dispute.

The memorandum's main questions and the answers given (orally) by their Soviet interlocutors, Suslov and Ponamarev (both members of the Central Committee of the CPSU), were as follows:[37]

Question: Is there a basic truth in the declarations made by the Arab rulers that the establishment [of Israel] was an imperialistic conspiracy against the unity and national liberation of Arab nations and that the solution to the Palestine problem is to be found in the liquidation of Israel as a state and the expulsion of the Jews who have lived in its territory since November 1917 (The Balfour Declaration) – in accordance with the PLO Covenant confirmed by all Arab states?

Answer: The establishment of Israel was not an imperialist conspiracy and the solution to the Palestine problem is not in the liquidation of the State of Israel, and it is necessary to act against the return of a Jewish-Arab war.

Question: What is the USSR's attitude towards the PLO and the Palestine Liberation Army, despite the PLO's incorrect covenant, whether it be towards a legitimate representative of the Arab Palestine people or towards organizations that reject the principles of peace and each nation's right to independence.

Answer: The USSR's attitude towards the PLO and the Palestine Liberation Army is negative. The USSR does not recognize the PLO as the legitimate representative of the Arab Palestinian people because its covenant is not correct.

To a range of questions the Soviet interlocutors avoided giving direct answers under the pretext that they did not want to analyze separately the views of the two factions to prevent the deepening of the split between them. They referred, however, to the Jewish problem in the USSR from the point of view of 'anti-Soviet propaganda'.

Suslov gave both factions the following directives on 19 November 1965:

Radical change in the foreign and internal policy of Israel's Government;

The struggle for an Arab–Israeli peace 'that is of tremendous importance' should stem from the assumption that Israel has no other alternative to secure good neighborliness in the region;

A struggle against nuclear weapons, particularly against the production of an atomic bomb in Israel. Such a bomb will cause a national disaster for Israel and will create an uncompromising opposition in the region as well as deep enmity towards Israel.

To struggle against anti-Soviet incitement; no concession to Zionism.

Ponamarev added:

> The Communist Party of the Soviet Union considers Israel as a capitalist state, its government conducting a pro-imperialist policy with aggressive aims towards its neighboring countries (the Sinai Campaign is one of the examples) and oppressing the Arab minority; helping imperialism in the Middle East and Africa; pursuing a struggle against the democratic forces within Israel. The government of Israel and the Zionist movement pretend to appear on behalf of all Jews in the world, and the organisation of Zionist congresses in Israel does not help lead to an understanding and does not help relations with the Arabs and with the Socialist States. But, the USSR recognizes the existence of an independent State of Israel and does not mix the regime with the masses of the people.

A large part of the summing-up was devoted to the necessity to re-unite the two factions as a guarantee for their successful struggle among the Israeli masses. It could be assumed, from Mr Mikunis's evidence, that in the dispute between both factions the Soviets tended to support Maki (consisting of a majority of Jewish members), attaching importance to their activities among the Jewish population.

Mikunis remarked that he sensed a change in this approach at the 23rd Congress of the CPSU, in 1966, following the accession to power of the left wing of the Syrian Ba'ath Party and Soviet support shifted to Rakach (the majority of whose members were Arabs). From the contents of the talks held by Soviet representatives with Israeli representatives on different levels, the following conclusions can be drawn:

The USSR adhered to the principle of Israel's right to existence, despite its Government's policy being – by Soviet definition – pro-imperialistic. Conversely, this policy was of aid to the Soviet Union in acquiring strongholds in the Arab world.

Israeli–Soviet relations were an integral part of East–West relations, which included the Arab–Israeli dispute. There was no Soviet inclination to separate the two systems.

Though the USSR tended to accept Israel's political and economic reliance on the West, particularly on the USA, Israel went some way too far in its dependence upon it. The USSR had no objection to Israel's continuous reliance upon the West, as long as this reliance was not grounded on an anti-Soviet basis in the field of inter-bloc relations.

Israel could advance its relations with the USSR, if it would help reduce international tension and use its influential channels in the Western world in this direction, meaning in Soviet concepts: the avoidance of pursuing anti-Soviet propaganda, abstaining from voting on pro-Western resolutions in the international arena, voting in favor of Soviet proposals intended to relax tension, and the avoidance of pursuing a policy of force towards Arab states within the framework of the Arab–Israeli conflict.

On the European plane the USSR advocated that Israel should avoid conducting a policy which would strengthen West Germany.

In exchange for a balanced Israeli policy regarding East–West relations, the USSR would increase its influence amongst the Arabs to convince them to accept Israel's existence and would consider acting as a mediator between the conflicting sides. Also, the problem of issuing exit permits to Jews in the USSR who wished to emigrate to Israel would be favorably considered.

There was no Soviet willingness to revise its ideological stand on Zionism.

Any Israeli activity aimed at strengthening the position of Western powers in the Middle East would encounter Soviet opposition whereas any Israeli activity intended to neutralize their stance would enjoy Soviet sympathy.

Israel's foreign policy was a primary determining factor in forging the chances of a Soviet–Israeli *rapprochement*. Israel's internal policy held only a secondary level of importance.

Under the existing circumstances it could be concluded: diplomatic relations between the USSR and Israel would be maintained; the USSR recognized an independent State of Israel; the continuation of a political dialogue with Israel and the cultural exchanges – on a limited scale – was the best possible situation. Any improvement in this situation was contingent upon a change occurring in Israel's policy, from an active pro-Western one to an active policy towards reducing tension between the two blocs.

SIXTH STAGE: MODERATE AND BALANCED TONES TOWARDS ISRAEL

On 22 September 1965 K. Katz, Israel's new Ambassador to the USSR, presented his credentials to the President of the Soviet Union, A. Mikoyan. At the presentation ceremony, the Ambassador said, among other things:

> The people of Israel will never forget the deep understanding displayed by the USSR in their struggle to establish a sovereign nation ... A special place is occupied by the USSR in Israel's history. My nation will always remember the glorious war the Soviet peoples fought against the Nazi foe ... your enemy and ours ... The USSR has made an immense contribution to the establishment of a workers' society based on the fundamentals of social justice ... The Soviet government's effort to ensure peaceful co-existence between nations and countries deserves praise ...[38]

These were truthful and candid words, which pleased the Russians. The President thanked the Ambassador and in his reply stressed the principles of peace which governed Soviet foreign policy.

A short biography of Israel's new ambassador accompanied by his photograph was published that week in the widely-read weekly *Novoe Vremya*.

The day after Mr Katz had presented his credentials to the Soviet President, the newspaper *Sovietskaya Rossia* published an interview with the Ambassador, again with his photograph. The article included the following statement from him:

My job, like that of any foreign ambassador in Moscow, is to work diligently at improving relations with your country. I will search out ways to improve the economic and cultural ties between our two states. Yes, I will have to explain the policy of Israel to the Soviet authorities. I will strive to work towards improving mutual understanding and maintain good relations with your official institutions so that I will have the opportunity of explaining Israel's stance more fully. Relations between our countries are steadily getting better and we must strive for even greater improvement and find methods for reaching new areas for suitable activity. In Israel all things related to Russian culture are highly esteemed and your state is admired as being a great power. I hope that my activities will cause me to be welcomed with understanding and good will ...[39]

The two articles, one in *Novoe Vremya* and the second in *Sovietskaya Rossia*, were exceptions to the rule and pleasantly surprising as such. The USSR behaved in this way only to countries whose sympathy it wished to gain. There may have been three possible motives for this: (a) to balance the unprecedented attack on the previous ambassador, Y. Tekoah, which had appeared about a year prior to this in *Izvestia*, and to indicate Soviet willingness to clear the atmosphere and start afresh; (b) to signal to Israel that the USSR was prepared to open a more moderate era towards Israel; (c) to create a favorable reaction in Israel towards the USSR, particularly in leftist circles, which had worked very actively towards building friendly relations between the two countries.

Israel in The Great Soviet Encyclopedia, *1965*[40]

The entry 'Israel' surveys Israel's internal and foreign policy in 1964. In presenting statistical data on Israel's economy and industry, there is a positive tendency in comparison with the entry in the 1963 annual. Also, some negative expressions and definitions were omitted in comparison with previous annuals. For instance:

1. *Population*: In noting the size of the Jewish population in Israel, the phrase in brackets 'the majority immigrants' was omitted.
2. *Economy*: The data on unemployment was omitted as well as the

definition that 'two-thirds of the workers earn an income lower than the vital income for a living'.

3. *Industry*: The present entry extensively surveys Israel's development. The same goes for the state economy.

4. *Internal Policy*: The statement which appeared in previous annuals that 'the state is dominated by a military psychosis and by a hostile attitude towards Arabs and towards Christian institutions' was omitted.

5. *Foreign Policy*: Israel's relations with African countries and with West Germany were reported in a less critical way. Two statements which had been repeated time and again were omitted this time: one, that Israel did not implement the UN resolution calling for the return of Arab refugees into Israel; second, that the government of Israel projected in the year under review 'a hostile policy towards the Soviet Union and the Socialist camp'.

The Israeli–Arab conflict was presented in an article by M. Kaspi, the *Kol Haam* correspondent in Moscow, published in *Novoe Vremya*, no. 46, October 1965. The article constituted a reply to one on this subject published several weeks previously in the same weekly by Seyful-Mulyukov. The essential points of Kaspi's article were:

1. *The diversion of the Jordan waters* – It should not be forgotten that Israel is also situated on the banks of the river Jordan and as such has the right to utilize its water too.

2. *Bourguiba's announcement* – His call to the Arab countries that they must recognize Israel cannot be ignored; it is an announcement that every Marxist must accept as it is aimed at lessening the tension between the Arab countries and Israel.

3. *Peace between Israel and the Arabs* – The other side (the Arabs) also threatens to use force, and the main item which Seyful-Mulyukov omitted to mention is the Soviet principle of solving controversial international problems by peaceful means, as in the case of India and Pakistan. It is regrettable that he did not propose solving the Israeli–Arab conflict within the framework of this principle.

The following editorial remark emphasized the significance of the article by stating:

> In publishing this article by the correspondent of the Israeli Communist newspaper the editorial board feels our readers

will be given the opportunity of forming a more complete and objective picture of Arab–Israeli relations.

Eshkol's government as viewed by the USSR

Reporting on Israel's election results, the weekly *Za Rubezhom*, no. 46, which appeared at the end of December 1965 under the headline 'A Modest Victory', wrote:

> Ben Gurion and his cohorts stood for extreme nationalism and did not conceal their aggressive plans towards neighboring Arab countries. The present Mapai leadership, headed by Prime Minister Eshkol, represents more moderate views and did not strive for the continued exacerbation of existing differences with the Arabs ...

This evaluation reflects the change in the Soviet approach to the Eshkol government , which is considered in a more favorable light than in June–July 1964. At that time statements such as 'The Eshkol government is continuing the previous [government's] policies' were made and it was claimed that nothing was being done to improve relations with the USSR. 'Moreover, it has condoned an anti-Soviet campaign in Israel based on the distorted pretext that anti-Semitism exists in the USSR.'[41] Also quoted then was the resolution passed at the plenary session of the Israeli Communist Party: 'There has been no significant change in the politics of the Eshkol government which are characterized, as in the past, by a *rapprochement* with the imperialist powers, and with the United States in particular.'[42]

The reason for the change in the assessment in 1965 was the policy of restraint of Eshkol's government compared to the policy of deterrence of Ben Gurion's government concerning the Arab–Israeli dispute as well as recognition of Eshkol's policy towards the Arab minority in Israel (the abolition of the post of Military Governor) compared with that of Ben Gurion.

The Palestine Problem in Soviet research

At the end of December 1965 a two-volume research study entitled *The USSR and the United Nations* was published in Moscow.[43] The authors' aim, as stated, was to examine the Soviet position during 20 years of UN activities and was the first research of its kind. The authors were lecturers at the Institute for International Relations of the Soviet Academy of Science and included N. T. Federenko, Head of the Soviet mission to the UN.

Volume A contained a chapter entitled 'The Palestine Problem' which described the USSR's approach to this problem between 1947 and 1950. In contrast to the books of Ivanov and Sheiniss and Nikitina, the facts are presented here objectively. The authors do not hide the USSR's part in the establishment of Israel, nor the fact that Arab armies invaded the territory designated for the State of Israel 'and thus began the conflict'.

Parallel to these publications, the Soviet media held back from publishing the Arab leaders' statements in which they condemned Israel. They also dealt, to a lesser degree, with the Arab–Israeli conflict.

Condemning anti-Semitism

In his speech given in Riga and published in the Soviet press on 19 July 1965, the USSR Prime Minister, A. Kosygin, stated:

> Lenin bequeathed us a national policy based on principles of Proletarian Internationalism, on non-restricted equality between races and nationalities. The capitalist system cannot exist without national disputes. The nationalistic remnants in whatever form, be it in manifesting extreme nationalism, powerful chauvinism, racialism, or anti-Semitism, all these are doubtless alien phenomena in our society and contrary to our world outlook.

Pravda, the organ of the CPSU, in its issue of 5 September 1965, in an editorial entitled 'Leninist nationality brotherhood', condemned manifestations of anti-Semitism: 'Lenin demanded that a constant struggle be waged against anti-Semitism which is merely a shameful exploitation of racial difference and national feelings of hatred … The imperialists are constantly attempting to revive the racial differences between our national minorities. This is hopeless.'

Several days afterwards, this article was copied in the majority of Soviet newspapers. It manifested to the Western world that the USSR was condemning anti-Semitism, and its condemnation in the Communist Party organ – after dozens of years of disregard – was an important event. (Several years earlier a phonograph record had been made of Lenin's speeches from the first years of the revolution. Of the eight speeches Lenin originally recorded, one was devoted to the condemnation of anti-Semitism – and that one was not included in the recording.)

The condemnation of anti-Semitism was an integral part of the general tendency towards improving the atmosphere in relations between the USSR and Israel against the background of the relative tranquillity in East–West relations, including the Middle East. The diversity of moderate expressions regarding Israel was evidence of this improvement, which comprised mutual relations in the fields of culture, tourism, the Jewish problem, and Middle Eastern affairs. This was the single 'Golden Era' in Soviet–Israeli relations and it ended with the Ba'ath revolution in Syria. This conciliatory tone did not apply to the discouraging of Jewish emigration to Israel, nor to the struggle against Zionism. On the contrary in October 1965 the USSR's representative on the Third Political Committee of the UN General Assembly proposed – for the first time in the international arena – to include Zionism together with anti-Semitism and Nazism in the ideological currents that should be condemned.[44]

SEVENTH STAGE: 1966–1967 SEVERE CRISIS AND THE SEVERANCE OF RELATIONS

The credit which the Soviets granted to Prime Minister Eshkol and his policy in the second half of 1965 expired in January 1966. Following Eshkol's statement in the Knesset, when presenting his new government, he expressed his hope that 'under the pressure of the Jewish people and enlightened world public opinion the Soviet authorities will change their stand regarding the Jewish problem'.[45] As noted, this statement aroused Soviet indignation and became a subject of expressions of anger on the diplomatic level both in Moscow and Jerusalem. The Soviet weekly *Novoe Vremya* made a new assessment at the end of 1966 regarding Eshkol's government policy, and it differed from what was published on the same subject one month earlier by the weekly *Za Rubezhom*. Israel's policy was once again identified as overlapping the anti-Soviet policy of the Western powers. It was noted that although the extreme right in Israel suffered a defeat, it would not be correct to state that the left scored a victory. Though Eshkol's pragmatic speech in the Knesset (when presenting his new government on 12 January 1965) included a sympathetic sentence regarding the USSR – on the Soviet policy in the Middle East and to its Foreign Policy principle – the Soviets disregarded it and noted that Eshkol's speech was evidence of a 'tendency to continue the previous political course', namely, pursuing a policy of dependence upon the Western powers. The article seemed to be disappointed with the election results and with Mapam's decision to participate in the government's coalition. An impression was created – writes the author Marcus – that with Mapam's joining the government, substantial policy changes would be introduced. But – the author notes – 2 ministers out of 18 would not be able to influence the foreign and internal policy of the government. On the contrary, the participation of Mapam's minister in the government would only be exploited by Eshkol to camouflage his reactionary policy.[46]

This reaction attested to a tendency to return to the period before credit was given to Eshkol and his policy. To a certain degree, it was an echo of those distant days on the eve of the USSR's severance of diplomatic relations with Israel, since a call to mobilize world opinion against the USSR resembled a declaration of a propaganda war against the USSR. (From the moment he became Prime Minister and until this statement made in the Knesset, Eshkol's public speeches had never included such a firm tone regarding the Jewish problem in the USSR.) We do not know if this statement, along with extensive activities pursued in the world, at Israel's initiative, for the sake of Soviet Jewry, had influenced Moscow policy to return to a firm course towards Israel. Yet, it may be assumed that Eshkol's statement left a negative residue in Soviet minds and influenced considerations for a turn towards Israel, following the rise to power of the left wing of the Syrian Ba'ath party in February 1966.

From this period until the USSR's severance of relations with Israel in June 1967, Soviet policy towards Israel focused on sending frequent and severe warnings aimed at deterring Israel from undertaking military action against Syria. The USSR's main fear was that such a step would cause the collapse of the new Ba'ath regime in Damascus, which had begun to conduct a pro-Soviet policy (also by including the Secretary of the Communist Party, for the first time in its history, in the Syrian government) aimed at diminishing American and British influence in the Middle East. This policy was accompanied by Syrian provocative acts along the Israeli–Syrian border, by aggressive declarations against Israel, and by Syrian leaders' frequent calls to fight Israel in order to wipe her out of the region.

Being concerned for the new Syrian regime's fate and determined to rapidly consolidate it, the USSR extended to the regime large-scale political, economic, and military support. Among other things, the USSR expressed its support by harshening the tone of its propaganda against Israel. During this period Israel was presented in the Soviet media as a war instigator in the Middle East in the service of the USA and as an assistant in stopping the 'process of social progressive changes in the Middle East'.[47]

The anti-Israel propaganda continuously occupied a large part of the Soviet media, in unprecedented volume, while concentrating on two new themes: first, expressing solidarity with the Palestinians 'in their just fight against Zionism';[48] second, from the beginning of the Six Day War, comparing Zionism to Nazism.

NOTES

1 I. B. Lutzky, *Problems of Economy* (Russian), no. 10, Oct. 1949, pp. 84–7, following a symposium held at Moscow University in June 1949 on the subject 'The Struggle for National Liberation in the Colonial States since World War Two'.
2 *The Great Soviet Encyclopedia* (Russian), Vol. 17, pp. 512–18.
3 Security Council Official Records, 642nd meeting, 24 Nov. 1953.
4 Paragraph 12 of the Western draft resolution notes: 'The Security Council requests the UN Secretary-General to put at the disposal of the UN observers an appropriate number of experts and in particular hydraulic engineers.' It could be assumed that it was this paragraph that caused the Soviet opposition to the proposal. The voting on this resolution took place on 22 Jan. 1954 (Security Council Official Records, 656th meeting, 22 Jan. 1954).
5 When Israel's complaint against Egypt was debated at the UN Security Council in Oct. 1950 and in Aug. 1951, concerning Egypt's discriminatory policy in relation to Israeli ships' transit and goods destined for Israel via the Suez Canal, the USSR abstained from voting on the draft resolution presented by the three Western powers, calling for Egypt to remove its limitations on free

international navigation and on cargo ships' passage through the Suez Canal. At the same time the Soviet press manifested a positive attitude to Egypt's demand for the nationalization of the canal and the imposition of its full control over the canal. The press then accused Britain of not respecting Egypt's sovereign right over the canal, as its territorial waters. In Jan. 1954, when Israel's complaint was again debated, the Soviets did not renounce their stand of 1951, under the pretext that there was no sense in the Security Council adopting an additional identical resolution which was not carried out. In fact, the USSR wished to avoid at that stage a resolution which might have infringed upon the right of Egyptian sovereignty over the canal. The voting on the draft resolution took place on 29 March 1954.

6 Security Council Official Records, 664th meeting, 29 March 1954; Security Council Official Records, 654th meeting, 29 Dec. 1953.
7 Ibid., 664th meeting, 29 March 1954.
8 On 24 Feb. 1955 the Baghdad Pact was established by Turkey and Iraq. On 5 April 1955 Britain officially joined the pact. That same day Pakistan's Foreign Minister announced his Government's intention of also joining the pact, which it did on 23 Sept. 1955. Iran declared its adherence to the pact on 11 Oct. 1955. Egypt announced its refusal to join on 22 Jan. 1956.
9 Quoted in Y. Ro'i, *From Encroachment to Involvement: A Documentary Study of Soviet Policy in the Middle East 1945–1973* (Tel Aviv: Israel Universities Press, 1979), p. 145.
10 M. Sharett, *Private Diary*, pp. 1272–5.
11 Ibid.
12 *Izvestia*, 30 Dec. 1955. Foreign Minister Sharett rejected Krushchev's statement in the Knesset (*Divrei Haknesset*, Vol. 19, pp. 677–8, 2 Jan. 1956).
13 MFA Arch. File 103.1 SSR. Partial report in A. Dagan, *Moscow and Jerusalem*, p. 96.
14 MFA Arch. File 103.1 SSR, Partial report, in A. Dagan, op. cit., p. 97.
15 Ibid.
16 MFA Arch. File 103.1 SSR.
17 A. Eban, *My Life* (Hebrew), Vol. 1, pp. 180–89.
18 The Czech–Egyptian arms deal was publicly announced by TASS on 1 Oct. 1955. Israel's proposal for a security alliance with the USA was brought up in the talks held with State Secretary Dulles during his visit to Israel in May 1953, and in continuation by Israel's Ambassador to Washington A. Eban (M. Zohar, *David Ben Gurion*, Vol. 3, pp. 1158–9). Moreover, Foreign Minister M. Sharett stated in the Knesset on 17 Feb. 1954: 'The fortification of [Israel's] independence and security could include, under certain circumstances, also the concern for the security and defense of the whole region [Middle East] including Israel in face of a danger which might be expected' (*Divrei Haknesset*, Vol. 15, p. 929).
19 *Divrei Haknesset*, Vol. 20, p. 1725, 23 April 1956.
20 'The extremists' conduct in Israel', *Izvestia*, 29 July 1956.
21 General Assembly Official Documents, 12th Session, 708th Meeting, p. 352.
22 *Divrei Haknesset*, Vol. 22, pp. 2039–47, 2056–8, 2063–7, and pp. 2072–6.
23 *Pravda*, 24 May 1957.
24 MFA Arch. File 103.1 SSR.
25 Expert on Israeli affairs. She published numerous articles on Israel including a book based on her doctoral thesis: 'The State of Israel', Moscow, 1968.
26 K. Ivanov and Z. Sheiniss, *The State of Israel: Its Situation and Policy* (Russian),

Moscow, 1959.

27 *Mezhdunarodnaya Zhizn*, 12 Jan. 1959; *Sovremeonyi vostok*, 18 Jan. 1959.
28 *Mezhdunarodnaya Zhizn*, 10, 1961.
29 A. Dagan, op. cit., Second Part.
30 Foreign Minister G. Meir's conversation with Soviet Ambassador Chuvakhin on 12 April 1965. MFA Arch. File 103.1 SSR.
31 Prime Minister Eshkol's talk with Soviet Ambassador Bodrov, 23 Sept. 1963. MFA Arch. File 103.1 SSR. Partial report, A. Dagan, op. cit., p. 148.
32 Soviet Ambassador Chuvakhin in his talk with the Director of the East European Division on 12 April 1965 following the conversation held with Mrs G. Meir. MFA Arch. File 351.1 SSR
33 Gromyko to Foreign Minister Meir, in the UN on 3 Oct. 1963. MFA Arch. File 103.1 SSR. Partial report by A. Dagan, op. cit., pp. 149–50.
34 Israeli diplomat's talk with a Soviet diplomat at the UN on 31 Oct. 1958. MFA Arch. File 103.1 SSR.
35 MK Abramov reported the details of his talk with MK Sneh to G. Avner, the Director of the US division of the Israeli Ministry of Foreign Affairs, end January 1962. MFA Arch. File 103.1 SSR.
36 MFA Arch. File 103.1 SSR.
37 S. Mikunis, General-Secretary of Maki recorded evidence, at the Davis Institute for International Relations, Hebrew University of Jerusalem, May 1976, pp. 495–517.
38 *Kol Haam*, 23 Sept. 1965.
39 *Sovietskaya Rossia*, 24 Sept. 1965.
40 *The Great Soviet Encyclopedia*, 1965 Annual, Moscow 1965.
41 *Asia y Africa Sevodnya*, April 1964.
42 *Pravda*, 31 July 1964.
43 *The USSR and the United Nations* (Russian), Nauka, Moscow 1965.
44 General Assembly, Official Documents, A/6181, Third Committee, 20 Oct. 1965.
45 *Divrei Haknesset*, Vol. 44, p. 348.
46 *Novoe Vremya*, No. 4, 1966.
47 *Sovietskaya Rossia*, 27 May 1966: a commentary entitled 'New bridge of provocations' deals with a news report that Israel had acquired jet fighters from the USA, noting 'And now there can be no doubt about the imperialist conspiracies. With the help of Israeli reaction they strive at exacerbating to the maximum the situation in the Middle East and to stop the process of progressive social changes in several Arab states.'
48 *Pravda*, 24 April 1966. A joint Soviet–Syrian communiqué published at the end of a Syrian State mission in Moscow, states: 'Both sides have confirmed their solidarity with the Palestinian Arabs, and expressed their support for their lawful rights in the just struggle against Zionism used by imperialist forces to increase tension in the Middle and Near East.' It was the first time that the USSR had expressed its solidarity with the struggle against Zionism in a joint communiqué with an Arab state.

5 · Trade relations

SHORTLY AFTER the renewal of Israeli–Soviet diplomatic relations in 1953 the Soviet authorities invited an Israeli delegation to Moscow for trade talks.[1] It happened even prior to the establishment of the respective embassies in Moscow and Israel. This initiative was part of the USSR's policy of extending its trade relations with foreign countries, with a double aim: to raise the living standard of the Soviet population and to develop its economic resources, on the one hand; and, on the other hand, to create a positive image regarding the principle of peaceful co-existence which was being propagated at that time by the USSR.[2] The Israeli delegation comprised 'Delek' (oil companies) and Citrus Fruit Board representatives. At the end of their discussions, November–December 1953, two agreements were signed (on the import of crude oil to Israel on 6 December 1953 and on the export to the USSR of citrus fruit and bananas at the beginning of January 1954) by both sides.[3]

See Table 5.1 for data on the volume of trade between Israel and the USSR, 1954–56.

Table 5.1 Volume of trade between Israel and USSR, 1954–56

Year	Mazut (tons)	Crude Oil (tons)	Total (tons)	F.O.B. Total $ (tons)	Total Israel Consumption of Petroleum Products
1954	175,000	100,000	275,000	3,650,000	1,092,000
1955	285,000	156,000	450,000	6,400,000	1,230,000
1956	285,000	185,000	470,000	7,000,000	1,350,000*
1957	300,000	220,000	520,000	8,100,000	1,500,000*
1958	350,000	280,000	630,000	11,000,000	1,600,000*

*Estimated according to the final trade agreement, signed July 1956

97

It is understood from the data published by Soviet sources that Israel imported 8–10 per cent of the total Soviet oil export at this time. Israel occupied fourth place (after Finland, Sweden, and Argentina) in the list of its oil exploration. Payments were made by clearings.

Citrus and banana fruit shipments from Israel to the USSR were valued as follows:

1953/4 season	$2,527,253
1954/5 season	$2,255,773
1955/6 season	$2,602,841

These sums were lower than the total value of Israeli purchases from the USSR. For that reason Israel had to pay for the difference in hard currency, or by transmitting clearance between Israel and other states, in payment of the debt. It was carried out with the USSR's consent. In July 1956, the last trade agreement (until the 1967 severance of diplomatic relations) was signed. Israeli authorities were satisfied with the trade results and it was noted that during the two-and-a-half-year continuance of this trading period 'no cases were registered to prove lack of satisfaction from the Soviet side in implementing the agreement in word and spirit'.[4] Only one incident occurred during this period which overshadowed the process of the normal trade. This was in January 1956 when Israeli police discovered at the Rehovot railway station, some anti-Soviet leaflets in citrus fruit boxes destined for shipment to the USSR.[5] The leaflets were written in Russian calling on the citizens of the USSR to establish an underground movement against the Soviet regime by setting up secret resistance cells. Israel's police found the suspects and issued warrants for arrest. During the interrogation it was learned that the leaflets were printed in West Germany by a group of Russian anti-Communist immigrants and refugees. Some of these leaflets reached the port of Odessa and on 9 April 1956 the USSR's Embassy in Israel submitted a note of protest to the Ministry of Foreign Affairs in Jerusalem, stressing the fact that the Soviet Union regarded this incident as being of the 'utmost gravity'. The political correspondent of the Israeli daily *Lamerhav* reported on the incident on 16 April 1956 noted that Israeli factors dealing with the exportation of citrus fruit had received a clear hint (presumably from the Soviet Embassy in Israel) that if such incidents were to occur again, there would be no alternative but to draw conclusions on behalf of the USSR regarding the Israeli fruit shipments to the USSR.

It was also learned that the legal adviser of Israel's Foreign Ministry applied to the legal adviser of the government requesting submission of a criminal claim against the suspects 'not later than within a week', in view of the Soviet hints that 'the affair may negatively affect Israeli–Soviet relations in general and trade relations in particular'. The incident was brought to an end only after it had been promised to the Soviet representatives in Israel that penalty measures would be taken against the guilty parties.[6]

The signing of the agreement on Soviet oil sales to Israel in July 1956 did not only bear commercial importance, but went beyond that: oil was considered to be first degree war material and its supply to Israel attested that the USSR did not believe that Israel would attack Egypt or use this oil for purposes of war. The USSR also did not take into account the Arab economic boycott against Israel.

We do not know if and to what degree the Arab states tried to influence the USSR to cancel its oil deals with Israel. However, from Soviet Foreign Minister Shepilov's answer to foreign correspondents on 21 July 1956, it could be concluded that such an attempt did indeed take place.

In referring to the signed agreement Shepilov said, 'The oil deal is nothing but a trade agreement of no importance to which unfortunately some people attach exaggerated importance; one should not emphasize here political aspects which do not exist.'[7]

The Soviet decision to cancel its agreements with Israel following the Sinai Campaign probably took into consideration the possibility that Israel would make military use of Soviet oil. The cessation of trade would have given credit to the USSR among Arab leaders who aspired to weaken Israel's economic and military potential. This consideration probably prevailed in the minds of Soviet decision makers immediately after the outbreak of the Sinai Campaign on 29 October 1956.

ISRAEL'S REACTION TO THE SOVIET CANCELLATION OF
TRADE AGREEMENTS FOLLOWING THE SINAI CAMPAIGN

On 16 December 1956 Israel's Ministry of Foreign Affairs sent a protest note to the Soviet Embassy: After recording the dates and details of the commercial agreements signed between the respective commercial companies of both countries it noted (paragraphs 5, 6 and 7, translated from Hebrew):

> (5) The Israeli companies related to the various commercial transactions have immediately informed their suppliers in the USSR that they do not accept the cancellation announcement, that they insist upon the full and agreed upon implementation of various commercial transactions and that they reserve all rights including the full right to be compensated for the damages and losses caused by the one-sided cancellation. (6) Since the suppliers base their position, *inter alia*, on the cancellation of export permits or on the announcement from the Soviet Foreign Trade Ministry that these permits will not be granted, for reasons of 'Force Majeure', and because the situation is related to the supply of goods agreed upon in signed agreements, still in force and with the knowledge of the Soviet government, the government of Israel is compelled to put the full responsibility on the USSR for the cancellation of the reserving of all its rights and the rights of its affected citizens by these deeds. (7) The Ministry of Foreign Affairs hopes that the government of the USSR will remove all the restrictions that have been imposed and will instruct the suppliers to implement agreements to which they are committed and to pay compensation for the damages and losses which the Soviet side has caused, directly or indirectly.[8]

Two conclusions could be reached from this note:

First, the process of canceling Soviet deals with Israel began prior to the Sinai Campaign, perhaps, as a result of Arab pressure on the USSR, following Shepilov's visit to Egypt in June 1956. (A hint of that is found in Shepilov's answer to correspondents on 21 July 1956 and in an article published in *Pravda* on 31 December 1957 denying the news regarding negotiations on the renewal of oil supplies to Israel 'aiming at forcing a wedge between the USSR and Arab States'.)

Second, the cancellation of the deals referred not only to the current year (1956) but also to 1957 and 1958. It was a definite cancellation on long-range scale – a kind of integration within the Arab boycott policy against Israel.

The USSR answered Israel's Note on 6 February 1957, saying: 'The supply of oil to Israel is impossible, resulting from the aggression against Egypt' and that 'the entire responsibility for that lies with Israel's government'.[9]

Since, in the Soviet reply – as in the Soviet announcements regarding the cancellation – there is no hint that after Israel's withdrawal from Sinai to the previous Armistice line, the situation would return to normal, it was understood that the Sinai Campaign was more used as a pretext for the breaking of trade relations than the true reason.

On 17 February 1957 the Israeli Ministry of Foreign Affairs sent the following reply (translated from the Hebrew) to the Soviet government:

> The government of Israel is taking notice of the Soviet government explaining the one-sided cancellation of the agreements concerning the supply of Soviet oil to Israel, for political reasons. This attitude of the Soviet government, particularly towards a small country, is contradictory to many Soviet declarations condemning the imposition of restrictions – for political reasons – on international trade and embargoes. These declarations must arouse doubts concerning normal relations with Soviet state companies when it becomes clear that their commitments are valid only as long as they suit the provisional political needs of the USSR. The government of Israel is taking notice that, in its Note of 6 February 1957, the government of the USSR is taking practically upon itself the responsibility for breaching agreements in force signed by Soviet companies and is reserving its rights regarding the damages that were caused to the State of Israel and its citizens as a result of the breach of these agreements.[10]

The purpose in mentioning that Israel 'reserves the right' was to bring up the matter in legal instances.

Israel submitted a claim for compensation to the Soviet companies for the damages caused in the wake of the cancellation of the agreements on the supply of oil. The amount of compensation claimed was estimated at some $2.4 million. According to the agreement between the two sides, the claim was submitted to the Soviet Arbitration Committee on Foreign Trade with its seat in Moscow.[11]

Israel's claim was discussed in 13 meetings of the committee made up of three Soviet judges which met periodically from 4 December 1957 to 19 June 1958. The Soviet defense stand was that the cancellation of the agreements was caused by 'Force Majeure' since the Soviet companies had no control over the Soviet Ministry of Foreign Trade in receiving export permits to foreign states.

Israel's representation claimed that the argument of 'Force Majeure' was not relevant in this case, since the Soviet companies were extensions of the Ministry of Foreign Trade and thus one department of a governmental institution did not have to get instructions from another department of the same institution; the Soviet companies did not even try – as the procedure required of an independent company – to protest against the cancellation of the permits for the export of oil to Israel. Israel's demand to prove this argument by inviting the Soviet companies' representatives to the committee was met with a firm rebuff. This is how Israel was prevented from proving the justification of its argument – and this is how Israel was prevented from inviting the legal adviser of the Soviet Ministry of Foreign Trade to the committee to clarify the procedure of issuing and cancellation of export permits.

In strengthening its legal claim Israel's representatives referred to legal convictions by known jurists in west European countries that had proved the justice of Israel's case. They also referred to the conclusions of the West German Max Planck Institute in Hamburg, which specialized in private international law, according to which 'Force Majeure' was not applicable in Soviet law, since the USSR was the exclusive owner of state property, and all institutes, enterprises, companies, and organizations acted as its agencies.[12]

Though the disputants were promised that political considerations would not constitute a basis for the determination of the verdict, the Soviet Note stressing that the cancellation of the agreements resulted from Israel's attack on Egypt was after all the main reason for rejecting Israel's claim. Not only that, but Israel was even required to pay the costs of the committee's work.

The verdict of the arbitration committee reverberated in the west European press, which sided with Israel by emphasizing the perversion of justice in the Soviet judgment and warned companies in the West not to fall into a similar trap in their trade relations with the USSR.

Had Israel expected such a verdict?

The arbitration committee was founded in 1932, and up to Israel's claim for compensation it had been known as a reliable legal authority. In the majority of the cases which were brought before the committee it had passed judgment in favor of foreign companies. True, the cases generally related to commercial details (for example, delay in the dates of goods' supply or protests concerning their quality). Israel believed that it had a simple legal case, presuming, probably, that whilst the USSR aspired to broaden its commercial ties with foreign countries, it would avoid creating an uncomfortable atmosphere by responding negatively to Israel's claim.[13]

The arbitration's results showed that Israel was mistaken in its presumption that Soviet trade was free of political considerations. Just as on the political plane Israel encountered a unique Soviet attitude towards itself, so it was in the commercial field. Israel apparently constituted a special category in the Soviet mind. Not only had the Soviet Union not severed its trade relations with Britain and France in the aftermath of the Sinai Campaign, but it also traded with states with whom it did not maintain diplomatic relations.[14] Israel's balance sheet on the legal plane showed that in the West it gained much sympathy, both because it had decided to test in reality the weight of Soviet commercial commitment and because of the validity of its claim. However, it could now be presumed that the Soviet authorities' enmity towards Israel was even stronger. The material of legal proof which Israel submitted to the arbitration committee was prepared by Western jurists and the undermining of trust in the sincerity of Soviet commercial deals with the West, which affected Western public opinion (particularly in the economic and legal circles), might have created in Soviet minds the impression that Israel was acting on a mission from the West. This did not help negotiations on the resumption of trade with Israel. Trade had been intentionally broken off on a long-term basis immediately after the Sinai Campaign. Moreover, the verdict of the arbitration committee encouraged the Arab economic boycott against Israel in its aspiration to weaken Israel's economic potential.

Responding to an interpellation of MK Ardity in the Knesset,[15] Foreign Minister G. Meir stated that, according to the rules of the arbitration committee, it was not possible to appeal against its verdicts and that, according to the constitution of the International Court of Justice in The Hague, only states were entitled to dispute before the Court. For that reason the Foreign Minister concluded that there was no sense in Israeli companies applying to the Court in this regard.

ISRAELI–SOVIET CONTACTS FOR THE RESUMPTION OF MUTUAL TRADE

On 21 August 1957, Ben Zion Razin, Secretary of the Israeli–Soviet League of Friendship, complained to Mr Avdayev, First Secretary of the Soviet Embassy in Israel, over the USSR not having renewed the oil supply to Israel. The Soviet representative reacted by saying that oil was considered strategic material. 'When Israel stops threatening its neighboring countries and declares its neutrality,' he said, 'no doubt the good relations which used to prevail between the USSR and Israel will be restored.'[16] This was a new argument, never heard before. On 3 April 1954 the Soviet representative at the Interparliamentarian Organizations Conference, held then in Geneva, demanded freedom of trade and the avoidance of all trade limitations of political nature. MK David Hacohen, who represented Israel at this conference, pointed out that the USSR itself had ceased its trading with Israel following the Sinai Campaign, whilst it did not stop trading with Britain and France, who also participated in that action. MK Hacohen stressed in his address that the USSR was 'making calculation' with small and weak countries, whilst strictly maintaining its normal relations with great and rich powers. Following this statement, another Soviet representative at the conference, Deputy Chairman of 'Gossplan', Zutov, assured MK Hacohen that trade between the USSR and Israel, in oil and citrus fruit, would be resumed adding: 'You can inform your government that the absence of trade (with Israel) will be annulled.'[17] Subsequent contacts between the Israeli Embassy in Moscow and Zutov led to nothing. It gave the impression that Zutov had just intended to calm the atmosphere of the Conference by giving his assurances to Hacohen, obscuring the contradiction between Soviet preachings to the Western states and its deeds towards Israel.[18]

On 4 July 1960, Israel's Ambassador in Moscow, A. Harel, discussed the subject of trade resumption with the Soviet First Deputy Minister of Foreign Trade, Borissov. The latter made it clear that from the point of view of commercial interest the Soviet Union could not be helped by Israel in two fields which were important to the Soviets: (1) the acquisition of equipment for chemical factories and for heavy industry enterprises; (2) the establishment of enterprises to speed up construction. This was the sort of trade that the Soviet Union maintained with the developed countries. As for other kinds of trade, Borissov noted, included in this category were underdeveloped countries with an ideological affinity with the USSR. The USSR was interested in helping them so as to accelerate their development. Israel, in his opinion, did not belong to either of these categories. In view of Borissov's clarification, Israel's Ambassador concluded that, at that stage, the Soviet decision not to resume its trade with Israel still prevailed.[19]

On 26 October 1960, Ambassador Harel noted, in conversation with Soviet Foreign Minister A. Gromyko, that he understood from his talk with Borissov that political considerations were preventing the USSR from renewing its trade with Israel. Whereupon Gromyko, in a long speech intended to prove that in commercial relations the only determining factor was commercial interest, reacted by saying that never had the USSR said 'Whether in a domestic or a foreign arena, that it did not have any trade with Israel because of political factors.' Gromyko promised to look into the matter and advised the Ambassador to contact the Ministry of Foreign Trade within two weeks. The Ambassador did indeed do that and found that there was no progress in the matter.[20]

On 30 August 1962, Israel's Ambassador in Moscow, Y. Tekoah, in conversation with the Director of the Near East Department of the Soviet Foreign Ministry, Schiborin, stated that, in accordance with advice he had received from Gromyko, his Deputy Lapin, and his interlocutor – who had stressed that trade relations with Israel were a purely commercial matter, he had submitted to the Soviet Deputy Minister of Foreign Trade, Borissov, a list of practical proposals for the resumption of trade relations but that he had received a negative answer from him. Director Schiborin thanked the Ambassador for this information, noted that he had proceeded correctly – as he was indeed advised – and that he hoped that the Ministry of Foreign Trade would study the proposals 'seriously'.[21]

On 5 September 1962, Ambassador Tekoah again discussed the subject with the Director of the Near Eastern Department of the Soviet Foreign Ministry, who informed the Ambassador that he had checked the subject with the Ministry of Trade which had replied that 'there was no possibility' of a basic revision of the trade policy with Israel, because the Ministry of Trade 'wasn't interested in changing the existing supply markets for citrus fruit'. He expressed, however, his hope that 'nevertheless' goods would be found which the USSR would be able to sell Israel and perhaps such that could be purchased from Israel. In his opinion, it would be desirable to continue negotiating with the Trade Ministry. The Ambassador argued: 'If, after all our proposals, we remain without trade relations, it would be difficult to distinguish between the considerations guiding the trade policy of the Soviet Union. It isn't clear how the USSR will demand in the UN trade relations between all nations with no discrimination, and how the USSR would raise its demand for a world conference to assure trade between all nations, if at the same time the USSR itself is alienating one of the UN members from the frame of its trade relations.'

Director Schiborin answered that ultimately general relations between states surely do influence trade relations between them and that up to 1956 the USSR had maintained normal trade relations with Israel. But after the Sinai Campaign the USSR understood that 'Israel is prepared to ally itself with imperialism without limitation'. The Ambassador reacted by saying: 'On the one hand we hear from Gromyko and his Deputy Lapin that there is no commercial discrimination against Israel', whilst on the other hand, it was clear from the Director's remarks 'that in the trade policy of the USSR non-commercial considerations do exist '. Hence 'it looks as if on two questions the USSR has a non-logical and non-justified complex – relations with Israel and the Jewish problem'. On this, the Director remarked, 'Here lies the main factor which separates us.'[22]

On 23 September 1963 Israel's Prime Minister Eshkol asked the Soviet Ambassador to Israel, M. Bodrov, what the reason was for the absence of trade relations between the USSR and Israel. The Ambassador replied that the Trade Ministry was afraid of renewing its commercial relations with Israel 'whilst from above the political level, there was no encouragement in this direction'.[23]

On 30 May 1963, the Deputy Director of the eastern European Division of Israel's Foreign Ministry, Mr D. Sattat, in conversation with the Trade Attaché of the Soviet Embassy in Israel, Mr Kuznetzov, raised the question of the absence of trade between the USSR and Israel. The Trade Attaché was of the opinion that the renewal of mutual trade was not expected 'neither this year nor before the end of mid next year'. He explained, contrary to Soviet high-level officials, that the reason for that was political and not economic since the USSR 'was interested in establishing its products well in the Arab market' and in that lay the political factor.

When the Deputy Director pointed out to the Trade Attaché the declared Soviet policy, according to which no political considerations were guiding it in commercial affairs, the Attaché answered, 'Indeed, it is true, but in the case of Israel the situation is slightly different.' The Attaché actually confirmed in his reply the unique course of the USSR's policy towards Israel, which was being expressed also in the domain of trade.[24]

On 4 March 1965 the USSR's Embassy Trade Attaché argued in conversation with the Director of the eastern European Division of the Foreign Ministry in Jerusalem that the difficulties in renewing mutual trade relations stemmed 'from the general atmosphere in Israel and the absence of political and security stability in Israel'. Atmosphere meant, in his opinion, 'the hostile attitude' of the Israeli press towards the USSR: Israel's activities on behalf of the Jews in the USSR, and so on. By 'absence of stability' he meant the war thoughts that were 'buzzing in the air'. The Soviets feared that, should 'the event of 1956' be repeated, the Soviets would find themselves connected with Israel in trade agreements and would be once again compelled not to respect them 'as a result of aggressive acts'.[25]

On 28 June 1965 Ambassador Tekoah went to say 'good-by' to Foreign Minister Gromyko upon completing his term of office in the USSR. At that opportunity Mr Gromyko noted that the USSR had no objection to having trade relations with Israel. He added, however, that 'Trade must be based on mutual interest.' If the Soviet Union was not purchasing goods from Israel, it meant that the Soviet trade organizations had no interest in this. 'The Soviet Union is definitely prepared to develop its relations with Israel, including trade.'[26] But it seemed that it was not interested in that.

Characteristically Gromyko attempted to diminish Israel's suspicions about political considerations that were blocking the renewal of trade relations with Israel. The lower level of the Soviet administration was, however, more open in revealing that there were political reasons for the non-renewal of trade relations, but each Soviet representative had his own pretexts. Yet, it seems that all of them came down to the same denominator: the USSR's interest in establishing itself in the Arab market, without incident, in contrast with its lack of interest in strengthening Israel's economic and military potential. These were the main factors which prevented the resumption of the commercial relations between both states.

AGREEMENT ON THE SALE OF SOVIET REAL ESTATE TO ISRAEL

Israeli and Soviet representatives held talks for a period of four years on the sale to Israel of real estate registered in Russia's name from the time of Tsar. The signing of the agreement on 7 October 1964 in Jerusalem was considered by Israel to be an important step which would lead to the renewal of trade relations between the two countries. It concerned properties of an exclusive secular nature (no properties of church institutions were included in the agreement) in exchange for which the government of Israel undertook to pay the USSR 4.5 million US dollars. It was agreed that this payment would be executed over a two-year period, starting at the date of the signing, and would consist of three equal parts of 1.5 million US dollars.[27] Paragraph 4 of the agreement, which noted that with a part of Israel's payment the USSR would purchase goods in Israel, served as a basis for the hope that this commercial deal would pave the way for the renewal of mutual trade.

The volume of Soviet purchases in Israel and its essence, in the frame of payments for the Russian property, were clarified later on.

On 28 June 1965 the Trade Attaché of the Soviet Embassy in Israel made the following clarifications to Mr E. Doron, Director of the eastern European Division of the Foreign Ministry in Jerusalem.

1. The USSR would use the Israeli payments to purchase Israeli goods, as from 1966 only, so that they would be included in the new import program.
2. There was no intention to purchase citrus fruit, since the USSR had prior commitments to buy citrus products from other countries.
3. The USSR would be interested in buying textiles from Israel.
4. As for Soviet exports to Israel, there was no intention of selling Israel oil, steel products and iron. Perhaps the USSR would be able to export wood to Israel, via Bulgaria.

This arrangement was reached, noted the Trade Attaché, after prolonged talks that he had conducted in Moscow at the USSR economic ministries, and he mentioned that the problem of mutual trade was raised in talks at the highest level, including Prime Minister Kosygin.[28]

Evidence shows that from the date of signing this agreement and up to the severance of Israeli–Soviet relations, the Soviets did purchase Israeli goods within the framework of the agreement, but there was no intention on their side to re-establish normal trade relations with Israel. It seems that the 'highest level', referred to by the Soviet Trade Attaché, decided to continue with the existing situation, though Soviet trade with Western countries increased considerably from the beginning of the 1960s and included a considerable increase in the import of citrus fruit products (which Israel was very interested in exporting to the USSR).

In conclusion, Israel's purchase of Russian property from the USSR remained, in effect, an isolated episode in the history of trade relations between both countries. It did not pave the way, as Israel had hoped, for the renewal of normal trade relations, because of those self-same factors which had tipped the scale towards severance of relations in 1956.

NOTES

1 *Kol Haam*, 12 Oct. 1953.
2 *Izvestia*, 15 Jan. 1954, carries an article entitled 'For the sake of normalization of international trade'. Its authors noted that the USSR signed, in 1953, a trade and payments agreement with France, Italy, India, Argentina, Finland, Denmark, Norway, Switzerland, Iceland, Greece, Iran, Afghanistan, and Egypt. The authors called for the ending of discrimination in international

trade and emphasized the economic benefit in economic co-operation between all states, irrespective of their social regime, which would lead to a relaxation of international tension.

3 *Kol Haam*, 6, 8 Dec. 1953.
4 MFA Arch. File 103.1 SSR.
5 *Divrei Haknesset*, Vol. 19, p. 893, 25 Jan. 1956. Minister of Police answering Maki's proposal to bring up the subject in the order of the day in the Knesset.
6 MFA Arch. File 103.1 SSR.
7 *Davar*, July 1956. In that interview Shepilov gave to foreign correspondents in Moscow, he also said that the USSR had no particular interest in Israel, except the interest of peacemaking in the Middle East.
8 MFA Arch. File 103.1 SSR.
9 *Kol Haam*, 8 Feb. 1957.
10 MFA Arch. File 103.1 SSR.
11 The Soviets insisted that for any dispute arising in trade relations between foreign and Soviet companies, arbitration between the parties would take place in Moscow through the 'Arbitration committee on foreign trade', which based its operation on Soviet law. This procedure was automatically included as a binding paragraph in the USSR's trade agreements with foreign states.
12 *Berlingske Tidende*, Copenhagen, June 1958, carried an article entitled 'The Soviet verdict is a warning on trade with the USSR'; *Manchester Guardian*, 27 June 1958, editorial 'Soviet Agreements'; *Financial Times*, 27 June 1958, 'Arbitration in Moscow'; *Economist*, London, 27 June 1958, 'Justice in Moscow'.
13 *Berlingske Tidende*, Copenhagen, 23 June 1958.
14 Spain is a good example. The USSR preferred to import citrus fruit from Franco's Spain rather than import it from Israel after the Sinai Campaign.
15 *Divrei Haknesset*, Vol. 26, p. 1949. The interpellation was submitted on 26 June 1958. The Foreign Minister's answer was given on 10 Feb. 1959.
16 B. Z. Razin's report to the Ministry of Foreign Affairs. MFA Arch. File 103.1 SSR.
17 MK Hacohen's report to the Ministry of Foreign Affairs. MFA Arch. File 103.1 SSR.
18 The USSR's Note to West Germany of 6 July 1957 stated *inter alia*: 'The Soviet government proceeds from the premise that the development of trade and economic ties is a basis for good relations between states and is of great importance for strengthening peace and co-operation among nations. The absence of a desire by state leaders to develop trade and economic relations with other states on the basis of reciprocity and objective favorable opportunities for this cannot be assessed otherwise than as an actual unwillingness to promote such relations between countries.' (Published in *Pravda*, 9 July 1957.)
19 MFA Arch. File 103.1 SSR.
20 Ibid.
21 Ibid.
22 Ibid. Also partial report in A. Dagan's *Moscow and Jerusalem*, p. 145.
23 Ibid.
24 MFA Arch. File 103.1 SSR.
25 Ibid.
26 Ibid.
27 *Reshumot, Kitvei Amana* (Hebrew) 593, Vol. 15.
28 MFA Arch. File 103.1 SSR.

6 · *Cultural and scientific relations*

THE DEVELOPMENT OF RELATIONS

CONTRARY TO the intensive development in Israeli–Soviet trade relations lasting from 1954 to 1956, cultural relations between both countries evolved slowly and gradually. They lasted almost through the whole period of diplomatic relations and were their most active domain. The volume of cultural exchanges in the 1950s was very limited but began to increase, in small steps, from the beginning of the 1960s. The most significant shift to their increase occurred in 1963, continuing until autumn 1966. These years were considered to have been the most fruitful period in the history of cultural relations between the two countries. Exactly as the development of Israeli–Soviet trade relations was a function of the domestic and foreign needs of the USSR – and reached its end because of political considerations – so did cultural and scientific relations between both countries develop within the framework of the general Soviet policy of extending cultural, scientific and technological ties with foreign countries, which included increasing Soviet activity in the hosting of international events, in some of which Israel participated. This tendency showed in liberal cultural activity more than it had done in the past, for instance in the inclination inside the USSR to give more objective description – in comparison with the past – of the cultural and scientific life of Israel in Soviet periodicals dealing with culture and science. These ties, as with the trade relations, came to an end because of political considerations – even before the USSR broke off its diplomatic relations with Israel in June 1967.

The cultural and scientific exchanges were expressed in the

growing number of performances by Soviet artists in Israel and by Israeli artists in the USSR; the translation of Hebrew works into Russian; and Israeli participation in international events held in the USSR such as festivals and exhibitions. The exchange balance-sheet was always in favor of the USSR. The traffic from the USSR to Israel was much heavier than in the opposite direction.[1] Nevertheless, the process was greeted in Israel and the USSR with much satisfaction.[2] Israel saw this as leading to a dual goal: providing actual content for the system of mutual relations and a national mission to Soviet Jewry. The USSR regarded this endeavor as a nuisance for itself, while considering the Soviet cultural presence in Israel as an important venue for spreading its cultural values there, helping, at the same time, the bearers of Soviet propaganda in Israel.

Israel's attempts to raise the cultural exchanges to the level of a formal cultural agreement – as usually done by both parties where other countries were concerned – met with a flat refusal by the Soviet authorities. The Soviet argument against such a proposal was that 'apart from exceptional cases stemming from specific considerations' – which were not defined – 'the USSR maintains cultural ties with foreign countries in two ways: the *first*, being exchanges with most of the developed countries, implemented via the relevant professional institutions such as "Goskonzert"; the *second*, general agreements with the underdeveloped countries, on a non-business basis'. Israel was included in the first category. The cultural traffic with Israel was from the very beginning conducted not at the state level, but through private organizations on Israel's side, and 'Goskonzert', or other Soviet institutions, were authorized by the Soviet organs to act in this domain.

To facilitate the cultural traffic in both directions, there was established on 30 March 1963, the Association for Israeli–Soviet Cultural Relations,[3] at the initiative of the Soviet Embassy in Israel. The majority of its founders were members of Maki and Mapam. This association received the blessing of the Presidency of the Union of Soviet Friendship Organizations with Foreign Countries.[4] Indeed, all the cultural activities which took place from then on, at the bilateral level, were executed by the members of the Association and known impresarios in Israel.

Proposals for cultural exchanges submitted by 'official' Israel, whether through Israel's Foreign Ministry in Jerusalem or through the Israeli Embassy in Moscow, did not receive any reply. We can learn from this procedure – imposed on Israel by the USSR – about the Soviet objectives in developing cultural relations with Israel, namely:

(a) by-passing the Israeli state institutions responsible for cultural exchanges with foreign countries, in such a way that the exchanges had an unofficial character;
(b) evading the principle of mutuality that obliges an equilibrium in the volume of cultural exchanges. Thus the USSR could send a large number of artists to Israel and receive from Israel a small number of artists;
(c) inspecting the ideological character of the Israeli exhibitions earmarked for the USSR, choosing the artists, literary works and the composition of delegations according to Soviet choice;
(d) strengthening the status of the Association founded by Maki, as part of the Israeli–Soviet Friendship Movement, by entrusting it with cultural exchanges and utilizing it for pro-Soviet propaganda purposes within Israel.

On the Israeli side, the state institutions in Israel were directly involved in organizing Israel's participation in international events that took place in the USSR. In this domain, Israel enjoyed a status equal to the other participating foreign states in those events (such as the International Film Festival, scientific conferences, agricultural and industrial exhibitions). Israeli organizers of the exhibitions and Israeli participants in the international events used to arrive in Moscow equipped with informative material, in the field of their profession and specialization, for distribution among the visitors and used to organize a Day of Israel within the framework of the National Day, the organization of whose events for the visitors was made possible by the hosts. For those Soviet Jews who came *en masse* to these events, Israel's presence was a source of excitement and national pride. During these events, not only was Israel able to demonstrate its capabilities and achievements in the domains of culture, science and technology, but it was also able to impart information about Israel to all those who were interested.

ISRAELI LITERARY WORKS PUBLISHED IN THE USSR

In January 1964 an anthology entitled *Poeti Israelia*, containing 100 works by 40 Israeli poets, was published in Moscow with a preface surveying 'Israeli contemporary poetry'.[5]

This was the first Israeli anthology to appear in the USSR in Russian and it included a comparatively broad spectrum of Israeli poets with various, and occasionally, opposing political views regarding Zionism and Communism. Although there undoubtedly was a certain trend in the choice of poems, this enterprise was received with great satisfaction because it was an innovation and because of the interest it aroused in both Jewish and non-Jewish circles in the USSR.

A year later a collection of poems by A. Penn, in Russian translation, was published in Moscow, entitled *Lev Baderekh* ('A Heart on the Way'). The collection included poems devoted to the Land of Israel and poems on the Holocaust.[6]

In the autumn of 1965 an anthology of Israeli authors was published in Russian translation in Moscow.[7] Here, a broad spectrum of writers was included. The anthology was prefaced by a broad review of Israeli literature and its resources, written by the editor of *Sovetish Heymland*, A. Vergelis. The review aimed at proving the existence of two literary streams in Israel: one, 'chauvinistic' (that is, nationalistic), the other, 'progressive' (that is, with pro-communist tendencies). Despite its inconsistencies and contradictions, it contained much information on the course of Hebrew literature from its beginnings 3,000 years ago to today. The reader could perceive the historic continuity in Hebrew literature, despite the dispersion of the Jewish people all over the world.

In autumn 1966 a third anthology appeared in Moscow. This one, devoted to Hebrew short stories, was called *The Pearl Diver*.[8] Many of the authors in this anthology had been featured in the anthology of Israeli stories published one year earlier. It was also prefaced by a review of 'contemporary Israeli literature'. The selective choosing of Hebrew stories describing the sadness of life in Israel was conspicuous. The stories by S. J. Agnon and M. Shamir, which use the symbolism of the 'Return to Zion', were the exception. This was the last anthology to appear in the USSR of Israeli literary works.

During the same period that these works appeared, considerable room was devoted to Hebrew literature in the *Short History Encyclopedia* published in Moscow between 1964 and 1966. The innovation here was the objective presentation of Jewish literature as the heritage of the Jewish people in Israel and in the Diaspora, thereby stressing the uniqueness and unity of the Jewish people.

Of particular importance was Israel's participation at an international festival of youth and students held in Moscow. Israel's representatives demonstrated their presence in songs, dances and talks which filled many Soviet Jews, especially the Jewish youth, with enthusiasm. For them these were their first encounters with Israeli youth, who were not only a source of encouragement but also an exposure to common Jewish roots and attachment to Israel as the historic homeland of the entire Jewish people.

Also of significant importance was the appearance of a Hebrew–Russian dictionary in Moscow in 1963, the first enterprise of its kind, initiated and edited in the USSR with the assistance of dictionaries of the Hebrew language published in Israel.

THE REDUCTION IN CULTURAL RELATIONS

Great expectations grew in anticipation of the proposed program of concerts by the Israeli Philharmonic Orchestra, due to perform in 15 cities throughout the USSR, whilst Moscow's State Philharmonic Orchestra was to perform in Israel. This program was first drawn up in Moscow by the Director of Israel's Philharmonic Orchestra and the cultural authorities in Moscow in February 1966. The date for the performance in Moscow was set for November 1966. This was the second time that a date had been fixed. The first date had been earlier and the presumption was that the Soviets postponed the concert owing to Prime Minister Kosygin's forthcoming trip to Egypt in July 1966 within the framework of intensified Soviet activities in Arab states with the aim of strengthening the new leftist regime in Damascus.

On 22 September 1966, it became clear that the postponement was actually a total cancellation of the program under the pretext of a reaction to the 'anti-Soviet campaign waged in Israel concerning the Jews of the USSR'.[9] Even though the arrangements for the program had been made by the Director of the Philharmonic Orchestra and the cultural authorities in Moscow, the announcement of the cancellation of the program was passed on at the official level.[10] Thus the cancellation of the program became an official act.

Undoubtedly, the Soviet fear that a new wave of Jewish national awakening would follow in the wake of the proposed concerts – in the same way that many Jews in the USSR had been stirred whenever they met with Israeli delegations and artists at international and national events in the USSR – deterred the 'competent authorities' from the planned tour of the Israeli Philharmonic Orchestra throughout the USSR. This fear also placed a question mark over the worthwhileness to the Soviets of the continuation of cultural relations with Israel on the bilateral level in face of the enthusiasm – at times unrestrained – that gripped the Jews in the USSR with every encounter with the real Israel. If the performances of the Israeli orchestra had taken place as planned, the 'competent authorities' would have had to confront unprecedented dimensions of Jewish national awakening and the demonstration of Jewish national solidarity. The cancellation of the tour spared them all that.[11]

The program of orchestral exchanges was worked out in a relatively calm period in the Middle East, when cultural relations between both countries were running smoothly. In contrast, the dates planned for the performances in the Middle East landed in a stormy period. The Soviet Union was at that time striving to strengthen its position in the Arab states, particularly by consolidating the new Ba'ath regime in Damascus. By that time the Soviet authorities had come to recognize an increasing Jewish national awakening which was being inspired to a degree by Israeli–Soviet cultural relations.

Since the Soviet authorities could not prevent Israel from participating at the international events hosted by the USSR, it was then decided to prevent Israel from being active in the domain of culture, on the bilateral level, and thus to diminish Israel's active presence in the USSR.

It should not therefore be surprising that with the cancellation of the orchestral exchange, the process of cultural relations between both countries came to an end. Its final halt attested to the dominant place of the Jewish factor along with the Middle East factor in shaping the system of Israeli–Soviet relations and as an integral function of it. Just as the beginning of the process symbolized a new state of *rapprochement* in mutual relations, so the end of the process symbolized a new phase in the deterioration in Israeli–Soviet relations.

If it had not been for the strong connection between Soviet hostility towards Israel because of its role in the intensification of

Jewish national awakening and increased Soviet activity of the Arab states – aimed at strengthening its footholds there – it is doubtful whether the process of cultural relations would have come to an end at that time, about half a year before the severance of diplomatic relations between both countries.

This period between 1964 and 1966 is justifiably considered as the golden age of fruitful cultural ties between Israel and the USSR and was unprecedented in the relations between the two countries.

NOTES

1 For further details see Y. Govrin, 'Israeli–Soviet Relations 1964–1966', pp. 64–73. Research paper 29, The Soviet and eastern European Research Center, The Hebrew University of Jerusalem, 1978.
2 Israel's Foreign Ministers, G. Meir and A. Eban, and Prime Minister L. Eshkol expressed their satisfaction concerning the cultural exchanges and hope for their expansion, from the Knesset podium and in interviews given to the Israeli press in the years 1964–1966.
3 *Kol Haam*, 31 March 1963.
4 *Kol Haam*, 12 June 1963.
5 Published by Inostranaya Literatura.
6 Published by Khudozhestvennaya Literatura, Moscow, 1965.
7 Published by Progress, Moscow, 1965.
8 Published by Nauka, in co-operation with the Institute for Asian Nations, Leningrad University, Moscow, 1966.
9 On 22 Sept. 1966 the Government Press Office in Jerusalem published the following announcement: 'The competent Soviet authorities have decided to withdraw from their previous consent concerning the visit of Moscow's State Philharmonic Orchestra in Israel, and to cancel the program for November 1966. The reason given for this act is the anti-Soviet campaign conducted in Israel and connected to the problem of the Jews in the USSR.'
10 The Chargé d'Affaires of the Soviet Embassy in Israel came to Jerusalem to hand over the announcement of the cancellation to the Director of the eastern European Division of the Ministry of Foreign Affairs. Following his announcement the Government Press Office published the statement in n. 9 above.
11 In June 1966 the 'Israeli Trio Geula Gil' appeared in the main cities of the USSR. The trio, especially the singer Geula Gil herself, gained notable success and stirred a wave of great excitement among Soviet Jews, and particularly among the Jewish young people. In some of the cities where the trio performed, many were detained because of the enthusiasm of the young Jewish people, which could not be controlled by the local security organs of the USSR. It could be assumed that this wave of excitement prompted the Soviets to reconsider their decision to enable the Israeli Philharmonic Orchestra to perform in the USSR, and as a result of that it was decided about the cancellation.

7 · Aliya, *emigration from the USSR and eastern Europe to Israel*

EMIGRATION ACCORDING TO THE SOVIET VIEW

*A*LIYA (emigration to Israel) as the central objective in Israel's policy was voiced to the Soviet Minister of Foreign Affairs and his high-ranking assistants as early as the first talks that Israel's envoy held with them in Moscow, shortly after diplomatic relations were established between the two countries. And although the subject was raised, in principle, it immediately became clear from the Soviet reaction that the USSR favored immigration of Jews to Israel from Western countries only. Immigration from the USSR was ruled out entirely. In the official Soviet view, Israel's task was to absorb the survivors of the Holocaust in Europe and those Jews in the 'capitalist states', who were living – from the Soviet point of view – under conditions of oppression and humiliation. Jews in those countries who would not be able, or would not want, to immigrate to Israel should take upon themselves the task, again according to the Soviet position, of struggling for the sake of democracy and for the establishment of a socialist regime in the countries where they dwelt.[1]

Ilya Ehrenburg's article of 21 September 1948 developed this conception by stressing the lack of motivation among the Jews in the USSR and the rest of the socialist states to immigrate to Israel, since they had integrated, he noted, as equals amongst equals in the socialist society where they were living.[2]

The theory happened to be in total contradiction with the

impressions of Israel's representatives in the USSR gathered from the talks and brief encounters they had with local Jews, who expressed their expectations of Israel – as the representative of the Jewish people – to act for their redemption. About two years passed from the time the matter was initially brought up at the diplomatic level until Israeli Prime Minister David Ben Gurion first issued a public appeal to the USSR to allow any Jew within its borders to immigrate to Israel and 'join those building the country'.[3] This demand was accompanied by Foreign Minister Sharett's appeal to his Soviet counterpart, A. Vyshinsky, in the autumn of 1950. Vishinsky rejected this demand under the pretext that emigration from the USSR contradicted the socialist system.[4]

In December 1951 the government of Israel made this appeal – for the first time in an official note – to the Soviet government (in reply to a Soviet note addressed to the Middle Eastern countries, including Israel, with a warning not to join the Middle East Command initiated by the Western powers) which, among other things, stated (translation from the Hebrew):

> As the government of the USSR is aware, the return of the Jews to their historical Homeland is the paramount mission of the State of Israel. The government of Israel knows that only by maintaining peace in the world and normal relations between nations, shall we be able to develop our country and to absorb all Jews who wish to return. It is in this respect that the government of Israel is appealing to the government of the USSR to enable the Jews in the USSR, who wish to do so, to immigrate to Israel. The government of Israel believes that this desire is in complete accord with the Soviet policy, which is based on national equality and the right to self-determination of every people.[5]

This demand rested on two fundamental principles:

first, the historical connection of the Jewish people to the Land of Israel (Palestine), which was recognized by Gromyko at the UN General Assembly on 14 May and 26 November 1947;[6] and
second, the right of the Jews to immigrate to Israel (which was established with the help of the Soviet Union and which received immediate and full recognition from it).

The first shift from airing the appeal for *aliya* on a bilateral level to sounding out for the international level was expressed pointedly for the first time in 1953 by Israel's leaders from the Knesset podium and in the UN, as already noted, following the anti-Semitic campaign in the Soviet Union and eastern Europe, during the Prague trials (November 1952) and especially with the disclosure of the 'Doctors' Plot' in Moscow (January 1953).[7]

From the renewal of Israeli–Soviet diplomatic relations in July 1953 and up to the beginning of 1960, Israel refrained from voicing the demand for *aliya* publicly, and even held back on raising the matter at the diplomatic level. However, from the mid-1950s onwards Israel was demanding, at first indirectly and then openly, that the Soviet authorities permit Jews in its sphere of influence to immigrate to Israel, and this was part of Israel's struggle, begun in the Western world, for the sake of the Jews in the USSR.

ALIYA IN ISRAEL-SOVIET TALKS

In his first talk with Foreign Minister Gromyko, shortly after he presented his credentials as Israel's new Extraordinary and Plenipotentiary Minister to the USSR, Minister S. Elyashiv raised Israel's request to permit Jews from the USSR to immigrate to Israel. Gromyko flatly rejected the idea.[8] His answer probably resounded for a long time in the realm of Israeli–Soviet relations and the subject was not raised at that level again. As from 1958 only Israel's Prime Ministers brought up the matter in their talks with Soviet Ambassadors, and so did Israel's representatives in Moscow, at the level of officials in the Soviet Ministry of Foreign Affairs.[9] Also, on the public level, it was noticed that the government of Israel refrained from carrying out open confrontation with the USSR on the subject of *aliya*.

Opposition members criticized the government's policy for silencing the struggle for *aliya* and that it did not condition the renewal of relations with the USSR upon permitting Jews from the USSR to immigrate to Israel.[10] Cabinet Ministers used to answer in a restrained manner. Foreign Minister Sharett stated on 15 November 1954 that 'the demand for *aliya* from the USSR and eastern European countries is always on our agenda' and that 'in the meanwhile we can note a slight relief in the present year, in the immigration of elderly parents of Israeli citizens from the USSR'.[11] In comparison to Sharett's moderate statement, MK M. Argov of the Mapai party and Chairman of the Foreign and Security Committee demanded that the USSR 'recognize the right to emigration of all Jews, not only of the elderly' stressing that the 'key to true friendship between the USSR and Israel, is in the hands of the USSR'. Argov summed up his demand with the appeal, 'Just as we fought against the closing gates for *aliya*, so will we call day by day and hour by hour against closed exit gates.'[12] The firm demand of Argov, compared to the moderate words of Sharett, members of the same party, reflected perhaps the desire at the Israeli government level to leave the public confrontation with the USSR at the party level, less compromising but enough to reflect the public mood in this matter. Minister of the Interior, I. Rokah, who declared in the Knesset on 27 June 1955 that 'the government of Israel will act in the future as in the past, to the best of its ability, to achieve the right to emigration of our brethren living in eastern Europe', explained that *aliya* was being carried out in the framework of 'unification of families' and that there was no reason to fear that this *aliya* would stop.[13] From the statistics he presented in the Knesset regarding the volume of immigration from the USSR and eastern European countries, a total of 597 persons in a period of one year (31 March 1954 – 1 April 1955), one could see:

(a) an important shift took place in the dimensions of *aliya* from those states, in comparison to previous years;
(b) the number of immigrants from each country was not in direct proportion to the total size of the Jewish population within their borders. Hence, the immigration quotas were fixed in each individual country according to the local authorities' consideration, and according their internal requirements.

These statistics tended to show that the restraint shown by the government of Israel towards the outside world did not reflect the quiet diplomatic activity that had resulted in the said shift.

At the opening meeting of the Zionist Executive Council, on 23 August 1955, Sharett used a restrained but also prophetic language when he stated: 'It is our heartfelt wish that with the opening of a new era in the relations between nations a new dawn will also break for the Jews of the USSR' and that as 'a result of the easing of international tensions and greater facility for mutual contact between the two blocs, the ties between that great Jewry which has suffered so sorely and the remainder of the Jewish people will be restored, and the right of every Jew to settle in this country will be afforded full recognition'.[14] Hence, Sharett believed in the prospect of immigration from the USSR with the relaxation of tension between both blocs and as a direct function of it.

The Executive Council itself used a similar language in its resolution on the matter of *aliya*, noting with satisfaction the improvement 'in recent months in issuing exit permits for emigrants from the USSR to Israel'.[15]

At the annual conference of MAGEN (an Israeli organization dealing with the immigration of Jews from the USSR to Israel) in 1955, an attempt was made to adopt a firm resolution against the USSR on account of the small volume of immigration to Israel; however the attempt was restrained because of 'an excessive harshness towards the Soviet Union – at a time when in all the Soviet bloc countries a thaw is being noted'.[16] Indeed, the declaration of MAGEN published on 16 March 1955 was much more restrained than had earlier been envisaged.[17] The reasons for restraint presumably were:

1. The fear of the Soviet Union accusing Israel of interfering in its internal affairs.[18]
2. The fear of halting *aliya* because of excessive firmness against the USSR.[19]
3. The absence of public and governmental consciousness concerning this matter in the Western world, particularly in the USA.[20]
4. Hesitation regarding the effectiveness of this action in face of a stubborn Soviet position[21] and in view of the belief that *aliya* will be possible in conditions of relaxed tension between the two blocs.

The period of indirect activity

The need to change the tactics of the policy regarding the struggle for the immigration started to arise among *aliya* activists in Israel, already in August 1955, but Ben Gurion did not agree with their view.[22]

A real turning point in Israeli tactics began when the murder of Jewish writers in the last year of Stalin's life became widely known after Krushchev revealed Stalin's crimes in his speech at the 20th Congress of the CPSU in February 1956. The first event revealed the magnitude of physical terror that Soviet Jews had faced in the last days of Stalin and increased the need to save them, in case the terror returned. The second event evoked the hope, in view of the openness that became visible in Krushchev's policy towards the West, that vigorous action for the sake of Soviet Jewry would bear fruit.

From this period onwards, the subject of *aliya* was raised with the Soviet leaders, at Israel's initiative, by Western personalities who made official visits to the Soviet Union, or by Western journalists who posed questions to the Soviet leaders during their official visits in the West. For the first time in the history of the USSR, Soviet leaders found themselves in a defensive position in the face of Western personalities who pressed them continually by asking for their explanations as to why it was forbidden for Soviet Jews to immigrate to Israel.[23] Although some of their answers repeated the argument that Soviet Jewry was not interested in immigrating to Israel, in substance, however, the answers showed greater commitment in comparison to Gromyko's reply given to Israel's Minister in Moscow in August 1953. These were the main answers:

The Soviet Union does not encourage the *aliya* to Israel because Israel is 'an anti-Soviet center', but would not prevent the immigration of those who wish to immigrate.[24]

The day will come when all the Jews who wish to immigrate to Israel, will be permitted to do so. The American security services use the Soviet Jews who reach Israel for their own needs. When Israeli–Soviet relations improve temporarily, difficulties will be removed.[25]

The Soviet Union does not permit every one of its citizens to leave the country. The Soviet Union, however, did enable a considerable number of Jews to leave for Poland, being aware of the fact that many of them would proceed to Israel.[26]

The time is not appropriate for permitting Jews or other citizens of the USSR to emigrate, but the day will come when the ban will be removed.[27]

These answers perhaps bear witness to Soviet preparedness to recognize the existence of the problem and the need to find a solution for it (though at that time no decision was taken as to how and when the problem would be solved). Hence the importance of Western personalities' involvement in this matter, which was initiated by Israel. From the Soviet answers to the Western questions it could be clearly seen that the Soviet argument that the Jews in the USSR didn't wish to immigrate to Israel contradicted the Soviet's own promise that a day would come when the immigration of Soviet Jews to Israel would be permitted. The ultimate meaning, of course, was the recognition of the fact that such a demand did exist.

The Soviet claim that the improvement of Israeli–Soviet relations would advance the settlement of the *aliya* problem is connected to another Soviet argument, namely, that Israel was hindering the advancement of *aliya*, by being an 'anti-Soviet center'. At that time this conception would not have included the struggle for the sake of Soviet Jews, since it had not yet been made public. Alternatively, perhaps what the Soviets had in mind was Israel's co-operation with Britain and France in the Sinai Campaign, and publications critical of the USSR and its foreign policy.

If this argumentation faithfully reflected the Soviet considerations regarding *aliya*, then it might have been assumed that Israel's efforts to improve its relations with the USSR would have assisted the advancement of *aliya*.

There is some proof of this considering the USSR's help with Jewish immigration from eastern Europe on the eve of Israel's independence and immediately afterwards. Yet, there is no proof with regard to subsequent periods; when relations between the two countries were broken off, and just then, there was an increase in the stream of immigration from the USSR to Israel. With this in mind, it may be that the Soviet argumentation was just a pretext to rebuff Western pressure. In any case, the Soviet claims only contributed to the continuous pressure on the USSR to change its policy in this matter.

The period of direct action

A major turning point in Israeli tactics came about in the early 1960s, when the demand for free emigration – as well as the demand for equal rights for Soviet Jews – intensified. It could be seen primarily:

1. in the frequent talks conducted by Israeli representatives with the senior echelons of the Soviet Foreign Ministry and with Soviet envoys throughout the world;
2. in statements by Israel's leaders from the Knesset podium or in public appearances, including interviews with Israeli and foreign media;
3. in statements by Israeli representatives at UN conferences on human rights;
4. in statements at world Jewish forums and at an international conference, the first of its kind, convened for this purpose in Paris in 1960;
5. in direct written appeals to Soviet leaders.[28]

This activity attested to an absence of any intention by the Israeli government to abandon the demand that Soviet Jews be allowed to emigrate to Israel, and it met with understanding and support from Western governments, including that of the United States, and from leftist circles around the world. Prime Minister Levi Eshkol no doubt took this fact into account in his forceful public appearances on behalf of *aliya* from the USSR and, on the other side of the divide, Soviet Prime Minister Kosygin took it into account when he told journalists in Paris on 3 December 1966: 'Regarding family reunification, if families wish to leave the Soviet Union or meet their families abroad, the Soviet Union will do everything in its power to open the gates for them. No question of principle is or will be involved.'[29]

The Soviet press published Kosygin's statement on 5 December 1966, with the omission of the statement that 'the government of the Soviet Union will do everything in its power to open the gates for them'.

Kosygin's statement took on historic meaning as it aroused new hopes among Soviet Jews that they would be able to emigrate to Israel. Israel's Foreign Minister Abba Eban welcomed it saying that it contained a 'definition of humanitarian policy that should be welcomed, and because of certain historic circumstances this declaration has a special significance for the citizens of Israel and Jews in the Diaspora'.[30]

The declaration did not lead to a swift change in the number of emigrants that year (although until the Six Day War, the number of exit permits issued by the Soviet authorities to Jews who wished to move to Israel was higher than in previous years). The statement, however, in a sense attested to a new trend of thought in Soviet policy-making on this issue, one that would subsequently leave its imprint.

What were the factors that guided Soviet policy-makers concerning the opening and closing of its gates in connection with *aliya* to Israel?

It may be that it played a certain role in the Middle East power confrontation, at a certain time.

A glimpse at past events shows us that during Israel's first year of independence the Soviet Union assisted in strengthening Israel's power, partly by letting Jews stream from the eastern bloc to Israel, aiming to diminish support for British influence in the Middle East. Afterwards their stance on *aliya* was used by the Soviet Union in its penetration of Arab states. In times of crisis in its relations with them it was careful not to let out Jews to Israel. When its relations with the Arab states were normal it did allow Jews to go to Israel.[31] The same went for its relations with the USA and the search for broader co-operation in the fields of economics, science, and technology. It also tended to take into consideration the sensitivity of American public opinion in the matter of *aliya*. Perhaps *aliya* played a certain role in the system of Soviet–American and Soviet–Western relations.

But in addition to the place of *aliya* in the considerations of Soviet policy towards the Middle East and the USA, we may find an explanation for the permitting of Jews to immigrate by surveying additional factors:

1. *Soviet sensitivity to its favorable image in Western public opinion.* In the view of many intellectual circles in the West, the Soviet response to the demand that Jews be allowed to leave for Israel was a litmus test of Soviet consideration for human rights.
2. *Soviet sensitivity to its status among Communist parties in Europe*, which considered the demand for *aliya* to be justified and intervened on more than one occasion with the Soviet authorities to enable *aliya*. The USSR undoubtedly needed their support and sympathy in its

confrontations with China. The Soviet response to their involvement was an indication of the extent of its willingness to take them into account.

3. *More Soviet openness towards Western Europe.* Beginning in the mid-1950s, the Soviet Union increased its involvement in politics, economics, and technology in Western Europe. Soviet leaders visited Western capitals, and Western figures visited the Soviet Union fairly often. In most of the encounters, the Western leaders raised the issue of Soviet Jewish *aliya*. The fact that Soviet Premier Kosygin made his statement concerning permission to leave the USSR while on a visit to Paris hints at consideration of Western European public opinion.

4. *Display of a more liberal attitude* by the Soviet authorities towards minorities, among them the Jews, in the USSR. It was this relative liberalization that made possible the Jewish national awakening and, in its wake, pressure from Soviet Jews wishing to emigrate to Israel, at the same time as external pressure was applied on the Soviet Union to the same end.

It is unimaginable that these sensitivities and developments could have existed in Stalin's time. The most important turning point in the post-Stalinist era was in the very willingness to take account of the existence of the *aliya* issue, and the need to resolve it in response to internal and external pressure. It was this watershed that brought about change in the Soviet attitude towards the emigration of Soviet Jews to Israel. The importance of the increase in the number of exit permits was that it proved that the struggle for *aliya* had been worthwhile and that the Soviets were willing to pay heed to it.

Table 7.1, showing immigration to Israel from eastern European countries between 1953 and 1967 shows:

Parallel to the low rate of immigration from the USSR, the immigration from eastern European countries flowed in a normal manner, and in some cases even in a broad stream.

The largest number of immigrants from Poland included Jewish repatriates from the Soviet Union who moved on to Israel, either immediately after arriving in Poland or later.

The relatively high numbers of immigrants from Romania during

1961–65 run parallel to the weakening of Soviet–Romanian relations.

The relatively high number of immigrants from Hungary occurred shortly after the Hungarian revolt.

Table 7.1 *aliya* from the USSR and Eastern Europe, 1953–67[32]

Year	USSR	Romania	Poland	Czecho-slovakia	Hungary	Bulgaria
1953	18*	61	225	16	224	359
1954	53	53	112	–	54	201
1955	105	235	206	40	274	192
1956	753	753	3,635	81	999	117
1957	149	595	31,854	16	7,408	116
1958	12	8,778	3,889	11	69	76
1959	7	9,672	3,889	19	133	51
1960	102	9,247	5,357	60	226	111
1961	128	20,778	901	21	82	71
1962	182	9,135	731	60	226	83
1963	338	11,461	374	75	160	81
1964	539	24,332	723	577	195	114
1965	1,444	9,905	863	409	163	88
1966	1,892	3,647	576	116	113	69
1967	1,162**	730	325	75	70	25

* Total number 1948–53.
** January–July 1967. With the outbreak of the Six Day War immigration from the USSR ceased. It was renewed in 1968.

Poland and Romania were the most distinct countries in permitting Jewish immigration from their territories to Israel in the second half of the 1950s, after a long interval. Our study will focus on the reasons for the change and its interrelationship with the USSR.

ALIYA FROM ROMANIA

The largest reservoir of *aliya* in eastern Europe (excluding the USSR) after World War II was in Romania. A considerable number of its Jewish population had not been uprooted from their places of residence during the Holocaust and thus escaped annihilation.[33]

By the end of World War II the Jewish population in Romania numbered 428,312[34] and in 1945–46 several thousand Jewish repatriates from the USSR arrived in Romania (within the framework of the Soviet–Romanian repatriation agreement) in the hope of moving on to Israel (then Palestine) or to Western countries.

After the collapse of the fascist regime in Romania on 23 August 1944, Zionist activities were openly renewed in the direction of emigration to Israel, preparing pioneer settlements in Israel and teaching national educational values. The Zionist activity stopped when the Communist regime came to power at the end of 1947. Immigration to Israel, however, continued to flow, initially in large numbers until it was considerably reduced, under Soviet influence, in the second half of 1952. From 15 May 1948 (the day Israel proclaimed its independence) until the end of 1949, 31,274 Jews emigrated to Israel; in 1950 – 47,000 persons; in 1951 – 40,625; and in 1952 – 3,712.[35]

Many of them were sent on ideological courses before their departure, with the aim of preparing them for communist activity in Israel.[36] Romania during this period was completely dominated by Soviet rule; in Prague, trials were held against the leadership of the Czechoslovak Communist Party, accused, among other things, of maintaining contacts with the World Zionist Movement; the eastern and western blocs were absorbed in a bitter confrontation. From 1953 until mid-1958, only a few hundred Jews were given permission to emigrate each year to Israel, whereas the pressure from Romanian Jews to emigrate was increasing at the same time as Israel's government was applying pressure at the diplomatic level, demanding that Jews be let out of Romania to Israel.[37]

The salient turning point in Romania's policy regarding *aliya* to Israel, during the period under review, occurred in August–September 1958. The Romanian authorities announced their readiness to accept applications for exit permits to Israel. Registration was opened and within a short time tens of thousands of Jews registered to leave. A mass exodus began and it seemed that the Romanian authorities had taken a decision to solve, in this way, their country's Jewish problem.

In his attempt to explain the essence of the turning point, Israel's Minister in Bucharest[38] asserted in his report to the Foreign Ministry in Jerusalem, on 10 September 1958, that the main reason for the change was a desire to crystallize the regime in Romania around loyal forces and to get rid of those elements considered to be alien and desirous of leaving the country. The Minister's impression was that the Soviets and the Chinese not only did not object to this course in the Romanian government's policy, but supported it. This fact had certainly made it easier for the Romanian authorities to decide to allow their Jewish citizens to emigrate to Israel.[39] A short time afterwards, the Minister confirmed his claim and added, 'As long as there is no serious opposition on the part of the Soviets and the Arabs, the Romanians will continue with this policy.'[40]

An internal report by the Jewish Agency, dated 16 November 1958, expressed the opinion that the volume of emigration and its components might show that it was not a matter of the Romanian government pursuing a humanitarian policy within the frame of 'family unification', but of a changing attitude towards the Jews by the Romanian government and that the reasons prompting this change were the following.

The (Communist Party) and the government of Romania had decided to remove from its files the Jews, who were considered to be 'alien ethnic factors'.

From the military-security point of view, it was desirable to remove Jews from key positions in the local society and economy.

New economic planning for the strengthening of Romanian heavy industry on the account of consumer goods had resulted in large numbers of dismissals of unneeded laborers and office workers, including Jews. An estimate put the number of unemployed at over 200,000.

The report based itself, in part, on information that had reached its authors, according to which the Senate of Bucharest University had held a meeting on 18 August 1958, in which university professors, students' representatives, and members of the central committee of the Romanian Communist Party had participated, to discuss new instructions 'to cleanse Romania from undermining elements'. At the meeting four categories of people who would be expelled from the party were defined:

1. Persons who held political and administrative functions during the regime of the monarchy, or who belonged to former bourgeois parties, as well as their relatives up to the fifth degree.
2. Members of and activists in former fascist organizations – Hitleristic and Zionist.
3. Persons who maintained contacts with foreign factors or expressed their willingness to leave Romania.
4. Persons who were sentenced or investigated for political offenses.

Another piece of information that the authors had obtained and now passed on was that, at the beginning of October 1958, the Federation of Jewish Communities in Romania had been urgently convened to a meeting with representatives of the Central Committee of the Romanian Communist Party to discuss 'negative manifestations among the Jews of Romania'. The spokesman of the Central Committee at this meeting denounced the Jewish committee leaders 'who are not vigilant enough in face of the undermining Zionist elements from within and without'. The spokesman said that Romania should rid itself of these Jews either by emigration 'or by other means'. To the remark of the President of the Federation of Jewish Communities that accused Jews could be brought to court, the spokesman replied, 'Romania ought to get rid of its Jews, and only those who would not wish to leave would be punished by other means.' In answer to a question on how many Jews the Romanian authorities were prepared to let live in Romania, the reply was that Romania was prepared to keep about 20 per cent of the (then) Jewish population 'who are working Jews making an honest living out of their labor'. The spokesman also added 'maybe it is an expulsion, but it is an expulsion with a happy end'.[41]

Additional information received by the Israeli Legation in Bucharest[42] from a reliable source held that at the meeting of the Central Committee of the Romanian Communist Party held on 26–28 November 1958, Romania's Prime Minister was asked about the government's policy regarding Jewish emigration to Israel, whereupon he summed it up, saying:

> When the popular democratic regime was established, the Romanian Jews were helpful in extending important support to the establishment of commercial entities in organizing the national economy, trade and industry. In that period we could not renounce their services in those domains. Today the situation is completely different. We have at our disposal (new) cadres who can assure continuation without disruption and without Jews. The Jews want to leave, so let them all leave, even those who do not want to.

From the evidence cited we can conclude that the anti-Semitic factor against the background of internal Romanian needs (the concentration of loyal cadres in the regime, party, economy, etc.)

was the decisive one in determining the Romanian policy of enabling the exodus of Jews from its territory after having received the USSR's acceptance. (There was always a rooted anti-Semitism in Romania, and the compulsion of the Jews to leave the country was always large.) In those days Romanian-Soviet relations were closely bonded.

It is certainly possible to argue that the anti-Semitic factor could have played a similar role in the Soviet Union, which was equally contaminated with anti-Semitism, and yet there was no mass emigration of Jews from the USSR. It seems a fundamental difference distinguishes between the two cases: Romania in the 1950s was still engaged in stabilizing its (Communist) regime and could afford to rid itself of 'alien elements' – primarily Jews, under the guise of 'family reunification' for those separated (as indeed they were, before, during and after the war), whereas the Soviet Union regime was already at a stage well beyond its consolidation. True, the Soviet Union also had to clear functions and posts for new national cadres, but it found its own way, in its vast territorial space, disposing of elements suspected of non-loyalty to the regime.

The Soviet Union had, no doubt, great interest in the stabilization of the Communist regime in Romania, particularly after the Hungarian revolt, and therefore it may be assumed that the Soviet Union took this into consideration in giving its acceptance to permit Jews to leave Romania (in addition to citizens of foreign nationalities) for Israel and the West. And, just as the Soviet Union influenced Romania to halt Jewish emigration to Israel, so it did not interfere in Romania's internal considerations to renew emigration in 1958. Both in 1952 and 1958 Romania was closely connected with the policy of the Soviet Union, and it would, therefore, be unthinkable that the emigration policy of Romania had not been coordinated in advance with the Soviet policy. Romania's dependence upon the USSR in this matter was also quite visible at the start of 1959 when Romania surrendered to Soviet pressure following Arab insistence on the temporary cessation of the mass emigration from Romania to Israel. It was, however, a tactical stoppage – and not one stemming from a basic Romanian policy change regarding the Jewish question, which would not have been pursued, at that time, without Soviet acceptance.

Arab pressure to stop emigration from Romania: its causes, results, and implications

The sudden spurt in emigration from Romania to Israel served as a subject of public statements by official Israeli personalities, expressing satisfaction and issuing calls to the Jewish population of Israel and the Diaspora Jews to make an effort in absorbing hundreds of thousands of immigrants, socially and economically. The statements created the impression that thousands of Jews are expected shortly to come to Israel from eastern European countries. They did not take into account the damage that would be caused to the *aliya* process by their declarations. By way of illustration, here are a few citations from them:

> *Aliya* is improving the security situation in Israel, is helping deter the Arab states from aggression, and is helping turn Israel into an active political factor capable of self-creativity … If Israel were to attain 3–4 million citizens and could mobilize a big army, no Arab state would dare to attack Israel. (Sh. Peres, then the Director General of the Defense Ministry, end of January 1959)[43]

> There is no basis to the rumors published in the Romanian press that the *aliya* from Romania has stopped. There are no signs to prove that this is true. Emigration will continue to grow and reach the number 100,000 this year. (Sh. Shragai, Director of the Immigration Department of the Jewish Agency, end January 1959)[44]

> The most important event that has occurred in the last two years (1957–58) has been the growth of *aliya* from eastern Europe, in 1957 from one country [Poland] and in 1958 from another country [Romania]. *Aliya* from that other country is growing larger and larger and it is to be hoped, to the best of our knowledge, not in thousands but in tens of thousands, and may reach even larger numbers. And although in these countries there is equality of rights, the Jews, however, like Jews in all these countries, are destined for destruction and their sole hope is to immigrate to Israel. It is not the hope of a few, or of tens of thousands, but the hope of hundreds of

thousands, and perhaps one could say without exaggeration, the hope of millions. (D. Ben Gurion, Prime Minister, February 1959)[45]

American reaction

The main American papers quoted American experts concerning this *aliya*. One of them said, 'There is no reason to believe that within a short period of time Jews will be permitted to immigrate to Israel. If, however, permission is given, it will not just solve an internal problem, but it will also be part and parcel of a Soviet movement to arouse disquiet in the Middle East and strengthen Arab apprehension about Israeli expansion.'[46]

Arab reaction

The Arab reaction was not slow in coming. *Davar*, 13 February 1959, was referring to London's JTA (Jewish Telegraphic Agency) report according to which Nasser, Egypt's President, and the Arab League were to file protests against the Soviet Union for permitting Jewish emigration from eastern Europe to Israel. *Davar* also reported that Egyptian politicians had told the correspondent of the *News Chronicle* in Cairo that 'the new wave of immigrants to Israel constitutes the greatest threat to peace since the days of 1948'. The correspondent added that Egypt and the Arab League would ask if and why the USSR was encouraging this immigration.

Similar questions were also to be addressed, according to sources of this British paper, to Romania, 'which is the main source of immigration' in those days. The British correspondent summed up, quoting Western diplomatic sources in Cairo: 'The Kremlin activated the immigration as a whip and bridle for Nasser' because of his persecution of the communists in Egypt.

A similar view was quoted in the name of the Arab League secretary Abdul Halek Hassuna,[47] who added that the Soviet Union had promised the League that it would not permit the immigration of Jews to Israel 'and that the emigration from Romania was limited only to humanitarian cases'.

There should be no doubt about Hassuna's evidence about the Soviet promise, which meant to say that the USSR did not permit

Jewish emigration from its territory to Israel, at that time, and that the USSR was acting as Romania's spokesman.

We do not possess Soviet evidence to confirm the assertions of the 'Western diplomats in Cairo' and Hassuna, according to which the Soviet Union permitted emigration from Romania in retaliation against Nasser for persecuting communists in Egypt.[48] The basis of this assertion is a Western one and it fits in, as we have seen, with the American tendency to incite the Arab states on the matter of *aliya* against the Soviet Union to widen the rift between them. However, the Soviet and Romanian reaction – following the Israeli declarations on the one hand and the Arab protests on the other – that led to the suspension of mass *aliya* for several months may attest to Soviet sensitivity towards the Arab states and to Soviet readiness to give in to Arab pressure, despite the persecution of communists in Egypt. If the Soviets' acceptance of *aliya* had been a 'retaliatory act' against the Arabs, the Soviet Union would not have been in haste to give in to Arab pressure.

The Soviet reaction

Izvestiya, on 21 February 1959, in an article entitled 'Provocative friction in America's propaganda' vented its anger about American policy, pursuing propaganda about 'Jewish mass emigration from the USSR to Israel', and about pro-American newspapers in Lebanon ascribing to the Soviet Union intentions of strengthening the military and economic potential of Israel against the Arabs. The newspaper regretted the fact that the editors of the Egyptian press fell victim to this plot, and noted the following:

> These fictitious lies are, presumably, intended for people of little faith, since it is well known that there is not and there has not been any emigration from the USSR to Israel. And as to the forthcoming Zionist Congress, it is also known that since 1917 the USSR's Jews have not participated in such congresses. They regard Zionism as a reactionary movement. They have never considered a change in their relationship towards Zionism, and there could be no such change ... Facts demonstrate that friendship between the USSR and Arab nations, including the UAR of Egypt, remain unchanged and will remain so in the future.

Though *Izvestia* did not promise that Jewish emigration from the Soviet Union to Israel would not take place in the future, it tended to pacify the Arabs and to accuse the USA of trying to push a wedge between the USSR and the Arabs by using the *aliya* from Romania to Israel.

The Romanian reaction

Agerpress – the Romanian official news agency – published a declaration on 25 February 1959 as a press release, headed as follows:

> In connection with the diversionist and provocative campaign unleashed by the Israeli press and Israeli official personages and by a number of Western reactionary papers regarding the so-called mass emigration of Jews from the Romanian People's Republic, a campaign which aims at slandering the Romanian People's Republic and its policy, at creating suspicion and sowing distrust between the Arab countries and the Romanian People's Republic and at disturbing the relations of friendship between these countries and Romania.

The main points of the declaration are listed below

The warm sympathy of Romania for the Arab countries fighting against colonialism and imperialism is well known. This sympathy was expressed by the firm position towards the Anglo-French-Israeli aggression against Egypt and towards Israel's 'aggressive acts aimed at maintaining a hotbed of unrest in the Middle East'.
The imperialist circles in the West are making strenuous efforts to isolate Romania from the Arab countries and to succeed in their goal 'they have resorted to old and faithful lackeys' – the ruling circles in Israel – and the leading circles of world Zionism, in initiating a provocative campaign of incitement concerning 'the departure to Israel of those Romanian citizens of Jewish origin who asked to be re-united with their families'.
The official circles in Israel 'are spreading worldwide the allegation that a real mass exodus of the Jewish population has started from the eastern European countries. In this connection they are quoting imaginary figures of hundreds of thousands and even millions of

persons.' They are asserting that 300,000 Jews are leaving Romania whereas the total number of Jews in Romania is 146,264 (according to the census carried out in 1956).

It is known that during and as a result of World War II, 'many Jewish families in Romania as well as in other countries, were scattered'. On the basis of humanitarian consideration the Romanian authorities permitted the departure of those citizens who have relatives in Israel or in other countries and who have insistently expressed their wish to be re-united with their families. Israeli and Western propaganda have blown up and distorted these facts, when speaking about the alleged departure of hundreds of thousands of Jewish immigrants from Romania to Israel.

The USA is behind this propaganda campaign, striving to undermine the friendship of the eastern European countries with Arab states. Moreover, its official circles are hinting at the intention of the eastern bloc 'to strengthen the military and economic potential of Israel', despite the fact that the whole world knows of 'the determined struggle of those countries against the aggressive and provocative policy of Israel' used by US imperialism 'as an instrument of its stance on a policy of strength aimed at undermining peace, at aggression and at subjugating the free peoples'.

There was no understanding between Romania and Israel regarding immigration. Israel's attempts in this direction were totally rejected. 'It is known that Romania's government firmly rejects any attempt, from wherever it may come, at interfering in its internal affairs'.

Zionist propaganda is using 'filthy and dishonest' means, as demonstrated in a recent statement made by Israel's Prime Minister D. Ben Gurion, 'who asserted provocatively that our state is aiming at getting rid of Jews, and even that the Jews of eastern Europe are threatened with destruction. A greater slander than this there cannot be.'

Romania has no reason to encourage emigration, since it is in need of manpower to develop itself. 'On the contrary, those who asked to leave were advised not to leave. Those persons who proved impervious to the explanations given and persevered in their wish to go to Israel in order to be re-united with their families were allowed to do so.'

Much regret has been caused to Romania by official personages of the United Arab Republic 'who let themselves be influenced by this malicious campaign'. Romania feels friendship and sympathy for the Arab countries and is convinced that 'this campaign can backfire on those who have inspired it'.

'Imperialist and Zionist circles must not and will not undermine the relations of friendship between Romania and Arab countries.'

This long declaration attempted to reconcile the Arabs, not only by using anti-Israeli terms accepted in the political lexicon of those times, but also by using terms of condemnation – towards Israel's leaders – which were not so common in the official eastern European announcements. Along with the effort at sealing the rift with the Arab states, the assertion that the allowing of Jewish migration was a 'humanitarian act' of 'family re-unification' was significantly notable in the sense that its cessation was not promised to the Arabs, and that this was a Romanian internal matter, namely, rejecting Arab pressure concerning future emigration. The declaration, however, did hint that Israeli statements would be detrimental to Israel, and it could be clearly understood that the Romanian intention was to stop emigration. The allusion that 'the campaign will backfire against its initiators' was widely quoted by the Soviet press whilst summarizing the Romanian declaration of 25 February 1959. Hence, it sounded as if the Soviets were in accord with putting a stop to emigration.

The emigration from Romania halted temporarily, to the deep sorrow of the Jews who had registered to emigrate, and to Israel's disappointment. Emigration was renewed, a year later (1961) to a similar extent (more than 20,000 persons) and in 1964 over 24,000 persons emigrated. At that time a turning point in Romania's foreign policy was noted towards being less dependent upon the USSR and more open toward the West, including Israel. Emigration did continue but at a gradually diminishing rate. Israel, on its part, had learned its lesson; its leaders and official representatives held back, for a long period, from expressing themselves publicly on matters of Jewish emigration from Romania. The Romanian government, for its part, knew how to turn a profit from its policy of permitting Jewish emigration to Israel, for both its internal and foreign affairs (for at the same time, Romania granted exit visas to the German minority to emigrate to West Germany). The continuous Jewish exodus from Romania to Israel – at a slow but set rate –

showed that this was an independent policy pursued with long-range goals for (a) the convenient solution of the Jewish problem in Romania; and (b) the stabilization of the communist regime in Romania with the participation of Romanian ethnic elements.

ALIYA FROM POLAND

Jewish existence in Poland after the Holocaust was constituted in part by those who had survived the Nazi annihilation campaign in Poland itself, and mainly by those Jews who had fled to the USSR during the Nazi invasion of Poland and had returned from the USSR after the war within the framework of the repatriation agreement signed between the two countries.[49]

And thus – more than any other eastern European State – Poland served, simultaneously, as a place of renewed Jewish concentration and also as a transit station, mainly to Israel, partly to the USA and other Western countries. This two-stranded process of concentration and dispersion would not have come into being if the USSR had not enabled Jews with Polish citizenship who had fled to the Soviet Union and stayed there during the war to return to their country of origin – even if it was aware of the fact that the Jews being repatriated were continuing on their way from Poland to Israel.[50] Also, their emigration to Israel would not have been possible had not the Polish (Communist) authorities permitted the Jews, at that time, to leave Poland, for Israel and the West.

The repatriation of 1945–46 differed from that of 1957–58 in the political circumstances in which it was conducted. It took place during Israel's struggle for political independence whereas at that stage the Polish regime had only begun to organize and consolidate itself. The later repatriation took place shortly after the Sinai Campaign, when Israeli–Soviet relations deteriorated, and Poland itself began to weaken its connections with the USSR.

The essence of the Repatriation Agreement of 1957

This agreement applied to Jews as well as to Poles who were Polish citizens prior to 1 September 1939 (the date of the outbreak of World War II). It did not apply to Ukrainians and Belorussians, even if they were at that time Polish citizens. The agreement also applied to the children of those who had the right to be repatriated, and who were born after 1 September 1939, or to children who had no relatives in the USSR but in Poland or whose relatives in the USSR were included in the category of eligible repatriates.

A person eligible for repatriation but who was serving at that time in the Soviet Army was to be released from his army service and returned to Poland. The same applied to a person under arrest or under an order of deportation, so they could leave Poland before the penalty term expired.

Women, children, and parents could join the repatriates, even if they were not Polish citizens and were not of Polish nationality.

Those who wished to return to Poland had to appeal to the local militia offices and present their documents confirming their Polish citizenship. Should any applicants not have been in a position to present the appropriate documents, their cases were to be brought before a joint committee of representatives of the Soviet Ministry of the Interior and the Polish Embassy in Moscow.

The applicants for repatriation to Poland would cease to be Soviet citizens upon leaving the Soviet Union and would be granted Polish citizenship after having reached Poland. Members of families who were not former citizens of Poland could choose before their departure either to remain Soviet citizens, or to renounce that status, and receive Polish citizenship, upon reaching Poland.

The acceptance of applications for repatriation was to continue until October 1958 and repatriation was to continue until 31 December 1958.

We do not yet know the details of the negotiations for the renewal of repatriation from the USSR to Poland. Still, we can examine some aspects of them as reflected in the paragraphs of the agreement.

The Jewish aspect

The importance of this agreement lies in the inclusion of a separate paragraph (14) asserting explicitly that persons of Jewish nationality should receive the same consideration as those of Polish nationality. Although a precedent for this is already found in the first repatriation agreement of 1945–46, the repetition of the precedent, in a different political situation, was very significant.

Moreover, the liberal phrasing defined those eligible for repatriation and enabled Polish citizens to be joined by Soviet Jews (assuming they could prove being related) who were given a free hand to choose their nationality – either Soviet or Polish.

The Polish aspect

Polish relations, since the Soviet authorities had decided to halt it in 1947, prior to the expiration date agreed upon. No doubt this angered the Poles, but as they were totally dependent upon the USSR (until autumn 1956), they did not dare raise their voices on this matter. The events in Poland in 1956 and Gomulka's rise to power, against the popular demand for a larger degree of independence, considerably changed the essence of the relationship between the two countries. It was this change that enabled the Poles to raise again the demand for the renewal of repatriation. The positive Soviet response to this demand tended to enhance the prestige of the new Polish leadership in the eyes of the Polish people by assisting it to stabilize its power.

It could be assumed that the Polish authorities insisted that the Jews be included in the general category of former Polish citizens eligible for repatriation, except for the Ukrainians and Belorussians, whose republics were incorporated within the USSR. Poland, rich in the experience of problems of national minorities during the inter-war period, was not quite happy to absorb within its borders, minorities whose territories were included in the USSR. As for the Jews, Poland knew that their numbers were limited to tens of thousands, and it could also assume, on the basis of the experience gained in 1946 and beyond, that the Jews repatriated to Poland from the USSR would continue on their way to Israel and the West.

The Soviet aspect

The assumption is that the USSR was aware of the former Polish citizens' drive to return to their country and of the Polish people's sensitivity to absorbing them there. After the Hungarian revolt in 1956 and the October events of 1958, the Soviet Union must have been interested in the consolidation of the Polish leadership and probably took into consideration that the renewal of repatriation would be one of the means to achieve it. Therefore, the USSR did not object to the Polish demand to include the Jews amongst those eligible for repatriation, as in the first agreement. To have them excluded in the second agreement would probably have aroused world public opinion against the discrimination pursued by the USSR in respect of the Jews – an accusation already voiced against the USSR in the not too distant past.

The USSR's agreement to include the Jews in the second repatriation agreement did not prevent the Soviet authorities, in the process of its implementation – apparently because of Arab pressure – from pressing Poland's government to not allow the Jewish repatriates to continue with an immediate departure from Poland to Israel.

We find an interesting reference on the danger then threatening the repatriation of Jews from the USSR to Poland, in a memorandum written on 27 March 1958 by Mr Benjamin Eliav, an Israeli official who at that time dealt (in Israel) with repatriation and Jewish immigration matters from eastern European countries. Mr Eliav writes:

> We have learned from reliable sources that the Russians are pressuring the Poles to agree that the stream of Jewish repatriates from the USSR to Poland should be reduced to zero, under the pretext that these Jews do not intend to settle in Poland but want to continue 'to another country'. Pressure in the same direction, and under the same pretext, was put on Poland's government by members of the Stalinist wing of the Jewish 'Kultur Gesellschaft' (Culture Society) in Poland, mainly Sh. Zahariasz, M. Mirsky and Y. Korman. Zahariasz spoke in this spirit at the Jewish party cell meeting of 'Kultur Gesellschaft' on 22 March 1958. The speech by Zahariasz was given in the presence of the head of the Minorities Committee, Slav, and Deputy Minister of the Interior, Schenk. Zahariasz explicitly demanded to appeal to the Soviet Union requesting the delay of the departure of the Jewish repatriates, because there are amongst them 'nationalistic elements whose intention is not to remain here but to continue elsewhere'. At this meeting another member of the party cell, one

of the Jewish Communist members, proposed halting through administrative means the entire emigration from Poland to Israel, but the representatives of the party and government explained that the Polish government had finally decided not to act on stopping emigration to Israel.[51]

Eliav also testifies in this memorandum that he had heard from his reliable sources that the Soviet authorities posed difficulties to Jews eligible to return to Poland, by demanding documents from them which they had not requested from Christian Poles, knowing they were unobtainable. Finally, the matter was settled after the Polish Embassy's intervention. Towards the end of April 1958 additional information reached Eliav from reliable sources about discussions held in Moscow concerning repatriation of Jews, in which the Soviets were inclined to reduce the number of Jewish repatriates, explaining their destination was not Poland, but somewhere else.[52]

We could detect from this evidence:

1. A reserved Soviet position on continuous Jewish repatriation from the USSR to Poland, because of the Jews' intention to move on to Israel.
2. The objection of Jewish Communists in Poland to the continuous repatriation for the same reason.

We do not possess sufficient data to prove who influenced whom. Did the Jewish Communists influence the Soviet position or vice versa? It might be reasonable to believe that it was the Jewish Communists who put pressure on the Soviet Union to revise its position on this matter, since they could testify to the national mood amongst the Jewish repatriates who were arriving in Poland from the USSR, and to the efforts of the repatriates to progress from Poland in the direction of Israel through the quickest and shortest route.

It seems that during the Polish-Soviet deliberations on this matter, the Soviets were pressured by the Arabs to 'not enhance the military potential of Israel', particularly after the Sinai Campaign, in consequence of which the Soviet Union itself stopped the emigration of Jews to Israel, temporarily. In 1956, up to the Sinai Campaign, the volume of immigration to Israel from the USSR had reached a climax never known before. When the immigration to Israel was renewed in 1958–59, its dimensions were much reduced. And along with the Arab pressure – perhaps to a lesser degree – the Soviets were put under ideological pressure by the Communist Jews in Poland, who considered the repatriates to be made up of nationalistic elements, not only in their striving to leave for Israel, but also because they were inclined to openly blame the Communist regime. The Polish authorities, unlike the Soviets, co-operated with the Jewish repatriates who wished to leave for Israel. As far as the Polish authorities were concerned the emigration of Jews from Poland to Israel liberated them from being concerned about the Jewish national implications for the non-Jewish society of Poland, and from supplying sources of living and housing to the Jewish masses. In addition to these aspects – social and economic – the emigration of Jews enabled Poland to demonstrate a sovereign and independent Polish policy.[53]

CONCLUSION

The policy of the eastern European countries concerning emigration to Israel, during the period under review, was a function of three major factors:

1. Recognition of the right of the Jews to repatriation to their historic homeland. This recognition was granted them in the period when the State of Israel was established. Despite the temporary stoppages in the flow of emigration, immigration to Israel was not totally halted, and the legitimate recognition of the right of the Jews to immigrate to Israel never abolished.

2. Considerations of internal policy (getting rid of national elements regarded as non-loyal to the regime, and their replacement by new cadres) and of foreign policy (demonstrating the capability of independent maneuvering, and later a means for gaining the sympathy of Western public opinion in order to achieve economic advantages).

3. Having regard for Israel's diplomatic pressure (called 'Zionist propaganda' in their language) and the Arab counterpressure (via the USSR).

As for Soviet interference in the issue of emigration, four stages are discernible:

First – (prior to the period under review) Encouragement of immigration to Israel (even before its independence) to strengthen the struggle of Palestinian Jews against the British Mandate.

Second – (also prior to the period under review in this book) Encouraging immigration to Israel, in the first years of its independence, aimed at strengthening its military power during its War of Independence and at influencing, ideologically, the character of its regime.

Third – Non-disturbance of emigration from east European states (Poland, 1957; Romania, 1958) due to consideration of their internal needs.

Fourth – Some Soviet disturbance, because of Arab pressure (Poland, 1958; Romania, 1959). At this stage, emigration became increasingly a function of their internal affairs. The weaker their dependence on the Soviet Union became, the more they permitted the Jews to leave for Israel and the West, according to their own interests.

The same went for Soviet policy towards the German minorities who wished to emigrate from Poland, Romania, and other eastern European countries to West Germany. As from the 1960s the USSR itself started to conduct a similar policy towards the Jews and the Germans who wished to emigrate from within its borders, the Jews to Israel, the Germans to West Germany.

NOTES

1 M. Namir, *Mission to Moscow* (Hebrew) (Tel Aviv: Am Oved, 1971) p. 52.
2 I. Ehrenburg, 'About One Letter' (Russian), *Pravda*, 21 Sept. 1948.
3 *Davar,* 23 May 1950.
4 M. Namir, op. cit., pp. 301–2.
5 The note was sent on 8 Dec. 1951 to the Soviet government and read by D. Ben Gurion in the Knesset plenum on 17 Feb. 1952. *Divrei Haknesset*, Vol. 11b, p. 1465.
6 UN General Assembly, 1st Special Session, 77th Plenary Meeting, 15 May 1947.
7 UN General Assembly, 7th Session, 1st Committee, 587th meeting, 25 March 1953; 596th meeting, 10 April 1953; 597th meeting, 13 April 1953.
8 A. Dagan, *Moscow and Jerusalem*, p. 75.

9 D. Ben Gurion told the Counselor of the Soviet Embassy in Israel on 17 July 1958, 'Unfortunately, we do not have any relations with the Jews in the USSR, and it's a pity. Krushchev said in one of his talks that the day would come and Jews would be able to immigrate. I hope it will be soon, if not we would be sorry about it. But this is the USSR's matter – We regret that the Soviet government does not permit relations with Soviet Jews, but this is a Soviet matter, though the USSR has another point of view and we cannot interfere, but we would like to have Soviet Jews permitted to come to Israel, to receive a Hebrew book. If it is not possible, we regret it. What can we do?' MFA Arch. File 103.1 SSR.

10 MK Altman's appeal against Israel's commitment to the USSR in exchange for the renewal of its relations (*Divrei Haknesset*, Vol. 14, pp. 2257–8, 13 Aug. 1953) as well as his appeal for the renewal of the struggle for *aliya* (*Divrei Haknesset*, Vol. 15, p. 1369, 29 March 1954; Vol. 78, 15 Nov. 1954).

11 *Divrei Haknesset*, Vol. 17, p. 67.

12 *Divrei Haknesset*, Vol. 17, p. 73.

13 *Divrei Haknesset*, Vol. 18, p. 2085.

14 *Davar*, 24 Aug. 1955.

15 *Davar*, 31 Aug. 1955

16 M. Sharett, *Private Diary*, Vol. 3, p. 830, 10 March 1955.

17 Declaration of MAGEN, 16 March 1955, Israeli Press.

18 At a debate held in the Knesset on 4 Nov. 1952, regarding the status of the Zionist Organization, Ben Gurion stated, 'Even if the State (of Israel) determines that the Zionist Organization represents two million Soviet Jews, it will be senseless, groundless and unrealistic and will encounter justified objection on the part of those who speak on behalf of Russian Jews, who would claim "who appointed you?".' *Divrei Haknesset*, Vol. 13, p. 24; see also n. 9 above.

19 See n. 16.

20 The US Deputy Secretary of State, Byroad, stated in May 1954, that if the USSR would open its gates for Jewish immigration to Israel, it would only result in the ignition of a bonfire in the region, following fresh turmoil in the Middle East. In the Knesset, Foreign Minister Sharett rejected this statement. *Divrei Haknesset*, Vol. 16, p. 1597.

21 M. Sharett, op. cit, Vol. 4, pp. 1121–3.

22 Ibid.

23 The foreign editor of the Italian newspaper *Corriera dela Sierra* asked Adzhubey, the chief editor of Izvestia, on 28 Feb. 1963, 'Why does the USSR not – contrary to the democratic states and to some Communist States – permit the emigration of Jewish citizens who wish to immigrate to Israel?' Adzhubey answered that the Jews in the USSR were happy and why didn't people leave them at peace? Wherever he paid visits, from Mexico to Rome, he was always asked the same question, whereas there were much more difficult problems in the world. MFA Arch. File 351.1 SSR. Partial report, *Maariv*, 1 March 1963; *Davar*, 3 March 1963.

24 A. Mikoyan, Deputy Prime Minister of the USSR, member of the Politburo, commented to a French Socialist Party delegation during their visit in Moscow, in May 1956, headed by Guy de Mollet. MFA Arch. File 351.1 SSR.

25 Krushchev to a group of Jewish leaders, United Press International, 27 July 1957.

26 *Davar*, 29 July, 4 Aug. 1957.

27 Krushchev, when visiting Los Angeles, *New York Times*, 25 Sept. 1959.

28 Letter of Israel's President Shazar to Soviet President Mikoyan of 7 July 1965. A. Dagan, op. cit., p. 164 as well as appeals by the Mapai leaders to the CPSU leadership.

29 *Le Monde*, 4 Dec. 1966; full details in Jews in Eastern Europe, 3, 8 (1967), p. 15.

30 *Kol Haam*, 22 Dec. 1966.

31 Y. Ro'i, 'The Standpoint of the USSR in relation to *aliya* as a factor in its policy towards the Arab–Israeli conflict (1954–1967)' (Hebrew), *Behinot*, 5 (1974) pp. 25–41.

32 Personal sources, according to registrations made upon the immigrants' entry to Israel. These statistics don't correspond 100 per cent with those of the Jewish Agency which includes numbers of immigrants who received exit permits to Israel but apparently left for other countries.

33 The regions from which the Jews were not deported were Wallachia, Moldova, and southern Transylvania.

34 *Encyclopedia Hebraica*, Vol. 14, p. 410.

35 MFA Arch. File 461.1 Rom.

36 I. Artzi, 'Romanian Jewry against the background of the last 25 years' (Hebrew), *Bitfutsot Hagola*, 11th year, nos. 1/2 (48/49), Jerusalem (1969).

37 MFA Arch. File 461.1 Rom.

38 At that time Israel was represented in Romania at the Legation level. The status changed to Embassy in 1967.

39 MFA Arch. File 461.1 Rom.

40 Ibid.

41 MFA Arch. File 461.1 Rom., report dated 30 Dec. 1958.

42 Ibid.

43 *Davar*, 1 Feb. 1959.

44 Ibid.

45 Ibid., 11 Feb. 1959.

46 Ibid., 2 Feb. 1959, according Hanna Zemer's report from Washington.

47 Ibid., 25 March 1959.

48 See Y. Ro'i's article, n. 31 above.

49 The first repatriation agreement after the war was signed on 6 July 1945. Within this framework 145,000 Jews returned to Poland, *Encyclopedia Judaica*, Vol. 13, p. 779 (Jerusalem: Keter, 1971). The second repatriation agreement was signed on 25 March 1957 (published in *Pravda*, 26 March 1957). The stream of repatriates started to flow until the end of 1956. Within this framework 25,000 Jews from the USSR left for Poland, *Encyclopedia Judaica*, 784. Some Polish sources that analyze the repatriation from the USSR to Poland: *Wielka Encyclopedia Powszechna* ('The Great Polish Encyclopedia') (Warsaw, 1967), p. 787; Christina Kerstein, *Polish Repatriation after World War Two* (Warsaw: Polish Academy of Sciences, 1974) p. 229.

50 See n. 26 above.

51 MFA Arch. File 351.1 SSR.

52 Ibid.

53 The Yiddish daily in Poland, *Volkstimme*, Warsaw, 4 Dec. 1958, published a summary of a lecture given by Schipek, the Chairman of the Nationalities Committee of the Polish Communist Party and Deputy Minister of the Interior, at a party meeting in Wroclaw, where he said, *inter alia*, that a considerable number of Jews left Poland in 1956–57 'because of increased anti-Semitism resulting from reactionary activity in Poland', and that their emigration was

also a result of national propaganda amongst the Jews. To that he added that the national question in Poland seemed to be a difficult problem, although they constitute only two percent of the total population. There was no hint in his presentation of any intention on the part of the Polish government to close the gates of departure on the Jews. See also the book (in Hebrew) by Katriel Katz, Israel's Minister in Warsaw at that time, *Budapest, Warsha, Moskva: Shagrir el Medinot Mitnakrot* (Tel Aviv: Sifriyat Hapoalim, 1976) pp. 76–9.

Part 3

The Jewish problem in the USSR

8 · Continuity and change in Soviet policy regarding the National Question and its attitude towards the Jewish nationality in the USSR

THE NATIONAL Question according to Lenin's and Stalin's theory was conceived as a temporary phenomenon of the capitalist era – that gave birth, according to Marx, to the various nationalities which would disappear in the communist era, when the nations would be amalgamated on the basis of political and civil equality into one communist nation, in one proletarian culture and one language. The process of *rapprochement* and amalgamation of nationalities would begin with the rise to power of the dictatorship of the proletariat and would then pave the way towards co-operation between them based on political and civil equality.[1]

The program of the Russian Socialist-Democratic party outlined at the Second Congress in 1903, headed by Lenin, asserted, regarding the National Question:

Recognition of the nations' right to self-determination.
Full equality of rights for all citizens, with no distinction of sex, religion, race and nationality.
The right of the population to be educated in its mother tongue.
The establishment of schools in their mother tongue, initiated by the government and the self-governing institutions.
The right of each citizen to explain himself in his own language at meetings and the introduction of mother tongues on an equal basis with the state language in all public and state institutions.[2]

This program was used as a basis for the 'declaration of principles of the Bolshevik government', formed in December 1917, promising:

Equality and sovereignty to the peoples of Russia.
The right of the peoples of Russia to self-determination until separation and the establishment of an independent state.
The abolition of privileges and national and religious limitations.
The development of national minorities' cultures and the ethnic groups in Russia.[3]

In theory, these principles were in force until the dismemberment of the USSR. In practice, however, they were given an interpretation which suited the character of the USSR's centralized regime, ignoring their (national) contents and concepts such as 'self-determination', which, Stalin asserted, is at times confronted by a more superior right of the working class in consolidating its regime.[4] Hence, a decision to separate in accordance with self-determination is subordinated to the party[5] and since the party rejected separation, apparently separation was, in effect, impossible.

The right to 'development of minorities' culture' did not mean, according to Lenin, that its contents should be national. The universal values, in its proletarian meaning of nationalities' culture, had the right to existence. The cultural values in themselves did not have any. As for the character of proletarian culture, Stalin gave it a theoretical interpretation, namely, that this sort of culture should be socialist in content and national in form. Proletarian culture did not involve replacing national culture, according to Stalin, but giving it universal content and, vice versa, national culture did not involve replacing proletarian culture but only giving it its form.[6]

DEFINING THE NATIONALITY CONCEPT

During Stalin's era

In his 1913 essay 'Marxism and the National Question', Stalin defined the concept Nationality as follows: Nationality is a constant partnership of people, marked off, historically, on the basis of a common language, common territory, common economic structure, and a common psyche expressed in a common culture.[7]

In asserting these four descriptors, Stalin stressed that the existence of only some of these signs was not sufficient to identify a nationality; in the absence of one of these signs 'a nationality ceases to be a nationality'.[8] Stalin totally rejected common destiny, religion and national character – characteristic to the Jewish nationality – as signifiers of nationality.[9] At the end of the 1920s, however, Stalin broadened the definition of the fourth descriptor by adding to it a national characteristic: 'common psyche expressed in common and unique features in national literature'. Even after the broadening of his definition it still remained within its rigid frame, raising no objections from Soviet theoreticians until the beginning of the 1960s.

In the post-Stalinist era

I. M. Zhukov, Soviet historian, member of the Soviet Academy of Sciences, was the first to launch an appeal, eight years after Stalin's death, for a renewed debate on Stalin's definition of nationality.[10] The basic point of this appeal was to say that Stalin's definition of nationality did not match reality. Nationalities in the USSR continued to exist despite some of the signs asserted by Stalin not applying to them. The deliberations, carried out in Soviet periodicals on history and ethnography, lasted for a number of years in the Soviet Union. Three fundamental points can be concluded from that debate:

1. It is not essential that a nationality be considered as such only if all four descriptors apply to it. A nationality will be considered as existing if only one of the characteristics apply to it;.
2. National consciousness is one of the most essential elements that characterize a nationality.
3. Nationalities will continue to exist for a long time, even after the establishment of a communist society.

In the course of the debate two Soviet historians proposed a new definition of nationality: According to S. A. Tokarev: 'Ethnic association is a partnership of people based on one or on several forms of social relations: common origin, language, territory, a sense of belonging to a state, economic connections, common culture, and religious structure (if preserved).'[11]

As defined by P. M. Rogachev: Nationality is an association of people that comes into being in the course of history, characterized by a stabilized association of economic life (under conditions of working-class rule) in a common territory, with a common language (particularly literary), a sense of ethnic belonging and some psychologically unique features, a common tradition and cultural environment, and a common desire for [apparently national] liberation.[12]

The need for new formulas to define nationality attests to the tension between Stalinist-Leninist theory and reality. More than 50 years of the Soviet regime (as at the 1960s) had neither annihilated nor concealed nationalities in Soviet society. The importance of the new formulations lies, however, not only in the theoretical undermining of previous definitions and attempts at broadening them by referring explicitly to 'social relations', 'ethnic consciousness' and 'national struggle', as elements of national existence, but in giving new recognition to an existing reality.

These definitions did not just remain academic, as witnessed by the definition of nationality in the *Great Soviet Encyclopedia*, 1972 edition, which completely ignored Stalin's definition by stressing national consciousness as a common element of nationality.[13]

THE PLACE OF JEWS IN THE DEFINITION OF NATIONALITY

In Stalin's era

Neither Lenin nor Stalin recognized, theoretically, the Jews as a nationality.[14] Although Lenin firmly condemned anti-Semitism and put himself in the position of a defender of the Jews, he denied the Jews the status of nationality in some of his essays. He praised the large role of the Jews in the socialist movement and their contribution to world civilization, as individuals. The solution of the Jewish problem he saw in their assimilation amongst the nations where they were living and thus he believed 'they will render their services as in the past'.[15]

Stalin did not find anything in common between the Jews in the East and those in the West to justify their identity as people of one nation. He mocked the 'Bund' when it demanded national autonomy for the Jews, saying that 'It suggests autonomy for a nationality that has not got a future and its existence at present must still be proved.'[16]

Hence, from the point of view of long-range policy Jews were destined to assimilation, being denied rights granted to every recognized nationality in the USSR. On the practical side, as a short-range policy, the Jews enjoyed – as will be further discussed – the status of nationality until the second half of the 1940s. From then until about the end of the 1950s their national status was stripped of content. The entry 'Jews' in the *Great Soviet Encyclopedia*, 1952 edition, asserted that 'the Jews are not a people and that they assimilate at a quick rate among the peoples of the USSR where they are living'.[17]

In the post-Stalin era

The theoretical debate on the definition of nationality that developed in the USSR at the beginning of the 1960s did not skip over the Jews. It should not be discounted that the fact of Jewish existence had caused the Soviet authorities to re-examine the question of how to make the definition congruent with reality. In some cases Jewish national existence served as an antithesis of Stalin's definition,[18] whereas the new definitions did apply to the Jews.

As in the case of the new definition of nationality, published in the *Great Soviet Encyclopedia* of 1972, so in the case of 'Jews', the definition underwent a notable change. There were no longer assertions that the Jews were not a nationality and no reference was made to the definitions of Lenin and Stalin in this respect. On the contrary, the entry in the encyclopedia presents the Jews as a nationality.[19] Possibly the major factor that influenced the Soviet theoreticians to re-examine the definition of nationality and its application to Jews was their recognition of the fact that, despite a large number of the Jews having assimilated into Russian culture, their national consciousness and sense of still belonging to the Jewish people remained a striking fact. Dozens of years of Soviet rule had not succeeded in obliterating it.

The importance of this re-examination is in recognizing the fact that closeness between Soviet nationalities does not abolish their uniqueness and therefore contradicts Lenin's and Stalin's assumption about the imminent disappearance of the Jewish nationality in the USSR.

The practical aspect

The theory that did not recognize Jews as a nationality significantly contradicted the pragmatic policy of the USSR towards Jews.

When the Bolsheviks came to power, the leadership encountered severe difficulties in dealing with the national question; it was therefore necessary to grant them many rights within Russia to national and cultural equality in order to avoid their separation and to secure co-operation with them in consolidating the Soviet regime. The right to separation in the frame of self-determination outlined before the October Revolution could not have advanced this goal. Therefore a pragmatic plan was outlined to obtain the immediate objective. Among other nationalities, the Jews benefited[20] in the framework of the general policy of establishing national institutions aimed at accelerating the social and economic integration of the population in the new regime.

First, it was necessary – as for all other minorities – to shift the Jews to productive occupations in industry and agriculture. Secondly, the Jews were discovered to be of specific value within the general population for their loyalty and faithfulness to the regime. Thirdly, because of its liberal attitude towards the Jews, by granting them national minority rights, the USSR could enjoy the sympathy of the USA and western Europe (and even influence Jewish communities throughout the world to strengthen the communist parties in their home countries).

The Jewish Council, The Jewish Commissariat and the Jewish Sections in the Soviet Communist Party in 1918, the Konset in 1924, the National Soviet Jews and the declaration of Birobidjan as a Jewish national autonomous district in 1932 – all these actually granted 'cultural autonomy to the Jews and enabled – through a network of Jewish schools, research institutes, cultural forums – a Jewish cultural flourishing of such size and essence as no one had expected in the course of the debates between the Bolsheviks and the "Bund"'.[21]

With the closure of Jewish institutions – either because of reorganization in the party or because of Stalin's fear of consolidating Jewish

1. Israel's Minister of Foreign Affairs Moshe Sharett (right) greeting the first head of the USSR's Legation in Israel Minister Extr. and Plenip. Pavel Yershov at the MFA in Tel Aviv, 1948.

2. Pavel Yershov presenting the greetings of the diplomatic corps to President Weizmann on the occasion of Israel's first Independence Day, Tel Aviv, 1949.

3. November 1956. Demonstration by Soviet citizens in front of Israel's Embassy on Vesnina St. in Moscow against Israel's involvement in the Sinai War.

4. The Great Synagogue on Archipova St. in Moscow, 1957.

5. The MFA, Jerusalem 1964. Signing an Israeli–Soviet agreement on the sale of Russian property to Israel. Front row (from left to right), M. Bodrov, Soviet Ambassador to Israel; Golda Meir, Minister of Foreign Affairs; P. Sapir, Israel's Finance Minister. Second row (from left to right), an assistant to the ambassador; A. Gilboa, Head of Protocol at the MFA; Y. Blum, Legal Adviser to the MFA.

6. Moscow, September 1965. Reception hall of the Supreme Soviet Presidency at the Kremlin, after the presentation of credentials of Israel's Ambassador to the USSR, Katriel Katz (sitting second from the right) to the President of the Supreme Soviet, Anastas Mikoyan (second from the left). The author is standing in the first row, fourth from the right.

7. Jerusalem, December 1965. The Soviet ambassador to Israel, D. Chuvakhin (left) after presenting his credentials to Israel's President Z. Shazar (centre). On the right is Abba Eban, Israel's Minister of Foreign Affairs.

8. The MFA, Jerusalem, 18 October, 1991. Soviet Foreign Minister Boris Pankin (left) and Israel's Foreign Minister David Levy (right) signing a joint statement on the restoration of diplomatic relations between Israel and the USSR, 24 years after having them severed by the Soviet Union. Second from the left is the author, then Deputy Director General of Israel's Ministry of Foreign Affairs. Second from the right is Israel's ambassador to the USSR, Aryeh Levin.

9. Yosef Govrin addressing a public meeting at the Municipality of Jerusalem in 1991 shortly after the resumption of diplomatic relations between Israel and the USSR.

10. Yosef Govrin in discussion with Mikhail Gorbachev during his official visit to Israel on 14–18 June 1992.

national existence beyond the functions that the Soviet leadership had entrusted to them – and the executions of Jewish national cadres in the second half of the 1930s, the process of strangulation of Jewish culture began. The USSR's annexation of sections of Poland, Romania and the Baltic states in 1939–40 – with a considerable Jewish population – prompted a new cultural blooming amongst the Jews which was abruptly and shortly cut off by Nazi Germany's invasion into the territory of the USSR.

The Soviet Union's war against Nazi Germany led to a revival of the Jewish national establishment embodied in the founding and activities of the 'Jewish anti-Fascist Committee' (within the USSR and amongst the Jews in the USA). The dismantling of the committee in 1948, the closing of the last Jewish schools throughout the USSR, the closing of the Jewish theater in Moscow (and in other cities of the USSR), the shutting down of the Jewish publishing house in Moscow (the only one to exist after the war), the closing of the Jewish press and periodicals, the arrest (and subsequent execution) of dozens of Jewish writers – all these expressed the objectives of Soviet policy under Stalin's leadership: the destruction of Jewish national existence in the USSR.

The main proof, however, of the continuing recognition of Jewish national existence in the period of 'the black years', 1948–53, was the continuous registration on the Soviet identity card of Jewish nationality – as was the case for all nationalities of the USSR – according to a law enacted in 1932. Since the identity card was the main means of identifying individuals in their contacts with the Soviet authorities, it was also a verified means for identifying someone's nationality.

Some six or seven years after Stalin's death the Soviet authorities began to rehabilitate Jewish culture, only in part and to a limited degree, with the appearance of: a periodical, *Sovetish Heymland*, a literary magazine in Yiddish; theatrical and vocal performances in Yiddish; the publication of numerous books in Yiddish by different authors; the publication of favorable reviews and survey articles on past and present Jewish writers and poets who worked creatively in the USSR and in Western countries, including Israel; the publication of anthologies of Hebrew short stories and Hebrew poetry in Russian translation; and the publication of a Hebrew–Russian dictionary (for the first time). All this was achieved as a result of pressure from world public opinion on the Soviet authorities to respect the rights of Soviet Jews in the domains of education, religion and culture against the background of changes occurring in Soviet internal policy after Stalin's death. If it were not for the pressure of world public opinion – as we shall see further on – it is unlikely that the few positive manifestations mentioned above would have occurred.

Since the ability of world public opinion to influence the Soviet authorities was adequately proven, the pressure continued to increase the rights of the Jews, both in scope and content. The pressure was based on the USSR's commitments, on its constitution, and on the International Treaty of Minorities' Rights, which upheld the right of minorities to cultivate their educational and cultural values. It was pointed out that the Jews were being discriminated against in the domains of education, religion, culture, and self-organisation in comparison to the other minorities in the USSR.

GENERAL CHARACTERISTICS OF THE LEGAL STATUS OF THE JEWS IN THE USSR AND OF THEIR NATIONAL SITUATION IN THE YEARS 1953–67

The 1959 census of the USSR, the first after World War II, counted 2,268,000 Jews, constituting 1.09 per cent of the general population.[22] Out of 108 nationalities counted in the census the Jews occupied eleventh place. The great majority of the Jews lived in the densely populated republics: Russia, 38 per cent; Ukraine, 37 per cent; Belorussia, 7 per cent. An additional 17 per cent were dispersed among the republics of Uzbekistan, Georgia, Lithuania, Moldavia, Latvia, and Estonia. The remainder were in the other six republics. Some 95 per cent of the Jewish population lived in the cities, and 20.8 per cent declared Yiddish as their mother tongue.

From the above data, the following conclusions can be drawn:

The Jewish population was a small minority in each of the 15 republics and hence lacked adequate representative weight. On the other hand, Jews occupied a notable place amongst the other nationalities because of their activity and disproportionate representation in the domains of medicine, law, science, technology, literature, the press, and administration.

The concentration of Jews in the cities of the Russian Republic exposed them to quick linguistic assimilation whereas in the rest of the republics they served as an important russification factor.

The percentage of Yiddish-speaking and -understanding people (including the Jewish dialect of Georgia, Bukhara, and Dagestan) was probably higher than that of people who had declared having Yiddish as their mother tongue. This percentage was much lower than it had been in the previous census conducted in the mid-1920s, but even if the percentage is taken to be accurate, it still constitutes a relatively high rate under conditions which lacked opportunities for learning the Yiddish language in state schools from the second half of the 1940s. Language assimilation is not an indication of national assimilation.

Since the question of religious affiliation was not asked in the census, it is not possible to learn what the percentage of believers in the Jewish religious faith was. The Chief Rabbi of Moscow, however, estimated them at half a million.[23] Such a number in a country like the USSR may also attest to a slow rate of assimilation (even though the estimated number might be exaggerated since it was reported for outside consumption).

DISCRIMINATION IN THE CIVIL DOMAIN

Declared policy

The declared policy as stated in Paragraph 123 of the Soviet Constitution of 1932 asserted: 'Equality of rights for all Soviet citizens, without national and racial distinction, in all the economic, political, governmental and public domains ... Every limitation of rights, direct or indirect, or vice versa, granting of excessive rights, direct or indirect, to citizens on the basis of their nationality or race is to be punished.'

'Propaganda or incitement directed at provoking national hatred or separation ... is met with punishment depriving personal liberty for a period of six months to three years, or with deportation for a period of two to three years' (Paragraph 74 of the Criminal Law of the USSR, in force from 1961).

The policy in practice (in the post-Stalin years)

The Jews enjoyed equal civil rights in a number of domains. There were no restrictions regarding housing, nor were there restrictions on membership in the Communist Party, trade unions, army service, social services, and so on. Equal opportunities were offered for working in the fields of science, medicine, law, literature, education, art, music, and journalism. In these spheres Jews enjoyed a distinguished position disproportional to their percentage among the population at large.[24] Discrimination against them was noted, however, in the following domains:

There was a large decline in the number of Jews in the Supreme Soviet of the USSR, the Soviet Councils of the Republics, Soviet government, and in the Central Committee of the CPSU, much lower than their proportional ranking in the general population.

There was a considerable decline in the number of Jews in the USSR's foreign service and army leadership.

Quotas were instituted on Jews being accepted as students at institutions of higher learning/universities, particularly in those republics with a large Jewish population.

In trials for economic crimes held in 1961–64 Jewish origin was mentioned together with the name of the accused. Jews were sentenced to more punishment than the non-Jews.

There was no information about any trials over anti-Semitic accusations.

Periodicals with anti-Semitic tendencies received wide distribution under the guise of anti-religious, anti-Zionist, and anti-Israeli information.

Jews were not allowed to perpetuate the memory of Jews who perished in the Holocaust within the territory of the Soviet Union and such enterprises (in art and literature) were condemned.

The Soviet arguments

The Soviet regime, in the past, had been assisted by a large number of Jews in advancing the development of the country, whereas other nationalities were considered to be culturally backward. In the 1950s new national cadres were ready to be integrated into such domains as management, administration, economy, science, and medicine.[25]

The fact that the percentage of Jews in key positions in managerial, administrative and higher institutions was much higher than their percentage in the population at large, and the local population, could have evoked envy and hatred towards them.[26]

There had never been an anti-Semitic policy in the USSR, since the very character of the USSR as a socialist and multinational country precluded such a policy.[27]

Assessing the arguments

The Soviet arguments constitute acknowledgment of a policy of discrimination dictated by the cultural authorities. While there was a strong, strained tendency to assimilate the Jews into Soviet society, there was no willingness to absorb them. Although the data in the period under review shows that the representation of Jews in the various management fields was still disproportionately high compared with their representation in the population at large, one must consider that this data reflected an ongoing process which had prevailed prior to the then current policy. A quota policy and limitation of rights showed themselves in the years after the period under review.

Denying the existence of anti-Semitism in the USSR, in the past and the present, was mainly aimed at Western public opinion to present a prettier picture of the Soviet regime. The denial of its existence, however, was in total contradiction, not only with the events that took place during Stalin's period, but also with the official appeals of Soviet leaders, including a warning article in *Pravda*,[28] prohibiting anti-Semitism. The need to have those appeals repeated only strengthened the argument about its existence. The criticism of its existence, voiced in Israel and by world public opinion, did indeed restrain its momentum, to a certain degree. But, when the anti-Israel policy in the USSR became stronger, the wave of anti-Semitic publications increased. It seems, therefore, that the anti-Semitic policy was a planned endeavor geared for internal consumption, and far from the declarations calling for its prohibition.

DISCRIMINATION IN THE DOMAIN OF RELIGION

The formal policy

The USSR's constitution assured freedom for religious cults and equal status for all religions.[29] The State Order of June 1944 that established the 'Council for Religious Cults' mentions the Jewish religion among a dozen faiths (except the Provoslav) that were granted official status.

Religious communities were given the right to establish religious centers.[30]

The policy in practice

The Jewish religion had neither a central nor a federative organization which would enable it – like the other religions in the USSR – to call conferences, oversee religious services throughout the country, publish a bulletin or periodical, and maintain contacts and meetings with co-religionists outside the country.

No religious objects were produced. The Bible was not published. The prayer book was printed only once, under pressure of world public opinion, in 3,000 copies. There were no current contacts with Jewish religious institutions abroad. Permission was not given to Jewish pilgrims to leave for the Holy Land – Israel – as was granted to the Provoslav and Muslim religions.

No centers existed for the training of cantors, ritual slaughterers, Jewish judges for rabbinical courts, or rabbis for religious services.

Limitations were introduced on the baking of *matzot* (unleavened bread for Passover) – in the course of time they were abolished because of outside pressure.

The Soviet arguments

There was no direct reference to discrimination in the religious domain, except for a general remark, saying that there was a general decline in the numbers of believers in religion – including the Jewish religion – as a result the move towards a materialist world view.[31]

Assessing the arguments

Discrimination in the religious domain, aimed at the asphyxiation of Jewry, was only one side of the coin. The propaganda conducted against Judaism as a philosophy for a way of life, often filled with hatred and national incitement, was the flip side of the coin. Unlike the anti-Catholic propaganda, which was not directed against any particular nationality, the anti-Judaism propaganda was aimed at the Jewish nation alone. The hatred revealed, at times, the anti-Semitic roots that were deeply embedded in the minds of the Russian theoreticians in the pre-revolutionary period.[32]

DISCRIMINATION IN THE FIELD OF EDUCATION

The formal policy

The Soviet Constitution asserted the right 'to teach in the schools in the mother tongue'.

A law enacted on 16 April 1959 in the Russian Republic asserted that 'education in schools shall be conducted in the mother tongue of the pupils' and that 'parents will be given the right to decide in which language to register their children at school' (assuming that there were schools where the language of instruction was that of the national minority).

The program of the CPSU, approved by its 22nd Congress in 1961, asserted the 'complete freedom of a Soviet citizen to speak, to educate and to teach his/her children in any language and prohibits any excessive right, limitation or compulsion in the use of this or another language'.

In August 1962 the USSR confirmed its adherence to the 'UNESCO Treaty' against discrimination in education which made it obligatory 'to recognize the rights of national minorities to continue with their educational activities, including the existence of schools, and the use of or teaching in their language'.

The policy in practice

Throughout the Soviet Union – including Birobidjan – there was not a single Jewish school nor even one class where Yiddish was taught.

The Soviet arguments

The establishment of separate schools in Yiddish for Jews dispersed all over the Soviet Union would be a great financial burden.[33]

If such schools were to have been established, only a few people would have attended them of their own free will.[34]

Assessing the arguments

There is no doubt that the re-establishment of a network of Yiddish schools would have required the training of teachers and educators, in large numbers, for assignment all over the USSR under appropriate pedagogical supervision and a central administrative staff in addition to the composing of new textbooks. All this would have probably required considerable expenditure and time in preparing the infrastructure. This does not mean, however, that the USSR could not have shouldered the burden. The USSR had proved itself to be up to implementing such a policy not only in the past but also at that time, regarding the German minority.[35] True, perhaps not many Jewish children would have streamed to Yiddish schools, but that does not mean that the few who would have done so would not have enjoyed them, if only the USSR had respected their rights as it had those of other minorities.[36]

It seems that the main reason for not reopening the Yiddish state schools was the USSR's policy of accelerating the Jews' assimilation process. The revival of Yiddish teaching and the administrative staff involved in the renewal of Yiddish teaching in the state schools would have reinforced national consciousness among the Jews and would have thereby delayed the assimilation process.

Although the number of those using Yiddish was declining in the world owing to the loss of millions of Yiddish-speaking Jews during the Holocaust, and to the process of language assimilation in different countries and to the revival of Hebrew, many Jews in the USSR continued to cultivate Yiddish as their mother tongue or to speak it as their second language, after Russian.

In the course of time, after the establishment of the State of Israel, the urge among the Soviet Jews to learn Hebrew overshadowed their devotion to Yiddish. But, to learn Hebrew, officially, was impossible, since Hebrew had no official status among the recognized languages of the USSR's nationalities. Thus, a vicious circle was formed. The Soviet authorities ceased cultivating Yiddish, although it was recognized officially as the language of the Jewish nationality in the USSR, whereas they did not make it possible to learn Hebrew, since it had no recognized status as the language of the Jewish nationality in the USSR.

There remained, then, the unofficial – almost underground – way to study Hebrew: through Jewish religious tradition and the history of the Jewish people. This way led those who were engaged in such activity to a confrontation with the Soviet authorities, who accused Israel that it was striving to influence the Jews to cultivate their national-Zionist consciousness and thus divert them from assimilating within Russian society. The confrontation began gradually to develop into an open struggle between those who forged the policy of forced assimilation and those among Soviet Jews who objected to it, both within the USSR and outside, under the organisation and leadership of Israel.

DISCRIMINATION IN THE DOMAIN OF CULTURE

Official policy

From the resolutions of the Party Congress in 1921: the CPSU would assist the nationalities 'to establish schools, newspapers, theaters, educational and cultural institutions, where the mother tongue will be introduced'.

Stalin, in his speech at the University of Tashkent on 18 May 1925: people's culture should be afforded the opportunity to develop, broaden and discover the hidden forces inherent in it, in order 'to create the conditions to be amalgamated into a unified, common culture, with one common language'.

The policy in practice

In reality the re-establishment of Jewish cultural institutions that had operated in the USSR until 1948 was avoided; information on the Jewish past was deliberately omitted, as it was on the contribution of the Jews to world civilization and to the development of the USSR itself; there was no information on the scale of the Holocaust against the Jews in the USSR and eastern Europe; there was no mention of the history of the Jewish people in the history textbooks and Jewish literature was not taught; the Jewish State

Theater in Moscow was not re-opened; there was no museum on the past of the Jewish people and its cultural and artistic values.

The Soviet argument

Justification for the absence of Jewish cultural institutions came from the very dispersion of the Jewish population all over the USSR.

Assessing the argument

The argument did not hold up to the examination of reality. Other nationalities were also scattered, yet they were enabled to cultivate their cultural values and historic heritage. Moreover, Jewish institutions operated until 1948. Hence, dispersion was not the reason for the non-cultivation of Jewish culture, but rather the lack of interest on the part of the Soviet authorities in its existence, probably in fear of how the Jewish cultural institutions might strengthen national consciousness among the Jews. The tendency to destroy Jewish culture suited the dream of 'the amalgamation of nationalities' culture' into a unified culture but contradicted the policy of developing the culture of nationalities, implemented in the USSR for every nationality except the Jewish one.

CONCLUSION

There is a distinct contradiction between the theoretical and practical policies towards the Jews in the USSR – making a mockery of the principles of national equality on which the Soviet laws were based and in effect contravening the international treaty of human rights, signed by the USSR.

The planned and vigorous policy of assimilating Jews by force into Russian society through limitation of their national rights stemmed from ideological considerations anchored in the Leninist-Stalinist heritage, in the way they perceived the status of Jews and their culture, and from psychological considerations stemming from the way the Jews were regarded as foreign implants in Soviet society, despite their contribution to the October Revolution and to its consolidation in advancing the USSR's development.

On the one hand, the leaders of the USSR condemned anti-Semitism as alien to communist ideology. On the other, they oppressed Jewish national manifestations and aspirations to preserving national Jewish existence in the USSR, through anti-Semitism, which is also alien to Leninist ideology.

Nevertheless, precisely because of national oppression, discrimination and forced assimilation, Jewish national consciousness was preserved to a greater extent than these policy makers had intended.

NOTES

1 Lenin's conception of the National Question was extensively discussed in B. Pinkus' article 'The National Problem in the USSR: Theory and Practice' (Hebrew), *Molad* 1, 24 (Oct.–Nov. 1967), Brochure 213, as well as in Franisek Silnitzky's article 'Leninism's Concept of Nationalism and the Jewish Problem' (Hebrew), *Shevut* 2, 19 (1974).
2 'The National Program of the Communist Party of the USSR' (Russian), *The Great Russian Encyclopedia*, 2nd edition (1952), Vol. 29, p. 291.
3 Ibid., p. 293.
4 I. V. Stalin, *Collected Works* (Russian) (Moscow: State Publishing House of Political Literature, Marx-Engels Institute, Central Committee of the CPSU, 1949), Vol. 5, p. 270: 'The right to self-determination should not be an obstacle to the working class regarding its right to govern.'
5 V. I. Lenin, *Selected Writings* (Russian) (Moscow: Progress, 1961–70), Vol. 26, p. 408.
6 I. V. Stalin, *Collected Works* (Russian), Vol. 7, p. 138.
7 Ibid, Vol. 2, pp. 296–7.
8 Ibid.
9 Ibid.
10 E. M. Zhukov, 'The 22nd Congress of the CPSU and the Role of Soviet Historians' (Russian), *Voprosy Historii* 12 (1961), pp. 3–13.
11 S. A. Tokarev, 'Problems of Characterization of Ethnic Groups' (Russian), *Voprosy Filosofii* 11 (1964), pp. 43–5.
12 P. M. Rogachev and M. A. Sverdlin, 'On the Concept of Nationality' (Russian), *Voprosy Historii* 1 (1966), p. 45.
13 *The Great Soviet Encyclopedia* (Russian), 3rd edition (1972, Vol. 9, pp. 10–14.
14 Lenin, *Selected Writings*, 4th edition, Vol. 19, p. 63: 'The Jews ceased to exist as a nationality, this concept is impossible without a territory.' Whereas in Vol. 7, pp. 84–5 (1903): 'If the Jews would be recognized as a nation, it would be an artificial nation, because the idea of a separate Jewish people is reactionary from the political point of view and does not stand up before scientific criticism.'
15 Ibid.
16 Stalin, op. cit., Vol. 2, p. 334. Also, Vol. 2, pp. 249–300, quoted from his essay on 'Marxism and the National Question': 'Bauer is talking about the Jews as

if they were a nationality, although "they do not have a common language", but about which common destiny and national connection can one talk regarding the Jews in Georgia, Dagestan, Russia and America who are entirely disconnected from each other, living in different territories and speaking different languages? ... If anything still remains in common between them, it is religion, common origin and some features of national characteristics ... And how is it possible to say, seriously, that some petrified religious customs and vanishing psychological remnants are influencing the "destiny" of the mentioned Jews, more than the living society, social, economic and cultural environment in which they live? Only under this assumption it is possible to speak about the Jews in general as unified nation.'

17 *Great Soviet Encyclopedia*, 2nd edition, Vol. 15, p. 378.
18 Tokarev, op. cit., p. 43.
19 *Great Soviet Encyclopedia*, 3rd edition, Vol. 9, p. 10.
20 The subject is dealt with in Prof. Altschuler's essay 'The Soviet Communist Party and Jewish National Existence 1918–1932' (Hebrew), *Molad* 1, 24 (1967), brochure 3 (213), pp. 324–32.
21 Stalin, op. cit. , Vol. 2, pp. 332–47.
22 See M. Abramovich's article 'The Jews in the 1959 Soviet Population Census' (Hebrew), *Molad* 18, 144–5 (1960), pp. 320–9.
23 According to a Jewish Telegraphic Agency report from Rome on 12 Jan. 1960, based on information provided by a member of the Soviet Committee for Religious Affairs, Vaschikov, in an interview to the news agency in Moscow. See also Jews in Eastern Europe 3 (Feb. 1960).
24 S. Rabinovich, *Jews in USSR* (English) (Moscow: Novosti Press Agency, n.d.) pp. 25–9.
25 N. S. Krushchev, in an interview with a delegation of the French Socialist Party, May 1956, published in *Réalité*, May 1957. See also, *The New Leader* (NY, 14 Sept. 1959).
26 Ibid.
27 E. Furtseva, Soviet Minister of Culture, in an interview given to the *National Guardian* (New York, 25 June 1956).
28 See page 91.
29 Law of the Soviet government of 23 Jan. 1918, and State Order of 8 April 1929.
30 State Order 8 April 1929.
31 S. Rabinovich, op. cit.
32 The Soviet Press on Judaism' (English) *Jews in Eastern Europe* No. 4 (May 1960); see also No. 5 (July 1964).
33 Krushchev to the delegation of the French Socialist party, May 1956.
34 Ibid.
35 *The New Leader*, 14 Sept. 1959, pp. 7–8; *Jews in Eastern Europe*, 3, 2 (May 1965) p. 3, and 3, 5 (Oct. 1966) p. 10.
36 *Jews in Eastern Europe*, 3, 5 (Oct. 1966) p. 9.

9 · The national awakening of the Jews in the USSR and Israel's dissemination of information among them

THE JEWISH national awakening in the USSR – which reached its peak after World War II – is unique against the background of a policy of oppression, hostility and discrimination on the part of the Soviet authorities towards the Jewish nationality on one hand, and the Jews' drive to search for their historic roots and national identification, on the other hand.[1]

Manifestations of national revival among the Jews in the USSR had already appeared in three contiguous periods prior to the period under review in this work:

1. *World War II.* First, the meeting – for the first time after the October Revolution – between a Jewry with a deep national consciousness living in the areas annexed to the USSR, in the years 1939–1940, and Soviet Jewry in the process of linguistic, cultural and social assimilation. Afterwards, through the contacts which were established – also, for the first time after the revolution – between the leaders of the 'Jewish Anti-Fascist Committee' and the Jewish communities in England and the USA during the war. The Nazi occupation of western areas of the USSR, with a dense Jewish population, and the Holocaust that befell them, kindled the national sentiments of the Jews in the USSR. The Soviet regime even encouraged these sentiments in the framework of its general policy to set the population in motion to fight the common enemy, and to

enjoy the support of the Jewish communities in the West and the USA. The war left very difficult memories in the minds of the Jews and bequeathed them a feeling of national unity and common destiny against the anti-Semitic enemies – domestic and foreign.

2. *The emergence of the State of Israel.* The USSR's support in the international arena for the establishment of the State of Israel could have been interpreted as a radical change in the Soviet attitude towards the Jewish national movement. The spontaneous mass welcome for Israel's first Plenipotentiary and Extraordinary Minister in front of the Great Synagogue in Moscow, even after the warning sounded by I. Ehrenburg in his *Pravda* article, was most probably a truthful expression of national feelings in the hearts of the Jews in the face of this historic event.

The emergence of a State of Israel not only served as a focus of national identity and national belonging for the Jews in the USSR, but probably evoked in the hearts of many a yearning to immigrate to Israel and become an integral part of the country.[2]

3. *The 'Black Years'.* During this period the sense of common destiny became stronger in the face of libels, threats of physical extinction and deportation plans (which did not materialize because of Stalin's death). Painting the Jews as a foreign, nationalistic, cosmopolitan element working on a mysterious intelligence mission for foreign powers aiming to undermine the Soviet regime and its leadership created in the minds of the Jews profound disappointment and despair in face of the regime's policy towards them in particular and towards Jewry in general.[3]

After Stalin's death, following the 'thaw', hopes stirred in the hearts of the Jews for the abolition of the anti-Semitic policy and anti-Semitic manifestations – but these hopes soon evaporated. Suspicion of the Jews as a foreign element did not vanish. Stalin's crimes towards the Jews as Jews were not condemned nor was any basic rehabilitation introduced in respect of Jewish cultural and educational institutions closed at the end of Stalin's era. To this a new dimension was added the anti-Israel and anti-religious propaganda, which probably stirred among the Jews a collective national resentment towards the regime. These manifestations only strengthened the national consciousness of the Jews in the USSR, nourished by pride in Israel's achievements – still in the early years of the state's existence – and by Israel's official presence in Moscow, which encouraged aspiration for Jewish life within the USSR and of hopes of being able to emigrate to Israel.

Testimony of the Jewish intelligentsia in the USSR about the motives behind national awakening among the Jews in the USSR places heavy emphasis on internal processes in Soviet society in general and in the Jewish sector in particular.[4] No doubt these processes were of a certain importance in the crystallization of the national awakening. Yet, it should be stressed that historical research had not yet paid sufficient attention to the role of Israel in influencing this stirring. Undoubtedly the very fact of Israel's being a focus of the Jewish people's identification, wherever they may be, and its extensive activity among the Jews of the USSR along with its active involvement in the struggle for their rights had a significant impact on this awakening.

Dissemination of information by Israel in the USSR is well deserving of thorough research. Here we will limit ourselves to the presentation of a general description of Israel's significance in the process of the national awakening of the Jews in the USSR.

THE ISRAELI EMBASSY IN MOSCOW

In contradistinction to all other places in the West, Israel's official presence in the USSR was uniquely significant. A. Harel, Israel's Ambassador in Moscow from 1959 to 1962, noted in his concluding report:

> The mere fact that an Israeli Embassy exists in Moscow, that Israel's flag is hoisted on one of the buildings in the center of the USSR, that the official Embassy car with its flag can reach the remotest town in the USSR ...The mere fact that a handful of people live in Moscow – Israeli diplomats who speak Hebrew among themselves, teaching their children in this language – forged emotional, sentimental and national influence, so deep and so far-reaching that few 'active activities' could have achieved such a range of influence. Starting with the Rosh Hashana (Jewish New Year) days of 1948, when Golda [Meir] met with tens of thousands of

171

>Moscow Jews at the outskirts of the Great Synagogue, to the
>crowding of dozens of Jewish children around the children of
>the Israeli Embassy on the Black Sea or Baltic beach, year
>after year, there is an unbroken chain of experiences that
>demonstrate the deep and powerful influence of the mere
>existence of the Israeli Embassy in Moscow. It is almost
>impossible to describe to those who haven't witnessed these
>experiences the enormous national value of a meeting
>between Jews in the USSR and official representatives of
>Israel.[5]

The presence of the Israeli Embassy in Moscow happened to be for
the Jews in the USSR living proof of realization of the Zionist idea,
the re-emergence of the Jewish State, in the Land of Zion, and a
living testament to the existence of an independent Jewish people
with whom Soviet Jewry shared deep historical links and a common
sense of destiny.

For the USSR the Israeli diplomat was one of the most coura-
geous among all foreign representatives in establishing contacts
and connections with local Jews. This stoked the anger of Soviet
authorities, who were in any case disturbed by the very existence of
an official Israeli representation in their midst, since this symbolized Jewish independence and the victory of Zionism over its
ideological enemies.

The activities of the Israeli Embassy, in the Jewish domain, included:

1. *Contacts with synagogues.* This contact became institutionalized,
over the course of time, and served as a natural link between Israel
and the 'religious Jewish communities' in the USSR. Through this
association the synagogues received ritual objects, prayer books,
prayershawls. A formal and permanent contact was established with
the directors of the synagogues, who were compelled to report to the
authorities on their encounters with Israeli representatives and to
serve at the same time as liaison officers between the Israeli representatives and the directorate of the synagogues. The representatives
used to go, on a regular basis, to the synagogues on Saturdays and
(Jewish) holidays and forge around themselves an atmosphere of a
mutual national link. When the service in the synagogue was over,
they used to speak with the worshipers' as far as circumstances
permitted, about Israel and the situation of the Jews in the USSR.

The holiday of Simchat Torah (Rejoicing of the Law) became a Jewish national mass holiday. Hundreds, even thousands, used to crowd together in front of the Moscow Great Synagogue, and Israeli representatives would mingle with them teaching them Hebrew songs and dances and conducting 'seminars' on Israel. The proportion of youngsters was very high. And the size of the crowd in front of the synagogue grew from year to year. These contacts were of great importance as a source of national inspiration and encouragement.

2. *Links with the Jewish intelligentsia.* Over the course of the years Embassy contacts with the Jewish intelligentsia and scientists, economists, writers and artists increasingly expanded. These encounters stirred Jewish consciousness in these circles and inspired them to search for the roots of their national belonging. In the course of time, these circles were the seedbeds for the Jewish activists who devoted themselves to national activity among Jews drawing many other Jewish youngsters into involvement in their activities.These circles used to receive written information from the Embassy about Israel and the history of the Jewish people, passing it on from one to another, and at times even making dozens of copies.

3. *Visits to Jewish centers.* Representatives of the Embassy paid scores of visits to Jewish centers throughout the Soviet Union. The purpose of these visits was: to become acquainted with the situation of the Jews in the USSR; to inform them about Israel, Jewish communities in the Diaspora, and the struggle for their rights, thus demonstrating the mutual link between Israel and the Jews of the USSR.

The following is a description of one of those many visits taken from a report by Y. Avidar, Israel's Ambassador in Moscow, after his visits to Minsk, Kharkov, Kiev, Gomel, Oriole, Poltava, Czernigov, and Bobroisk at the end of September 1955.

> The news of our arrival in each of the cities that we visited spread around among the Jews at unbelievable speed, stimulating curiosity and great interest. No doubt the car flying the Israeli flag was the first drawing card and significantly helped in passing around the news of our arrival and setting off the search for establishing contact with us. Everywhere we stopped, we were immediately surrounded by many people, some of them non-Jews, the majority Jews, who had

the courage to enter into a conversation, to ask for a Hebrew newspaper. Some of them were afraid of approaching us; they would stare at us and only listen to our conversations.

The most wonderful thing that distinguished itself in our contacts with Jews of Ukraine and Belorussia was the power of national and Zionist awareness and the yearning for Israel that were expressed openly, among the Jews – including youngsters – who had never learned a Hebrew letter and had not been influenced by Zionist propaganda. These were people born during the Soviet regime, students and graduates of its colleges, ex-military officers, laborers, craftsmen, drivers, workers in governmental commerce and in other professions.[6]

Many of Israel's official representatives who had made similar tours throughout the USSR, gathered the same experience. The results of these encounters flowed in two directions. The Israelis would instill within the local Jews good hope, while they themselves were encouraged by the 'strength of national consciousness' pulsating in the hearts of the Jews.[7]

EXHIBITIONS AND ISRAELI ARTISTS IN THE USSR

We have already noted that Israel's presence at international events held in the USSR was of great national and informational importance for the local public, particularly the Jews, who used to flock to them *en masse*. At these events, Israeli representatives – from the diplomatic staff and special representatives who came especially to attend these events – used to lecture about Israel's problems and achievements, correcting the negative image depicted in the Soviet press and distributing informative material on Israel relating in particular to that specific event.

ISRAELI TOURISTS

Significant importance is to be attributed to the Israeli tourism that started to reach the USSR, wave after wave, stretching from the beginning of the 1960s to the rupture of relations between the two countries in June 1967. The main purpose of this tourism was meeting with relatives who had been separated from each other for many years. At these meetings Israeli tourists were able to tell both adults and youngsters in their families about themselves and their experience of living in Israel. This tourism symbolized more than anything else the links between the Jews in the USSR and those in Israel and in the Diaspora.

KOL ZION LAGOLA (THE VOICE OF ZION TRANSMISSIONS TO THE USSR BY ISRAEL'S BROADCASTING AUTHORITY)

An informative and educational incentive unparalleled in its influence was Kol Zion Lagola, with its Russian, Yiddish, and Hebrew transmissions to the USSR. In addition to editions of the news, broadcast several times a day, these transmissions included regular programs such as: *The Week in Review*, economic surveys, assessments and political interpretations of a non-polemical nature regarding the USSR, current information on scientific institutions, scientific and technological achievements, the history of the Jewish people, episodes in the history of Zionism and the Jewish settlement in Palestine, education, culture and art, music, theater and events occurring in the Jewish world. The Hebrew programs included the study of Hebrew, the Bible and Hebrew songs.[8]

We do not possess precise statistics on the scale of listeners in the USSR to Israel's broadcasts. However, the assumption is that many listened to the Israeli transmissions'[9] which in the course of time became a reliable source of inspiration and reinforcement for national consciousness among Jews in the USSR.

CONCLUSION

The success of Israel's activities not only undermined Soviet theory on the solution of the National Problem in a communist regime, but might have constituted a threat in the form of the spread of nationalist currents among the Ukrainians, Belorussians, Estonians, Latvians and Lithuanians, whose nationalism was high in their consciousness. The Soviet fear of the upsurge of these currents apparently stemmed from concern about the integrity of the USSR.

This, perhaps, is the explanation for the Soviets' sensitivity about Israel's information activities, which at times prompted irrational angry reactions and led Israeli–Soviet relations to an ideological confrontation. Since this sensitivity developed within a conscious-ness replete with anti-Semitic overtones, the clash led to a harsh form of enmity towards Israel and its representatives in the USSR.

NOTES

1 See Sh. Ettinger's Hebrew essay, 'The National Awakening of the Jews in the USSR', *Parshiot* 33 (1972).
2 M. Namir, *Mission to Moscow*.
3 Y. Gilboa, *The Black Years of Soviet Jewry* (Hebrew) (Tel Aviv: Am Hasefer, 1972).
4 See, for example: M. Azbel,'An Autobiography of a Jew' (Hebrew) and A. Voronel,'The immigration of Soviet Intelligentsia' (Hebrew), in *The Jewish Intelligentsia in the USSR* (Hebrew), Tel Aviv, March 1976; also,'The Search for Jewish Identity in Russia', in *Soviet Jewish Affairs*, Vol. 5, No. 2 (1975), pp. 69–74.
5 MFA. Arch. File 103.1 SSR.
6 Report of the Israeli Ambassador to Moscow, 4 Oct. 1955, MFA. Arch. File 103.1 SSR.
7 Ben Ami (pseudonym of Lova Eliav, former First Secretary of Israel's Embassy in Moscow), *Between the Hammer and Sickle: Personal Experience amongst Soviet Jews* (Hebrew) (Tel Aviv: Am Oved, 1965).
8 Based on detailed programs of the Russian and Hebrew transmissions distributed for the information of Israel's Embassies abroad, 17 Sept. 1964. MFA. File 351.1 SSR.
9 L. Eliav's report of 14 Oct. 1958 following his visits to Kutaisi, Tbilisi, and Baku, 22 Sept. – 1 Oct. 1958, noted:

> In Tbilisi, Kutaisi and Baku we talked with many Jews who related that they were listening to Kol Israel Lagola. The transmissions are well received, clearly and without disturbances. Listeners told us about programs they follow during all hours, day and night, and according to what they reported, the Voice of Israel could be picked up on medium wave lengths with any ordinary receiver. Jews listen to Kol Zion Lagola on short wave but prefer, in this area, to listen to Kol Israel.

An additional report by Eliav on 16 Feb. 1959 following his visits to Ukrainian towns – Kurostan, Zhitomir, Berdichev, Vinitsa – noted:

> We talked in these towns with hundreds of Jews, mainly in the synagogues, but not only there. We talked with Jews whom we encountered on the train, in restaurants, hotels, cinemas, theaters, streets, barbershops, etc. We learned, without any doubt, that the full majority of people with whom we talked were listening to Israel's radio transmissions. Since this sampling seems to us a representational one not only quantitatively but also

qualitatively from the point of view of age, social status, and so on, it seems to me that our assumption is justified about the large part, and perhaps the decisive part, of the Jewish communities in the USSR who are clinging to the radio, listening, if not every evening, than regularly, to Israel's voice ...

In each town that we reached many Jews told us the previous day's news. Jews listen to all languages. They also try – without much success – to receive the radio transmissions. They listen (particularly the elderly ones) to the Hebrew transmissions. A lot of people listen to the Russian transmissions, which are still not disturbed, and there are people who even listen to European languages which they understand ...

... Listening to Kol Zion Lagola turns out to be unimaginably important for Soviet Jewry in general and for those in towns, even the remotest ones, who have no alternative.

It is not to be ignored that around these broadcasts gather circles or groups of listeners who establish links between themselves.

Following these visits it became clear to us – something we have been sensing for a number of months – that the transmissions are one of the most useful and strongest arms that we possess in the war for the social and spiritual existence of Soviet Jewry.

10 · The struggle on behalf of Jews in the USSR

THE FIRST public struggle on behalf of Jews in the USSR took place against the background of the 'Doctors' Plot'. This effort was characterized by the severe reaction of Israel's government and the Knesset, aimed at expressing the angry reaction of Israel's people to the news of the plot, and by the mobilization of world public opinion to bring about a retraction of the plot allegations and the cessation of the harsh anti-Semitic campaign conducted at the end of Stalin's era against the Jews in the USSR and Jews in the world at large. The struggle on behalf of Soviet Jews was unique in the sense that it was the first time a debate on this subject took place in the Knesset, and the issue was put on the agenda of the UN General Assembly as an unyet resolved international problem.[1]

True, the struggle was centered on the 'Doctors' Plot', but it exposed publicly, for the first time, the situation of the Jews in the USSR, calling upon the USSR to put an end to its anti-Semitic policy, to grant the Jews living within its borders the same rights as those enjoyed by its other national minorities, and to enable those who wished to do so to emigrate to Israel. The struggle subsided, following the Soviet government's announcement about the invalidation of the alleged 'Plot' attributed to Jewish doctors, who were accused of attempting to poison Stalin, and after its condemnation of the anti-Semitic manifestations in the USSR. The resumption of Israeli–Soviet diplomatic relations in 1953 also played a role in the cessation of the battle. It was a relatively short halt, since the struggle was renewed towards the end of 1955, when it became clear that there

178

was no substantial improvement in the Soviet Jews' status, in spite of the thaw after Stalin's death, and that the danger threatening the destruction of their national future had not yet passed.

In 1954 the US Congress in Washington pursued activity – the first of its kind – (not initiated by Israel), aimed at condemning Soviet policy toward the Jewish nationality. This activity was part of a campaign aimed at condemning the Communist regime in the USSR and in the east European countries. The Congressional Committee on Communist Aggression listened to hearings of non-Zionist Jewish organizations aimed at convincing the American public of their opposition to Communism, partly because of the persecution of Jews and their oppression in the USSR and east Europe. The Committee discussed a wide range of subjects related to the Jews in the USSR and east Europe, in the past and the present, particularly the elimination of Jewish culture and Jewish institutions, persecution of Jewish religion, the pursuit of an anti-Semitic policy and assimilation by force. The hearings, debates and evaluations were compiled in a House of Representatives report[2], which must have drawn public attention to the problem.

Israel's Ministry of Foreign Affairs had not asserted any official stance on those debates, presumably for fear that the Soviet Union would accuse Israel of assisting the USA in conducting an anti-Soviet propaganda campaign through Jewish organizations in the USA, though they were known for being non-Zionist.[3]

In the years 1954/55 the voices of various personalities and public organizations were heard in Israel forcefully demanding a worldwide struggle for the sake of Jews in the USSR.[4] Frequent news from the USSR was received in Israel regarding the physical and spiritual distress of the Jews and their expectations that Israel and the Jews of the world would act on their behalf.

In this atmosphere, on 10 August 1955, there met with Prime Minister D. Ben Gurion: S. Avigur, one of the heads of Mossad le-Aliyah Bet (the authority in charge of the 'illegal' immigration of Jews from Europe to Palestine, under the British Mandate) and Director of Nativ (the authority operating under the auspices of Israel's Foreign Ministry in charge of matters of *aliya*, the immigration to Israel of Jews from the USSR and east European countries – under Soviet domination) and Foreign Minister M. Sharett. They were to discuss the destiny of Jews in the USSR and of ways saving them. Both felt that the Jews of the USSR were destined to spiritual destruction and that only 'an increase in immigration could save them'. The question which Avigur and Sharett posed to Ben Gurion and to themselves was: 'Hasn't the time come to raise the problem full blast and with publicity in the international arena?' Both thought that the present timing was suitable, since 'the thaw between the eastern and Western blocs was increasingly' and under such circumstances it would be inappropriate for a new order of international relations to be established, and for an honest regime of co-existence be formed, without a solution to the Jewish problem'. Their conclusion was that the time had come to 'create a huge fuss' in the Western press over the distress of Jews in the USSR, assuming that the Soviet leaders, aspiring to peaceful co-existence, would be sensitive to public opinion and to their image in the West, which could be influenced by Western criticism of their policy towards Jews – 'deprivation of basic rights and oppression of feelings of nationality'.[5]

Ben Gurion agreed, in principle, with their position. The session of the Zionist Executive Council which convened in Jerusalem on 23 August 1955 discussed this issue – with the active participation of Ben Gurion and Sharett – and its resolutions called for the renewal of contacts between Jews in the USSR and Jews in the rest of the world as well as for recognition of the right of the Jews in the USSR to immigrate to Israel.[6] These resolutions were the signal to begin the struggle on behalf of the Jews in the USSR. Ben Gurion's and Sharett's personal involvement was proof of the importance which the highest political level in Israel attached to this matter.

INITIAL ORGANIZATION OF THE STRUGGLE

Following the resolutions of the Zionist Executive Council, and upon the instructions of Foreign Minister Sharett, a senior team from the Ministry held a series of discussions in the second half of August 1955, which were summed up in a decision 'to start a [world-wide] campaign for the sake of the Jews in the USSR and east European countries'. The decision-makers, headed by Sharett, regarded the campaign as an assignment demanding continuous effort over a long period of time 'being aware of its historical significance'.

On 5 September 1955 Israel's Ministry of Foreign Affairs instructed its missions abroad to start the campaign, and in doing so laid the foundations for a protracted and continuous struggle on behalf of the Soviet Jews' rights, by setting up the norms of its conduct, its ideological justification, and the political and informational means for reaching its goals.[7] The opening of the campaign was based on two major assumptions, namely:

The Soviet Union after Stalin was interested in the relaxation of the confrontation between the Eastern and Western blocs. Since Western politicians were suspiciously inclined towards the Soviet Union (as a result of the cold war), it was presumed that its leadership would invest much effort in gaining recognition for its true intentions. Hence, the Soviet Union would be dependent upon public opinion in the West, where the Jewish factor had significant weight.

The sensitivity of the Soviet Union to its positive image in the West opened an opportunity for influencing the Jewish-policy makers in the USSR, through Western public opinion, to improve the situation of the Jews in its territory. The interest of public opinion in the situation of the Jews in the USSR, and their harassment by the Soviet authorities, could in the view of the Foreign Minister, have motivated the Soviet Union to bring about an improvement in the social, national and cultural status of the Jews.

The authors of the instructions did not mention the assumption (though they were probably aware of it) of the unwillingness of the USSR Jews to assimilate within the Soviet population by force, nor did the authors note the aspirations of the Jews to maintain contacts with the Jewish world, including Israel. The avoidance of mentioning this assumption was probably based on three reasons: (a) Israel did not have the authority to represent Soviet Jewry in acting in its name; (b) the appearance of Israel acting on behalf of Soviet Jewry could have encountered fierce opposition from the USSR – under the pretext that Israel was interfering in the internal affairs of other States; (c) the fear that it might cause harm to Soviet Jewry as the Soviet authorities could have accused them of co-operating with those conducting this campaign. Therefore, the authors of the instructions used the pretext of the link with the Jews in the USSR, saying that Israel and world Jewry did not intend to give up their connections with an important part of the nation – Soviet Jewry; thus, the activity was not being initiated by Soviet Jewry, nor in its name.

Defining the aims of the campaign

1. Soviet Jewry should decide freely for itself about the expression it wants to give its Jewishness and the way it organizes itself.
2. Soviet Jewry will be given the right to come into contact with Jewish communities in other States, as they are part of the Jewish world.
3. The right of Soviet Jewry to immigrate to and maintain a direct relationship with Israel should be assured.

The ideological justification

1. For the State of Israel the question of maintaining free relations with every Jewish community in the world is a vital issue. Therefore, the State of Israel is obliged, when asserting the essence of its international relations, to take into consideration whether the Jews in the world are permitted to come into contact with Israel and participate in its development.
2. The situation of the Jewish people is not like that of other nations whose existence is assured. The Jews are a small nation; every loss of a member endangers its very existence. The absence of relations between Soviet Jewry and other parts of the Jewish people throughout the world is a heavy blow to its existence. The question, therefore, of contact between Jews in the USSR and the rest of the Jewish people is a basic problem. Contact means a strong co-operative relationship on every vital subject that might secure the physical and spiritual existence of the Jewish people. This relationship includes the participation of Soviet Jews in the consolidation of the State of Israel as a secure shelter for the Jewish people. Israel's concern is directed not only at the prevention of anti-Semitism, but also to the return of a vital part of the nation to its bosom, essential to the existence of the entire Jewish people.

'This argumentation', the authors of the instructions from the Ministry of Foreign Affairs asserted, 'comes to explain why the

Jewish people cannot keep silent in face of Soviet Jewry's status within the entire nation and to clarify the uniqueness of the Jews' struggle for their national existence.'

This statement on the uniqueness of the problem was intended to contradict the argument, if and when it were raised, that the interference of Israel and world Jewry in the internal affairs of the USSR could be harmful to the advancement of the peaceful co-existence process between the Eastern and Western blocs.

The norms in conducting the struggle

Three limitations were asserted in the struggle:

1. To avoid any incitement against the Soviet Union.
2. To avoid the creation of an impression that Israel intended to disturb the international effort to achieve a relaxation of the confrontation between the two blocs, by pursuing a policy of incitement against the USSR.
3. Non-exposure of Israel as the initiator and organizer of the campaign.

The means to achieve the goals

Israel's missions abroad were requested to act in accordance with the following guidelines:

Raise the problem in talks with representatives of the USSR, East European and Western countries.

Motivate the leaders of Jewish organizations towards systematic activity (in accordance with the resolution of the Zionist Executive Council), in direct appeals on this matter to the politicians of their home countries and to their local Soviet representatives.

Organize Jewish delegations and senior representatives of organizations to visit the USSR and meet with Jews, to collect information about them and to conduct talks with the Soviet leaders.

Devote special attention to the Jewish press, in increasing its awareness regarding the problem.

Gain access to known non-Jewish personalities who influence local public opinion on international matters.

Brief personalities who intend to visit the USSR to show interest in their talks with their Soviet interlocutors in the situation of the Jews in the USSR, particularly in the case of government missions.[8] Encourage important writers and journalists in Western countries to visit the USSR with the aim of becoming interested with this subject.

The organizational basis

Each mission was requested to appoint a diplomat from its staff who would take care of the subject. In Israel, the East European Division of the Ministry of Foreign Affairs was to co-ordinate the activity on the topic, while copies of the reports were to be sent to the senior team who worked out the program of the campaign.

Assessing the campaign's chances of success

In summing-up the instructions, it was said: 'We are not confident that the efforts will be successful. Yet, we are obliged to try out all possibilities.' Jewish unity on this issue was assessed as a good guarantee for its success.

To sum up

Calling this action by the name 'campaign' may indicate the intention to try it out for a limited period of time, until conclusions could be reached from its results. Three unanswered questions faced those who planned the action:

1. How would the Jewish world react in the Western countries, who did not bear the brunt of the problem in a way it was felt in Israel. Would Israel succeed in mobilizing them for this campaign? This should have been a top priority assignment, since without the unity and identification of the Jewish world with this mission, it would not be possible to secure the success of the campaign.
2. How would the USSR react to this campaign? On the one hand, it was necessary to neutralize the USSR by using careful tactics of a non-provocative nature. On the other, it should have been ensured that the Jewish and non-Jewish pressure in the Western countries

would be sufficiently effective to secure an appropriate Soviet response in the improvement of the situation of the Jews in the USSR and the east European countries under its domination.

3. Would the non-Jewish world co-operate in the achievement of these goals which were entirely strange to them? Would it accuse Israel that, by turning this issue into an international problem, it intended to undermine the basis on which hope was founded for strengthening the process of relaxation of tension between the eastern and Western blocs?

The Ministry supplied information – as much as it possessed – on the situation of the Jews in the USSR, to show the background to and intentions behind the definition of the three aims of the campaign, and in particular the first one, which strove for the granting of nationality rights to the Jewish minority promised in accordance with the USSR's constitution, on equal status to the rest of the nationalities in the USSR.

Fixing the timing for issuing the campaign's instructions attested to the considerations, based on appropriate political circumstances, which made it possible to start the campaign with a small chance of success. In the political circumstances prior to the chosen time, no chance to succeed could have been expected at all.

The only avenue to which Israel had access for conducting the struggle was world and Jewish public opinion, which in those days – before Stalin's crimes and the murder of Jewish writers had been exposed – was quite removed from being able to absorb the subject. Hence, the fears about support from world opinion were justified. When those two events became known publicly, Israeli access to world public opinion became easier and the understanding of the problem was quicker. But even then, without constantly nourishing public opinion the campaign would not have achieved the range of its results.

INSTITUTIONALIZATION OF THE STRUGGLE

Lessons of the campaign in its first year of activities

A first biannual report, which summarized the development of the campaign's activities, assessed[9] that important achievements were gained in the domain of the spread of information and the

185

establishment of contacts with people who had influence on public opinion. In the majority of cases, it was noted in the report, Israel encountered understanding for its demand for the granting of 'the right of self-determination to Jews as regards their national life' and the need 'to raise the voice [of world public opinion]' on their behalf. Also the demand for the right to immigrate to Israel was regarded as natural and justified by those who were informed about the plight of Soviet Jews. At times some doubts were heard as to whether the Soviet regime would accede to the demands might give in. But, after the exposure of Stalin's crimes and the changes introduced in the internal processes of the USSR, following the 20th Congress of the CPSU, it was easier to convince people that there was indeed a chance for a positive change in the status of the Jews and that the efforts made on their behalf were founded and justified.

The main problem which the activists encountered with their interlocutors was the absence of information on the situation of the Jews in the USSR. With the exception of the Prague Trials and the 'Doctors' Plot,' almost nothing had been published in the world press about the life, destiny, and aspirations of the Jews in the USSR. Hence, a realistic description of their situation, free of hostility, was well received with understanding as regards the difference between the process of assimilation by choice and the oppression of any national manifestation.

The author of the report recommended continuation of the struggle on two fronts: (1) by reaching the Jews in the USSR and East European countries through all possible ways, with the aim 'of establishing and preserving relations with them, by encouraging their national awakening as a means of pressure and objection to evil plots against them, to being isolated, silenced and annihilated by assimilation'; (2) by making an informational effort in the Western countries following the outlined aims of the campaign to activate free public opinion as a means of pressuring the USSR.

His final conclusion was that 'only internal awakening and external pressure are capable of moving the Soviet regime towards revising its stance concerning the Jews'.

Foreign Minister Sharett, in his survey to Israel's missions abroad, summarized the first year of activities of the campaign by asserting:

1. The assumption that the new Soviet government is looking for a way to world public opinion turned out to be true. Also, the assumption that the Soviet government is seriously weighing the Jewish factor in this respect was verified. There are clear proofs that the campaigning actions have had a considerable effect on the Soviet government. It is a fact that the Soviet government tried to portray during the current year that there has been a turnabout in stance concerning the Jewish question in the USSR.

We knew very well, that there were some pseudo-facilitations, such as permitting the printing of a prayer book, permission given to open a new rabbinical institute as well as the performance of several Yiddish concerts, and so on. We paid attention to the fact that the Soviet government had issued during this year, several times, press releases to the foreign press in an attempt at convincing public opinion that the Jews in the USSR enjoy equality of rights in the domain of cult and culture. We found it necessary, of course, to remind our missions abroad that these were pseudo-accommodations, which do not deserve serious consideration. The fact, however, that the Soviet government found it necessary to act in this way proves that the campaigning actions were wise and useful. One of the most important results was that the Soviet government felt it was necessary to permit some Jewish delegations from abroad to visit the USSR and to come into contact with Jews. The psychological results of these delegations' visits were not imaginary, though it is possible that the Soviet Union believed that it would exploit these visits for its own benefit. For a very long time there had not been such a rich and blessed year in direct contacts between Soviet Jewry and world Jewry.

2. Information that has reached us during this year has also proved that our assumptions about a positive awakening among the Jews in the USSR have turned out to be true.

It is said that the number of Jews in the USSR, according to the official Soviet census, is estimated at three million. It is clear that such a large Jewish community has a variety of attitudes. The main thing is, however, that there are sufficient proofs that within this large Jewish community there are circles, including young ones, whose interest in Judaism is very dear to them, and their interest in Israel is very close to their hearts. On the various occasions that we had this year for contact between Jews outside Russia and Jews inside it, we learned that a considerable part of Russian Soviet Jewry is awaiting any opportunity to demonstrate, even openly, its Jewish loyalty and its spiritual relationship with Israel. As a result of actions taken this year, the future of the Jews in the USSR appeared once again on the agenda of the Jewish people. Slowly, slowly, people are being successfully convinced that Soviet Jewry is continuing to struggle for its existence and future as an integral part of the whole [Jewish] nation.

3. There were various proofs during the course of the year that it was quite possible to interest non-Jews in this problem, and to make them test the sincerity of the Soviet government. It is interesting that, although the question of the USSR's involvement in the Middle East was primarily on the agenda, there were non-Jews who were prepared to deal especially with the Jewish question in the USSR. The stand of H. Gaitskell (leader of the British Labour Party), the French Socialists, Prime Ministers of Sweden and Norway, various non-Jewish journalists and Christian clergy of various countries – all of them proved that it was possible to bring the issue to the non-Jewish world, and that such informational activities were fruitful. There is no doubt that this year, for the first time in many years, the Soviet government has been given to understand, from many and various quarters, that the world was not prepared to remove the Jewish Question in the USSR from the agenda, and that if it wants to conquer hearts in the Western countries, it will have to give a rather convincing answer to the Jewish Question.

Foreign Minister Sharett concluded this part of his survey by saying: 'On the basis of this experience we now have to plan the second year of actions in the struggle for the sake of Jews in the USSR.'

In continuation Foreign Minister Sharett specified further campaign assessments aimed at deepening and expanding Israel's informational efforts on behalf of Jews in the USSR through world public opinion. Referring to the degree of Israel's exposure in the campaign's actions, Sharett noted:

The question raised during this year was as to whether Israel's diplomatic missions should act in a direct manner. In each country, obviously, the Mission would try to act through local people, Jews and non-Jews. They will pass on information to the Mission and will be the carriers of our informational explanations. But, even if a Mission were to reach such an ideal situation, it should be clear that without the Mission's permanent surveillance – including all the members of its staff – such people would not be found. Even then, when such people are found, members of the Mission will always have to look for appropriate occasions to expand the sweep of informational explanation by meeting new people and briefing them. In countries where such people are not to be found, members of the Mission should not hesitate to be themselves the bearers of the campaign, of course following all rules of discretion.

When the campaign started a year ago, we remarked and stressed that we have to be very watchful that this campaign not serve anti-Soviet objectives. The debate concerns only the status and future of the Jews in the USSR. We have no interest in giving any activity in the framework of this campaign an anti-Soviet character.[10]

In conclusion, the accumulated experience in the first year of the struggle seemed to have justified its initiation and establishment as a long struggle which would continue until the majority of the demands were met.

Sharett's perception, however, regarding the degree of Israel's exposure in the process of the campaign showed clearly that it was not the intention of Israel's government to enter into an open confrontation with the USSR on this subject, so as not to be exposed as an anti-Soviet factor. The institutionalization of the struggle and its dynamic development could not have maintained this delicate balance for very long. (After all, it was impossible to speak publicly and constantly about national oppression and the 'closed gates' barring Jews in the USSR who wish to immigrate to Israel without criticizing the regime which was pursuing those policies.) Therefore, it was unavoidable that this struggle would lead to an open Israeli–Soviet confrontation, even if there was no such an intention.

The organizational basis

The volume of the constantly increasing activities necessitated the establishment of a governmental apparatus for their implementation. This was set up towards the end of 1955 with the name of BAR under the auspices of the Ministry of Foreign Affairs. Conditions of its operations were secret, and its workers were, to a degree, anonymous persons. Its main tasks were:

Implementation of the policy struggle (asserted by a joint committee: Foreign Ministry, Zionist Organisation, World Jewish Congress). In the course of time the apparatus became an autonomous authority, with a strong link to the Foreign Ministry which meant: centralization, briefing, and controlling of informational activities in the Western countries.
Maintaining direct contact with its representatives who began to act in different world centers.
Mr Shaul Avigur was appointed director of this apparatus. He thus united this division with the one responsible for activity among Jews in Eastern Europe, for which he was also responsible.

In the course of time the apparatus become larger and wider ranging, in Israel and abroad. Its functions and authority were also extended with the spreading of the struggle in its two tasks: dealing with the Jewish subject at Israel's missions abroad, and leading the struggle for the sake of Jews in the USSR.

Motives of the struggle

The first memorandum from Israel's government about the situation of Jews in the USSR and the need to resolve it reached the Soviet leaders through Burma's Prime Minister U Nu in October 1955.

The memorandum, written by Foreign Minister Sharett on 10 October 1955, was transmitted to U Nu as background material, for his own perusal, acquainting him with the subject. U Nu was requested to raise the cause of Jews in the USSR in his talks with Soviet leaders in Moscow. Out of naivety U Nu handed over the memorandum to his interlocutors in Moscow. Thus, Soviet leaders received a detailed memorandum on the subject, without it being addressed to them.[11]

In this memorandum, Sharett surveyed, the plight of Jews in the

USSR, underlining the danger of cultural annihilation, with the threat of being disconnected from Jews in the Diaspora and Israel, and no opportunity to maintain a communal forum of their own aimed at preserving Jewish values and educating the young generation accordingly. All this, not because of an anti-Jewish policy pursued by the Soviet government, but as a result of the Soviet regime's influence on the life of the Jewish community. Other minorities in the USSR – mentioned in the memorandum – were enjoying their national life in the USSR but this was not the case with the Jews. Therefore, the Soviet government was requested to grant the Jews in the USSR threefold permission:[12]

(a) to live a Jewish life according to their historic heritage;
(b) to let those Jews who wished to do so immigrate to Israel;
(c) to allow free connections between the Jews of the USSR and the Jews of the rest of the world.

Unwittingly U Nu exposed Israel as trying to persuade high ranking personalities to raise the Jewish cause in their political talks with Soviet leaders. Hence the USSR was conscious, even at the first stage of the struggle on behalf of the Jews in the USSR, that the noise over the deprivation of their rights originated from Israel.

Faithful to the policy which he undertook, Sharett used in this memorandum relatively restrained language without accusing the USSR of pursuing an international anti-Jewish policy. This attitude was characteristic of the first stage of the struggle, namely: avoiding a direct or indirect confrontation with the USSR. Despite that the Soviet leaders reacted angrily. They totally rejected the description of the situation of the Jews in the USSR followed by Israel's demands, accusing Israel – according to U Nu – of interference in the USSR's internal affairs.[13]

On 25 April 1956 the leadership of the World Jewish Congress presented an official memorandum (the first of its kind) to the Soviet leadership, on the occasion of the State visit to England by the Soviet Prime Minister Marshal Nicolai Bulganin and First Secretary of the Central Committee of the CPSU, Nikita Krushchev. This was the first visit of Soviet leaders to England aimed at demonstrating the USSR's desire for peaceful co-existence with the Western countries. In Israel it was assumed that that this would be a fitting opportunity for the official hosts, the Jewish organizations and public opinion in England to bring up the plight of Jews in the USSR in talks with their official guests, to let them see that a true peace between East and West would not be possible without solving the Jewish question in the USSR.[14]

B. Eliav, special emissary of the Ministry of Foreign Affairs in Jerusalem, left for England to prepare the ground. His activity for the sake of Soviet Jews was of utmost importance.

Following are the main points of argument on which the above memorandum based itself and its principal demands to the Soviet government to improve the status of Jews in the USSR:

Jews throughout the world have a vital concern in peaceful co-operation between states. No other people suffered more than the Jews, proportionally to their numbers, from the two world wars. One third – 6,000,000 – of the entire Jewish people were annihilated by the Nazis.

Equally basic in their faith, tradition and culture is the entity of the Jewish people, who from time immemorial have preserved the deep roots and ties of kinship which unite them. This unity was brought to historic demonstration by the establishment of the State of Israel in 1948, with the USSR's support.

Jews of Russia were for many generations the main source and reservoir of the spiritual, traditional and cultural ideas which have inspired the Jews in their long struggle to survive, and to pursue their way of life.

World Jewry acclaimed the Russian Revolution of 1917 as marking the end of Tsarist anti-Semitic persecution. The Jewish people gained new hope and encouragement from the fact that the constitution of the USSR guaranteed the cultural autonomy of all nationalities and races and made racial hatred and incitement thereto a crime punishable by law. However, Jews in the USSR are cut off, physically and spiritually, from the rest of the Jews throughout the world – this is a source of deepest sorrow and disappointment. Whereas individual freedom and equality of Jews in the USSR are fully recognized, their communal, religious and cultural life have suffered grave deterioration. Jewish sorrow reached a climax at the disappearance of a large number of Jewish writers who, as is known, were executed despite their innocence of any crime.

The World Jewish Congress is convinced that the restraints upon the maintenance of Jewish religious, traditional and cultural life in the Soviet Union are not in conformity with the principles upon which the USSR was founded and upon those enunciated in its constitution, providing for full freedom for ethnic groups to pursue their way of life.

The Congress is convinced that the removal of these restraints and the granting of facilities to the Jews in the USSR to renew and continue their ancestral Jewish life, their religion and their culture, in equality with other ethnic or religious groups, as well as the facility to meet their fellow Jews abroad, would not only be in accordance with justice and democratic freedom, but would also constitute a major contribution to the cause of international peace, good will and understanding, which the USSR had demonstrated its desire to achieve.

'In the spirit of the foregoing considerations' the World Jewish Congress requested the government of the USSR to give its approval to the following facilities and opportunities to be granted to the Jews in the USSR:

1. To pursue their religious and cultural life and to that end, to establish and maintain their religious, scholastic, cultural and artistic institutions and organizations.
2. Printing and distribution of religious literature and the publication of Jewish writers and scholars on Jewish subjects and of Jewish periodicals in Russian, Yiddish and Hebrew.
3. Communication and interchange of views on matters of common Jewish concern between the Jews of the Soviet Union and Jews and Jewish organizations abroad.
4. Reunion of Jews and Jewish families with their relatives in Israel and other countries.

The Jewish Congress also requested to proclaim officially the injustice of the execution of the Jewish writers and to rehabilitate their memory.

This position, as presented in the memorandum, became a pattern or points for argumentation in talks held with representatives of the USSR and or demands to improve the status of Jews in the USSR, mainly in three directions:

1. Their right to enjoy the rights of a national minority, equal to that of the other national minorities in the USSR.

2. The right to maintain contacts with Jewish communities around the world in the same manner as applied to the institutions of the other religions in the USSR which did have open contacts with their counterpart institutions outside the USSR.

3. Their right to be reunited with their families in Israel and throughout the world. This demand was based on the principle of family reunification for those separated during World War II and on Soviet recognition of the Armenians' right to immigrate from abroad to the Soviet Republic of Armenia and on the right of Poles and Germans to repatriation from the USSR to their homelands.

These arguments – whether in full or in part, in detail or in summary – were presented to Soviet representatives in the West, by heads of States, parliamentarians, parliamentary delegations, personalities, writers, Jewish and non-Jewish organizations. As time passed the demand for 'family reunification' was broadened to free immigration to Israel, and added to the package of demands was that the Soviet Union put a halt to its anti-Semitic campaign as expressed in anti-Jewish propaganda literature, in the blood libel of Dagestan in 1969, and in economic trials held in the USSR towards the end of the 1950s and at the beginning of the 1960s.[15]

TACTICS OF THE STRUGGLE

Three fundamental principles of policy were asserted at the beginning of the struggle:

(a) avoiding incitement against the Soviet Union;
(b) separating the issue from the confrontation between the eastern and Western blocs;
(c) non-exposure of Israel as the initiator, or the conductor, of the struggle.

These three principles were vigorously pressed during the period under survey (1953–67). However, a certain devaluation affected them as from 1962, when Israel moved from a stage of non-exposure to a stage of gradual revelation as the leader of the struggle. Here are the stages:

First stage: The mobilization of the Jewish world to a wide, systematic action, while concealing its active part in this initiative. The purpose was to evoke a sensation of anxiety among part of the Jews in the world over the fate of Soviet Jews and a need for urgent action to rescue them.

Second stage: Arousing world opinion (through the communications media), partly by reporting the activities carried out in the past – but not those on the diplomatic level.

Third stage: Persuading Jewish and non-Jewish organizations, parliamentarians, activists of socialist parties and politicians to talk with the leaders of the USSR about the rights of the Jewish minority in their country, to express concern for their fate, to explain that the problem distresses public opinion, and disturbs the climate of *rapprochement* between East and West, and especially perturbs the friends of the USSR in the Western countries. From 1960 there were more frequent official statements on this by representatives of member states in the UN, by high ranking personalities and by international organisations. These statements included a resolution adopted by the Socialist International,[16] Bertrand Russell's letter to Krushchev,[17] a statement by the President of the USA on 28 October 1964,[18] and the Council of Europe's report of 26 January 1965.[19]

Fourth stage: Embarrassing the Soviet leadership by placing it in a defensive position, by recognizing the existence of the problem and the need to find a solution to it.

The importance of the policy stages was to create continuous pressure, from as many directions as possible, to generate at the appropriate political time a shift from the frozen situation of the Jews in the USSR toward some positive action.

TRANSITION FROM A RESTRAINED TONE TO AN AGGRAVATING ONE

The internal discussion

From the beginning of the struggle for the sake of the Jews in the USSR, Nahum Goldmann, President of the World Jewish Congress and President of the World Zionist Organisation, co-operated closely with the organized struggle in Israel. This co-operation was of great importance. For Goldmann's actions, his prestige in the Jewish and non-Jewish world, his statements on behalf of the Soviet Jews in the World Jewish Congress and the World Zionist Organisation as well as his initiative to convene the first conference of intellectuals in Paris on 15 September 1960 – all gave the struggle a universal-Jewish and non-Jewish character.

The conference was held under Goldmann's chairmanship, with the participation of 40 intellectuals and politicians from 14 states who from than onwards played an active role in the struggle. Israel assisted in organizing the conference.

The first rift between Goldmann and the organizers in Israel became discernible, against the tactical background, following the debate on the question of Jews in the USSR held in the United Nations Sub-committee for the Prevention of Discrimination and Defense of Minorities on 12 and 27–28 January 1961. This debate was held on the basis of a complaint made by the co-ordinating committee of Jewish organizations against the policy of discrimination and anti-Semitic manifestations towards the Jewish Minority in the USSR, submitted to the sub-commission and accompanied by documentary material. This was the first debate held on this subject in the United Nations since the beginning of the campaign. Representatives of the US and other countries, all of whom had been briefed in advance by representatives of Israel and Jewish organizations, took an active part in the debate. At the end of the discussion, which created a very important echo in the American media, Goldmann found it necessary to reserve his opinion on the line undertaken in the debate regarding two topics. He expressed his reservations at a press conference which he gave on 8 February 1961 in New York:

1. In his view the USSR did not pursue a policy of discrimination towards the Jews as individuals, but the Jewish minority as such did not enjoy a status equal to that granted to the other minorities in the USSR.
2. Though it was true that anti-Semitism prevailed in the USSR, it would, however, be unjust – in his opinion – to accuse the Soviet government of conducting an anti-Semitic policy. Moreover, this accusation distorted the 'true problem' of Jews in the USSR.

In his letter of 14 February 1961 to Avigur, Goldmann explained his stand, noting:[20]

> I did not deny that anti-Semitism existed in Russia [the USSR], but I did say that we cannot proclaim that Soviet Russia [the Soviet Union] is an anti-Semitic country and I said that the main and most important thing for those for whose sake we are fighting is that the Jewish community [Diaspora] in Soviet Russia [the Soviet Union] be free to live as Jews. I always thought that we agreed upon this line. If not, then we will have to act separately. I will not change this line.
>
> I would have regarded the development of a cold war between the Jewish people and Soviet Russia [the Soviet Union], as a historic disaster, especially, as I am confident that the power of the Communist bloc is constantly growing in comparison to the West. It is bad enough for us that Russia [the USSR] is an anti-Israel power; to make it become an anti-Jewish power would be a big disaster for Russian [Soviet] Jews and a tragedy for the whole Jewish people.

This was a controversy over tactics for the conduct of the struggle and the question of their future implications. In Goldmann's view, accusing the Soviet Union of conducting an anti-Semitic policy was, presumably, a deviation from a line agreed at the beginning of the struggle. He feared, we should think, that the struggle for the rights of the Jews in the USSR would develop into an open confrontation between the Jewish people and the Soviet Union, which the Soviet Union would. There was a reference to this in the reaction by the Soviet Ambassador, Sapozhnikov, in UNESCO, to the complaints of the Jewish organizations submitted to the UN Sub-committee for the Prevention of Discrimination and Defense of Minorities, accusing them of conducting an insidious policy towards the USSR.

In contrast, Israel's leadership probably felt that there was no escape from aggravating the struggle in face of the anti-Semitic manifestations in the USSR accompanied by an anti-Semitic propaganda campaign organized in the press.[21] Still at the beginning of the struggle, Israel's leadership believed that Jewish public unity around the struggle would compel the Soviets to reconsider their policy towards the Jews in the USSR. Goldmann wanted to adhere to the agreed principle and cut a clear limit to the measure of its aggravation, but since the struggle developed according to its own dynamics, whilst new circumstances were created, it was vital, in the opinion of Israel's leadership, to adjust to reality.

Goldmann did not change his stand. He repeatedly warned of the danger in deviating from the basic principles of the struggle. At the end of January 1964 he met with the President of Israel with the participation of the Ministry of Foreign Affairs, Golda Meir, M. Sharett, Sh. Avigur, and A. Eban in order to convey: (a) that he did not agree with the policy of the struggle, which might, in his view, endanger the situation of the Jews in the USSR; (b) that he did not wish to be a partner in conducting such a policy; (c) that he had hopes for direct negotiation with the Soviets; (d) that he wished to convene a world Jewish conference on peace with the participation of delegations from the Soviet Union and Eastern Europe. Under such a conditions it would be possible to maintain official direct links with a Jewish delegation from the Soviet Union.

In the course of the meeting, Goldmann withdrew from the first three positions outlined above, and even from his intention of resigning from the leadership of the struggle. As for his idea about the conference (which was not accepted by Foreign Minister Meir, since she did not believe that the Soviet authorities would permit a Jewish delegation to participate in it), he was determined to convene it, under the condition that a Jewish delegation from the Soviet Union and Eastern Europe would participate in it.[22]

Since this conference did not take place, presumably Goldmann's groping with Soviet representatives lead nowhere. It should not be excluded that an additional reason behind the idea to convene the conference was to manifest before the Soviets the vital interest of the Jewish people in the cause of peace and thus to distinguish between the struggle for the rights of Jews in the USSR and the confrontation between the Eastern and Western blocs.

Even though a rift was avoided at that stage, the differences of opinion still prevailed, whilst the feeling of Israel's leadership towards aggravating the struggle was stronger than that of Goldmann.

Raising the problem of Soviet Jews in international organizations

In July 1966, a team of Foreign Ministry officials convened in Jerusalem to discuss Israel's policy in the United Nations regarding the problem of Soviet Jews, with the participation of Israel's Ambassador in Moscow and other people from the Ministry who were dealing with the organisation of the struggle. The team focused on three questions:

1. What is the usefulness of raising the problem of Jews in the USSR at the United Nations and other international organizations?
2. What content and form should be adopted when dealing with the problem within these frameworks?
3. What has been the effect of the statements made by Israel's representatives within these forums on Israeli–Soviet relations?

On Question One

All participants in the discussion were of the opinion that bringing up the problem in the United Nations and other international organizations, constituted a vital part in the total action and tended to evoke world sympathy for Jews in the USSR. Stopping the campaign, or even pausing, would harm the struggle outside the international arena, since the debate within that framework granted the struggle an international moral dimension.

Whereas in the past representatives of Israel had avoided addressing the subject before international organizations, from 1962 the policy changed (on 29 October Israel's Ambassador addressed, for the first time, ECOSOC in the United Nations), based on the conviction that without Israel's representatives' mobilization in this battle, it would be difficult to persuade representatives of other countries to speak out. Statements made by Israel's representatives came to constitute 'a catalyst for evoking interest in this problem ... and encourages broad actions taken outside the UN ...'.

An assessment was made that after Israel's address in the international area, it could be noted that Soviet sensibility increased, 'either to the mere existence of the problem, or to its manifestations and the necessity to devote to it the utmost attention'. The subject of Soviet Jews found its legitimate place among the general problems debated in the UN on human rights, especially the prevention of racial discrimination. Hence, it was useful to bring up the subject in the international arena; this action therefore should be continued.

On Question Two

1. To strictly avoid the possibility of Israel's action being interpreted 'as assistance extended to factors who are confronting the USSR against the background of cold war', Israel's appearance in the UN should be defined and termed as stemming from a concern oriented exclusively to Jews in the USSR.

2. The aim of any statement should not be a voting contest with the USSR, but the strengthening of international consciousness of the problem. Therefore, it was recommended that having the issue put to the vote should be avoided.

3. In presenting the complaints factual precision should be strictly respected. The wholesale accusation that the USSR was pursuing an anti-Semitic policy would miss the aim. (Echo of Goldmann's stand.)

On Question Three

The team asserted that the fact should not be ignored 'that the criticism voiced by the Israeli representatives about the Soviet Union is making mutual relations difficult and could contribute to their further aggrevation'. However, the team believed that 'the Soviet Union is determining its essential relationship with Israel, and the orientation of its policy in the region, on the basis of considerations fundamentally unrelated to this problem'. The international pestering as a result of the struggle for the rights of Jews in the USSR could – according to the team – inspire the USSR, in the course of time 'to negotiate with Israel, not only to express anger and grievance, but to embark on a constructive dialogue' regarding the means to resolve the problem. Hence, it could be concluded, in its view, that the international annoyance did not only affect mutual relations badly, but could even advance them by a mutual necessity to find a solution to the problem of Jews in the USSR.

The findings and recommendations of the discussion were compiled by Gideon Rafael (Israel's future Ambassador to the UN) and submitted for the perusal of A. Eban, Minister of Foreign Affairs, on 17 July 1966.[23] It seems that the Minister agreed with the team's evaluations and conclusions, which corresponded with the policy of Israeli statements in the course of that year at the United Nations and its organizations.

200

The importance of the conclusions was that Israel's official activities for the sake of Jews in the USSR constituted a useful (and even vital) incentive, in strengthening the world's public consciousness of the matter and in deepening Soviet sensibility to it, and that the Soviet Union's relations towards Israel would not worsen at that stage.

These conclusions had probably influenced Prime Minister Eshkol who, contrary to his prior statements, attacked the USSR in his address in the Knesset, on 12 January 1966, in a sharp tone which clearly symbolized the turn in Israel's tactics in the direction of aggravating the struggle for the sake of Jews in the USSR.[24]

It seems that in asserting its assessments the team based itself on two presumptions:

1. The important goals achieved in the struggle: not only the winning of world public opinion and the support of distinguished politicians, but also the gaining of concessions from the USSR in its policy toward Jews, which was mainly expressed in the gradual increase in exit visas issued to Jews who emigrated to Israel (1965 saw the largest number in emigrants, during the existence of diplomatic relations between the countries).
2. The broadening of bilateral relations in the spheres of culture and tourism, which too reached its peak in 1965.

Hence, the belief that although the struggle was making mutual relations more difficult, it was not the main determining factor. Nevertheless, at the beginning of the 1960s a clear Soviet policy was being noted in the direction of aggravating the political and ideological clash with Israel against the background of the struggle for the sake of Jews in the USSR.

In the United Nations arena

In addition to the USSR's constant support for the Arabs in their conflict with Israel (in consequence of Soviet policy in the Middle East), its representatives on the UN Committee for Human Rights started to attack Israel for its discriminatory attitude toward its Arab minority in answering the complaints of Israel's representatives regarding the discrimination against Jews in the USSR.[25]

We have already mentioned that in 1965 the USSR attempted to condemn Zionism in the same bracket as Nazism in the Third UN Committee. This attempt failed, but after ten years, when it was presented again, it succeeded. It was the first time that Zionism was compared in the international arena to anti-Semitism, Nazism and other racial movements.[26]

In the Soviet internal arena

The USSR opened a constant and systematic campaign to denigrate Israel's social regime, accusing it of exploitation, poverty, hunger, religious law overruling civil law, ethnic gaps, militarism, nationalist fanaticism and a hostile attitude towards immigrants. Though these allegations were directed to deterring Jews from fostering illusions regarding Israel, they did express the USSR's hostility towards Israel, which exceeded that towards any other country in the West.

THE USSR'S REACTION AND ITS IMPLICATIONS ON ISRAELI–SOVIET RELATIONS

The reactions of Soviet leaders to the harassment of journalists, politicians, leaders of socialist parties and emissaries of Jewish organizations were mainly:[27]

There is no Jewish problem in the USSR; anti-Semitism is forbidden; all nationalities in the USSR are equal before the law.
Jews are not interested in educational and cultural institutions of their own as they tend to assimilate into the local population wherever they live.
Jews are not sentenced to harsh punishments because of their national origin but because of their crimes.
Jews occupy, in comparison to other minorities in the USSR, a prominent place in the academic professions. Their striving in this direction is recognized better among them than with others. There were among them collaborators with the Nazis during the German occupation (as there were also among other minorities).
They have no interest in emigrating to Israel, which is a 'capitalist country', servant of American imperialism.

The day will come for those who wish to leave the USSR. Finally, all those who wish to reunite with their families outside the USSR will be able to do so.

The importance of the Soviet reactions, from Israel's point of view, was that they attested to the USSR's sensitivity to its image in the eyes of world public opinion and its attempts to defend itself. The unreliable contents of the Soviet leaders' reactions brought about negative criticism in this respect – especially against Krushchev's anti-Semitic remarks – encouraging the activists to continue with their struggle. The publication in the Soviet press of the Russell-Krushchev exchange of letters served as a source of encouragement for Soviet Jews, as they learned that in large parts of the world extensive activity was being carried out on their behalf.

The harassment diminished the prestige of the USSR which was probably aware of it. This was particularly so among those circles considered progressive by the USSR, such as leftist parties and personalities in culture and thinking. In no other political matter were Soviet leaders so harassed as over the Jewish cause. For the USSR, Israel was one of the main world factors – if not the only one – that was constantly striving to expose the behavior of the Soviet regime towards the Jews in the USSR. Israel was paramount in undermining, in the eyes of the world, the credibility of Soviet declarations on 'fraternity' prevailing in the USSR, emphasizing the gap between Leninist theory and Soviet reality on the national problem.

On the diplomatic and political plane

The Soviet authorities reacted to the international activities of the Israeli Embassy staff in Moscow among the Jews in the USSR in three stages: voicing protests (called verbal announcements) to Israeli Ambassadors in Moscow; defaming Israeli diplomats and discrediting them in the Soviet press; expelling them from the USSR as *personae non grata*.

The protests of the Soviet Ministry of Foreign Affairs referred to 'complaints' made by worshipers that reached the Council for Religious Affairs of the Soviet Prime Minister's Office about 'non-suitable behavior' of the Israeli Embassy staff in Moscow during their visits to synagogues in various towns in the USSR.

Substance of the complaints: Distribution of Israeli printed material, including propaganda brochures from the Jewish Agency; exploiting visits (of Israeli diplomats to various parts of the USSR) for encounters with suspected persons, in order to receive parcels from them and conduct propaganda talks with them.

The protest: The worshipers protested against this behavior 'which insulted their religious feelings'.

The authorities' conclusion: The staff of the Israeli Embassy is visiting the synagogues not for worship but for purposes 'which have nothing to do with praying'.

Warning of the Ministry of Foreign Affairs: Such behavior does not correspond with the known and accepted norms of diplomatic representatives and 'is about to lead to undesired results'.

The protest which the director of the Near Eastern Department of the Soviet Ministry of Foreign Affairs submitted to the Israeli Ambassador in Moscow on 5 September 1958[28] followed a pattern typical of similar protests submitted later on. In due course another complaint was added: an accusation of persuading worshipers to emigrate to Israel.[29] Changes were made to the wording of the complaints: 'propaganda of the Jewish Agency', was replaced with 'anti-Soviet propaganda;[30] 'other purposes of visits' was replaced with 'engaging in underground work;[31] and in place of 'undesired results' was a tone threatening expulsion.

In the introductory words prior to the protest, it was noted 'that this means was chosen in order not to create difficulties', with an additional remark that the 'worshipers' were pressing to publish the affair publicly but it was the Ministry of Foreign Affairs that prevented them from doing so.

Clearly the 'worshipers' were none other than the people of the security services of the USSR (the KGB) who were 'pressing' to publicize the event, whereas the Ministry of Foreign Affairs served, in this respect, as a factor of restraint, so to say, in order not to damage the mutual relations by giving an opportunity to the Israeli Embassy staff to improve its ways. When the security services came to the conclusion that warnings did not help, they then initiated the publication of defaming articles in the press.

This tendency became apparent in 1961, increased during 1964–66, and gradually toned down after the break in Israeli–Soviet relations in the aftermath of the Six Day War, in June 1967.[32] The articles were entitled by disgraceful words, such as: 'Rotten Merchandise under the Dress';[33] 'Israeli Diplomats at Their "Work"';[34] 'Merchants from Israel';[35] 'Presents of Poison';[36] 'Diplomats Taking Off Their Mask';[37] 'Dirty Propaganda from the Cellar';[38] 'Scandal in the Synagogue';[39] and disgrace without titles — 'An Event with the Diplomats in Odessa';[40] 'Another Event with Diplomats in Odessa'.[41]

In the course of time they were accused of conducting poisonous anti-Soviet propaganda and even of espionage. The name of an Israeli diplomat was publicly discredited. He suffered jibes of mockery and insults that no foreign diplomat ever had experienced. The Soviet authorities' arrows of criticism were aimed in two directions: first, at suppressing the national aspirations that evoked among Jews in the USSR whenever they met an official Israeli representative, and second at deterring Israeli diplomats from any contact with Jews in the USSR. And the goal was – to suppress the national common link between Israel and the Jews in the USSR.

Declaring representatives of the Israel Embassy as *personae non grata* was an expression of utmost severity. It was reported in the press, in a short, succinct manner, when the reason for that was 'espionage'. At first Israel's Foreign Ministry reacted in a restrained manner 'so as not to further damage the relations and strain them up to renewing the danger of breach'.[42] But in the course of time, when the declarations of *personae non grata* became frequent, Israel began to counteract by expelling Soviet diplomats. When this displeased the Soviet authorities, they lowered the number of those expelled from the USSR down to zero, and began, in return, to focus mainly on the publication of defaming articles in the press.

It seems that none of the three modes of reaction towards Israel, especially the articles poisonously attacking the Israeli Embassy staff in Moscow, succeeded in deterring Israel from information activity among Jews in the USSR and from the scope of the struggle for their sake. They also did not deter Jews in the USSR from looking for connections and contacts with the Israeli Embassy, in spite of the danger involved in it. The articles, however, gradually caused a deterioration in the relations between the two countries. Israel, though, revealed readiness to go on with the order of the day, being conscious that this was the price for its activity, whereas the Soviet authorities did not display a similar attitude but tended to worsen their relations with Israel in return for its deeds.

In political talks held by the Israeli representatives with the Soviet representatives in Jerusalem, Moscow and in the West, Soviet diplomats repeatedly rejected the accusation of anti-Semitism prevailing in the USSR and condemned the struggle of Israel and the West for the rights of Soviet Jews. In some of the talks they pointed out the negative impact of the struggle on Israeli–Soviet mutual relations.

Following are some of their main comments and warnings:

Israeli–Soviet relations cannot be improved as long as Israel regards Soviet Jews as if they are its own citizens and as long as an anti-Soviet propaganda is being conducted around Jews in the USSR.[43] The main factor separating Israel from the USSR is the Jewish one. The mere idea of Zionism contradicts the fundamental perception of the Soviet Union, which cannot accept the idea that the future of Soviet Jewry is in Israel. The Jews in the USSR are good citizens and they should be allowed to continue their contribution to the Soviet enterprise.

Israel's activities in the USSR (among Jews) and the informational material that it distributes have no other intention but to persuade the Jews that their future is in Israel. The Jews Problem in the USSR arose only after the establishment of the State of Israel. For example, the Jewish Theater in Moscow was closed when it came under considerable Zionist-Israeli influence from Israeli representatives and is not interested in Israel.

The Soviet Union supported the establishment of the State of Israel because it recognized the right of the Jewish population in Palestine to political independence, but it rejects the view that Israel emerged for the sake of the Jews in the rest of the world.[44]

The noise which has been evoked in the USA in the last two years (1962–1964) has convinced the Soviet authorities that the issue is not concern about the situation of Jews in the USSR, but a campaign directed at aggravating the cold war. If the campaign does not stop the Soviet authorities will be compelled to undertake the following counteractions:

(a) recognizing Shukeiry and the PLO;
(b) establishing a Soviet organization for the defense of the rights of Arabs in Israel.[45]

(Referring to this, E. Doron, Director of the East European Division of Israel's Ministry of Foreign Affairs, commented in his memorandum to Foreign Minister A. Eban, on 31 March 1965:

> The Soviet authorities did not recognize Shukeiry and did not invite him to Moscow; not out of love for Israel, not because of hatred for Shukeiry. The basic political line of the USSR is that the United Nations is an organization of sovereign states only. Also, because the Soviet stance does not recognize exiled groups, it seems that the Soviet authorities have interest in Shukeiry and his requests. Should they decide to recognize Shukeiry, it would not be because of Israel's activity for the sake of Jews in the USSR, but because of their political considerations in support of the Arab cause.[46]

When the Director wrote this letter he did not know that a Palestinian delegation would visit Moscow in February 1966.)[47]

Israel should know that its activity on behalf of Jews in the USSR is the main obstacle to the improvement of relations between both countries.[48]

In conclusion, it seems:

(a) Improvement of Israeli–Soviet relations was conditional on Israel's stopping activity for the sake of Jews in the USSR;
(b) The Soviet warnings (until 1966) did not include threats to severe relations with Israel or to aggravate them. However, some counteractions could be possible, such as *rapprochement* with the PLO.
(c) Until 1962, the Soviet authorities believed that Israel's activity together with that of the Jewish organizations stemmed indeed from keen concern about the fate of the Jews in the USSR, but as from this year (during which Israel's representatives in international organizations raised the problem of Jews in the USSR for the first time after the 'Doctors' Plot') this activity began, in the Soviet view,

to be integrated into the anti-Soviet propaganda of the West, which made it difficult for the USSR to come to terms with the West.

In 1966 a considerable worsening was noted in the USSR's attitude towards Israel, against the background of the activities on behalf of Jews in the USSR. First expression of this appears in the angry reaction to Prime Minister Eshkol's speech in the Knesset (12 January 1966) regarding Jews in the USSR. Later, an even angrier response followed the decision by Israel's Ministry of Education and Culture, June–July 1966, to introduce 'a week of identification with Jews in the USSR' during the month of October that year in all schools in Israel. Also, notice should be given to the decision taken by the Soviet authorities to expel an Israeli diplomat from Moscow, as a *'persona non grata'* (as it had stopped doing at the end of the 1950s) as an expression of displeasure and as a warning sign to the Jews). From the point of view of the USSR, the decision to introduce 'the Week' – for the first time in Israel – placed Israel in a public and official manner at the head of the campaign for human rights in the USSR.

The organization of 'the Week' within a state framework – the Ministry of Education and Culture – no doubt added a new dimension to the struggle. It could possibly be that the USSR feared having this pattern copied in other countries, which might mar its image even more among nations.

In the protest submitted by the Soviet Ambassador in Israel to the representative of Israel's Foreign Ministry, he stressed that such an action was interpreted by the USSR as an anti-Soviet act, warning that it could be harmful to mutual relations. It could have been felt that this act upset the Soviet authorities more than any other act. The political commentary on Radio Moscow on 6 July 1966 (published the following day in a summarized form by the BBC) remarked:

> The USSR aspires to develop relations with all countries, but it is important to stress the anti-Soviet campaigns do not contribute to the development of such connections ... Their initiators should act more carefully. They should ask themselves in particular if such acts are in the interest of Israel and its people, since their inevitable result must be a deterioration in relations with the USSR. And who will gain from it?

In 1966 cultural relations between Israel and the USSR ceased, quite a while before the severance of diplomatic relations between the two countries following the Six Day War. It may well be that the rupture of cultural relations resulted from Israel's activities among Jews in the USSR, which were assisted by those relations.

The 12-year balance sheet of Israel's activities among Jews in the USSR (1955–67) and the struggle to ensure their national rights, including the right to emigrate to Israel, is summarised below.

From Israel's point of view

The positive side

A constantly growing national awakening of Jews in the USSR that nourished the struggle on their behalf in the world and constituting a moral basis for its continuation. The struggle strengthened the Jewish national consciousness.

The goals chosen at the beginning of the struggle were achieved: creating world consciousness of the problem of Jews in the USSR, inclusion of the issue in the permanent agenda of talks held by Western politicians with the USSR, and making it an international problem.

A shift was marked in the status of Jews in the USSR: the publication of *Sovetish Heymland* (a Jewish periodical of Jewish literature); performances of Jewish song; publication of distinguished books of Jewish classics as well as contemporary works. Anti-Semitism was officially condemned (including Kitchko's book *Judaism without Embellishment*)[49]; economic trials against Jews were stopped; matzot (unleavened Passover bread) were baked; there was a gradual increase in the number of Soviet Jews allowed to immigrate to Israel and the Soviet Prime Minister expressed the willingness of his government to enable 'family reunification', which meant in practical terms the opening of Soviet gates for increased exit of Jews to Israel.

The negative side

There was no improvement in the domains of education and religion. The isolation from the outside Jewish world continued. The Jewish Theater was not rehabilitated. No Jewish umbrella organisation was established. The anti-Israel-Jewish-Zionist campaign deteriorated and caused much tension in Israeli–Soviet relations.

Israel's policy towards its Arab minority was condemned in the organizations of the United Nations, through demonstration of their being discriminated against politically, socially and economically.

An attempt was made in the UN organizations to condemn the Zionist movement in the same bracket as anti-Semitism and fascism.

'Zionism' was presented as the 'enemy of humanity' and Israel's policy as a factor disturbing the process of *rapprochement* between East and West.

From the USSR's point of view

The positive side

Intensive condemnation of Zionism and Israel gained the sympathy of Arab countries. It added a new dimension of ideological confrontation between communism and a 'reactionary' movement – a product of 'Capitalism' and 'Imperialism'.

In spite of the pressure of world public opinion on the Soviet Union, the changes that it introduced in the status of the Jewish nationality were only cosmetic ones.

In practice, the Soviet Union did not change its basic policy towards the Jewish nationality, aimed at assimilating it among the peoples of the USSR.

The negative side

National fermentation increased among the Jews, consequently the Soviet Union was compelled to increase the number of exit permits to Israel.

The changes introduced towards the Jews almost did not evoke the expected sympathy in the international arena. The more the Soviet authorities tended to give in, the more the international pressure increased. For the first time after Stalin's death, the USSR was compelled to defend its policy towards Jews at the UN. The campaigning over this matter went on constantly, damaging its image.

Western politicians exploited the Jewish Problem in their bargaining with the USSR. Israel and the world Jewish and Zionist organizations were an obstacle in the way of the USSR's achievement of its political targets in the West.

APPENDIX 10.1
ADDRESSES MADE BY REPRESENTATIVES OF ISRAEL AND
JEWISH ORGANIZATIONS AT THE UNITED NATIONS ON
THE PROBLEM OF JEWS IN THE USSR

12 January 1961	Sub-committee for the Prevention of Discrimination and Defense of Minorities Dr Morris Perlzweig, World Jewish Congress (WJC)
25 January 1962	Sub-committee for the Prevention of Discrimination and Defense of Minorities W. Kory, Co-ordinating Committee of Jewish Organizations
29 October 1962	Third (Political) Committee of the UN General Assembly Michael Comay, Ambassador of Israel
16 January 1963	Sub-committee for the Prevention of Discrimination and Defense of Minorities Dr M. Perlzweig, WJC
22 January 1963	Sub-committee for the Prevention of Discrimination and Defense of Minorities L. Katz, President of B'nai B'rith Dr M. Rosenne, Consul of Israel
5 July 1963	ECOSOC, Geneva M. Bartur, Ambassador of Israel
January 1964	Sub-committee for the Prevention of Discrimination and Defense of Minorities Dr Y. Barromi, M. Comay, Ambassadors of Israel
10–12 March 1964	Committee on Human Rights M. Comay, Ambassador of Israel
30 July 1964	ECOSOC, Geneva M. Bartur, Ambassador of Israel

12–14 January 1965	Sub-committee for the Prevention of Discrimination and Defense of Minorities
	D. Marmor, Representative of Israel
	Dr M. Perlzweig, WJC
24 March 1965	Committee on Human Rights
	H. Cohn, Judge of the Supreme Court, Jerusalem
29 March 1965	Dr M. Perlzweig, WJC
30 March 1965	D. Marmor, Representative of Israel
20 October 1965	Third (Political) Committee of the UN General Assembly
	M. Comay, Ambassador of Israel
	Judge Hadassa Ben-Ito, Representative of Israel
19 January 1966	Committee on Human Rights
	Dr M. Rosenne, Consul of Israel
12 October 1966	ECOSOC, Geneva
	D. Marmor, Representative of Israel
12 October 1966	Third (Political) Committee of the UN General Assembly
	G. Avner, Ambassador of Israel
16–17 January 1967	Sub-committee for the Prevention of Discrimination and Defense of Minorities
	Dr M. Perlzweig, WJC
	Judge S. Zeltner, Representative of Israel
22 March 1967	Committee on Human Rights
	H. Cohn, Judge of the Supreme Court, Representative of Israel

APPENDIX 10.2
REGIONAL AND INTERNATIONAL CONFERENCES ON
BEHALF OF JEWS IN THE USSR

Paris, 15 Sept. 1960	First International Conference of Intellectuals
Rome, 23 March 1961	Italian Intellectuals' Conference
Paris, June 1961	Second International Conference of Intellectuals

London, 15 Sept. 1961	Land Conference of British Intellectuals
Rio de Janeiro, 15 Sept. 1961	Latin-American Conference of Intellectuals
Rome, 1 Oct. 1963	Second Conference of Italian Intellectuals
New York, 12 Oct. 1963	100 Religious Leaders Conference and US Intellectuals
Washington, 8 April 1964	Founding Committee for the Sake of Soviet Jewry by 24 Jewish Organizations in the USA
Paris, 29 Oct. 1964	Conference of French, Belgian and Swiss Intellectuals
Stockholm, 24 April 1965	Conference of Scandinavian Intellectuals
Philadelphia, 17 April 1966	Second Conference of the Jewish Organization in the USA
Mexico, 13 May 1966	Regional Conference of Central American Intellectuals

APPENDIX 10.3
THE PROBLEM OF JEWS IN THE USSR IN THE COUNCIL OF EUROPE

6 Nov. 1964	Belgian representative raised the problem of anti-Semitism in the USSR
25 January 1965	Representative of Norway lectured on the situation of Soviet Jewry
19 March 1965	Representative of Luxembourg submitted a report on the situation of Jews in the USSR and a draft resolution on action to be taken
6 May 1965	The Advisory Assembly of the Council adopted a unanimous resolution condemning Soviet policy towards Jews in the USSR and calling upon the Soviet leadership to improve the situation

APPENDIX 10.4
THE PROBLEM OF SOVIET JEWRY IN THE SOCIALIST
INTERNATIONAL

29 April 1960	Resolution unanimously accepted by the Council [convened in Haifa] condemning Soviet policy toward Jews and calling upon the Soviet leadership to improve their situation
10 Sept. 1963	Conference in Amsterdam called upon the Soviet authorities to stop their discriminatory policy towards Jews in the USSR
April 1964	A working group of the International published a comprehensive report on the situation of the Jews in the USSR
5 May 1966	A session of the International in Stockholm established an investigation committee on the matter
1 June 1966	The Eighth Socialist International Congress in Vienna adopted a Swiss resolution demanding religious and cultural freedom for Jews in the USSR and reunification of families
18 Dec. 1966	The Bureau of the Socialist International in Paris decided to set up a working group of the Labour parties from Britain, the Netherlands, Norway, Sweden, France and Belgium to investigate the situation of Jews in the USSR
20 March 1967	In London the Socialist International decided to set up a committee of representatives from Britain, France, Italy, Sweden, the Netherlands, Belgium, and Norway to investigate the situation of the Jews in the USSR
9 October 1967	A report on the situation of Jews in the USSR was submitted to the Session of the Socialist International in Zurich

APPENDIX 10.5
A TEXT FROM THE PRESIDENT OF THE USA,
LYNDON B. JOHNSON TO ROBERT KENNEDY

This text was read out by Kennedy at the New York Conference for the Sake of Soviet Jewry, 28 Oct. 1964.

The position of the Jewish community in the Soviet Union is a matter of deep and continuing concern to me, to this administration and to millions of thoughtful people throughout the United States. We cannot ignore the existence of religious or racial persecution anywhere in the world.

Anti-Semitism in Russia is a long-standing historical tragedy: its roots go deep into the Czarist era. There have been periods of relative restraint in the more recent past, but in the Soviet Union today there is a grave governmental, social and economic pressure against Jewish culture and religious identity. There is harassment of synagogues and interference with training in the great cultural heritage of Judaism which has given the Jewish community such vigor and endurance through many centuries.

All responsible officials in our government continued to search for practical methods of alleviating the position of Soviet Jews. Thus, in February of this year I instructed Mrs Marietto Tree, the US representative to the Human Rights Commission, to propose an article on anti-Semitism in the draft Convention on the elimination of all forms of racial discrimination. Over the vigorous objections of the Soviet delegate the following article was adopted for consideration by the United Nations General Assembly this fall: "States-parties condemned anti-Semitism and shall take action as appropriate for its speedy eradication in the territories subject to their jurisdiction."

We continue to believe that the official actions available to us must be reinforced by the pressures of an aroused world public opinion. It is my hope that citizens and organizations of all faiths will join in an overwhelming expression of moral concern for the Jews of the Soviet Union. The moral judgment of millions of people throughout the world cannot be ignored by any government.

Lyndon B. Johnson

215

NOTES

1 *Divrei Haknesset*, Vol. 13, p. 738, pp. 820–21; GA 7th Session, First Committee, 597th Meeting, 13 April 1953.
2 Special Report, No. 1, No. 2, *Treatment on Jews by the Soviets, Seventh Interim Report on Hearings before the Select Committee on Communist Aggression*, House of Representatives, 83rd Congress Second Session (NY, Sept. 22–4, 1954).
3 In an internal Memorandum, dated 4 May 1955, Mr S. Leibovich of the East European Division in Israel's Ministry of Foreign Affairs, made the following assessment: 'There is a fairly well-based fear that such publications could harm the cause of the Jewish people at large, because: (a) the Soviet authorities and the east European People's Democracies would certainly not hesitate to use this material, on appropriate occasions, against Jews and the State of Israel; (b) the anti-Semites, also, in the Western world, could easily seize various details of the hearings to strengthen their anti-Jewish claims.' MFA Arch. File 351.1 SSR.
4 MK A. Altman (Herut party), *Divrei Haknesset*, Vol. 15, p. 1369, 29 March 1954; also Vol. 18, pp. 1324–5, 28 March 1955. On 13 April 1954 *Davar* reported on and also devoted an editorial to a convention of Magen (a society for supporting people persecuted for being accused of Judaism, Zionism and national Identification in the Soviet Russia) held in Tel Aviv on 12 April 1954.
5 M. Sharett, *Private Diary* (Hebrew), Vol. 4, pp. 1121–3.
6 *Davar*, 24 Aug. 1955, published the greetings of D. Ben Gurion. The resolutions of the Zionist Executive Council were published in *Davar* on 1 Sept. 1955.
7 MFA Arch. File 11/131/Z. Circular letter by Deputy Director General of the Ministry, A. Harman, to Israel's Missions abroad.
8 On 13 July 1955, two months before the beginning of the campaign, Foreign Minister Sharett instructed Israel's missions in friendly countries to use the visits of parliamentary delegations to the USSR to raise the Jewish subject with their Soviet interlocutors. MFA Arch. File 11/131/Z.
9 Written by N. Levanon, 25 April 1956. MFA Arch. File 350.1 SSR.
10 M. Sharett in a circular letter to Israel's missions abroad, 27 Aug. 1956. MFA Arch. File 350.1 SSR.
11 M. Sharett, op. cit., Vol. 4, pp. 1200–1201.
12 A summary of the memorandum was conveyed to Israel's Ambassador in Moscow, on 13 Oct. 1955. MFA Arch. File 351.1 SSR.
13 M. Sharett, op. cit., Vol. 6, p. 1712.
14 The memorandum was addressed to Bulganin and Krushchev, Claridge's Hotel, London, and was signed by M. Sieff, Chairman of the European Executive of the WJC and by A. L. Easterman, Political Director of the WJC.
15 On the blood libel in Dagestan, see *Divrei Haknesset*, Vol. 30, p. 344, 29 Nov. 1960. On the economic trials, see *Jews in Eastern Europe*, Vol. 11:2, May 1963.
16 *Haaretz*, 3 May 1960.
17 *Izvestia*, 28 Feb. 1963, Exchange of letters, Russell-Krushchev.
18 On 28 Oct. 1964, a meeting was held in New York of leaders of Jewish organizations and President Johnson's telegram was read out. It was the first time that he declared publicly his concern about the situation of Jews in the USSR and the first time that an American President referred openly to this issue. The text of the message, published the following morning, contained: (a) a commitment by the US government to act officially to stop the persecutions; (b) the underscoring of the need for public protests against Soviet policy

towards the Jewish nationality; (c) an accusation against the Soviet government of discriminating against Jews.

19 The report was unanimously approved on 5 May 1956. Council of Europe, Document 1912, Strasbourg.
20 MFA Arch. File 351.1 SSR.
21 *Jews in Eastern Europe,* No. 3, Feb. 1960; no. 7, 7 March 1960.
22 MFA Arch. File 351.1 SSR. Letter from the Director of the East European Division, dated 14 Feb. 1964, addressed to Israel's Ambassador in Moscow.
23 MFA Arch. File 103.1 SSR.
24 *Divrei Haknesset,* Vol. 44, p. 345, 12 Jan. 1966.
25 Addressing the Human Rights Committee of the UN Economic, and Social Council (ECOSOC) on 24 March 1965, the Soviet Ambassador reacted to the statement made by Israel's representative on the committee, Judge Haim Cohn, in saying: 'In Israel Arabs and other groups of the population are facing all kinds of discrimination, including religious discrimination. Lands are taken away from Arabs in Israel. They have only five high schools and the percentage of Arab students at the universities is very low. Only 1.5 per cent of civil servants are Arabs. They are treated like slaves and their occupations are limited to manual labor.' ECOSOC, Doc. 819, 24 March 1965.
26 In the debate on an 'International Treaty to eliminate all forms of racial discrimination', 20 Oct. 1965, UN, General Assembly, Third Committee, Doc. A/6181.
27 *Jews in Eastern Europe,* Vol. 3, Dec. 1955; Vol. 4, June 1966.
28 MFA Arch. File 103.1 SSR.
29 In a verbal announcement given by the Director of Near Eastern Affairs of the Soviet Ministry of Foreign Affairs to the Israeli Ambassador in Moscow on 31 Aug. 1959. MFA Arch. File 103.1 SSR.
30 Soviet Deputy Minister of Foreign Affairs to Israel's Chargé d'Affaires in Moscow, on 28 June 1961. MFA Arch. File 103.1 SSR.
31 The event was repeated on 4 Jan. 1960, warning that in the future it would be punished. MFA Arch. File 103.1 SSR.
32 Y. Govrin, 'Activities of Israeli Diplomats among Jews in the USSR as Mirrored in the Soviet Press' (Hebrew), *Shevut* 8, 1981 as well as in *Jews in Eastern Europe,* Vol. 3, Dec. 1965 as 'The Israeli Diplomats/Motives behind Hostile Press Attacks' (English).
33 *Trud,* 17 March 1961.
34 *Trud,* 11 March 1964.
35 *Znamya Kommunisma,* 7 July 1964.
36 *Trud,* 30 Aug. 1964.
37 *Zarya Vostoka,* 28 May 1965.
38 *Izvestia,* 6 Sept. 1966.
39 *Pravda Vostoka,* 2 Sept. 1966.
40 *Izvestia,* 11 April 1965.
41 *Izvestia,* 22 May 1965.
42 M. Sharett, op. cit., Vol. 4, p. 1139, 18 Aug. 1955.
43 Counselor of the Soviet Embassy in Ottawa in his conversation with the Israeli Ambassador there, April 1962. MFA Arch. File 351.1 SSR.
44 Director of the Near Eastern Department of the Soviet Ministry of Foreign Affairs in his talk with Israel's Ambassador in Moscow, 5 Sept. 1962. MFA Arch. File 103.1 SSR.
45 Soviet Ambassador in Washington in his talk with Dr N. Goldmann, on 23 Feb.

1965. MFA Arch. File 351.1 SSR.
46   MFA Arch. File 351.1 SSR.
47   K. Katz, 'Budapest, Warsaw, Moscow: an Envoy to Unfriendly Lands' (Hebrew), p. 121
48   Director of the Near Eastern Department of the Soviet Ministry of Foreign Affairs in his talk with Israel's Chargé d'Affaires in Moscow, 21 July 1965. MFA Arch. File 103.1 SSR.
49   See *Jews in Eastern Europe*, Vol. 2, No. 5, July 1964.

Part 4

The impact of the East–West superpowers' confrontation on the Arab–Israeli conflict and on Israeli–Soviet relations

11 · The Middle East in the Soviet strategy

THE FUNDAMENTAL FACTORS CHARACTERIZING THE
PERCEPTION OF SOVIET STRATEGY IN THE MIDDLE EAST

Geopolitical

THE MIDDLE EAST was geographically close to the USSR. Some of the Middle Eastern countries, such as Turkey and Iran, had a common border with the USSR. Instability in the region or a country partly or entirely dominated by regimes and powers hostile to the USSR could in times of crisis constitute a direct threat to the security and peace of the USSR. The shock of Nazi Germany's sudden attack on the USSR in June 1941 and its fears of NATO's war plans led the USSR to consider the importance of the Middle East's security in relation to itself. The security belt around its borders with the Middle Eastern countries became for the USSR a matter of utmost importance.

The Middle East is an important crossroads between three continents. Free passage for its fleet was of the utmost vital interest for the USSR. This crossroads branched off into:

The Bosphorus and the Dardanelles – the only outlet of the Soviet navy to the Mediterranean Sea from the Black Sea. The presence of Western powers' navies, mainly the US Sixth Fleet, in the Mediterranean after World War II, had increased the importance of the Mediterranean Sea for the USSR, which needed, among other things, permanent home ports for the functions of its navy.

The Suez Canal – vital passage to ships and tankers from the Mediterranean Sea to the Indian Ocean.
The Bab-El-Mandeb Straits – vital passage from the Red Sea to the Persian Gulf.
The Strait of Hormuz – the only maritime route to carry oil from the Persian Gulf.

Economic

For the USSR's economy the Middle Eastern oil producing countries did not constitute a decisive economic factor, whereas for Western powers and Western industrialized countries, free access to the oil-producing countries was a basic matter of existence and development – because of their dependence upon the oil reservoirs of these countries. Barring access to this region to the West could have been decisive in any possible confrontation between East and West. The same applied to domination of or influence on these countries: stoppage of the oil supply would have been like blocking access to this region.

GOALS OF SOVIET STRATEGY IN THE MIDDLE EASTERN REGIONS

First stage – Supporting the Middle Eastern countries in the process of their liberation from Western domination.
Second stage – Undermining the political, economic and military status of Western powers in the region, increasing the USSR's popularity with the area's countries as their supporter in their struggle against Western powers' influence and attempts to set up military alliances in the region.
Third stage – Strengthening anti-Western regimes in the regions; bringing them nearer to Soviet policy; giving them military, political and economic assistance. The ideological factor was not decisive though it could at times be helpful. A regime would not be marked progressive according to ideology, but by the degree of its opposition to US policy in the world.
Fourth stage – Supporting those regimes on the 'non-capitalist' road of development and ensuring their total immunity to the influence of Western powers.

Fifth stage – The gradual inclusion of the Middle Eastern regimes in the military, political and ideological sphere of influence of the USSR and its satellite countries.

For many years the Middle East was under the influence of Western powers – a region possessing a huge potential wealth relative to its poverty and backwardness, where nations clash with each other, Muslims with themselves and they with Israel. The USSR's striving for concretization of the above stages of its strategy in the Middle East most certainly would have led to a confrontation with the Western powers, who had a vital interest in this region's political and social regimes ensuring the normal flow of oil for their economies.

In the years 1945–50, Soviet policy on the Middle East was characterized by extending support for the achievement of political independence of the region's countries. In the years 1950–55, the USSR continued with the process of liberating the countries from the rule of Western powers, acting to prevent the return of those powers to the region in the guise of military alliances under their leadership. When the USSR did not entirely succeed in preventing Western attempts in this direction, it penetrated into the region under the cover of the arms deal with Egypt, and from then on it worked to maintain its presence by political and military means, so it could be an influential factor in the course of events in the region, according to its strategic needs.

This study will not deal with the stages of Soviet policy in the Middle East, but rather with its stance on the Arab–Israeli conflict as part of its Middle Eastern policy, and the way this influenced Israeli–Soviet relations.

ATTEMPTS BY WESTERN POWERS TO ESTABLISH MILITARY ALLIANCES IN THE MIDDLE EAST

On 13 October 1951 the governments of the USA, Britain, France, and Turkey appealed to the government of Egypt proposing it join the Middle East Command as a founding member on an equal basis for defense of the region against foreign aggression. Parallel to their appeal to Egypt, they informed Israel and the other Middle Eastern countries on the same day about their initiative. On 15 October 1951 Egypt informed them of its refusal to accept the proposal.[1]

On 10 November 1951, the Western powers published a joint statement saying that in spite of Egypt's negative response, they were proceeding with their declared intention of establishing the Command and that each state to join would do so on the basis of equality with the Western powers and with the preservation of its own sovereignty. They promised the joining states military assistance in developing their capacity 'to play their proper role in the defense of the area as a whole against foreign aggression', whereas the Command 'would not interfere in problems and disputes arising within the area'.[2]

Though the source of 'foreign aggression' was not defined, it was clear that the intended reference was to the USSR. Also, the link between the intention to establish the Command and NATO defense plans was not concealed. On the contrary, it was stressed that the decision to establish the Command was taken by NATO. The reference to 'not interfering in disputes within the area' was presumably directed to the Arab states. First, their joining the Command was not conditional upon their acceptance of Israel's existence. Secondly, it was not the aim of the Western powers to act in settling the conflict between them and Israel. Hence, it could have been understood that the Arab–Israeli conflict did not disturb the Western powers in establishing the Command and that in their view the conflict could continue.

The Soviet reaction

On 24 November 1951 the Soviet Union sent identical notes to the USA, Britain, France, and Turkey in which it reacted sharply to their intention of setting up the Command. It called their plan 'aggressive' accusing them, *inter alia*, of setting themselves 'the object of turning the countries of the Middle East into bridgeheads for the armed forces of the Atlantic bloc', 'subordinating their armed forces, military bases, communications, ports, and other installations' to the command of NATO and 'drawing the countries of the Middle East into the aggressive war measures of the Atlantic bloc' with the groundless excuse of an external threat to the security and peace of the region and the need to defend it collectively.

In this note the Soviet Union warned the Western powers that 'it cannot overlook these new aggressive plans', 'in an area located not far from the frontiers of the USSR', and that 'the responsibility for the situation which may arise as a result of this will rest with the initiators of the Command'.[3]

In its notes of 21 November 1951 to Egypt, the Soviet Union expressed its full appreciation for the stand taken by Egypt in rejecting the invitation of the Western countries to join the Command, which fitted in with 'NATO's aggressive plans against the USSR and people's democracies' and which 'cannot but lead to the loss of independence and sovereignty' of those countries who would join the Command, which 'would cause serious damage to the relations existing between those countries and the USSR' as well as to the cause of peace and security in the area.[4]

Verbal notes of similar content were sent by the Soviet Union to Israel and Arab States.[5]

ISRAEL'S REACTION TO THE USSR'S APPEAL NOT TO JOIN WESTERN MILITARY ALLIANCES

In its reply to the Soviet appeal of 21 November 1951, Israel reacted with the following verbal note on 8 December 1951.

> (1) Israel has not been invited to join the 'Middle East Command' and no question concerning its participation has arisen. Therefore the government of Israel has not defined its views on the nature and the form of the Command. It is therefore apparent that the government of Israel has not decided to join this Command. At the same time, Israel has received a statement from the powers involved in organizing the 'Middle East Command' to the effect that this Command has no aggressive intent or purpose.
>
> Israel considers its predominant security problem to be the threat posed by Arab countries that refuse to make peace with it. Since peace is indivisible, all members of the United Nations, especially the great powers, are obliged, in Israel's opinion, to take practical steps and vigorous action to remove this threat to the peace of Israel and the Middle East.

Israel has not agreed and will not agree to assist aggressive acts or preparations against the Soviet Union or any other peaceloving country.

Israel draws the attention of the government of the USSR to the news items repeatedly published during the last two years or so throughout the Soviet press, including the most responsible Soviet organs, on the ostensible establishment of foreign bases in Israel. These items are absolutely untrue, since no foreign military bases exist in our country; to our regret these news items are liable to damage relations between our two countries. The government of Israel, on the other hand, has a strong desire to maintain cordial relations with the Soviet Union.

In the other paragraphs of Israel's reply it was also noted that 'Israel views the preservation of peace throughout the world as the loftiest objective of international policy', that 'Israel will remember and will not forget, that at a critical political stage of its struggle for independence [it] enjoyed the generous and most important support of the USSR' and that 'the government of Israel requests that the USSR allow those Jews in the Soviet Union who so wish to emigrate to Israel'.[6]

By comparison with the answers sent to the USSR by the USA[7] and Britain,[8] Israel's answer is formulated in a cordial and non-polemical tone. This is explained by the following:

Israel's stand regarding the Western proposals to establish the Middle East Command was not negative. Israel believed that the proposals did not harbor aggressive intentions against the USSR. Israel's formal reply would be given when it was formally invited to join the Command. Hence, Israel neither rejected it nor accepted it.

Compared to the threat that the Soviet Union underscored would be the result of the Command's establishment, the Arab threat against Israel was real and its removal would secure peace in the region.

Israel invited the Soviet Union to take an active part in the removal of the threat against Israel, together with the rest of the powers and all the UN members. Thus, Israel granted the Soviet Union a status equal to that of the Western powers in solving the Israeli–Arab conflict.

An explicit commitment that Israel would not assist in anti-Soviet plans was included. (This paragraph was the basis for Israel's commitment to the USSR in exchange for its agreeing to renew diplomatic relations with Israel in 1953, and was often used by Soviet diplomats as an argument against Israel, which they felt did not implement this commitment, both in its Middle Eastern policy and in its struggle for the rights of Jews in the USSR.)

Israel's denial of the alleged existence of foreign bases on its territory. No promise was given that such bases would not be placed, in the future, at the disposal of Western powers.[9]

ISRAEL'S STRIVING FOR A DEFENSE ALLIANCE WITH THE USA

The efforts by Western powers to establish the Middle East Command failed. The Arab states' refusal to join the Command – in particular Egypt's rejection – had practically determined its fate. US Secretary of State Dulles explained the failure – after returning from a visit in the Middle East – on 1 June 1953. 'The Defense organization was a failure rather than an immediate possibility.' He had found only 'a vague desire' for a collective security system. No such system, he added, could be imposed on the Middle East by the Western powers and little could be done in this direction until the Arab states and Israel had settled their differences.[10]

At the meeting of the Mapai Political Committee, held on the eve of the Dulles visit to Israel, Ben Gurion summarized the main points he felt should receive the main effort invested in convincing the USA to conclude a defense alliance with Israel, even if it were necessary to place military bases at their disposal. After having been disappointed by Britain's position on this, Ben Gurion concluded by saying that Israel had no interest in a regional security arrangement, but in one with the USA or with NATO.[11] He believed that by obtaining such an arrangement, the threat to Israel's security would dissolve, since the Arab states would be deterred from attacking Israel. Ben Gurion's main concern was the problem of security. He saw it as a guarantee for the mere physical existence of the people of Israel, and upon that existence depended the future of the entire

227

Jewish people. In explaining, in the Knesset, the way he saw Israel's security during all the years of its existence, he stated:

> As Israel's security problems differ from those of other nations, so do our security means and needs, whose range is much larger than any other state. We have to look, with cruel clarity, at the fateful difference between us and our enemies. Our foes believe that they are capable of totally resolving, once and for ever, the Problem of Israel, by our total annihilation. We will not be able to achieve such security by a military victory, even a complete one. We do not want to, we are not entitled to, and we cannot liquidate tens of millions of Arabs in the Middle East, and our security lies in our constant and overall increase in power in all domains and on all fronts.[12]

The need to lean upon a friendly power – in order to remove the danger of the physical threat from outside and to enable the state to absorb new immigrants, to increase the number of settlements throughout the country, to develop scientific, medical and technological research for the economic, social, cultural and physical stabilization of Israel – is the explanation for Israel's leaders, particularly Ben Gurion, striving at that time to reach a Defense Alliance with the USA.

At the Mapai Political Committee meeting held on 12 May 1954, Foreign Minister M. Sharett asserted two facts: (1) that no state had asked for military bases in Israel; (2) that although Israel was interested in a security arrangement with the Western powers, none of them was willing to make one.[13] Nevertheless, Israel's diplomacy concentrated during 1953–55 on the effort to convince the USA to conclude a defense treaty with Israel.[14] This treaty was supposed to guarantee Israel's frontiers with a commitment to defend Israel, if attacked, and to extend military aid to Israel to balance Israel's force with the total power of the Arab states.[15]

Israel's efforts failed even after the balance of power in the region shifted against it, following the conclusion of the Baghdad Pact and the Czech–Egyptian arms deal. Israel abandoned these efforts at the end of 1955. In February 1956, Dulles said that the USA had never seriously considered the possibility of concluding an alliance with Israel, since the USA was not in a position to guarantee 'frontiers that were not fixed by mutual agreement'.[16] It was clear, beyond any doubt, that the courting of the Arab states prevented at first Britain and then the USA from concluding an alliance with Israel.

On 30 October 1955, Sharett summarized in his diary his words to Dulles: Israel has lost all credit with the Soviet Union because of its efforts towards a security treaty with the USA without having gained anything from the USA.[17] This was rather a sad summary of Israel's diplomatic activity on this matter in the years 1953–55.

Israel's striving for a defense treaty with the USA was not perceived in the minds of the Israeli leaders as contradictory to its commitment to the USSR not to support anti-Soviet plans. (1) they did not regard such a treaty as a regional, anti-Soviet alliance, but rather as a bilateral arrangement between two States. (2) they believed that as some of the European states had defense agreements with the USA, and their relations with the USSR suffered no harm, so no harm would befall Israel either.[18] But this was not the way the Soviet Union saw it. In Europe a security belt of people's democracies defended the USSR, whereas in the Middle East the USSR itself bordered the states under the influence of the Western powers. In the face of Western attempts to establish Defense Alliances, the USSR probably looked with concern at the expansion of the Western powers' activities in the Middle East, close to its borders. Therefore the Soviet Union did not distinguish between a collective defense arrangement and a bilateral one as long as one of the Western powers directed it. The decisive point for the Soviet Union was the range of possibility granted or not granted to the Western powers to establish military bases in the territories of the Middle Eastern states. This Soviet fear was expressed more than once to Israeli representatives,[19] who did not attach much importance to it as the USSR ignored Israel's fears when Syria and Egypt were strengthened by Soviet political support and by great quantities of arms that violated the military balance to Israel's disfavor.

Israel's official statement on its attempts to reach a defense treaty with the USA[20] probably created in the eyes of the Soviet Union an image of Israel as an ally of the USA (even if it was not), aspiring with all its power for the extension of US presence in the Middle East for the sake of Israel's security needs ('exaggerated' in the Soviet view) without taking into consideration the Soviet interest in halting Western powers' activity, particularly that of the USA, in an area which it saw as being close to its borders.

This clash of interests between Israel and the Soviet Union developed against the background of Western attempts to establish military alliances in the Middle East and Soviet activity against them. Arab states, headed by Egypt, exploited the confrontation between the Eastern and Western blocs in advancing their aspirations to destroy Israel.

THE REACTION OF THE SOVIET UNION TO THE BAGHDAD PACT

1. On 15 April 1955 the Soviet Ministry of Foreign Affairs published an official statement condemning in harsh terms the Pact and the continuous attempts by the Western powers to set up arrangements in the Middle East, against the will of the peoples in the region. In this statement the Soviet Union repeated the principal accusations it had previously addressed to the Western powers. However, the new element of the declaration was in the expression of Soviet readiness to co-operate with the nations of the region in assisting to strengthen peace (namely in renouncing the pressure of Western powers) and 'support any steps by the countries of the Middle East' towards putting into practice 'principles of equality; non-interference in domestic affairs; non-aggression and the renunciation of encroachment on the territorial integrity of other states; and respect for sovereignty and national independence'.[21]

The main importance of the Soviet statement was not in the reiteration of the Soviet aim of deterring the Middle Eastern states from joining military alliances in the region, but in Soviet support of states that would reject pressure by Western powers promising to defend their freedom and independence. Evidently, there was an intention to switch from a policy of deterrence to a policy of direct co-operation with them for attaining 'national independence', meaning, in the Soviet view, the removal of Western powers' influence and then moving towards a pro-Soviet orientation. This statement, published on the eve of the 'Bandung Conference', paved the way for the announcement of the Czech–Egyptian arms deal.

2. In surveying events of the year 1955 at the Supreme Soviet of the USSR, on 29 December 1955, Krushchev, First Secretary of the CPSU, referred to the Baghdad Pact in the following words:

> As it is known the sponsors of the Baghdad Pact are devoting all their efforts to inveigle the Arab countries into this aggressive bloc. But they are coming up against the mounting resistance of the peoples of those countries. Soviet public opinion has been following with sympathy the valiant struggle of the people of Jordan against the attempts to force their country into joining the Baghdad Pact. We understand the yearnings of the peoples of the Arab countries who are fighting for their full liberation from foreign dependence.

In continuation, Krushchev bitterly attacked Israel, by saying 'one cannot fail to condemn the actions of the State of Israel which from the first days of its existence began threatening its neighbors and pursuing an unfriendly policy towards them',[22] in spite of the fact that Israel opposed the Baghdad Pact and even condemned it publicly. Foreign Minister Sharett rejected Krushchev's accusations from the Knesset podium[23] by quoting Soviet statements in the United Nations in the years 1948–49 which then asserted that Israel was a victim of Arab aggression.

SOVIET STATEMENT ON THE SETTLEMENT OF THE ARAB–ISRAELI CONFLICT

This was the first statement by the USSR's Ministry of Foreign Affairs that was entirely devoted to the question of settling the Arab–Israeli conflict.[24] It was published on 17 April 1956, about six months after the Czech–Egyptian arms deal became known (regarded by Israel as a real danger to its existence, for the first time since its independence) and only a few days before the Soviet leaders, Krushchev and Bulganin, left for a State visit in Britain.

Following are the main excerpts of the statement:

The main cause of the 'deterioration of the international situation in the Middle East' is the continuing attempts to establish military alliances in the region 'which serve the aims of colonialism and are

231

directed both against the independence of the peoples and against the security of peaceloving countries'.

The establishment of such alliances 'has become the source of international friction and conflicts in the Middle East and the cause of deterioration of relations between the Arab states and Israel' ... that is 'one of most the dangerous elements of the situation in the Middle East'.

'Certain circles of some states ... are seeking to use the Arab–Israeli conflict for their own aggressive ends, going so far as to introduce foreign troops into the territory of the countries of this region and to create military complications ...

The Soviet Union has regarded with sympathy and warmly supported the efforts of the countries of the Middle East aimed at establishing and consolidating their independence. (Israel is included among the countries mentioned.)

The Soviet Union supported and continues to support the striving of Arab states to secure the further strengthening of their national independence and the advancement of their economic well being.

Desiring to secure the consolidation of peace and the development of international co-operation and taking into account the just national interests of the peoples of all countries, the Soviet government has invariably opposed the violation of peace in the Middle East and any actions which could entail the outbreak of armed conflicts ...

The Soviet Union adheres to the principle of 'respect for national independence, sovereignty and non-interference in the domestic affairs of states and the settlement of international disputes by peaceful means'.

The Soviet government considers that an armed conflict in the Middle East can and must be avoided and that it is in the interests of all the states of the Middle East not to allow themselves to be provoked into being involved in hostilities.

The Soviet government regards as unlawful and impermissible, the attempts to make use of the Arab–Israeli conflict for intervention from outside in the domestic affairs of the independent Arab states or for introducing foreign troops into the territory of the Middle East.

In connection with the aforesaid, the Soviet government stated:

1. The Soviet Union will support United Nations activities aimed at the strengthening of 'peace in the Palestine area' and implementing corresponding decisions of the Security Council.

2. The Soviet Union considers that measures should be taken 'to ease the existing tension in the Palestine area without interference from outside'. The Soviet Union urges the parties concerned to abstain from any actions which might aggravate the situation of the existing demarcation line established by the armistice agreements between the Arab countries and Israel, and to 'make the necessary efforts to improve the hard lot of the hundreds of Arab refugees, deprived of their shelter and means of livelihood'.

3. In the interest of strengthening international peace and security the matter must be handled in such a way as to lead to a lasting and peaceful settlement of the Palestine issue 'on a mutually acceptable basis taking due account of the just national interests of the parties concerned'.

4. The Soviet Union expresses its readiness to facilitate, 'together with other states, a peaceful settlement of outstanding questions'.

Israel's reaction

In the Knesset debate of 23 April 1956, Foreign Minister Sharett reacted cautiously to the Soviet statement. He found in it 'a certain turning point' which in the continuation of his response could be interpreted as a positive shift towards Israel, as he enumerated its positive and negative aspects.[25]

Among the positive aspects: the statement admitted that the threat of war was looming over the Middle East and it had to be thwarted; there was an obligation to prevent it. The Soviet Union had supported Israel's independence and continued to do so, opposing the introduction of any changes – by force – of the armistice lines. The Soviet Union insisted upon the necessity for a peaceful settlement of the Arab–Israeli dispute 'on a basis acceptable to both parties'.

Among the negative aspects: The statement did not mention that the settlement of the Arab–Israeli conflict should be achieved through direct negotiations (a principle the USSR always adhered to in the settling of international disputes). The statement ignored the disruption in the military balance between Israel and the Arab states, consequently endangering Israel's existence. The statement did not take any stand on the root of the Arab–Israeli conflict, and it did not say how to prevent a war. On the one hand, the Soviet Union was calling for a reduction in tension, while on the other, it supplied arms to Egypt in large quantities, increasing tension in the region. The statement 'did not propose how to improve the factual situation, but on the contrary it contained hints of a danger of further aggravation'.

Sharett assessed that the statement aimed at 'asserting and demanding for the USSR, a status in the Middle East, which has been the guiding line for Soviet policy for a very long time now'. In general, Sharett referred positively to the statement in the hope that would bring about 'a favorable change in the climate of relations' between the USSR and Israel, which would have 'to pass the test of reality'.

In the Arab states the statement was given a cool welcome, and perhaps because of that *Izvestia* published, four days later, on 21 April 1956, an article signed by 'Observer' stressing extensively the existing friendship between the Soviet Union and the Arab states, whilst accusing Israel of 'grossly violating' the United Nations Charter by its acts along the armistice lines, which were not the permanent frontiers between Israel and the Arab states. Israel was presented in the article as 'an instrument of the US and British aggressive circles'. The article covered up the positive aspects toward Israel in the statement, emphasizing the negative ones. On the diplomatic level Soviet representatives emphasized, to their Israeli interlocutors, the positive aspects of the statement.[26]

The statement's aims

The aims of the statement may be defined as follows.

1. To prevent a flare-up between Israel and Egypt, following the Czech–Egyptian arms deal.
Toward Israel, calming words, in the light of the noises made in Israel itself and elsewhere, stressing that its very existence was in danger and calling dramatically for defensive arms,[27] by alarming world public opinion and putting pressure on Western powers to supply it.
Toward Egypt, words of restraint, meaning that the arms it received were supplied for defense purposes in the event of outside aggression and not for opening an attack on Israel, whose sovereign and independent existence the USSR recognized.

2. To correct the negative image of the USSR created mainly in the Western world as a result of the arms deal, and in particular on the eve of the forthcoming State visit of Soviet leaders in Britain. To emphasize its good will in settling the Arab–Israeli conflict by peaceful means and thus demonstrating its responsibility as a power aspiring to mediate in establishing peace in the world.

3. To prevent the USA and Britain from concluding a defense alliance with Israel in response to Israel's desperate calls about the disturbance in the military balance between Israel and the Arab states and because of the USSR's military and political support of Egypt.

4. To stress that the USSR was ready to support all countries in the Middle East in preserving their independence and sovereignty, on the condition that they liberate themselves from the influence of Western powers.

5. To stress that Arab–Israeli conflict would not be settled by military means, but by mutual agreement based on mutual concessions, without the interference of Western powers (in the original, 'outside interference'), who might determine the line in Israel's favor.

6. The USSR's readiness to co-operate in settling problems outstanding between Israel and Arab states, together with the United Nations and other countries (it did not say Western powers, so it may be presumed that the reference was to the member states of the Bandung Conference) – a settlement which would strengthen peace in the region.

7. To demonstrate its political and moral authority, its status as a power involved in the region, and thus to hint to Israel, the Arab states and the Western powers that the road to settlement of the Arab–Israeli conflict led not only through the Western capitals but through Moscow as well.

The importance of the statement

The statement's significance is in:

1. Raising the USSR's prestige as a power initiating ways to settle international conflicts and working towards alleviating tension in the world (this against the background of the Czech–Egyptian arms deal).

2. Presenting a balanced Soviet position on the Arab–Israeli conflict and in calling for its settlement by peaceful means on the basis of: (a) Israel's right to an independent existence; (b) the settlement of the Arab refugee problem; (c) mutual consent.

3. Stressing that the USSR supported the Arab states not on the basis of their aspirations to destroy Israel, but on the basis of their rejection of the attempts by Western powers to establish military alliances in the region, including Israel.

4. Fostering public consciousness that in its confrontation with Western powers against the background of their attempts to establish military alliances in the Middle East, the USSR had gained a considerable measure of success.

5. Asserting that the Arab–Israeli conflict could serve not only Western powers, but also the USSR, in strengthening its status and deepening its presence in the Middle East.

The reaction of Western powers

On 18 April 1956, one day after the USSR's statement was announced, Soviet leaders Krushchev and Bulganin paid a State visit to Britain. In the talks with their British hosts, the Middle East situation held a place of predominance against the background of Britain's joining the Baghdad Pact and the Soviet arms supplies to the Arab states.

In a joint declaration published in London, at the end of their visit, a clause was included regarding the Near and Middle East, emphasizing the agreement between the two governments 'to do everything in their power to facilitate the maintenance of peace and security in the Near and Middle East ... in accordance with the national aspirations of the peoples concerned with the necessity of ensuring their independence'.

The governments of the two countries also called on the states concerned 'to prevent the increase of tension in the area of the demarcation line, and stated that they would support the United Nations in an initiative to secure a peaceful settlement on a mutually accepted basis' of the Arab–Israeli conflict.[28]

The majority of the accepted paragraphs in the joint declaration were taken from the Soviet statement (of 17 April 1956). Hence, not only were they acceptable to Britain's leaders, but they were fostered by Britain, and formulated in the joint declaration between both powers and thus received an international dimension. From Israel's point of view this was of political importance, since two of the declared principles – Israel's right to an independent existence and the need to settle the Arab–Israeli conflict by peaceful means – had been acceptable to Israel's policy from the beginning of its independence.

This was the first time that the Soviet Union had referred to the Middle East problems and the Arab–Israeli conflict in a declarative joint document with a Western power, as a partner on equal footing. From the Soviet Union's point of view it was, probably, of considerable importance since this document legitimized the status which the USSR wanted to obtain.

On 27 April 1956 Bulganin stated, in London, to the representatives of the press that in the talks with their British hosts the Soviet leaders had expressed their point of view that the main reason for the heightening of the situation in the Middle East, the main source of international conflict and friction in this area, and the deterioration of relations between the Arab states and Israel as well as other countries is the creation of military alliances such as the Baghdad Pact. Bulganin added that 'the British side did not share the Soviet view in this question'.[29]

Thus, Bulganin noted the different stand taken by each of the two powers, which was not expressed in the agreed upon subjects of the joint declaration.

On 19 May 1956 at the end of the French visit of the Soviet leaders (Krushchev and Bulganin), a joint French-Soviet declaration was published in Paris, containing a clause repeating most of the paragraphs of the Soviet statement regarding the right of all countries in the Middle East to an independent existence, and the need to settle the Arab–Israeli conflict by peaceful means, on a mutually acceptable basis. Thus, two Western powers practically expressed their accord with the Soviet Statement.

CONCLUSION

Western attempts at establishing military alliances in the vicinity of Soviet borders aggravated the confrontation between the powers of the Eastern and Western blocs, while the Soviet Union on one side and the Western powers on the other were fighting over winning the hearts of the Arab leaders, since without their agreement the alliances could not be established.

As a result, the weight of the Arab countries increased in the inter-power bargaining. The refusal of the Arab countries to join the alliances (except Iraq in 1955) credited them with considerable Soviet support, in the military and political domain, against the Western powers, and in their conflict with Israel. It was this support that had helped the Soviet Union to acquire status and authority in the Middle East and become, gradually, an influential factor in the region.

Israel, fearing for its physical existence – in face of the increasingly unfavorable balance of power between Israel and the Arab states owing to their becoming stronger with Soviet arms, and in light of the frequent threats made by Arab leaders (especially the ruler of Egypt) to destroy Israel – was striving for security arrangements with the West to restore the military balance and serve as a deterrent against the Arab leaders' aspirations to destroy Israel. For this reason, the Soviet Union hardened its stand against Israel, since it interpreted these security arrangements as American–British attempts at strengthening their status in the Middle East, which from the strategic point of view might have threatened Soviet security.

With its dependence on the West and its struggle against Arab aggression, Israel became, paradoxically, an important asset for Soviet policy in the Middle East. Thus, one sees the ambivalent attitude of the Soviet Union towards Israel, in the Middle East domain – extending support to Israel's enemies, on the one hand, and support for Israel's right to existence in the region, on the other.

NOTES

1 See Yaacov Ro'i's book, *From Encroachment to Involvement: Documentary Study of Soviet Policy in the Middle East, 1945–1973*, pp. 89–94.
2 *American Foreign Policy*, Vol. 2, pp. 2180–5.
3 *Izvestia*, 25 Nov. 1951.
4 Soviet news, 27 Nov. 1951, reprinted in *Document on International Affairs*, 1951, pp. 429–31.
5 *Divrei Haknesset*, Vol. 11, 27 Feb. 1952, p. 1465.
6 State of Israel, *Documents of Foreign Policy of Israel, 1951*, Companion volume,

Vol. 5, pp. 357–8.

7 *Middle East Affairs*, May 1956, pp. 14–16 (Documents).

8 Ibid., pp. 188–90.

9 Soviet reports on British military bases in Israel were tendentious and untrue. They had, however, a certain grasp of reality, since in the course of 1951, Ben Gurion negotiated with British senior officers on mutual security arrangements. See M. Bar Zohar, David Ben Gurion (Hebrew), Vol. 2, pp. 900–905.

10 *Keesing's Contemporary Archives*, 1952–54, 6–13 June 1953. Also see, *Davar*, 3 June 1953.

11 M. Bar Zohar, op. cit., Vol. 2, pp. 912–13.

12 Ibid.

13 Protocol of the meeting, 12 May 1954, p. 20, Mapai Archive File 26/54.

14 M. Sharett, *Private Diary*, pp. 697, 712, 794, 881, 939. A. Eban, *My Life*, p. 1984, as well as statements by Sharett in the Knesset, *Divrei Haknesset*, Vol. 16, p. 25449, 30 Oct. 1954; Vol. 17, p. 65, 15 Nov. 1954; Vol. 18, p. 1758, 1 June 1955; Vol. 19, p. 88, 18 Oct. 1955; and Ben Gurion's statement in the Knesset, *Divrei Haknesset*, Vol. 19, p. 283, 3 Nov. 1955.

15 M. Sharett, op. cit., Vol. 3, p. 1213, 9 Feb. 1955.

16 *Divrei Haknesset*, Vol. 20, p. 1213, 19 Feb. 1956, MK H. Landau in the debate on Israel's Foreign Policy.

17 M. Sharett, op. cit., Vol. 5, p. 1266.

18 Sharett's statement in the Knesset, 1 June 1955, *Divrei Haknesset*, Vol. 18, p. 1758. Also, Sharett's briefing to Yosef Avidar upon his nomination as Israel's Ambassador to Moscow. M. Sharett, op. cit., Vol. 3, p. 251, 21 March 1955. See also Ben Gurion's statement in the Knesset, *Divrei Haknesset*, Vol. 20, p. 2067, 10 June 1956.

19 Conversation between Eban and Molotov in San Francisco, 24 June 1955, in A. Eban, op. cit., pp. 195, 198.

20 Ibid.

21 Izvestia, 17 April 1955. English translation in *The USSR and the Middle East* (Moscow: Novosti Press, 1972), pp. 58–65.

22 *Izvestia*, 30 Dec. 1955; also *New Times Supplement* (English), pp. 30–31, 5 Jan. 1956.

23 *Divrei Haknesset*, Vol. 13, pp. 677–8, 2 Jan. 1956.

24 *Izvestia*, 18 April 1956; also in English, *The USSR and the Middle East*, pp. 66–71.

25 *Divrei Haknesset*, Vol. 20, pp. 1725–6, 23 April 1956.

26 A. Dagan, *Moscow and Jerusalem*, pp. 100–101.

27 Sharett's statement in the Knesset, *Divrei Haknesset*, Vol. 19, pp. 86–8, 18 Oct. 1955 as well as Ben Gurion's statement, Vol. 19, p. 232, 2 Nov. 1955.

28 *Keesing's Contemporary Archives*, 28 April – 5 May 1956, p. 14835.

29 Associated Press and *Davar*, 29 April 1956.

12 · *The USSR's policy during and after the Sinai Campaign*

ROM THE development of events in the first half of 1956, it follows that the diplomatic activities of the powers[1] – as reflected in their statements – did not have any influence in stopping the deterioration of Israeli–Arab relations nor on the USSR's relations with France and Britain. Two events that occurred in the course of 1956 paved the way to the Sinai War: (1) penetration of fedayeen gangs from Egyptian territory, in accordance with the decision of Egypt's President, into Israel's territory to carry out acts of sabotage and murder, and to tighten the sea blockade in the Gulf of Aqaba; (2) Egyptian government decisions to nationalize the Suez Canal (after British forces had left its territory by Egyptian demand) in reaction to the US refusal to finance the Aswan Dam.[2]

The first event brought about acts of retaliation by Israel in the territories of Jordan and Egypt, causing a considerable escalation of tension in Israeli–Arab relations. Though these acts were aimed at restraining the Arab leaders from organizing fedayeen penetrations into Israel, it was proved, in the course of time, that this goal had not been reached. On the contrary, they evoked and intensified Arab hostility towards Israel. Among the Israeli leadership two approaches could be discerned: the one led by Foreign Minister Sharett, desirous of reducing Israel's retaliatory acts, because of the damage caused to Israel's position in the world, the other, headed by Prime Minister Ben Gurion, wishing to enlarge the scale of the attacks to deter the enemies.[3]

With Sharett's resignation from the government, the tendency towards striking the Egyptians intensified, the aim being to remove the fedayeen threats to Israel, to reopen the Straits of Tiran in the Gulf of Aqaba to Israeli shipping, to destroy Soviet arms in the hands of the Egyptian army before its absorption, and to remove Nasser from his post as President of Egypt.[4]

The second event was the rejection by Egypt of recommendations from two international conferences (with the participation of the USSR but with its abstention from voting) to place the operation of the canal in the hands of an international body. This refusal infuriated Britain and France and prompted them to seize the canal to ensure free shipping and bring about Nasser's removal.

The evolution of these events brought Israel, on the one hand, and Britain and France on the other hand to co-operate in the forthcoming war against Egypt. If it had not been for the joint interests of the three states, it could have been that Israel alone would not have gone to war against Egypt. And it could well have been that Britain and France would not have gone to war by themselves if Israel had not promised them its co-operation. And if the three of them had foreseen the reaction of the USA and the USSR to this war, perhaps the three of them would have decided not to proceed.[5]

The USSR, which regarded the nationalization of the Suez Canal as an important achievement in its struggle to remove Western strongholds in the Middle East, supported Egypt in its conflict with Israel and Britain – even prior to the start of the Sinai Campaign – to deter them from any possible co-operation which might delay or obstruct the process of nationalization.

The Soviet Union used a threatening tone towards Israel on the propaganda and diplomatic levels. In an article signed 'Observer' published in *Izvestia* on 29 July 1956, the Soviet Union claimed that the 'stand of the extremists in Israel is similar to the stand of colonialists who are afraid of strengthening peace and independence of the Near East countries'. The 'Observer' based his argument, in part, on Ben Gurion's statement that Israel would not be in a position to tolerate for long the 'so-called' violations of the armistice agreements by the Arab states, and on intimations by 'the ruling circles in Israel' that if a war was to break out it would not just be a local one. The article attested to the nervousness and concern, hence its warning to Israel:

Israeli–Soviet relations, 1953–67

> The ruling circles in Israel probably don't take into consideration that the preservation of tranquillity and peace in the Middle East corresponds to the interests of all nations in this region – and not least – Israel itself. Being pushed by aggressive imperialist circles, these extremists in Israel are placing their country and its future in a difficult position by their attacks and hostile actions towards Arab independent states.

Such actions, noted 'Observer', could bring about 'poisonous results first of all to Israel itself'.

There was no evidence that the Soviet Union was trying to restrain the Arab states from the continuous sabotage acts by fedayeen within the territory of Israel. A. Chelouche, Chargé d'Affaires of Israel's Embassy in Moscow, brought up this question in his talk with Soviet Deputy Minister of Foreign Affairs, A. Zorin, who replied: 'One could interpret the Arab actions as retaliation for retaliation, and it would be difficult to assert which was earlier and which later in this chain of retaliatory acts.'[6] This was in complete disregard of Israel's vital interests and accompanied by a deterioration in bilateral relations, which was marked by the cancellation of commercial deals with Israel, refusal to use the option of increasing oil exports to Israel, a decline in exit permits for Jews wishing to emigrate to Israel, and so on, all this in an impolite tone toward Israel[7] and combined with a propaganda campaign against it aimed at presenting Israel as one who tends to be the spearhead for Western powers for returning the 'colonialist regime' to the Middle East.

On the other hand, towards the Western powers the Soviet Union, in its statement dated 15 September 1956 'on the need for peaceful settlement of the Suez Question', argued:[8]

> The Soviet government considers it necessary again to declare that it supports the view that freedom of navigation through the Suez Canal should be ensured for all countries and that such a situation can, and should be brought about only by peaceful means, taking into account the inalienable rights of Egypt as well as the interests of the states using the Suez Canal.

This was a balanced appeal whose main purpose was to prevent a local flare-up and gradually bring about a positive development which would serve Egypt's interest.

In this statement it was also noted:

> Moreover the Soviet government expresses support for the view that all countries which signed the 1888 convention should be represented at the Conference, including the successor states of countries which signed the above-mentioned Convention, the Arab countries which are territorially situated in direct proximity to the canal and are vitally interested in the peaceful settlement of this question, and other countries using the Suez Canal.[9]

Israel was not included in any of the detailed categories mentioned above. The Soviet Union was of the opinion that this was a question between Egypt and Israel, thus it attributed Israel's right to use the canal to a bilateral and not an international dimension.

And then came the warning:

> The USSR as a great power cannot stand aloof from the Suez question and cannot fail to display concern at the situation which has come about at the present time as a result of the actions of the Western powers. This is understandable, because any violation of peace in the region of the Middle East cannot but affect the interest of the security of the Soviet State.

The leaders of Israel and France did not consider in advance what the USSR's reaction to a war against Egypt would be.[10] At any rate, none of them presumed that the USSR would be prepared to carry out its threats, on the basis of its deterring statements publicly published and of its talks with Israeli representatives. Judging from the evidence at our disposal, it seems that the Soviet factor by itself did not play any determining role in the decision to go to war. Had it been taken into consideration, it might have been, as the then Chief of Staff M. Dayan said, that Israel would not have gone to war.[11]

Let us examine the USSR's relation to Israel during the war, according to its official statements, which reflected, faithfully, its relations in reality on the bilateral and Middle Eastern level.

MAIN POINTS OF SOVIET GOVERNMENT STATEMENT 'ON ARMED AGGRESSION AGAINST EGYPT' ON 31 OCTOBER 1956

Israel's invasion of Egypt was used as an excuse by Britain and France to conquer the Suez Canal.

The government of Israel 'operating as a tool of imperialist circles bent on restoring the regime of colonial oppression in the East has challenged all the Arab peoples of the East fighting against colonialism'.

'The path chosen by the extremist ruling circles of Israel is a criminal one and dangerous, above all to the State of Israel itself and its future.'

The statement ended with an appeal to the United Nations Security Council that it must 'take prompt measures' towards ending the 'aggressive actions' by Britain, France and Israel against Egypt and towards the immediate withdrawal of the interventionist forces from Egyptian territory.[12] At this stage the appeal did not contain concrete threats except that the Soviet government held 'that all responsibility for the dangerous consequences of these aggressive actions against Egypt will rest entirely with governments which have taken the line of aggression'.

The statement testified to the prime Soviet fear that the campaign of conquering the canal might become a precedent regarding other areas, previously ruled by Britain and France, and would return 'the colonialist regime', which may endanger, from the Soviet point of view, the progress of the decolonization process in the world generally, and in the Middle East particularly. Israel was portrayed in the Soviet statement as one who assisted the Western powers to achieve their goal and consequently increase their threat to the USSR's security.

The statement did not specify what kind of danger Israel was facing. It could, however, be presumed that it had a double intention. Firstly, Israel itself had emerged as a result of a process of liberation from the yoke of colonialism, and if a precedent were to be created of colonial States returning to conquer areas they had previously ruled, then Israel itself would be endangered by such a possibility. Secondly, the Arab states too could have behaved towards Israel in the same manner by invading its territory to conquer it and consequently pursue their aspirations to destroy it.

IDENTICAL MESSAGES FROM THE SOVIET PRIME MINISTER
TO THE PRIME MINISTERS OF BRITAIN AND FRANCE
ON 5 NOVEMBER 1956

After having harshly condemned Britain and France for their involvement in the war in co-operation with Israel, the USSR posed a question: 'In what situation would Britain/France find themselves, if they were attacked by stronger states, possessing all types of modern weapons ... for instance rocket weapons?' The note stated that 'the Suez Canal issue was only a pretext for British and French aggression, which has other and far-reaching aims ... of destroying the national independence of the States in the Middle East and re-establishing the regime of colonial slavery'. It concluded by saying that 'the war in Egypt can spread to other countries and turn into a Third World War' and that the Soviet government was fully determined to crush the aggressors by the use of force and to restore peace in the East.[13]

The messages hinted that the claim that the motive to attack Egypt was to assure freedom of navigation through the Suez Canal was 'absolutely fallacious' since the USSR itself and other nations (it did not specify which) would have seen to it that Egypt respected its commitments to freedom of navigation, since they themselves were interested in it no less than Britain and France. Therefore, the note stated that the main object for the British-French attack was not the question of freedom of navigation but the aspiration to return the domination of the canal to the hands of Britain and France – an allegation already made against Britain and France.

The main negative thrust of the messages was in the open threat against Britain and France of using force against them, and seeking UN support and USA co-operation in that. Yet, the proposed involvement, in all its severity, had to be approved by the Security Council and agreed to by the USA. Had it been raised for discussion at the Council, a veto would have been cast against it, not only by the powers directly involved in the war but also by the United States. That meant there was no chance of it being accepted, and perhaps because of that the USSR limited itself, in advance, by saying that it was seeking the Security Council's acceptance for its intervention in repelling the 'aggressors'. In addition, the threat to the powers was not accompanied by a call to the Soviet Ambassadors in London and Paris to return to Moscow, nor by any announcement of the breaking off or freezing of commercial, economic, cultural and scientific relations. It seemed, therefore, that on the one hand it was a psychological threat for propaganda purposes aimed at frightening the powers – which were in any case being pressured by the USA to stop the war – and on the other hand it was intended as a demonstration to Egypt and the Arab states of the range of Soviet support for them.[14]

MAIN POINTS OF THE MESSAGE SENT BY THE SOVIET PRIME MINISTER TO THE PRIME MINISTER OF ISRAEL ON 5 NOVEMBER 1956

The government of Israel is acting as an instrument of outside imperialist forces ... challenging all the peoples of the East who are fighting against colonialism for their freedom and independence.

The activities of Israel's government show 'the worth of all the false assurances about Israel's love for peace and her desire for peaceful co-existence with the neighboring Arab states. With these assurances the Israeli government has in fact only tried to blunt the vigilance of other peoples while preparing a traitorous attack against her neighbors.'

Fulfilling the will of others, acting on instructions from abroad, the Israeli government 'is criminally and irresponsibly playing with the fate of peace, with the fate of its people. It is sowing a hatred for the State of Israel among the peoples of the East such as cannot but make itself felt with regard to the future of Israel and which puts in jeopardy the very existence of Israel as a State.'

The Soviet government 'is at the present time taking measures in order to put an end to the war and curb the aggressors' and is expecting that the government of Israel 'will change its mind, while there is still time' to discontinue its military operations against Egypt ... and withdraw its troops from Egyptian territory.

The message concluded: 'Taking into account the situation that has arisen, the Soviet government has decided to instruct its Ambassador in Tel Aviv to depart from Israel and leave immediately for Moscow' in the hope that the government of Israel 'will properly understand and assess this warning'.[15]

The text of the Soviet message addressed to Israel is very harsh and resolute in comparison with those sent to the Prime Ministers of Britain and France. Its main severity is the danger threatening the future of Israel, though it did not attest to the Soviet Union itself constituting that danger, whereas in its messages to Britain and France, the Soviet Union hinted, clearly, at the use of military force against them. The threat of taking measures in order to bring about a cease-fire and withdrawal of Israeli troops from Egyptian territory could have been interpreted as a threat to take political and economic measures, but not necessarily military measures. But harshest of all was the hint of delegitimization of Israel's right to exist as a state.

When the Soviet message was received in Israel, some saw it as containing a direct Soviet threat to Israel (only Israel's Ambassador to Moscow, Y. Avidar, thought differently and called it 'fraud').[16] Perhaps, the rumors, for which Krushchev himself was responsible, on the consigning of volunteers to Egypt were the source of that assessment. The USA assisted the formation of that impression, since it was interested in the government of Israel interpreting the Soviet threat to its existence as a real one.[17]

As in its statement of 31 October 1956, so in this message the Soviet government refrained from noting the source of the danger for Israel. It may be presumed (as in the case of the statement of 31 October 1956) that the source of the danger was to be related firstly to the Western powers who aspired, in the Soviet view, to again dominate the countries where they had previously ruled – and, again in Soviet perception, Israel was assisting them in this direction. From this it followed that Israel might fall victim to these ambitions, ones it had itself helped bring to fruition. Secondly, the hatred of the Arab states towards Israel had considerably intensified after the Sinai Campaign, and their hopes to destroy it would perhaps thus appear justified. Since the statement hinted that the hatred towards Israel stemmed from the countries in the East (meaning the Arab states), and in face of the tone of Soviet 'anxiety' for Israel's existence as a sovereign and independent state (otherwise it would not have found it necessary to warn Israel of the danger lurking before it), it could be presumed that the threat to Israel's future was not coming from the USSR. That is, contrary to suppositions rife upon receipt of the message, its contents did not inform Israel that it would be crushed by Soviet forces.[18]

The recall of the Soviet Ambassador to Moscow intimated that it was not the intention of the Soviet Union to break relations with Israel. Thus, it could also be understood that the Soviet threat was not of operating force against Israel, but rather a sign of protest and perhaps a gesture towards Egypt.

In his 8 November 1956 reply to Soviet Prime Minister Bulganin, Israel's Prime Minister Ben Gurion rejected a Soviet accusation claiming that Israel, by invading Egypt, had acted in the interests of the Western powers. He reminded Bulganin of the organized infiltration of the fedayeen gangs into Israel's territory, according to Nasser's instructions, and the Egyptian blockade of the Suez Canal to Israeli navigation – all to prove Egypt's provocations against Israel. Ben Gurion also informed Bulganin of Israel's decision to respond favorably to the United Nations General Assembly's appeal to stop fighting against Egypt and withdraw from Egyptian territory as well as Israel's readiness to negotiate with Egypt a peace arrangement with no preconditions. At the end of his reply he expressed his surprise and regret at the threat to Israel's existence and integrity that was embodied in Bulganin's message of 5 November 1956. Ben Gurion also stressed that Israel's Foreign Policy was independently determined, without intervention from foreign interests. That reply revealed no sign of giving in to the Soviet threat nor any evidence of fright.[19]

THE SOVIET THREAT

The Soviet Prime Minister's messages of 5 November addressed to the Prime Ministers of Britain, France and Israel were accompanied by two dramatic appeals, one to US President D. Eisenhower, and the second to the President of the UN Security Council, proposing that the USA co-operate with the USSR, with UN support, in taking immediate measures to 'curb the aggression' of Britain, France and Israel against Egypt. The Soviet Union told of its readiness to open immediate negotiations on the advancement of its proposal.[20]

It was probably part of the general political offensive aimed at neutralizing the USA, so that it would not extend political support for Britain, France and Israel, and at putting on pressure so that the USA would influence these three states to stop fighting in light of the threat of direct Soviet involvement to support Egypt.

The Soviet Union continued to use the weapon of a threat of direct involvement, even after the three states had already announced their willingness to accept the appeals of the UN General Assembly regarding the cessation of fighting and withdrawal of their troops from Egypt. The excuse for the threat was that the withdrawal might be delayed, beyond the agreed timetable. Following are two passages from a Tass statement in this respect, of 10 November 1956:

> A graphic expression of the warm sympathy of the Soviet people for the Egyptian people as well as for the other peoples of the East fighting for their national independence and freedom is provided by numerous statements of Soviet citizens, among whom are many pilots, tank men, artillery men, and officers of the reserve-participants in the Great Patriotic War – who ask to be allowed to go to Egypt as volunteers, in order to fight together with the Egyptian people to drive the aggressors from Egyptian soil ...

> It has been stated in the leading circles of the USSR that if, in spite of the UN decisions, Britain, France and Israel do not evacuate all their troops from the territory of Egypt and should they, under various pretexts, delay the implementation of these decisions and accumulate forces creating a threat of resumption of military operations against Egypt, the appropriate bodies in the Soviet Union would not hinder the departure of Soviet citizens – volunteers who have expressed their desire to take part in the struggle of the Egyptian people for their independence.

The Soviet Union justified its involvement by stating that 'the Soviet people have never been, nor will they be, passive onlookers in the event of international outrages, when some colonial powers or others are trying to re-enslave by force of arms the states in the East which have become independent'.[21]

This threat had a double purpose: the one, to create panic among the Western powers and Israel, and the other, to demonstrate 'real' support for Egypt. Except for its psychological impact it lacked any acceptable basis of credibility (fighting ceased five days prior to the publication of the statement and the decision to withdraw was taken two days earlier). Nevertheless, this statement was used, over the course of time, for Soviet propaganda purposes as a means of pressure to force the decision for withdrawal.

Message from the Soviet Prime Minister addressed to Israel's Prime Minister on 15 November 1956

This message was a reply to the letter of 8 November 1956 from Israel's Prime Minister. It was polemical but less harsh than his previous Message, sent on 5 November 1956, and devoid of all threats to Israel's future. The main points were as follows:

The fact that Israel attacked Egypt many times because of its military actions in the territory of its neighbors contradicts Israeli arguments that these countries were endangering its existence.
Israel not only failed to heed the appeal of the UN General Assembly for an immediate cease-fire and the withdrawal of troops, but even openly announced its annexationist intentions regarding the Gaza Strip, the Sinai Peninsula and the Tiran and Sanefir islands in the Gulf of Aqaba. Israel also announced that the armistice agreements concluded between Israel and the Arab states are invalid.
Even when compelled to withdraw its troops from Egypt, Israel demanded that 'satisfactory agreements must be concluded with the UN' with regard to international forces entering the Suez Canal Zone. All this obviously contradicts the assertion that the policy of Israel is dictated by a longing for peace and the 'vital needs' of Israel.
'The Soviet government is convinced that Israel's current policy, intended to incite hostility against the Arabs and to suppress them, is really dangerous for the cause of universal peace and lethal for Israel ... This policy is only in the interests of the external forces seeking to restore colonialism in this region. The Soviet government is profoundly convinced that it runs counter to the interests or all peoples in the Middle East.'
The aggression against Egypt 'undermined Israel's international position, aroused deep hatred towards it on the part of the Arabs and other Eastern peoples, worsened Israel's relations with many states and has brought about new economic and other difficulties.'
The Soviet government considers it necessary, for the sake of

stabilizing the situation in the Middle East and eliminating the consequences of aggression against Egypt, that measures be taken to rule out any probability of new provocations by Israel against the neighboring states and to ensure a stable peace and tranquillity in the Middle East.

'Justice demands' that Israel, Britain and France compensate Egypt for the loss of property. International UN forces should be stationed on both sides of the Israeli–Egyptian demarcation line.

The Soviet Prime Minister concluded his Message by expressing his hope that 'the government of Israel will draw the proper conclusions from the lesson of recent events' as 'a participant in the aggression against Egypt'.[22]

This message disregarded the Israeli security situation prior to the Sinai Campaign; it follows that the demand to settle disputes between states by peaceful means applied to Israel only and not to the Arab states.

As for the annexation of the Sinai Peninsula to Israel, the Soviet Message was referring to Ben Gurion's speech in the Knesset on 7 November 1956 in which he surveyed Israel's motives for the Sinai Campaign and its hopes for the future, including its conditions for peace.[23] He hinted that it was not Israel's intention to return to the previous armistice lines with Egypt (later on Ben Gurion revealed that it was indeed possible to understand from his words that he really intended to annex territories from the Sinai Peninsula and the islands of Senfire and Tiran).[24]

There were two new elements in the message:

(a) Israel should return Egyptian property – meaning mainly Soviet arms captured by Israel during the war – and compensate Egypt for material damages;
(b) a UN force should be stationed on *both* sides of the Israeli–Egyptian border line.

However, it seems that the main warning which the Soviet Union wanted to pass on to Israel was related to its policy in the Middle East; namely, Israel's integration into the Western powers' plans in the Middle East might result in a disaster for Israel and to the peace and security in the region. The lesson which the Soviet Union

251

wanted to impart to Israel, following the Sinai Campaign, was that Israel's policy in the Middle East had the power to intensify the confrontation between the eastern and western powers, or that this confrontation had a decisive influence on Israel's relations with its neighboring states, and this should be a fundamental Israeli national consideration, which should serve Israel's interests in the region. This should be one of Israel's main considerations.

The Prime Minister of Israel's answer of 18 November 1956 to the Soviet Prime Minister's message

Ben Gurion explained at length the background to Israel's motives for the Sinai Campaign and rejected vigorously the Soviet demand that Israel compensate Egypt and return property gained through the war, as well as its proposal that UN forces be stationed on both sides of the Israeli–Egyptian armistice lines. He also noted that Israel had no intentions of annexing Egyptian territories.[25] This was the last exchange of notes between the two Prime Ministers regarding the Sinai Campaign.

THE AFTERMATH OF THE SINAI CAMPAIGN

Whilst the negotiations were being conducted between Israel and the USA regarding security guarantees for free Israeli and international navigation through the Straits of Aqaba and the stationing of UN forces in the Gaza Strip – as a condition of Israel's full withdrawal to the Israeli–Egyptian armistice lines – US President D. Eisenhower presented on 5 January 1957 a plan defining the new policy of the USA on the Middle Eastern states.

This plan, endorsed by the US Congress (9 March 1957) and called the Eisenhower Doctrine, included the following three principles of importance to Israel:[26]

1. The US will co-operate with and assist any nation or group of nations in the general area of the Middle East in the development of economic strength dedicated to the maintenance of national independence.
2. The President will be authorized to undertake in the same region

programs of military assistance and co-operation with any nation or group of nations which desires such aid.

3. Such assistance and co-operation includes the employment of the armed forces of the US to secure and protect the territorial integrity and political independence of such nations requesting such aid against overt armed aggression from any nation controlled by international communism. These measures would have to be consonant with the treaty obligations of the US, including the UN Charter, and with any action or recommendation of the UN.

The third principle contains the new main element of the plan, granting the President the authorization to use military force in order to assist an attacked Middle Eastern State, if it so desired, should he find it necessary. Doubtless the background to this plan was the Soviet penetration into the Middle East.[27]

The Soviet Union's first official reaction appeared in a Tass statement on the Eisenhower Doctrine on 13 February 1957. The statement sharply denounced the goals of the plan, which in the Soviet view contained a great danger to peace and security in the Middle East, since its main aim was to 'impose on the region nothing but a regime that was a kind of military protectorate and set back the development of these states for many years'. It asserted that the plan 'goes much further than the notorious tripartite 1950 declaration by Britain, France and the United States and the 1951 plan for the establishment of the so-called Middle East Command' and was even more dangerous.

As for Israel, the statement noted:

> The US interference in the internal affairs of the Arab countries, and the crude threat to employ force against those countries, can only encourage the aggressive tendencies of Israel's ruling circles with regard to the Arab countries. These extremist circles, closely connected to American monopolies, will seek – relying on US support – to carry out their predatory plans, which in turn could aggravate the situation in the Middle East even further and greatly heighten the danger to peace in that area.

In summing up the statement, it was declared that the operation of the plan 'which envisages the possibility of employing US armed forces in the area, might lead to dangerous consequences, the responsibility for which will rest entirely with the US government'.[28]

There was nothing new in the Soviet reaction. Not even in its Israeli paragraph which was probably addressed to Arab leaders to deter them from seeking any assistance through the US plan by activating the 'Israeli threat' in permanent use by Soviet propaganda after the Sinai Campaign. Just as the attempts by Western powers to set up military alliances in the region gave birth to the USSR's peace plan of 17 April 1956 for the settlement of the Arab–Israeli problem, so also this time following the Eisenhower Doctrine, the USSR presented the Western powers, on 11 February 1957, with 'Basic Principles for a Declaration by the Governments of the USSR, USA, Britain and France, on Peace and Security in the Middle East and Non-Interference in the Domestic Affairs of the Countries of that Area'.

The principles were:[29]

1. The preservation of peace in the Middle East through the settlement of all issues by peaceful means alone, and by means of negotiations.
2. Non-interference in the domestic affairs of the Middle East countries; respect for their sovereignty and independence.
3. The renunciation of all attempts to involve these countries in military blocs in which great powers would participate.
4. The removal of foreign bases and the withdrawal of foreign troops from the territories of the Middle East countries.
5. Reciprocal refusal to deliver arms to the Middle East countries.
6. The promotion of the economic development of the Middle East countries without the attachment of political, military or other terms incompatible with the dignity and sovereignty of these states.

This declaration of principles, proposed for the signature of the four powers, was aimed at serving the needs of Soviet propaganda in order to demonstrate the constructive position of Soviet policy in the Middle East, *vis à vis* the military plans of the USA, with a declared goal of preventing a power to act in the Middle East whenever it might think it necessary. For this reason, no doubt, the proposed declaration did not receive a positive response from the Western powers. Moreover, at that stage the Western powers were not prepared to give up their attempts at establishing military alliances in the Middle East and refrain from supplying arms to their allies in the region. From Israel's point of view, the proposed declaration presented a contradiction between the calling for increased economic relations between the countries of the Middle East and the powers, and the Soviet break of such relations between the USSR and Israel for purely political reasons.

ISRAEL AND THE EISENHOWER DOCTRINE PLAN

In the course of January 1957, Egypt, Syria and Saudi Arabia rejected the plan. (Saudi Arabia later switched from rejection to support.) Iraq, Jordan, Iran, Lebanon and Pakistan supported it. In June 1957 Israel, too, expressed its support for it. Prime Minister Ben Gurion, in his statement in the Knesset, noted that the reason Israel supported the plan was not because it was anti-Soviet inclined, but rather owing to the feeling of security it granted Israel in the face of the growth of Egyptian and Syrian military strength due to arms received from the USSR and because it might deter those two neighboring countries of Israel from undertaking aggressive acts against it.[30] Ben Gurion added that, unlike the other countries expressing support for the Doctrine, Israel's written announcement of acceptance stated that 'it opposed any attack, no matter by whom, it had no aggressive aim against any state of nation and did not condemn any state ...' This explanation was intended at removing the sting of 'anti-communism' from the Doctrine. This was a genuine gesture to the USSR on Israel's part aimed at not worsening mutual relations in light of the inter-power confrontation and Israel's commitment given to the USSR in 1953 that it would not join any aggressive pact against the USSR.[31]

In the course of 1957–58 the USSR pursued an extensive and active policy in the Middle East and in UN forums intended to prevent Britain and America from gaining footholds in the region. It sent Israel several sharp notes containing warnings about its fate and future in the region after permitting British and American troops to cross its air space into Lebanon.[32]

Also in diplomatic talks Soviet representatives repeatedly stressed that Israel's co-operation with Western powers was the main factor hindering its *rapprochement* with the Soviet Union.

Sometimes it seemed in this respect that by raising its arguments against the Soviet Union, because of its one-sided policy in the Arab–Israeli conflict and its disregard for Israel's security needs and Israel's aspiration for peace with its neighboring States, Israel was also disregarding Soviet interests in the Middle East, as noted in writing (as for instance Bulganin's last message to Ben Gurion and in the Soviet government's notes addressed to Israel's government with regard to Jordan and Lebanon) as well as orally. That is, Israel did not properly grasp the Soviet message on the link between Israel's policy towards the Western powers in the Middle East and the USSR's relations with the Arab states and Israel. This follows from Ben Gurion's statement in the Knesset on 21 October 1957.[33]

Israel's foreign policy, according to Ben Gurion, was outlined first of all according to the national needs of Israel and not according to the needs of the USSR. These needs were based fundamentally on the constant enforcement of Israel's security, by strengthening the relations with those countries that assisted Israel economically and militarily, and by enabling the Jewish communities in the Diaspora to join the build-up of the State and maintain free contact with it. The USSR was not included in this category, both because of its attitude towards Israel and because of its policy towards its Jewish citizens.

Ben Gurion confessed on that occasion that from the beginning of its independence, Israel was compelled to act in two circles: the regional and the international. Israel was facing a dual battle, military and diplomatic, without either of them being able to come to a conclusion. 'Because in this double battle forces who act in the big circle are interested and involved to a greater or lesser degree.' Had the small circle been separated from the big one, then the military power would have had the upper hand. However, according to Ben Gurion's summing up, based on the history of the State, it was not in the power of a military battle alone to tip the scale because 'the Middle East circle, more than any other world region, is integrated within the world circle, and the balance of power in the world differs from the balance in regional military relations'.

Ben Gurion asserted that 'immense outside powers' (namely, the USSR) are aggravating and increasing tension in the region and only 'parallel world powers [namely, the USA] could ease tension in the region'.

It follows that the initiative for an inter-power confrontation came from the USSR and that Israel would find its peace and security in the region when the inter-power confrontation ceased when the powers were on a basis of equal footing, either by dividing the spheres of influence between them or by reconciling with each other, which meant – a notion Ben Gurion had raised in his talk with the Soviet Ambassador in Israel[34] – granting security guarantees to all States in the region on behalf of both rival powers.

Ben Gurion did not believe that Israel's contribution to the process of reducing inter-power confrontation should be by declaring a policy of neutrality,[35] but by being a forceful factor in the Middle East which by its military and economic power would deter those who wished to destroy it.

There was not much new in his theory, since he had already expressed its main points when he first outlined the principles of Israel's foreign policy.[36] However, the pivotal point in his address – Israel's security – is interesting, even after Israel had proven its military strength in the Sinai Campaign, and had consequently become a decisive military factor in the Middle East. He considered the security of Israel's existence as a decisive question so long as Israel's neighbors did not recognize its right to exist in peace and security.

From this standpoint, Israel's acceptance of the Eisenhower Doctrine coincided with the security needs of Israel. It was the first time that Israel's aspiration to be in the same camp as two of its neighboring Arab states (Jordan and Lebanon) was fulfilled, though it was a loose security framework. It was also the first time that Israel's links with the USA became stronger, on the regional basis, without having relations with the USSR broken off, in light of its commitments to the USSR before these relations were resumed in 1953.

The Sinai Campaign created the first clash between the security interests of Israel and strategic interests of the USSR in the Middle East. The total balance sheet showed that Israel came out as a the one who gained – for the first time after its War of Independence – as a decisive military factor among the states in the region, whereas the powers ought to have taken it into account in their military considerations of the region. The Soviet Union too came out having gained both in the international arena and in the Middle East (which was considered to be under the exclusive influence of the West) as a political force that should be taken into account in the regional considerations. Yet, Israel's impressive achievement in the battle-field had not raised it in the eyes of the Soviet Union to a level equal to that of the Arab states as a factor which would be important to cultivate and to mold closer relations with. On the contrary, in the eyes of the Soviet Union, the importance of the Arab factor seemed to be greater than that of Israel. Moreover, Israel's military might and its co-operation with Britain and France were exploited by Soviet propaganda for three purposes:

1. Deepening Soviet presence and involvement among the Arab states (mainly Egypt and Syria).
2. Demonstrating its loyalty to the Arab world and the non-aligned nations.
3. Pushing aside the settlement of the Arab–Israeli conflict, intending to perpetuate it as a guarantee of an increased Arab dependence upon the USSR.

The Soviet propaganda apparatus did this by presenting Israel as an instrument of Western imperialism and neo-colonialism and denigrated it as a state living by its sword for purposes of expansion and the oppression of peoples. Israel was compelled to pay this price in exchange for its alliances with Britain and France in the Sinai Campaign, the peace it enjoyed along its border with Egypt (until the Six Day War in 1967) and the free passage of its ships through the Straits of Tiran.

NOTES

1 Statement by the Soviet Ministry of Foreign Affairs, 17 April 1956, and joint declarations with Britain of 25 April 1956 and with France on 19 May 1956. Also statements by the Soviet government of 9 Aug. 1956 and 15 Sept. 1956 (concerning the Suez Canal).
2 On Egypt's decision to nationalize the Suez Canal, see: *Encyclopedia Hebraica* (Hebrew), Vol. 25, pp. 458–62; Y. Ro'i, *From Encroachment to Involvement*, pp. 174–81; A. Eban, *My Life*, pp. 204–5, noting that Israel acted in the USA to frustrate Egypt's request to receive American aid for building the dam.
3 On the different attitudes to Israel's security policy, see: M. Sharett, *Private Diary*, Vol. 5, pp. 1507–20; Y. Yissaharov, Maariv, 20 Feb. 1974. At the meeting of the Mapai Political Committee on 27 Dec. 1955, Sharett explained his

objection to Israel conducting a preventive war with the following arguments.

There was no assurance of Israel's victory. The war could expand and not remain restricted to the Israeli–Egyptian frontiers. A foreign power could interfere. A war initiated by Israel – which would escalate a small incident into retaliation on a forceful scale – would stir world public opinion against Israel. UN steps against Israel should be taken into consideration. The War of Independence was imposed: the UN supported Israel then because it stood up to fight in defense of its decision. The Jewish population (in Israel) was different. To sum up, he did not accept that the war was imperative. Mapai Archives, Protocol of the meeting, pp. 37–8, 27 Dec. 1955, File 26/35.

4   Y. Rabin, *Pinkas Sherut* ('Service Card', Hebrew), Vol. 1, p. 92, on the failure of retaliatory acts.

5   M. Dayan, *Yoman Maarekhet Sinai* ('Diary of the Sinai Campaign', Hebrew), p. 166.

6   A. Chelouche, First Secretary of the Israeli Embassy. The talk took place on 24 Sept. 1956. MFA Arch. File 103.1 SSR.

7   According to Israel's Ambassador in Moscow, Y. Avidar, report to the Ministry of Foreign Affairs in Jerusalem, 3 Oct. 1956. MFA Arch. File 103.1 SSR.

8   *Izvestia*, 16 Sept. 1956. English version in *The USSR and the Middle East,* p. 80.

9   Referring to the Soviet statement of 15 Sept. 1956 that stipulated freedom of navigation in the Suez Canal for all states. Soviet Deputy Foreign Minister Semyonov told Israel's Ambassador in Moscow, Y. Avidar, on 7 Oct. 1956, that the statement was of a general nature and did not go into 'the particular aspects of the problem', and that in denying Israel shipping in the canal, Egypt bases itself on paragraph 10 of the Constantinople Treaty of 1888. It follows from his words that the USSR accepted Egypt's stance on Israel's shipping in the canal. This stance corresponded with the Soviet veto in the Security Council on the resolution treating this on 29 March 1954.

10 M. Dayan,*Avnei Derekh* (Hebrew), p. 234. On the question by Israel's delegation to the French delegation a fortnight before Israel attacked Egypt, 'What would be the Soviet stand, if the Soviet Union were to send its troops to aid Egypt?' the French answered that 'they did not believe that the USSR would send its troops to Egypt and that in their view, it would satisfy itself with sending military equipment ... the shorter the battle were to be, the greater the chance that the USSR would not intervene in practice'.

A. Eban, op. cit., p. 230, quotes G. Meir: 'I think D. Ben Gurion believed that we would be able to stay in Sinai and Gaza. He did not take into consideration, nor did any one of us, that the USSR would react as it did'.

11 M. Dayan, *Yoman Maarekhet Sinai* (Hebrew), p. 166.

12 *Izvestia*, 1 Nov. 1956; English version: *The USSR and the Middle East*, p. 85.

13 *Izvestia*, 6 Nov. 1956; English version, The USSR and the Middle East, pp. 90–93.

14 This impression could be gained in Krushchev, *Krushchev Remembers* (London: Andre Deutsch, 1971), pp. 434–5.

15 *Izvestia*, 6 Nov. 1956; English version in *The USSR and the Middle East*, pp. 96–98.

16 M. Bar Zohar, *Ben Gurion*, Vol. 3, p. 1271.

17 According to A. Eban, op. cit., p. 230, Israel's Minister in Washington was called to see the US Deputy State Secretary on 7 Nov. 1956, who told him that if Israel were to stop fighting and not withdraw to the Israeli–Egyptian armistice line, Israel would be the first to be swallowed up by Soviet penetration. The USA, too, would halt its state and private aid to Israel. The

United Nations would impose sanctions on Israel and ultimately expel it.
18 On Ben Gurion's fear of a Soviet involvement which might lead to a world war, see M. Bar Zohar, op. cit., Vol. 5, pp. 1282–3.
19 M. Dayan, *Yoman Maarekhet Sinai* (Hebrew), p. 165.
20 *Izvestia*, 6 Nov. 1956.
21 *Izvestia*, 11 Nov. 1956; English version, *The USSR and the Middle East*, pp. 98–101.
22 *Izvestia*, 16 Nov. 1956; English version, *The USSR and the Middle East*, pp. 102–5.
23 *Divrei Haknesset*, Vol. 21, p. 198, 7 Nov. 1956.
24 A. Eban, op. cit., p. 230.
25 Information Division of Israel's Ministry of Foreign Affairs – exchange of notes, between Israel's Prime Minister D. Ben Gurion and Soviet Prime Minister N. Bulganin (in French), Nov. 1956.
26 Ben Gurion's statement in the Knesset on the Eisenhower's Doctrine and the visit to Israel of the US President's emissary. *Divrei Haknesset*, Vol. 22, pp. 2039–47, 2072–6, 3 June 1957.
27 For full text, see Y. Ro'i, op. cit., pp. 198–204.
28 *Izvestia*, 13 Jan. 1957; also English version, *The USSR and the Middle East*, pp. 105–15.
29 *Izvestia*, 13 Feb. 1957; also English version, *The USSR and the Middle East*, pp. 116–23.
30 See n. 26, above.
31 Israel's commitment was a condition for the resumption of diplomatic relations between the two countries. This fact was mentioned in *Pravda* on 25 May 1957 as a warning that Israel's joining the Eisenhower Doctrine contradicted Israel's commitment to the USSR that it would not join aggressive acts or alliances directed against the Soviet Union.
32 The USSR's statement of 29 April 1957, *Izvestia*, 30 April 1957; the USSR's statement, *Izvestia*, 2 Aug. 1958; Soviet Foreign Minister Gromyko's statement at a press conference in New York, *Izvestia*, 24 Aug. 1958; Soviet note to Israel, *Izvestia*, 7 Sept. 1958.
33 *Divrei Haknesset*, Vol. 23, pp. 1–3, 21 Oct. 1957.
34 M. Bar Zohar, op. cit., Vol. 3, p. 1336.
35 *Divrei Haknesset*, Vol. 22, p. 2075, 3 June 1957.
36 D. Ben Gurion, *Hazon va-Derekh* (Hebrew), Vol. 3, pp. 285–90 (based on his Knesset address on 4 Feb. 1952).

13 · Soviet proposals for the prevention of world war and improvement of relations between states

THE 1957 PROPOSAL AND ITS EVALUATION

ON 10 December 1957 the Soviet government addressed a note to the government of Israel, with a proposal for action in the UN 'for the prevention of a new war and the use of nuclear arms [and] for taking measures to improve relations between states'. The motive for sending the note – which was probably sent to all member states of the UN with whom the USSR maintained diplomatic relations – was the assembly of the NATO Council in December 1957, which the Soviet Union thought would discuss 'ways and means to increase the arms race; planning new strategic programs; making extensive use of nuclear arms; and turning the territories of NATO members into US storage bases for nuclear and projectile armaments'.

Though the note focused on issues such as NATO's armament and the inter-power confrontation, it also referred to the Middle East problem as part of the inter-power confrontation, mentioning the Eisenhower Doctrine and the Baghdad Pact, which had turned the Middle East 'into 'one of the most dangerous focal points of tension in international relations'. This was the only region outside Europe mentioned in the note.

The concrete proposals of the note related to military confrontation questions: turning the military alliances in Europe – NATO and the Warsaw Pact states – into a system of collective military

261

security with US participation and the signing of an agreement of non-aggression between countries included in this association. As to the Middle East, the note repeated the Soviet government's proposal to conclude an agreement between the four powers for strictly safeguarding 'the principle of non-interference in domestic affairs of states in the region and of non-use of force to solve its problems'.

The means to reach these goals, according to the note, should be in convening a meeting of heads of the powers, similar to the Geneva summit conferences, with the aims of strengthening economic and cultural relations and co-operation between states, and, first of all, 'to renounce the use of force or threats of force in solving problems; to cease hostile propaganda conducted through the press and radio towards other states'. It claimed that 'the positive solutions to these problems depend first of all upon the big powers', but other states too could contribute to a considerable degree in restoring the international situation 'that is developing in a dangerous direction'. Had member states of the UN opposed the arms race 'in their own way', they would have served, in the Soviet view, 'the cause of peace', since these states had a growing weight in international relations. Finally, the note expressed the hope that the government of Israel 'will do anything it can to assist in preventing the danger of a new war and consolidating peace and friendly co-operation between states'.[1]

Between the lines of the note, whose main goal was to create for the Soviet Union a positive image throughout the world as a peace-loving power that initiated practical proposals aimed at attenuating inter-power tension, some other considerations could also be distinguished:

1. A desire to frighten the concerned states into seeing that in co-operating with NATO or the Eisenhower Doctrine, or by joining any other military alliances of Western powers, they were endangering themselves in time of war.
2. The Middle East was next in importance, after Europe, to the USSR's global policy. Just as an inter-power understanding was needed to ease tension between the two military blocs in Europe, so it was necessary to reach a similar understanding between the Eastern and Western powers on the Middle East.

3. Agreements reached between the USSR and Western powers had direct influence on the security and peace of other states. Moreover, the reciprocal relations between the other states and the main powers could influence relationships among the powers themselves.
4. Western public opinion was of significant weight in the formation of Soviet government policy, and in determining the USSR's image in the West.

From Israel's standpoint there was an outstanding gap, in the note, between the preaching about correct mutual relations between states, based on commercial and cultural ties and a non-hostile press, on one hand, and reality, on the other. In two cases the USSR had taken quite an opposite stand towards Israel: the USSR had not renewed its commercial relations with Israel, severed unilaterally during the Sinai War, to the point of negating Israel's right to exist as a State, a campaign which had certainly not contributed in the direction of *rapprochement* between Israel and its neighboring countries and certainly was not an expression of Soviet will to maintain normal relations with Israel. In the Middle East, the Soviet Union had armed the Arab states with modern arms, without any condition that the arms should not be directed against Israel, which those states openly declared they wished to destroy.

ISRAEL'S ANSWER

Replying on 19 January 1958, the government of Israel presented its views regarding the ideas included in the Soviet note, both as regards the question of preventing a world war and as regards the Arab–Israeli dispute and the need to expand commercial and cultural relations between Israel and the USSR.[2] Following are the main points of Israel's reply:

The government of Israel agrees with the 'constructive principles' included in the Soviet note aimed at strengthening peace throughout the world in the Middle East.
Israel, as a small state unlinked by any political alliance with the world powers, is refraining from expressing an opinion as regards 'the causes of international tension, because it agrees with the points of the Soviet government in this respect'.

Israel will do anything it can to prevent a new war and strengthen co-operation between states.

Israel believes that peace is indivisible. Peace should prevail everywhere. Small and local wars could lead to a world flare-up.

Israel agrees with the USSR that relations between states should be based on principles of peaceful co-existence and co-operation.

In May 1957 Israel informed President Eisenhower that it recognized the need 'to invest every effort for the achievement of long-lasting peace in the Middle East and throughout the world, and that for its part it would be ready to co-operate with the USA and other friendly countries in order to achieve this goal'. In this respect Israel's government expressed its desire 'to co-operate with the USSR, to reach this end'.

Contrary to the UN Charter and to the Soviet principles of peace, the Arab states declined to negotiate with Israel for the establishment of peaceful relations and co-operation with it. Israel had not requested anything else from its neighboring countries.

Israel was convinced that the USSR could have assisted in the achievement of peace in the Middle East, if it had called on the Middle East states to maintain co-existence based on co-operation and peace, respect for the territorial integrity of all states in the Middle East, and if in this respect it had advised Israel and Arab states in the East, 'to open direct negotiations towards the conclusion of a peace agreement and the establishment of co-operation between them'.

Israel appealed to the USSR to increase bilateral relations and to improve relations between them as part of improving the international atmosphere. The government of Israel was convinced that such an improvement in their mutual relations would strengthen peace in the Middle East and contribute to reducing international tension.

Israel's reply indicated its government's tendency to answer the Soviet call in its attempts to spread its principles of peace and co-operation, presuming that these principles were also applicable to the Arab–Israeli conflict and to the USSR's relations with Israel. Israel refrained from giving a polemical answer regarding the causes of tension in the Middle East and presented its link with the Eisenhower Doctrine in a positive light with regard to the USSR.

Thus Israel granted the USSR a status equal to that of the USA in an effort to establish peace in the Middle East. Finally, Israel passed the ball to the Soviet court, hinting that its principles would be applicable when the USSR itself pursued them.

THE SOVIET PROPOSAL TO DEMILITARIZE THE MEDITERRANEAN BASIN OF NUCLEAR WEAPONS AND ISRAEL'S REPLY

On 20 May 1963 the Soviet government addressed a note to the government of Israel (and to governments of all the states of the Mediterranean basin) proposing to demilitarize the Mediterranean basin of nuclear weapons, and expressing readiness to offer security guarantees, together with the USA and other Western powers, so that the area of the Mediterranean Sea would be outside the area of nuclear weapons use in times of war.

The background to the Soviet appeal was linked to the entry of American nuclear submarines, equipped with Polaris missiles, into the waters of the Mediterranean Sea, and to the opening of the road for West Germany to nuclear arms, according to the decision of NATO's council in Ottawa a short time earlier. It was proposed to Israel, as a state situated in the Mediterranean basin, that it supports the Soviet proposal.[3]

The aim of the proposal was to weaken the strategic position of the Western powers in the Mediterranean. However, the Soviet proposal did not have any chance of being accepted, since some of the member states of NATO were situated in the Mediterranean basin, and they would certainly not have accepted the proposal. Therefore, it seemed that the proposal was intended to embarrass the USA and its allies, by presenting them as war instigators on the one hand, and on the other, by showing that in the area of Mediterranean Sea the USSR had a status equal to that of the Western powers, and by initiating the offer of security guarantees to the states of the basin.

In its reply of 30 May 1963, the government of Israel started by drawing the attention of the USSR to two flaws in its appeal. Firstly, the Soviet note recalled the sufferings of the nations around the Mediterranean Sea as from ancient times – Ancient Egypt, Rome,

Greece, and Carthage – but ignored one nation, whose place and historical, cultural, and political influence in region were not less than those of the states mentioned (in the note), namely, the people of Israel. Secondly, when the Soviet note described the feelings of millions of people, residents of this region, facing the danger of nuclear arms close to the 'walls of the Vatican, Jerusalem, Mecca and Medina' the note mentioned Christians and Moslems who have an interest in the well-being of these towns, with all that they signify for them. 'But, the note did not mention the Jews, whose historic capital is Jerusalem, a town sacred to the entire Jewish people, from ancient times to this day.'[4]

Following are the main points of Israel's answer:

The government of Israel has repeatedly, at every opportunity, voiced its warning against the danger of nuclear armament, stressing that it supported all means to be taken in order to prevent such danger in every place on the globe, including the Mediterranean Sea. The area of the Mediterranean Sea is not calm. The danger to its well-being stems from the desire of Arab governments to destroy Israel. These states 'are accumulating many arms and are intensifying their preparations for war with Israel. The supply of arms in great quantities to Arab governments, particularly since the end of 1955 to Egypt , disregarding the belligerent policies of these states, causes under the existing circumstances a direct threat to Israel and undermines international peace.'

If there is a possibility that the USA and the USSR will co-operate together, towards general disarmament in Israel and the Arab states, and guarantee the territorial integrity of all states in the region, it will be one of the greatest peace enterprises throughout the world. Israel believes that the USSR and the USA are capable of bringing peace to the Middle East.

The government of Israel believes that every peace-loving power should assist in reaching peace between Israel and the Arab states. Israel is not a member of any military alliance. It does not possess nuclear arms, and there are no foreign military bases on its territory, either nuclear or any other kind. The safeguard of peace is of vital interest for its existence, and its policy is based on that perception. Israel will regard very positively every useful initiative 'that would remove war dangers from the region in which it is situated'.

It was not just incidental that the USSR, in its note, disregarded the past of the Jewish people in the Middle East and the historic link of the Jewish people with Jerusalem; after all, this did not fit its pro-Arab policy in the Arab–Israeli dispute, nor its policy towards the Jewish minority within its borders.

Israel's reaction (similar to that regarding the Soviet proposal to prevent a nuclear war) was probably aimed at convincing the USSR that lessening tension in the Middle East would have a positive influence on the process of reducing tension on the inter-power level. For Israel, the reduction of regional tension came before the reduction of global tension, whereas the Soviet Union's priorities were the opposite. Regional tension served the USSR as a bargaining card with Western powers, when the USSR was interested in the existence of a controlled tension. Israel, in its reply, attempted to expose this position by stressing the gap between the Soviet preaching in theory and its real policy in practice in the Middle East. Even if Israel refrained from declaring its support for the Soviet proposal, the USSR and its supporters would have, in any case, suspected that it supported the stand of Western powers and not that of the USSR.

A SOVIET PROPOSAL FOR PEACEFUL SETTLEMENT OF INTERNATIONAL CONFLICTS AND THE QUESTION OF APPLYING IT TO THE ARAB–ISRAELI CONFLICT

On 31 December 1963 Soviet Prime Minister N. Krushchev sent a note to Israel's Prime Minister L. Eshkol proposing that 'an international agreement be signed to refrain from the use of force, and to use peaceful methods in settling territorial conflicts and border disputes between nations'.

According to Soviet press reports, Krushchev's note was dispatched to all heads of states. Their names were not specified, but from the phrase 'problems causing frequent friction between countries in various parts of the world', it is possible to conclude that this was an identical text addressed to all those countries with which the USSR maintained diplomatic relations at that time, including the State of Israel. The nature of 'these problems' was, in Krushchev's view, 'territorial conflicts and border problems between countries and the mutual or unilateral claims of countries regarding areas'.

The Soviet proposal was an additional link in the chain of the USSR's political initiatives, which had been unsuccessful as far as propaganda was concerned. It had been preceded by The International Treaty for Outlawing the Testing of Atomic Weapons in Air, Space or Underwater, and the American–Soviet agreement 'calling upon states to refrain from placing in orbit around the earth any objects carrying nuclear weapons'.[5]

The Soviet proposal was aimed, first and foremost, at serving Soviet interests by paving the way for obtaining the agreement of the various countries to the European and Asian borders which had emerged after World War II. Corresponding to this, another important objective of the note was the definition of the character of the territorial problems of the times, while suggesting proposals for their peaceful solution. Herein rested the note's significance for Israel with regard to its conflict with the Arab states. In their contacts with the Soviets and in their public declarations, Israel's leaders repeatedly referred to this proposal as one of the important fundamentals on which it would be possible to build Israeli–Soviet relations in the future.

The Arab–Israeli conflict was not mentioned explicitly in Krushchev's note, but it is known that when the Soviet Ambassador, M. Bodrov, delivered Krushchev's note Prime Minister Eshkol asked him whether the Soviet proposal applied to Israel and its neighbors as well. The Soviet Ambassador replied in the affirmative and added that the proposal would bind Israel to conduct verbal and written negotiations with Egypt as well as with all the other Arab States.[6] The operative part of the note stated that the purpose of the Soviet proposal, which would be discussed by all nations, was to lead to an international agreement regarding the renunciation of the use of force as a solution to territorial conflicts and border problems. An agreement of this nature would require the following basic preconditions:

1. The solemn undertaking of participant states to refrain from using force to change existing frontiers.
2. The assurance that territory belonging to other states should not be even temporarily the object of invasion, attack, military

occupation or any other forcible measure undertaken directly or indirectly by other states for political, economic, strategic or other reasons.

3. The guarantee that differences in social and political systems, the refusal to grant recognition, the absence of diplomatic relations, or any other pretexts should not serve as the basis for the violation by one state of the territorial integrity of another.

4. A commitment to solve all territorial disputes solely by such peaceful means as negotiations, mediation, conciliation procedures or any other peaceful method chosen by the parties concerned, in accordance with the United Nations Charter.

Each of these four preconditions had a direct connection with the situation prevailing between Israel and the Arab states. From this point of view, these proposals provided a balance between Israel's position and that of the Arabs. While the proposals would safeguard Israel from Arab attacks motivated by the desire for vengeance, they would also protect the Arab states from Israeli attacks on military or strategic pretexts.

In another section of the note, Krushchev mentioned four exceptional cases which could not be viewed as border conflicts. The first of these was *Taiwan* which , 'in ancient times was an inseparable part of China. The illegal conquest of Taiwan by the American Army must cease. The island is an integral part of the Chinese National Republic, and would have been united with it long ago were it not for external interference by another country.' In addition there was the problem of the unification of *Germany*, *Korea*, and *Vietnam* since 'after the war each of these countries found itself separated into two states, under different social regimes'. The fact that these instances were noted is important for our study since it indicates that the Arab–Israeli conflict was not included in this category, according to the Soviet political outlook, and that it belonged in the category of 'territorial conflicts and claims in connection with political borders which have been formed and established'.

From the Israeli standpoint, there were at least three important elements in the note which accorded with Israel's foreign policy: that national boundaries established by armed conflict could not be altered, that national sovereignty could not be damaged, and that territorial conflicts should be resolved peacefully, through negotiations, mediation, and so on. Although Israel was aware of the note's propaganda purpose, the decision was made to reply positively. This was done, firstly, because it was regarded as desirable 'to get on the same wavelength as the Russians', and secondly, and more importantly, because the note reiterated the principle which Israel had always upheld, namely, that the Arab–Israeli conflict should be solved peacefully on the basis of the borders formed in the 1948 Arab–Israeli war.

In his reply of 16 January 1964, Eshkol welcomed the Soviet proposal and expressed the Israeli government's agreement with them. He mentioned the paragraph in Krushchev's note which referred to the Asian nations and the fact that their economic and social development was dependent upon peace on their borders, indicating that Israel regarded itself as falling into this category. He noted that the Foreign Minister, Golda Meir, had made similar proposals on the podium of the UN. In referring to the Middle East, he noted that 'general and global commitment' would not suffice and that it would be necessary to work towards the 'activation of these principles with regard to special parts of the world as well'.

> My government believes that action must be taken to reduce tension in our region on the basis of an undertaking by all States of the area to respect the territorial integrity of each and every one of those States as its exists today. We have subscribed in the past as we do today to the principle expounded in your letter to the effect that territorial disputes should be settled without resort to force. All the States in the region must, therefore, refrain from the threat or use of force, must put an end to policies of belligerency and settle all their disputes by peaceful means and by negotiation.
>
> In view of the special circumstances which prevail in our region, it is essential to prevent changes of the frontiers and the territorial situation of the States of the area, unless such changes are effected as a result of negotiations and of free agreement between the States and on condition that they do not endanger the peace and security of any other State in the region.
>
> In the light of these considerations, and in pursuance of its declared policy, my government welcomes the proposal of

the government of the Union of Soviet Socialist Republics that an international treaty or covenant be concluded on the abandonment of the use of force for the solution of territorial disputes and frontier questions and on the settlement of international disputes by peaceful means. (Published by the Israeli Government Press Bureau, 27 Jan. 1964, in English)

Israel's affirmative reply, 'in view of the special circumstances which prevail in our region', was based on the supposition that the principle underlying the Soviet proposal applied to the Arab–Israeli conflict. It was accepted as such by the Soviets, who tended to acknowledge the historical formation of borders rather than historical claims, and perhaps for this reason Israel's reply concentrated more on the general aspect of the Arab–Israeli conflict than on the clarification of its background.

Israel's reply was welcomed in Moscow. *Izvestia* published it only in part, omitting Eshkol's words and the reference to Golda Meir's statement regarding the principles of Israel's policy in the Arab–Israeli conflict. It did, however, emphasize Israel's agreement to the proposal, stressing Israel's suggestion that these fundamentals be applied to various areas – hinting at the Middle East – and 'not limited to general and global commitments only'.[7]

In contrast to the partial publication of the Israeli government's reply, the Soviet press published Nasser's reply in full. This included the reference to Israel, which fundamentally negated the application of the principles outlined in the proposal to the Arab–Israeli conflict. The relevant section read as follows:

> ... It is well known to you that the Arab world is suffering from the conspiracy which imperialism has imposed within the heart of the Arab homeland. Through the conquest of a large part of Palestine, we are witness to a crude and cruelly imperialistic attempt, which ... does not limit itself to the expulsion of the Arab people from its land but has also established an imperialistic base within the heart of the entire Arab nation. This has impeded the unity of the Arab nation and constitutes a threat to it, as was proved by the tripartite aggression against Egypt in 1956.[8]

The publication of this missive caused the Israeli government to send Krushchev another letter, on 26 March 1964, clarifying Israel's position in the light of Egypt's reply. Israel also feared that the full publication of Nasser's statement in the Soviet press could be interpreted as tacit Soviet agreement to it. This is stated quite clearly in Eshkol's letter to Krushchev:

> While your note justly stressed that the solution of international conflicts should not be achieved through the use of military force, the President of Egypt says that he is not prepared to agree to this idea or conduct himself accordingly in relation to Israel. In his reply to your letter, as published in the Soviet press, the Egyptian President stated that he is not prepared to discuss any possible solution to the dispute with Israel by peaceful means, without resorting to threats or force. The Egyptian President's claim, in his reply to your letter, that the Soviet government supports his belligerent aspirations towards our country and favors his destructive policy, negating the principles of co-existence and the peaceful solution of conflicts as regards Israel, is particularly dangerous. This assertion of his cannot be disregarded ...

Elsewhere, Eshkol's letter describes the sequence of events leading to the 1948 Arab–Israeli war, including Gromyko's announcement made in the Security Council on 21 May 1948 that the object of the Arab action was 'the suppression of the National Liberation Movement' in Israel. The letter states that 'since then, Egypt has continued to maintain a state of war with Israel, notwithstanding continuous calls for peace by Israel', and despite Egypt's clear commitment towards Israel according to the armistice agreement, signed by both states. Eshkol adds that 'The Egyptian government openly declares that the purpose of its military preparations is in order to attack the State of Israel', noting in this connection that, '... on 14 February 1964, Cairo Radio announced, in connection with the Egyptian President's reply to your letter of 31 December 1963, that one of the most important items in Nasser's reply was the section stating that the clash between Israel and the Arabs is unavoidable, while the President of Egypt made it quite clear, in a speech given on 22 February 1964, that the prospect for the future is war against Israel, the time and place to be set by ourselves'. These declarations, noted Eshkol, should be taken seriously.[9]

The Soviets never published the letter.

Because of technical reasons in Moscow, this letter was presented to the Soviets with a considerable delay.[10] Even though the subject was still valid as far as Israel was concerned, the Soviets were not interested in publishing it at that time, probably because the planning for Krushchev's State visit to Egypt was then in full swing. The publication of even part of Eshkol's letter, provided the Soviets agreed with it at all, would have harmed the chances for the success of the visit from the outset. At the same time, the Israelis were interested in clarifying this problem with Krushchev on the eve of his departure for Egypt.

The Soviets never replied to the letter. Israeli leaders began to suspect that the underlying principle of the proposal would be waived with regard to the Arab–Israeli conflict. Two Soviet officials who were consulted on this topic denied this suspicion. The first, P. Rodakov, First Secretary of the Soviet Embassy in Israel, stated: 'Krushchev's note also applies to the Arab–Israeli conflict. However, the actual solution to the conflict is first and foremost a matter for the Israeli and Arab nations.'[11] The second, the editor of *Izvestia*, Alexei Adzhubei, gave a similar reply in response to questions posed by a diplomatic correspondent in Paris.[12]

Finally, it was Krushchev himself who declared in an interview in *Izvestia* on 5 May 1964, a few days before his departure for Cairo: 'The USSR's policy towards the Middle Eastern countries, and the Mediterranean Near East, is the same as it is towards all the rest of the world, being based on the fundamentals of peace and co-existence among nations of different regimes ...'. Although the topic of the interview was the Cyprus problem, an indirect allusion to the Arab–Israeli conflict (as requested by Eshkol from Krushchev) can be perceived within this declaration, although this was not made explicit.

The question of applying the principle of 'the peaceful solution of border conflicts' to the Middle East continued to occupy Israeli representatives, who took advantage of every suitable opportunity to induce the Soviets to make a clear and unequivocal public statement. However, the Soviets succeeded in evading this issue and the Israeli efforts did not have the desired results.

When the Soviet Foreign Minister submitted this proposal to the United Nations Assembly for ratification, towards the end of 1964, the Israeli representative proposed that the Middle East be specifically named as an area to which this principle would apply. When Deputy Prime Minister, A. Eban, raised this issue with Gromyko in a meeting held on 18 December 1964 in the UN, he noted that Israel would support the Soviet proposal, and that in Israel's view the USSR should make it clear that this principle applied to the Middle East as well. Gromyko replied evasively, declaring that his government wished for peace and normal, neighborly relations between Israel and the Arab nations, and that in the USSR's view the lessening of tension in the Middle East would serve to prevent the interference of the imperialist powers. Eban expressed the hope that the Soviets would tell this to the Arab governments too, adding that the USSR could play a decisive peacemaking role in the Middle East by applying the principles of honoring sovereignty and territorial integrity and upholding the peaceful solution of conflicts in the area. These general principles would stand the test, Eban said, when the need arose for their application to specific cases. They would have little value if certain nations were to ratify them while at the same time rejecting their application to the specific conflict in which they were engaged, as the Arabs had done regarding their dispute with Israel. Gromyko did not give an affirmative reply and noted that bilateral Israeli–Soviet relations were correct 'even though they are not warm or friendly'. He claimed that this was because of 'unfriendly' official Israeli declarations 'regarding Soviet foreign policy and the critical attitude of the Israeli press towards the Soviet Union'.[13]

On 29 March 1965 Foreign Minister Golda Meir devoted an important part of her speech in the Knesset to Israeli–Soviet relations, emphasizing Soviet arms shipments to Egypt in the light of the Soviet Union's declaration regarding the need to solve territorial conflicts peacefully. She said, 'We say again that we do not understand how supplying weapons to those who openly declare that these weapons are needed for attacking another state is compatible with the policy of peace declared by the Soviet Union'. However, she expressed the 'hope that these principles will guide the policy of the Soviet Union in our region also, for we are convinced that the Soviet Union is in a position, by using these principles, to contribute to the lessening of tension and to bring peace nearer'.

But she also indicated that the apparent contradictions in Soviet foreign policy in the Middle East were in fact a reflection of Soviet strategy, which aspired to eliminating Western influence in the area. This being so, the USSR preferred to guarantee its dominance of the Middle East by supplying arms to Egypt at the expense of peace, rather than ensuring peace at the expense of losing its ascendancy in the area.[14]

The Soviet way of avoiding making an explicit statement that the Arab–Israeli conflict was an international question, at the same time as declaring principles which could be applied to it, did not mean that these principles were not applicable to it. If it were so, the Soviet Union would have said it. It is more likely that the USSR took a technical approach, in order not to arouse Arab anger, presuming that it would declare that its principles did apply to the Arab–Israeli conflict at an appropriate time. This Soviet switch of tactics, expressed in voicing fewer calls for the settlement of the Arab–Israeli conflict, through political negotiations, and taking measures to renounce the military option, began to be felt after the Sinai War.

From the Soviet standpoint, the conflict served the interests of the USSR in the region. For this reason the Soviet Union was interested in continuing with the conflict, if not to perpetuate it. After all, it was better for the USSR to secure its domination in the Middle East region – by sending mass armaments to Egypt and Syria – than to ensure peace by settling the Arab–Israeli conflict without its domination.

NOTES

1   MFA Arch. File 103.1 SSR.
2   Ibid.
3   MFA Arch. File 103.1 SSR.
4   MFA Arch. File 103.1 SSR.
5   Ibid.
6   Ibid.
7   *Izvestia*, 1 Feb. 1964.
8   *Izvestia*, 13 Feb. 1964.
9   A. Dagan, *Moscow and Jerusalem*, p. 153.
10   Ibid., 154.
11   *Kol Haam*, 16 March 1964.
12   *Jerusalem Post*, 9 April 1964.
13   A. Dagan, op. cit., p. 158.
14   *Divrei Haknesset*, Vol. 42, p. 1668, 29 March 1965.

14 · Intensification of Soviet activity in the Arab states and intensification of tension

DETERIORATION IN THE SOVIET ATTITUDE TOWARDS ISRAEL FOLLOWING THE RISE TO POWER OF THE BA'ATH PARTY IN SYRIA

THE LEFT-WING Ba'ath faction in Syria gained the almost immediate support of the USSR after its rise to power in February 1966, particularly after it became clear that the new regime intended to base itself on co-operation with the Syrian Communists and that its objective was to develop close ties with the USSR. The return to Syria of Haled Bagdash, Secretary of the Syrian Communist Party, and the inclusion of a Communist in the government, signified a meaningful development. This was the first time this had happened in any Arab country, including Egypt, which had enjoyed more Soviet economic and military assistance than any other Arab state.

The Soviet press began to describe the 'progressive' nature of the Syrian regime and to be impressed by its enmity to the Western powers, which was seen through manifestations of hostility towards Israel against the background of the Arab–Israeli dispute. Soviet delegations began to visit Syria frequently and they included high officials. The visit of a Syrian delegation to Moscow in May 1965 heralded a period of close relations between the two countries. Syria gradually became the central pivot point of Soviet foreign policy in the Middle East. Official announcements and articles in the press indicated that the USSR was prepared to make every effort to guarantee the stability of this regime, and assure its continued existence as the USSR's foothold and mainstay in the Middle East in light of the strategic importance of its proximity to the USSR. Since the Ba'ath government in Syria professed a policy of open support for the Al Fatah terrorists calling for a 'war of national liberation' with Israel, the USSR did not refrain from utilizing Arab hatred to enhance its position in the region. In this connection the USSR embarked on an intense anti-Israel campaign – unprecedented since the days of the Sinai War – which gradually led to the sequence of events preceding the Six Day War.

Visit of the Syrian state delegation to Moscow, 18–24 April 1966

On the eve of the visit the Soviet press highly praised the social changes anticipated in Syria and the close co-operation expected between Syria and Egypt, Algeria, and Yemen, 'which was to become a strong anti-imperialist factor in the Middle East'. Expressions were voiced and quoted, which in the course of time became part and parcel of the anti-Israel propaganda in the USSR, such as:

> The Palestinian tragedy is the outcome of colonialist policies on the part of the Zionists and the colonialists, who are striving to dominate the Arab East and subvert Arab unity ...[1]

> The leaders of Israel, who are the allies of the imperialist states and especially those of the USA and West Germany, have transformed Israel into a military arsenal and a base for aggression and blackmail against the national and social liberation movement of the Arab people. The leaders of Israel have not even recoiled from extending their hands to Nazism, to the leaders of Bonn, in order to obtain arms to fight the Arab nation ... These adventures ... intensify the tension in the region and threaten the Arab world ...[2]

> The restoration of the legal rights of the Arabs of Palestine and the implementation of the 'imperialist-supported Zionist programs for expansion and aggression constitute the most important problems facing Syria, which is supported by all progressive forces'.[3]

277

> It is vitally important to unite all the progressive forces of the Arab world in order to hinder the plan to establish the 'Islamic Alliance' to repel the plots of imperialism and Zionism and to support the legal rights of the Arabs in Palestine ...[4]

The frequent use of these terms is worthy of note:

1. 'Zionism' and Zionists were mentioned in one breath with imperialism and colonialism. This was a phenomenon unprecedented since the last period of Stalin's days. Although these statements were not attributed to Soviet leaders, but to their Arab guests, the fact that they were published may bear witness to Soviet identification with the quoted statements, and thus encourage the ones who voiced them to pursue an extreme anti-Israeli policy.

At any rate there was no hint of any Soviet reservations about the extreme Arab declarations.

2. Israel as a 'base for aggression' constituted a threat to 'the national and social liberation' of the Arab people. In other words as long as Israel existed in the region, it would be a factor preventing the advancement of 'progressive' and left-wing ideology in the Arab world.

3. 'The restoration of the legitimate rights of the Arabs in Palestine' and Israel's existence were the central problems preoccupying the new Syrian regime. According this definition, they took precedence over the problems of economic, social progress of Syria. The elimination of Israel, therefore, came before the implementation of social reforms aimed at putting Syria 'on the road to non-capitalist development'. Israel was perceived and presented as the main hindrance to achievement of this goal.

4. Only 'Arab unity' could save the Arab people from their Zionist foe. From this propaganda line it transpires that this 'unity' would succeed in its tasks if it were compounded of 'progressive' forces in the Arab world acting with the guided support and inspiration of the USSR and not by 'reactionary' forces are acting on behalf of Western powers in co-operation with Israel.

In the course of the Syrian State visit to Moscow, the Soviet leadership's expressions on Israel were relatively moderate. Prime Minister Kosygin even included in his welcome speech in the Kremlin in honor of Syrian Prime Minister Zeayn on 19 April 1966 the following passage: 'There is no, nor could there be any, controversy on the question of the independent development of the states in the Middle East, because we consistently and firmly support the principle of the sovereignty and equality of all nations' (from which one could have understood that the USSR did not strive for Israel's elimination). However, the Soviet media published the answering speech of Syria's Prime Minister Zeayn, in which he referred to Israel as 'occupied Palestine' serving 'as a major threat' that 'takes up unlimited energy, which could be diverted to the creation of a national Arab homeland, the fulfillment of which would end imperialism and reaction in this region' ... He added that the Arab people of Palestine 'are paying for Nazi crimes in Europe ...'[5] – and implied the guilt of those who had supported the establishment of the State of Israel, including the USSR. In the joint Soviet–Syrian communiqué published at the end of the Syrian delegation's visit was the statement:

> Both sides have confirmed their solidarity with the Arabs of Palestine and expressed their support for their lawful rights in the just struggle against Zionism used by imperialist forces to increase tension in the Middle and Near East.[6]

This was the first time that an official Soviet communiqué (issued in conjunction with an Arab state) had expressed solidarity with the Palestinian Arabs and support for their just struggle against Zionism. For the Syrians, this was an extremely meaningful achievement paving the way for Soviet recognition of the Al Fatah organization and its activities against Israel in exchange for consolidating Soviet influence in Syria.

For Israel this paragraph, more than anything else, marked a serious deterioration in the Soviet attitude towards Israel and the intensification of tension on the Israeli–Syrian frontier as a result of Al Fatah activity with Syrian organization and blessing.

Prime Minister Eshkol referred to this paragraph in his speech in the Knesset on 18 May 1966. In rebuffing the attack on Zionism and after having explained the essence of the Jewish National Movement, he added:

> Arab rulers who identify Israel with Zionism can interpret joint communiqués of this nature as constituting an

> acceptance of their hostile and aggressive policies. The USSR, who maintains that the solution of conflicts must be achieved by peaceful means, would contribute more to the reduction of tension and the improvement of the atmosphere in the Middle East by avoiding such expressions and definitions.[7]

Explaining the essence of Zionism, from the podium of the Knesset, something no Israeli leader had been required to do for a long time, indicated how deep was the shock caused by the joint Soviet–Syrian communiqué and the Israeli government's fear in face of the attack against Zionism and the negation of the Jewish people's right to the Land of Israel. Although Eshkol's words were addressed to the Soviet leader, they were phrased in a relatively restrained tone. They contained sufficient material for accusing the USSR of encouraging Syrian aspirations to eliminate Israel – even if this was not its intention – and of playing its part in increasing tension in the Middle East, following Soviet encouragement.

The Soviet prime minister's visit to Egypt

On 10 May 1966, Kosygin left for Egypt accompanied by Foreign Minister Gromyko, the Minister of Energy and Electricity, the Chairman of the Council for Economic Relations with Foreign Nations, the Vice-Minister of Defense and the Head of Naval Forces, Admiral Gorshkov, as well as senior officials of the Soviet Foreign Office. It was understood that the object of this visit was to co-ordinate positions with the Egyptians in the light of the political developments in Syria, and to attempt to create a consolidated bloc of Arab nations with the participation of Syria. Kosygin adopted a relatively moderate tone regarding the Arab–Israeli conflict during his appearances in Egypt. *Pravda* of 18 May quoted Kosygin's address of 17 May as follows:

> ... All those who follow developments on the international scene closely can see that many complicated problems and various issues have arisen in the world. It will be dangerous to leave them unresolved. In these circumstances no country can allow itself to be indifferent. The government of the USSR is striving to settle these issues peacefully for the sake of world security ...

Although the Arab–Israeli conflict was not mentioned here specifically, there is some reference to it nevertheless. The call to solve territorial conflicts peacefully, which paralleled Krushchev's proposal, was not made regarding Syria, as paradox would have it. This reflects the tactics adopted at the time by the USSR concerning its Middle East policy, which adapted itself to the conditions in Egypt on the one hand and to those in Syria on the other. *Pravda* of that day presented Kosygin's speech to the Egyptian Parliament as follows:

> ... We understand the ardent interest of the Arabs in the Palestine problem and we are in favor of solving it on a fair basis. The USSR, as before, aligns itself sympathetically with the struggle to restore the legal and inalienable rights of the refugees of Palestine ...[8]

The joint Soviet–Egyptian communiqué published on 19 May 1966 included the following reference to the Arab–Israeli conflict:

> ... The Soviet side fully supports the legal and inalienable rights of the Arabs of Palestine. It supports the struggle and the efforts of the Arab states against the aggressive plots of the imperialist forces, aimed at exploiting the Palestinian problem to intensify tension in the Middle East ...[9]

Kosygin's two declarations in Egypt indicated Egypt's demand that the Soviet Union show greater involvement in the 'struggle for restoring the legitimate rights of the Arabs of Palestine' and take practical measures against Israel. Neither of the declarations indicates that the 'Soviet side' had moved to an extreme anti-Israeli stand. Kosygin's reference about the need to solve the Palestine problem 'on a fair basis', indicated a balanced intention, namely, the settlement of the Arab refugee problem, on the one hand, and granting recognition to Israel's right to existence, on the other. The joint Soviet–Egyptian communiqué is more moderate than the Soviet–Syrian one in which both sides expressed solidarity with 'the struggle against Zionism'. Perhaps, there was a deliberate retreat from the hostile tone towards Israel because the Soviets felt they had gone too far in hurting Israel in their joint declaration with the

Syrians. Finally, the fact should be taken into account that the Soviet–Egyptian communiqué employed the phrase 'the Soviet side' indicating that the Egyptian side did not acquiesce to the moderate definition of the situation.

The moderate tone of the communiqué was significant, since it maintained, at that stage, the calm between Egypt and Israel, without intensifying tension between them.

The common denominator of the two joint declarations may indicate a characteristic line of the Soviet tactics in utilizing the Arab–Israeli conflict to advance its goals in the Middle East. When it was important for the USSR to strengthen a local regime on an 'anti-imperialist and anti-Zionist' basis, as in the case of Syria, it joined in giving its voice to hostile expressions towards Israel, as the Syrians probably demanded it. And, when it did not have a special need to stabilize a regime on an anti-Western basis, as regards Egypt who in any case was anti-Western inclined, there was no need to use hostile expressions against Israel.

Intensified Soviet activity within Arab states

Intensified Soviet activity among Arab states was particularly noted during the first year of the Ba'ath regime in Syria. This activity aimed – as indicated by Kosygin himself at an election speech he gave in Moscow on 8 June 1966 – at strengthening the Syrian-Egyptian link and preparing the basis for the addition of other Arab countries 'who have thrown off the yoke of colonialism and under new circumstances continue to act against imperialism and reaction …'. 'Reaction' – alluded to those states, such as Saudi Arabia and Jordan, and organisations within the Arab states opposed to pursuing a pro-Soviet line.[10]

Following is a summary of the main events in illustration of the volume of Soviet activity:

1. The inauguration of direct Moscow-Beirut flights. (Tass, 14 June 1966)
2. A Soviet State delegation left for Algiers to participate at its national holiday, headed by Deputy Foreign Minister J. Malik. (Tass, 3 July 1966)
3. A delegation of the Soviet Committee for Afro-Asian Solidarity

left for Beirut. (It was announced that the delegation would discuss questions regarding the strengthening of national solidarity in the struggle for peace and against colonialism and imperialism.) (Tass, 5 July 1966)

4. Egyptian Deputy Foreign Minister Ahmed Fiki visited Moscow, at the invitation of the Soviet Foreign Ministry. (Tass, 13 July 1966)

5. The Moroccan Minister of Foreign Affairs arrived in Moscow at the invitation of Foreign Minister Gromyko. (Tass, 17 July 1966)

6. Iraqi Prime Minister Al Bo-zaz, arrived in the USSR on 27 July 1966, at the invitation of Prime Minister Kosygin, for an official visit.

7. A delegation from the Arab Socialist Union of Egypt arrived in the USSR on 21 August 'to become acquainted with the practical work of the CPSU'.

8. In September 1966 the first delegation from the Egyptian–Soviet Friendship League arrived in Moscow (Tass, 8 September 1966); a convention of organizations for friendship and cultural ties with Arab states was held in Moscow (Tass, 20 September 1966); Soviet experts in economic planning visited Egypt (*Pravda*, 21 September 1966); Soviet Deputy Foreign Minister Semyonov visited Egypt between 20 and 22 September 1966 (*Pravda*, 26 September 1966).

9. On 9 October the Kuwaiti Minister of Public Works concluded a visit to the USSR. Upon his departure he said, 'The aim of my visit – to establish economic ties with Soviet experts – was achieved'. (*Izvestia*, 10 October 1966)

10. A joint Moroccan-Soviet communiqué, issued on 29 October, included the following paragraph:

> In the opinion of both sides, the Arab people's movement for unity aids them to unite on an anti-imperialist and anti-colonialist basis, to win their common struggle, to guarantee the legitimate rights and interests of the Arabs, and to strengthen the sovereignty and independence of the Arab nations.

11. At the end of October 1966 a Komsomol (Young Communist League) delegation left for Tunisia, and an official Soviet delegation headed by Soviet Deputy Foreign Minister J. Malik arrived in Algiers 'to participate in celebrations marking Revolution Day'.

12. On 22 November 1966, following the signing of a Syrian-

Egyptian defense pact, *Pravda* noted that 'it not only constituted a deterrent factor but was also a cause of consolidation and laid a strong foundation for a bloc of progressive nations'.

13. On 22 November 1966 Egyptian Prime Minister Amar arrived in Moscow for an official visit.

14. An agreement was signed between the USSR and Jordan for the construction of a hydro-engineering plant on the Yarmuk River. (Tass, 30 November 1966)

15. A Soviet delegation left for Algiers to initiate a direct air route between Moscow and Algiers. (Tass, 30 November 1966)

This activity, which continuously intensified after 1966, was certainly an expression of Soviet efforts to deepen the co-operation between the USSR and the Arab and newly liberated African states on the government and party levels aimed at strengthening neutral and anti-American tendencies – at the first stage – and at deepening Soviet presence among them on the economic and military levels – at the second stage.

There was no innovation in this effort nor in the outcome of the 23rd Congress of the CPSU, which acted under the slogan of Soviet intensified support for the 'movement of Arab unity'. It was rather an over-stressed effort of a continuous USSR policy, acting at that time under the pressure of three challenges:

1. The need to consolidate the Ba'ath regime in Syria.

2. The need to hinder the Saudi Arabian plan, under USA inspiration, to establish the Islamic Pact, regarded by the Soviet Union as – if established – endangering its interests in the region and in Africa (since the pact's religious basis could have given Saudi Arabia a good chance of mobilizing many nations in a broad people's movement against communism and socialism).

3. The need to introduce a revision of its policy towards the national liberation movements in order to intensify its support for them and for the liberating states in light of the damage caused to the USSR's status in Ghana and Indonesia at that time.

In all these three challenges the USSR utilized the Arab–Israeli conflict to advance its goals in the Middle East and in the Arab world.

INTENSIFICATION OF THE SOVIET ANTI-ISRAEL CAMPAIGNS
AND EXACERBATION OF THE SECURITY SITUATION
BETWEEN ISRAEL AND SYRIA

From the beginning of May 1966 there was an intensification of the campaign against Israel in the Soviet media, presenting Israel as 'an imperialist strategic base' which constantly threatened the Syrian regime. The visit to Israel during that period of the West German Prime Minister and senior officials of the American State Department, as well as Israel's purchase of United States combat planes, led to the still greater force of the campaign against Israel. This was exploited by Soviet propaganda to entrench the Soviet presence in Syria as the Arabs' only protector against the 'Zionist' foe.

A review of the gradual escalation of the anti-Israel propaganda as mirrored in the Soviet press at that time is given below.

1. *Izvestia* of 8 May 1966 contained an article headed 'A Useless Lesson', which condemned Israel for organizing 'frequent armed provocations' against neighboring Arab nations and for raising them to the level of 'official policy' on the pretext that 'terrorist gangs were using these countries as bases from which they conducted their attacks'. The article claimed that Israel had embarked upon an extensive campaign against Syria and that Israel's leaders had 'apparently' established that Syria was responsible for the activities of 'mysterious' terrorist gangs.

The article asserted that the imperialists who were utilizing Israel in order to strike at Syria were concerned at the rise of progressives to power in Syria and concluded: 'The Soviet people cannot help expressing its fear and concern at the deterioration of the situation in this area and at the provocative acts against nations with whom the USSR maintains friendly relations ...

2. Al Fatah terrorists, who frequently carried out acts of murder on Israel's northern border, were presented as 'mysterious gangs' whose identity was unknown to the USSR, whilst Syria and other Arab states had nothing to do with them. Israel was represented as a threatening Satan, who should be warned very seriously and at the same time to support Syria, whose 'only desire' was to pursue a domestic 'progressive' policy.

3. An article in *Izvestia* on 18 May 1966 pointed out that 'the flow of economic and military infiltration into Israel is intensifying. This constitutes a dangerous bridge-head of imperialism in the Near East.' The author listed three imperialist fronts in the Middle East which were acting against the Arab nations: first, the unification of monarchical and reactionary regimes within the framework of the Islamic Alliance; second, the activation of reactionary forces within Egypt and Syria; third, Israel, in whose economy the Western capitalists were investing ever-increasing means, supplying it with the most modern arms and encouraging it to initiate 'constant provocations and border incidents'.

4. An article in *Pravda* commentary on 21 May 1966 called 'Provocation Schemes' accused Israel of initiating 'provocative activity against the borders of its Arab neighbors and against Syria in particular' and of conducting an intense anti-Syrian campaign in the press, 'making belligerent demands for intervening in Syria's internal affairs'. It also stated that the 'dissidents of Syria had such deep hatred for the new regime that they were prepared to co-operate with the imperialists and the Israeli extremists'. The article concluded by saying: 'The Soviet people has a great love for the freedom-loving Syrian nation, which has started on the broad path to independent development, and is by no means indifferent to the fate of this friendly nation and to the sovereign State of Syria.'

It can be deduced from this that any co-operation between Arab elements or states and Israel was rejected from the outset by the Soviet authorities if undertaken without its blessing, and that it would naturally be considered a betrayal of the Arab cause. Once again Israel was admonished and Syria encouraged. The new Syrian regime was promoted as being on 'the path to independent development', which meant in the Soviet lexicon the beginnings of an anti-Western character to the regime.

5. *Pravda* published an article on 21 May 1966 which strongly condemned Israel for the purchase of planes from the United States, stressing the fact that the United States had acted in accordance with its rule of 'aiding Israel secretly in making military preparations against the Arab nations'.

6. *Sovietskaya Rossia* of 21 May 1966 published an article headed, 'False Accusation and Armored Cars', containing the following passage:

Declarations have been made in Tel Aviv that Syria is responsible for acts of sabotage supposedly perpetrated by groups from Syrian territory. These groups are explicitly unidentified. However, Israel's so-called acts of 'retaliation' are extremely practical and are motivated by unprincipled intentions.

It also said:

No doubt Israel's ruling circles continue, as always, to constitute a lackey of the imperialist forces, whose main concern is with the way things are developing in Syria.

Mine-laying and terrorist activities along Israel's border with Syria by the Al Fatah terrorists were termed again 'mysterious forces' by the USSR, which the Israeli's had apparently invented in order to justify the attacks on Syria as proved by the anti-Syrian campaign in Israel. On the other hand, the Soviet authorities did not publish threats to destroy Israel made by the Syrian leadership (*Pravda*, 24 May 1966, quoted Atasi's speech to Syrian officers deleting the threats against Israel).

7. *Sovietskaya Rossia* of 27 May 1966 published an article under the heading, 'A Bridge to New Provocations', which referred to Israel's purchase of new fighter planes from the United States as follows:

... It is not difficult to understand the true aims of this unsavoury transaction. This is not the first time that the Israeli leadership has demanded the right to fulfill the role of a spearhead ... oriented by imperialism towards the heart of the Arab national movement.

There can no longer be any doubts concerning the imperialist plots which with the help of the Israeli reactionary forces strive to exacerbate the situation in the Near East and curb the process of progressive social change in some of the Arab states ...

The implications regarding Syria are clear. 'The Israeli reactionary forces' are presented as a factor which curbs 'social change'. Thus, they have been attributed with another ideological 'task' in the

Middle East, in addition to the usual one of serving imperialism as Soviet propaganda has attempted to show.

There was an additional escalation in the Soviet accusations against Israel in the Tass announcement of 27 May 1966. This included a serious warning to anyone attempting to overthrow the Syrian regime, which was a clear reference to Israel. While this announcement cautioned those concerned not to take it upon themselves to act as they had in the Suez Campaign of 1956, no mention whatsoever was made of the Syrian leaders' threat against the security, peace and sovereignty of Israel. The announcement read as follows:

> The Government of the Syrian Arab Republic has appealed to the member states of the Security Council concerning the aggravation of the situation around Syria and in the Near East in general, as a result of the activation of imperialist and reactionary forces in this region.
>
> Syria's appeal has been studied carefully by the guiding circles of the USSR. The peace-loving nations connect the activation of subversive acts by the imperialist powers and their reactionary allies in the Near East with the fact that a number of Arab states have adopted an increasingly independent political course as sovereign nations. The Syrian Arab Republic is included amongst these nations.
>
> Not long ago the military-colonial bloc of 'Santo' was called to an urgent session in Ankara. A consultative meeting of US Ambassadors in the Near East was held in Beirut. US ships of the US Sixth Fleet appeared in the territorial waters of Lebanon. It is also known that talks were recently held between high officials of the USA and the Israeli government and Chief of Staff.
>
> It seems that in this connection the aggressive and extreme forces of Israel were activated against the neighboring Arab states. The number of provocations from the Israeli side was increased in the border area with the Arab states. According

to press reports, the Israeli army is in a state of emergency, leave for the soldiers and officers has been canceled and there are Israeli military concentrations on the border with Syria. The Israeli Chief of Staff, Rabin, has made provocative speeches against the Arab countries, presuming that Israel can determine which policy should be adopted by its neighbors.

According to the reports, extremist circle in Jordan and Saudi Arabia which are not satisfied with Syria's policy are, with the help of the USA and England, plotting against this Arab nation.

These facts testify to the fact that the aggressive circles in some imperialist powers and their agents are beginning to forget the shameful lessons of the aggression against Egypt and their other defeats in the Near East. It seems that the colonialists have not abandoned their programs of regaining the positions they may have lost in the countries of the Near East and are doing their utmost to disrupt the free development of these countries.

The people of the Arab states understand well what danger is presented to the cause of peace and to their free development, by the new plots of the imperialist powers and their reactionary agencies in the Near East, and of the ruling circles of Israel, and especially the attempts to interfere in the internal affairs of the Syrian Arab Republic.

The Soviet Union certainly cannot remain indifferent to the attempts to violate peace in an area neighboring immediately close to the frontiers of the USSR.

The most important element in the announcement is the warning that the USSR 'cannot remain indifferent' to what was happening on its border. This can be interpreted as constituting a clear threat that the USSR would not hesitate to intervene if the situation seemed to be endangering peace in the vicinity of its border, on the pretext that geographical proximity gave it this right. The doctrine that intervention in the area on the USSR's part was justified was considered strategically vital by the Soviet authorities.

As in the case of the Sinai War, once again the USSR was threatening to intervene when peace in the area was endangered – meaning when the Syrian regime was in danger on the way to its consolidation.

Israel's reaction

Levi Eshkol, Israel's Prime Minister, was *en route* for a State visit in Africa when this declaration was issued. (The question can also be asked: How could Israel have been planning a war at the very time that its Prime Minister was abroad? The Soviet government may have feared that particularly during his absence the leaders of the Israeli Defense Forces would take matters into their own hands and this may have been why they issued the warning to Israel.) From Paris the Prime Minister made the following statement in reaction to the Tass announcement:[11]

> Israel categorically denies the implications and libels contained in the Tass announcement that Israel acts as the agent of other countries. The references to Israel's concentration of its army on the Syrian border, the cancellation of leave in the army, etc. are a complete fabrication. Israel's sincere desire as a sovereign nation in the Middle East is for peace with its neighbors, as has been declared many times from the Knesset podium and in many international forums. It is Syria which is causing constant provocations on Israel's border and from Syrian territory murderers have crossed into Israel, killing farmers, as happened recently in Almagor. It is Syria which repeatedly declares its intention of attacking Israel. Presumably it would not be difficult for the USSR to find out about Syria's aggressive activities on Israel's border, expressed in concentrations of arms and troops which have been forbidden by the Armistice Agreement. There are grounds for believing that these Syrian acts are intended to disguise their true purpose. Israel's powerful desire for peace on its borders often compels it to restrain itself to the limits of human and civilized strength. It should be clear to Syria,

its friends and the entire world, that it must avoid provocative actions, sabotage and murder on the borders.

Ten days ago I clarified our policies thoroughly in the Knesset. As I said then, we do not envy any strengthening of the bonds between countries of the Middle East and the great powers, so long as this does not encourage the aggressive tendencies of the Arabs. I also proposed at that time that were Moscow to refrain from making damaging announcements this would help strengthen peace in the area. Unfortunately this Tass statement and similar articles in the Soviet press of late have not contributed in this direction.

There was no reaction in the Soviet media to Eshkol's reply. Moreover, Tass published an article on the situation in the Middle East under the heading, 'A Dangerous Game by the Enemies of Peace' on 30 May. The author stressed the favorable reactions to the Tass announcement of 27 May in Arab capitals, except for certain groups in Jordan and Saudi Arabia, and stressed the significance of the fact that there had been no attempts to deny assertions made in this announcement by Israel or the capitalist states. Thus, the furious reaction of the Israeli public, Eshkol's statement in Paris and the criticism voiced by Foreign Minister Eban to the Soviet Ambassador in Israel, were all blithely ignored.

It is quite possible that the Soviet campaign against Israel, both in the press and on the diplomatic level, was the outcome of a well-planned policy aimed at establishing and strengthening Soviet influence in Syria. The descriptions of Israeli threats to attack Syria, by creating provocative border incidents with Syria, including the concentration of Israeli military forces along this border and Israeli consultations with American experts, were all designed to frighten the Syrians, to mobilize help for them from Egypt and other Arab states and to deter the opponents of the regime in Syria itself from taking any action against it. Thus the USSR aimed to achieve a greater unity within the Syrian people around its new government. The Soviet policy of deterrence was undoubtedly aimed at frightening the Western and Arab states, such as Jordan and Saudi Arabia, not to interfere in Syrian domestic affairs and at demonstrating to Syria the importance of the defense and political protection extended to Syria by the USSR.

291

It is doubtful, however, whether this calculated Soviet policy made sufficient allowances for the vehemence of Arab instincts, fanned by its unconditional support of Syria and foremost the Syrian passion for waging a holy war in order to achieve the destruction of Israel. It is also doubtful whether the Soviet leaders estimated at that time the eventual outcome of the inflammation of these emotions, taking into account the nature of the Arab–Israeli conflict in the short and long run.

ISRAELI–SOVIET DIALOGUE ON THE SITUATION IN THE REGION

On 25 May (two days prior to the Tass announcement) K. Katz, Israel's Ambassador in Moscow, was summoned to Soviet Deputy Foreign Minister Semyonov, who read out a message from the Soviet government addressed to the government of Israel. This included the main accusations listed in the Tass announcement on Israel's intention to attack Syria, accompanied by a warning to Israel of the danger to its existence should it initiate a war against Syria.

Following are excerpts that were not included in the Tass announcement:

> The Soviet government is certainly also aware of the peace-loving declarations made by Israel's leaders. However, these declarations are in contradiction to the mentioned facts, which therefore put them in doubt. The question is, are the Israeli extreme circles, who undertake extreme and hostile stands towards the neighboring states, again capable of subordinating Israel and its people into being a blind instrument of imperialism and neo-colonialism in the Middle East?

> The government of the USSR would have liked to hope that the government of Israel revealed a realistic attitude in assessing the possible result of implementing the dangerous plans directed against independent Arab States, including the Arab Republic of Syria.

> The Soviet government expresses its hope that the government of Israel would not permit outside forces to play with the

destiny of its people and State. In expressing these thoughts
the government of the USSR is guided only by the desire to
strengthen peace and tranquillity in the Middle East region,
which is in direct proximity to the borders of the USSR.[12]

The main tone in the message – such as was lacking in the Tass
announcement – was the Soviet awareness of the fact that Israel's
leaders wanted peace – as it were in contradiction to the tendencies
within the Israeli military circles, headed by Chief of Staff Y. Rabin,
to whom the message attributed the voicing of threats 'to undertake
military actions' against Syria. This meant that the USSR
distinguished between the policy of Israel's Government on the one
hand and Israel's Defense Forces and its Chief of Staff on the other.
The Soviet hope for 'a realistic attitude' on behalf of Israel's government in assessing the situation could have been interpreted as an
appeal for restraint, but also as a serious warning of what was
expected of it if it decided to attack Syria. The assurance that the
USSR was guided by a desire to 'strengthen peace' could have hinted
that the Soviet Union was acting to restrain the Syrians in face of
the Syrian threats to Israel's security and well-being.
   Indeed, in the course of the next weeks, at least until mid-July
1966, the Soviet press revealed signs of restraint, mainly by omitting
extreme statements made by Arab leaders concerning Israel.
   It could also be that the reaction of Israel somehow had an
influence in restraining the Soviet behavior. Israel's reaction was
transmitted on 31 May 1966 to the Soviet Ambassador through A.
Levavi, the Director General of Israel's Foreign Ministry. In its
reaction to the Soviet message, Israel's government emphatically
rejected the main Soviet accusations of Israeli troop concentrations
along the Israeli–Syrian border; of its responsibility for the border
incidents, caused by acts of murder and sabotage carried out by
infiltrators from Syrian territory; and of the alleged pronouncement
by the Chief of Staff, General Y. Rabin, 'who in fact never made it'.
   Israel's message in response referred to the Syrian President's
declaration on 17 and 22 May about waging a war of extermination
against Israel in face of Israel's principles of peace. The message
proposed to the Soviet Union that it asserts its influence on Syria,
and finally noted 'with satisfaction the Soviet assertion that the
policy of the Soviet Union was guided by the desire to support peace

in the Middle East – a desire which is in complete harmony with the policy and interests of Israel, and for whose realization Israel was ready to co-operate with the USSR'.[13]

Israel's reaction was presumably intended not only to reject categorically the accusations leveled against Israel in the Soviet message, concerning Israel's intentions to bring down Syria's new regime, but also to uproot such suspicions from the hearts of the Soviet leadership and prevent a rift with the USSR, arising from its support for the new Syrian regime. Moreover, Israel invited the USSR, officially, to co-operate in the relaxation of tension along the Israeli–Syrian border, this with a clear intention of restraining the Syrian leadership. It is doubtful whether the role offered to the Soviets fitted their intention to demonstrate one-sided support for the new Syrian regime, even though this invitation contained a complimentary element in presenting the USSR as an influential factor in the Middle East.

This was the opening round in a series of messages between Israel and the USSR, following the rise to power of the left wing of the Syrian Ba'ath party that gave rise to the crisis in Israeli–Soviet relations arising from the Soviet accusations about Israel's intentions to attack Syria. This crisis subsided and revived in the course of time until reaching a climax in the Six Day War. It subsided to some extent when the Soviet government felt it had succeeded in assisting the new Syrian regime to become stabilized and in preventing the domestic and foreign forces to overthrow it. The crises flared up again whenever the Soviet government did not succeed in restraining terrorist activity by Syria in the territory of Israel and when Israel retaliated for these acts to such an extent that, from the Soviet standpoint, its achievements in Syria were endangered.

A second and third round of exchanged messages followed in October and November 1966.

At the beginning of October 1966, a new crisis emerged. The Soviet print media aggravated their hostile tone against Israel. An article published in *Pravda* on 3 October 1966, entitled 'General Rabin's Sabre Rattling' set the tone for the other Soviet media, which attacked Israel in sharp terms. The author of the article noted that 'the reactic.ary and militarist circles in Israel do not limit themselves anymore in initiating provocations of border incidents, but consider and take decisions to undertake plans for military invasions deep in Syrian territory aimed at overthrowing the government of this state'. The author based himself on a statement made by Rabin, Chief of Staff of the Israeli Defense Forces, to an Israeli weekly, *Bamahane*, in this respect and stressed that 'the Syrian people would not be alone in case of a provocative aggression against it, violating its sovereignty and national independence'.

The mere fact the newspaper had to voice such a warning, invoking the proximity of Syria to the USSR's borders, indicated the USSR's fear for the fate of the regime in Syria, in face of dangers from Israel.

The background to the new crisis was indeed an interview given by the Chief of Staff to *Bamahane*, published on 12 September 1966. In this interview Rabin analyzed the level of confrontation between Israel and Syria:

confrontations connected with agricultural work in the demilitarized zone;
confrontations connected with securing free fishing in Lake Kinneret;
confrontations connected to Syrian plans to divert the flow of the Jordan;
confrontations connected to terrorist acts of mining in Israel by Al Fatah groups trained in Syria and sent on its behalf to carry out assignments in Israel.

Rabin asserted that the conflict with Syria was essentially a confrontation with the regime. Since Syria had adopted the decision to wage war-like activity against Israel, in contrast to other Arab states, including Egypt, and since Syria had been the one to plot the level of confrontation with Israel, Israel's reaction – in Rabin's view – should have been against both those who carried out the terrorist acts and those who controlled the regime that supported such deeds. Israel's aim should have been, in his opinion, 'to change the regime's decisions and remove the motives for these activities'.

This assertion confirmed, in fact, the Soviet suspicions about Israel, that its aim was to overthrow the Syrian regime. To be sure, Prime Minister Eshkol made it clear in an interview with *Haaretz* a week later, on 9 October 1966, that the Chief of Staff's words had not been properly understood and that the State of Israel had no intentions of interfering with Syria's domestic affairs, but this clarification was to no avail. The Soviet Ambassador in Israel, Chuvakhin, brought an urgent message addressed to Prime Minister Eshkol concerning Rabin's interview and Israeli troop concentrations along the Israeli–Syrian border. 'Actions of this kind', the message stated, 'bear witness to the existence of unceasing efforts on the part of extremist circles in Israel to step up activities against those neighboring Arab states who follow a line of political independence, and above all against Syria ... These Israeli actions create threats to peace and tranquillity in the Middle East and are not in harmony with the promises given by Israel's government that it would work for peace and on its borders ...'[14]

Prime Minister Eshkol rejected the accusation regarding troop concentration but did not refer to Rabin's interview quoted in the Soviet message.

The tone of the message, similar to that of May 1966, without the threats to Israel's future, was contradictory in the context of Soviet Foreign Minister Gromyko's remarks in his talk with Israel's Foreign Minister A. Eban, held on 30 September 1966. Gromyko then said:[15]

The USSR is prepared to maintain friendly ties with several Arab nations as well as with Israel.

The USSR has supported the establishment of Israel and recognized its right to exist.

The USSR is not a party to the aspirations to obliterate Israel (indicating that Soviet support of Syria did not extend to denying Israel's right to exist).

There was no polemical tone in his words. On the contrary, there was a tendency to calm his Israeli colleague. Another calming hint – the only one in the series of exchanged messages – could be discerned in the Soviet message of 9 November 1966, handed over to Israel's Ambassador in Moscow, K. Katz.[16]

Soviet message to Israel of 9 November 1966

Upon presenting this message to the Israeli Ambassador in Moscow, Deputy Foreign Minister Semyonov noted that his government was aware of the hostile declarations made about Israel by Arab politicians but did not take them seriously, and Israel should do likewise. The intention of the message was to advise Israel that its government should act wisely and carefully. It was sometimes wiser to avoid an immediate reaction in favor of long-term interests. Despite their declarations Arab leaders knew they would not benefit by thrusting a war into the region.

In comparison to previous messages, this one did not contain any reference accusing Israel of concentrating troops along its borders with Syria. Also, there was no accusation of Israel's intention to attack Syria and overthrow its government. This goal had not been attributed directly to Israel. From its last paragraph, it could be understood that the USSR acted indeed in restraining the Syrians (as Prime Minister Eshkol had requested of the Soviet government, through the Soviet Ambassador in Israel, Chuvakhin).

Kol Haam of 15 November 1966 continued a report by its political correspondent, based on 'reliable sources', on three objectives embodied in the Soviet message:

1. To reduce the fear that the USSR is hostile to Israel.
2. To clarify that in the opinion of the USSR the responsibility for the tension on the Israeli–Syrian border was not Syria's but that of the imperialist forces which were meddling in the concerns of others.
3. To warn the Israeli government not to allow itself to become involved in the schemes of the imperialist powers by attacking Syria.

These supposed aims were actually in accordance with the content of the message. Answering a question from *Kol Haam*'s correspondent, published on 27 November, Prime Minister Eshkol clarified that the source of tension in the region was the refusal of the Arab leaders to recognize Israel's right to existence, and that 'once our Arab neighbors cease the infiltrations, terrorism, bloodshed and the protection of those who undermine our security, there will be peace in the area'.

> I have no doubt that if all the great powers who helped to establish our State were to unify their efforts to obtain peace, they could make an appreciable contribution to harmony and

stability in our area. I know that the Western powers wish to maintain the status quo in this part of the world. I welcome the Soviet announcement asserting its concern for peace in our region. Because of this concern the USSR has, in my opinion, a moral and political responsibility to exert its influence on the Arab states, with whom it is now on friendly terms, in order to prevent terrorism and aggressive acts and to ensure the strict observation of the cease-fire agreement.

What caused the Soviet Government to transmit a pacifying statement to the Israeli Government, at the height of an intense anti-Israel campaign? It seems that there were at least two factors at work here: (1) an attempt to induce members of the Israeli government, and first and foremost Prime Minister Eshkol himself, to conduct a restrained policy towards Syria; (2) the message was transmitted a week after the signing of the Syrian-Egyptian defense pact, which the USSR considered a significant achievement for its diplomatic efforts, in view of the mutual suspicions and the breach between Syria and Egypt. The USSR considered it to be both a deterrent factor and an important nucleus, to which the USSR would be able to add other Arab states and thus strengthen its influence in the region. Thus, paradoxically, as long as the USSR was sure of its influence in the area its obdurate attitude towards Israel was relaxed, while as long as it felt weak and insecure, it intensified its unyielding attitude towards Israel.

The USSR's accusations against Israel, as reflected in the anti-Israel propaganda campaign, on the one hand, and the moderate tone of the Eban-Gromyko talks and the 9 November message on the other, symbolized the USSR's ambivalent policies in the Middle East. On the one hand, it aggravated the Arab–Israeli conflict in order to advance its presence in the area and to advance its global interests. On the other hand, it acted to prevent a war in order to impede the possibility of a Western intervention because of the worsening situation. Thus, the Arab–Israeli conflict fulfilled a decisive role in the complex of Soviet strategy in the Middle East. Israel served as the main component, constituting a constant threat to the Arab states, whose sole protector was the USSR. The mischievous image of Israel was a product of the Soviet tactics, and therefore the USSR was so concerned in cultivating it, constantly.

A restrained, submissive Israel, indeed, would have decreased the prospects of a local flare-up, but it would not have served the USSR's interests in the region in same way it did in the guise of upstart rebel. Hence, the Soviet messages to the government of Israel that were officially published were actually directed towards the Arab states to demonstrate that the USSR was vigorously defending their position in the conflict with Israel. They were also directed to the Western powers to deter them from any idea of interfering militarily in the region's affairs. What motivated the Soviet government during this period to act in the way it did? The answer may be found in four features which were manifesting themselves concurrently at that time:

1. *Syria as strategic foothold.* For the first time communist elements were part of the new Syrian regime (even more than in Egypt, though this country had been linked to the Soviet Union since the early 1950s) and Syria had opened its doors to penetration by the USSR and the eastern bloc. Industries were nationalized and far-reaching social reform was begun. Soviet influence in the economic, educational and military fields grew from day to day. It was natural that the USSR would endeavor to preserve this achievement, both because of Syria's proximity to its borders and because of the prospect of alienating the Western powers' influence in the area. Because of the USSR's fervent desire to strengthen the Syrian regime and attach Syria to the anti-American alignment, it found itself supporting its slogans literally, merely in order to maintain unity and remove internal and external opposition.

2. *Preventing the establishment of the Islamic Pact.* In view of Faisal's activities against Egypt and his support of the nationalist forces in Yemen, the USSR aspired to create a bloc of states within the Arab countries which would oppose him and prevent him from establishing the US-inspired Islamic Alliance. This alliance was considered by the USSR to be a new American–British attempt to establish an anti-Soviet alliance in the Middle East and this time against a Moslem background. For this reason the USSR attempted to establish a bloc of 'progressive nations' (Syria-Egypt-Iraq-Algeria), on an anti-American basis, to consolidate them and obtain their confidence by supporting the Palestinian cause, although this support did not extend to the USSR's denial of Israel's right to exist.

3. *Striving for a foothold in the southern Arabian peninsula.* In February
1966 Britain declared its intention of pulling out of the southern
Arabian peninsula. The USSR, for strategic reasons of its own (this
geographic area was vital for it in its confrontation with both the
West and China), wished to extend its influence in this region,
fearing that unless it acted quickly Saudi Arabia, with the help of
Britain and America, would become pre-eminent and the USSR
would have no foothold there. Consequently, the USSR tried to
present Israel and Saudi Arabia as the enemies of the Arab
independent nations and thus to isolate Saudi Arabia from the Arab
nations 'independent' bloc.

4. *Deterring the Sixth Fleet from intervening in Syria.* The USSR
constantly feared that the American Sixth Fleet would intervene in
Syria and that Israel might also attack, along the lines of the Suez
Campaign of 1956, in order to overthrow the pro-Soviet regime in
Damascus. Because of these fears and because of the USSR's own
tendencies to penetrate into the Mediterranean as a power equal
in status to the USA, Brezhnev declared, at a convention of east
European Communist leaders held in Karlovivari, that the time had
come to clear the Mediterranean of the Sixth Fleet. In addition,
fear that the Suez Campaign scenario would recur was always
present in the Soviet propaganda. The danger that this could
happen again, with a different balance of powers, since the United
States, unlike in 1956, would be backing Israel, was very real to the
USSR. The declaration about the clearance of the Sixth Fleet was
no doubt connected to the lack of political stability in Syria.

In this situation the Arab–Israeli conflict constituted a crucially
important instrument for the USSR in its efforts to increase its
influence in Syria, and thence to other Arab nations. In fact,
summarizing the first year of the Syrian regime's existence, the
USSR had already achieved two vital objectives: the new Syrian
regime was becoming established and Syria and Egypt were linked
by a mutual defense pact brought about through the active intervention of the USSR. This pact was considered to constitute an
additional deterrent against an Israeli attack on Syria. The Islamic
Pact did not come into being. Regional fighting on a large scale was
prevented. Soviet popularity had grown among Arab and African
states. Its hopes increased for creating a bloc of 'progressive' Arab

states, under its guidance, as support in its confrontation with the Western powers in eliminating their influence and footholds in the area.

The Soviet Union hoped to make political capital from any future event. Should Israel not attack Syria the USSR would attribute that to its own speedy and effective reaction in support of the new Syrian regime as well as to its deterrent power. Should Israel attack Syria, in spite of everything, the USSR could move in its troops, according to the situation, in one of the three following ways or with all three together:

1. Put an immediate end to the fighting through the intervention of the United Nations Security Council and the threat of imposing sanctions on Israel, isolating it in the international arena.
2. Activate Egypt in defense of Syria, in accordance with their mutual defense treaty; Egyptian involvement would certainly endanger Israel's achievements in the Sinai War, diminishing the danger of an imminent Israeli attack on Syria.
3. Intervene itself, directly, in the fighting, in the hope of preventing the possibility of Western powers intervening in support of Israel.

In each instance, the USSR would emerge as the sole defender of Arab interests and would therefore intensify Arab dependence upon itself in the military, economic and political spheres.

In either event, the USSR expected to gain from this policy. The only party to lose as a result of these considerations would be Israel. In the first event, the number of incursions by Syrian-trained terrorist groups into Israel's territory had increased and its security was in serious danger. In the second event, Arab forces would have defeated Israel because of their military superiority.

The USSR's ambivalent attitude, however, had probably not taken sufficient account of its own inability to fully dominate the situation – into which the conflicting parties had been pushed as a result of the Soviet support of Syrian aggression against Israel in order to advance its own interests in the area.

The USSR failed either to restrain the inflamed emotions of Syria against Israel, or to reckon with the Israeli government's sensitivity to and responsibility for the security and well being of its citizens. This equivocal attitude of the USSR paved the way for the events which precipitated the Six Day War.

THE SYRIAN–ISRAELI INCIDENT OF 7 APRIL 1967

A series of terrorist attacks on the northern zone of Israel, launched from Syrian territory,[17] led to a sharp Israeli reaction unprecedented in its scope and force. It was on the morning of 7 April 1967 that Syrian fire was directed at an Israeli tractor working some land in the demilitarized area on the Israeli–Syrian border near Kibbutz HaOn. The Syrian positions were fired on in return, whereupon the Syrian army began bombarding Israeli settlements in the vicinity. In the course of the day, the exchanges of fire developed into large-scale fighting, with the armour and air force taking part on both sides. Seven Soviet-made Syrian planes were shot down – some in fighting on the Jordanian border and some over Damascus. This was the first air battle to take place between the two sides and it raised the tension between them to a new pitch. As a result events now moved swiftly towards the Six Day War.

The outbreak of fighting stemmed from the confrontation that had developed between the two sides. Israel, for her part, was determined to exercise her right to work the land in the demilitarized area on the border between her and Syria. In the mid-1960s moves were made for the first time to assert this right from the purely political calculation that not to work the land in this area would look to the Syrians as if Israel had relinquished sovereignty over it. This was a matter of principle and prestige. Israel had been pursuing a policy of relative restraint in the face of an increasing number of Syrian attacks, and this particular reaction was presumably intended as a tangible demonstration that Israel was disinclined to go on with this policy, and to warn Syria that if it did not put an end to the terrorist attacks on Israel there would be dangerous consequences. Developments after the air battle showed that instead of preventing escalation it was actually the cause of further deterioration.

Syria, for her part, was not going to acquiesce to Israel working on the land in the demilitarized area that had been abandoned since the signing of the Armistice Agreement between the two countries, and, in fact, she interpreted the Israeli move as deliberate provocation. Syrian interference with the work on the land went together with a policy of letting guerrilla units infiltrate Israeli territory under the slogan of 'freeing the "pillaged" lands from Israeli rule'. In reality, Syria was the only Arab country maintaining such a policy.

She apparently drew encouragement from the Soviet Union's military, economic and political support, as well as from her army's topographical advantage opposite the Israeli forces. She saw no reason to refrain from exacerbating the situation with Israel and took the lead in Arab anti-Israel belligerence on the assumption that the other Arab countries and the Soviet Union would stand by her in a war against Israel.

The Soviet Reaction

Without question, the downing of the planes embarrassed the Soviet Union because the French-made Israeli planes had performed better in battle than the Soviet planes, or because of a fear that the incident might seriously weaken the Syrian government, which would be open to attack from opposition forces for its ineffectual showing.

The Soviet media reported the facts of the incident with the addition of the familiar propaganda accusation that the 'imperialists' were behind it all, and were conspiring against the Syrian regime because of its anti-American inclinations. But only two weeks later, on 21 April 1967, the Soviet Deputy Foreign Minister handed the Israeli Ambassador in Moscow a sharply worded note which described the Israel Defense Forces' (IDF) action of 7 April as 'dangerous playing with fire in an area adjacent to the frontiers of the Soviet Union' and demonstrating that Israel wanted to settle her disputes with the Arabs 'from a position of strength and by military means'. (The contents of this note were published in the Soviet press on 27 April 1967 in the form of a foreign ministry announcement, with changes in the wording that made it a still weightier condemnation of Israel accompanied by a serious warning.)[18]

The note was mainly concerned with warning Israel against a policy towards her neighbors that was liable to lead to 'serious consequences' for her. The Soviet government expressed the hope that the Israeli government would prevent certain 'IDF circles', which manifested a lack of political restraint, 'liable to endanger the vital interests of their people and their States', from serving as a tool in the hands of 'inimical external forces'. The content of the note implied that these 'IDF circles' were headed by the Chief of Staff, who was quoted in the note as saying that the IDF action would not be the last in the series of reprisals, since Israel herself would choose the methods and forms of 'similar actions' in the future.

On 25 April 1967 another note to the Israeli government was transmitted to the Israeli ambassador in Moscow. The note was more moderate in tone than the previous one and stated that the Soviet Union was aware of 'peace-loving declarations' made by personalities in Israel in contrast to the Chief of Staff's threatening declarations against Syria. The main subject of the new note was, however, the contention that the IDF was concentrating forces 'with offensive intentions' on the frontier with Syria.[19]

Both notes completely ignored the Syrian attacks on Israeli territory and bore witness to Soviet fears lest the IDF action against Syria proved to be part of a general plan of attack aimed at putting an end to the pro-Soviet regime in that country. The Soviet accusations and the threats to Israel, direct and indirect, were nothing new, but it is nevertheless surprising that the Soviets should have taken two weeks to wake up to the need to transmit an alarmed note to Israel, reverting for some reason to accusations about military concentrations on the Israeli–Syrian border, when in fact there were not any. The grounds for this seem to have been the following events.

On 17 April 1967 the *US News and World Report* published an interview with Prime Minister Eshkol. The interviewer asked, 'Would Israel expect help from the USA, Britain and France, if she were attacked by her neighbors?' to which Eshkol replied, 'We would certainly expect such help, but we rely mainly on our army. Of course, I would expect help, especially taking into account all the solemn promises given to Israel. We are given these promises when we ask the USA to supply us with arms and we are told, "Don't waste your money. We are here. The Sixth Fleet is here." My reply to this advice is that the Sixth Fleet is liable not to be quick enough for one reason or another, and so Israel has to be strong enough. That's why we waste such a lot of money on arms purchases in proportion to the size of our population.'

Eshkol's emphasis was on the need for Israel to be strong, but his words could be interpreted as a declaration that:

1. the USA was ready to come to the aid of Israel with the Sixth Fleet the moment it was asked to, and
2. Israel did not rule out the possibility of getting the Sixth Fleet

to intervene in her conflict with the Arab countries. All she wanted was to be able to hold out by means of the arms she was asking for until the Sixth Fleet could come to her aid.

The Soviet media presented what Eshkol had said as confirmation of the danger they were constantly admonishing Israel about – the danger of intervention by the US Sixth Fleet, which would threaten the independence of the Arab states in general and pro-Soviet Syria in particular.

At the conference of the European Communist Parties in Karlovy-Vary on 24 April 1967, the CPSU Secretary-General Brezhnev declared that there was no justification for the presence of the US Sixth Fleet in the Mediterranean 20 years after the end of the Second World War. It could only be viewed as 'a threat to the independence of the Middle East states and the time had arrived to demand that the Sixth Fleet "quit the Middle East"'.[20] From then on the Soviet Union waged a vigorous propaganda campaign to get the Sixth Fleet out of the Mediterranean. Soviet reservations over the presence of the Sixth Fleet were already sufficiently well known, but the dates of the Eshkol interview and the Brezhnev declaration were remarkably close to each other and the views expressed markedly opposed. Even if there was no direct connection between the two, it cannot be overlooked that the timing of Brezhnev's demands stemmed from apprehension over the fate of Syria, with Eshkol's statement serving as the pretext in this connection, at least on the propaganda level.

Some time after the 7 April incident, news was published of attempts being made in Jordan to overthrow the Damascus regime with the help of exiled Syria officers. It was noted that the IDF attack of 7 April had supposedly been known to them beforehand and the people concerned had been put on alert to exploit the opportunity and try and take over in Syria, but the Syrian response spoiled their plan.[21] Whether this report was true or not, the very fact of its publication in Western sources – and it must be assumed that it was known to the Soviets even before its publication – testified to Soviet apprehensions about the fate in store for the Syrian regime. On 30 April, *Pravda* found it necessary to revert to the subject of the 7 April incident and its consequences, and to affirm that 'the Israeli action was intended to assist the fifth column in Syria' while relying on the US Sixth Fleet. The *Pravda* commentary concluded with the warning that Egypt would stand at Syria's side if the latter were attacked in accordance with the Egyptian–Syrian defense agreement. From this it would appear that the reason for the belated Soviet reactions to the 7 April incident was not vacillation nor the absence of a defense minister (after the death of Marshal Malinovskii), but the conclusion reached by Soviet leadership (on the strength of these events reported shortly after the incident) regarding a possibility that had not presented itself in former incidents on the Israeli–Syrian border: that beside the IDF, Arab units might also act against Syria from Jordanian territory. Apparently it was only when this danger threatening Syria became known that the Soviet leadership decided to issue warnings and take preventive measures. This seems a more reasonable explanation than the assumption that the Soviet reaction came late in the day because of the struggle for the succession to the post of defense minister. Some theorists saw the warnings as connected with the efforts of Marshal Grechko to obtain the post (which he held in the interim) by alarming the Soviet leadership over the possibility of a dangerous deterioration of the situation on the Israeli–Syrian border, which would supposedly necessitate the appointment of a military man as defense minister rather than a civilian from the party and state hierarchy such as Ustinov.[22]

Soviet apprehensions increased in the course of the second week of May 1967 when religious uprising occurred in the big cities of Syria for the first time since the Ba'ath took power. The risings were ferociously suppressed, but it is reasonable to assume that even then it did not look as if the threat to the regime was over. At this time too, terrorist actions were on the increase inside Israel and on 11 May 1967 Premier Eshkol declared that Israel would have no choice but to take more drastic steps than those of 7 April if Syrian terrorist activity did not stop.[23]

It would appear that the risings in Syria and the Israeli declarations at the same time made the Soviets move on from warnings to preventive action. On May 12, the Egyptians were told of Israeli army concentrations on the Syrian border and that Israel intended to attack Syria on May 17: this was the Soviet contribution to raising tension. Thus the foundation was laid for the Six Day War. On 13 May 1967 on the strength of the Soviet news that reached him from various sides (but from a single source), Nasser decided that action was needed to get the Israeli army away from the Syrian frontier towards the south. The UN Emergency Force had to be expelled from Sinai so that his own army could go in and then the Straits of Tiran could be closed to Israeli shipping. It was with the intention of getting the Egyptian president to bring about a 'thinning out' of the IDF in the north of Israel that the Soviets fed the Egyptian leadership falsified information: first on increased IDF concentrations on the Israeli–Syrian border, and second on Israel's intention to attack Syria on a date between 16 and 22 May 1967.[24] These two false pieces of 'information' were never confirmed, either before the war or after it.[25] The Soviet-inspired false 'information' was clearly responsible for the sudden change in the Egyptian president's strategy on 13 May 1967, as he himself testified. The line of complete abstention from entering confrontation with Israel (followed since Israel withdrew from Egyptian territory in 1957) changed to his being drawn into a fresh confrontation, without preparation, on the basis of false information received from the Soviet Union.

Developments leading up to the outbreak of the war have been dealt with at length in research literature. The data at our disposal enable us, however, to assess how far the Soviet Union influenced Egypt in taking these two decisions – to get the UN Emergency Force to leave Sinai and the Gaza Strip and to close the Straits of Tiran – and how far it supported these decisions when and after they were taken.

THE SOVIET POSITION IN THE CRISIS OVER EGYPT'S EXPULSION OF THE UN EMERGENCY FORCE FROM SINAI AND THE GAZA STRIP AND THE BLOCKADE OF THE STRAITS OF TIRAN

The question that emerges at this point is what the Soviet leadership's expectations were regarding the steps Nasser would take when the false information was transmitted to him concerning Israel's intention to attack Syria. Did the Soviet Union expect that the Egyptian army would enter Sinai without the evacuation of the UN Emergency Force, as had already happened before, and thereby lower the tension on the Syrian–Israeli border? Or was it in fact the Soviet intention that Nasser should act as he did: first by getting the UN Emergency Force to leave, and then blocking the Straits of

Tiran to Israeli shipping? And if it was the latter, then what kind of reaction from Israel and the Western powers did the Soviet leadership expect?

Hassanein Heikal, at this time editor-in-chief of *Al-Ahram* and close confidant of President Nasser, testified that, contrary to the opinions prevailing after the Six Day War, the Soviet Union had not advised the Egyptians to expel the UN Emergency Force from Sinai and close the Straits of Tiran, and that the Soviets were taken by surprise 'just like every other factor', and were 'full of apprehension on this account at a later stage'. Heikal did not make it clear when it was that this 'later stage' had arrived and the Soviet Union had second thoughts on the wisdom of the Egyptian action. It can be assumed, however, that it was on the eve of the outbreak of war that the Soviets realized that the situation had deteriorated beyond control.[26] We have no data contradicting this testimony of Heikal's. On the contrary, two more pieces of evidence, one from Heikal himself and the other from Nasser, strengthen his affirmation:

1. The presumption that, during Gromyko's visit to Egypt (a week before the 7 April incident) an agreement was reached to expel the UN Emergency Forces, is not confirmed by Heikal (who testifies that the visit was intended to clarify the Soviet position on Iran, which was held to be an enemy of Egypt's at this time on account of her active support of the establishment of an Islamic alliance).[27] This does not of course rule out the possibility that the entry of Egyptian troops into Sinai in the event of an aggravation of the situation on the Israel–Syria border may have been discussed on this occasion.
2. After the war Nasser admitted that he had received the news of Israel's intention to attack Syria from the Soviet Union, but he intimated that the responsibility for the decisions, taken as a result of this information, was his alone.[28]

From these sources we can therefore conclude that the Soviet Union did not propose the expulsion of the UN forces and was not a partner to the decision taken in this respect. The same holds good for the related decision to close the Straits of Tiran. There is, however, no evidence at all that the Soviets warned Egypt *not* to take these steps.

Another piece of evidence comes from an unidentified Soviet diplomat, who is stated to have told a journalist representing the

Nouvel Observateur early in June 1967 that Soviet intelligence had fully believed that Israel planned to attack Syria on 15 May 1967 with the double objective of destroying the nests of Palestinian terrorists and advancing on Damascus to overthrow the Syrian government. So President Nasser stationed the Egyptian army on the Sinai–Israel frontier, in agreement with the Soviet Union, in order to prevent an Israeli attack on Syria. The other two serious decisions, however – to demand the evacuation of the UN forces and to close the Straits – 'Nasser took on his own and only told us about them afterwards'. The Soviet diplomat is reported as saying that the Soviet Union warned Egypt of 'the possibility of undesirable reactions'. 'We made it clear that our one and only undertaking was to neutralize the United States inasmuch as we would react to any action on their part by one of ours – but no more than this.'[29]

This testimony must be accepted with caution. The person interviewed may have wanted to excuse Soviet non-intervention in the war by presenting this alleged pre-condition about America's intervention. However, his statement has not been denied, as far as is known, by the Egyptians, and it does fit in with Heikal's testimony. It does add something fresh by its clearer definition of what was, and what was not agreed on between the Soviet Union and Egypt: the intelligence information was transmitted to Egypt because the Soviet Union wanted to secure the stationing of Egyptian forces in Sinai as a force threatening Israel from the south, while Nasser's decisions taken as a result were his alone.

Presumably the Soviet Union could not know beforehand that UN Secretary-General U Thant would decide to accede to the Egyptian demand and more[30] – that is, total evacuation of the UN forces – and so could not have planned it in advance. With the entry of Egyptian forces into Sinai – as had been done in the past – the Soviet Union would be in no danger if there was a confrontation between Israel and Egypt, and it would get what it wanted as regards the thinning out of Israeli forces in the north.

Getting the UN to leave Sinai and the Gaza Strip

Once Nasser's decision to have the UN Emergency Forces removed had been made public and the UN Secretary-General had complied with total evacuation, there were two distinct phases in the Soviet

309

attitude: first, receipt of the news was met with a certain disquiet, the step neither excused nor praised nor condemned;[31] and second, backing for the Egyptian decision was evidenced in the following ways:

1. On 24 May 1967, the government of the Soviet Union published an announcement, 'Regarding the Situation in the Middle East', which stated *inter alia*

> Honouring her commitments under her Mutual Defense Agreement with Syria, the United Arab Republic [Egypt] has taken steps to halt the aggression. In consideration of the fact that the presence of the UN forces in Gaza and the Sinai Peninsula could in this situation lend Israel an advantage effectuating its military provocation against the Arab countries, the Government of the UAR requested the UN to remove its forces from the area.[32]

2. On 25 May 1967, Soviet Foreign Minister Gromyko told Shams ad-Din Badran, the Egyptian Defense Minister, that Egypt had been right to request the evacuation of the UN forces. Badran was told the same thing the next day by the head of the Soviet Government, Kosygin himself, 'The political calculation behind your action was correct'.[33]

Closing the Straits of Tiran

Here too it is possible to discern two stages in the Soviet response: first, giving the information unadorned, with a tendency to ignore it in official public statements (this was the case in the above-mentioned announcement of 24 May 1967 in the Soviet Ambassador's appearance at the Security Council session on 29 May 1967); second, backing the Egyptian move on the official and diplomatic level. The latter stage was evidenced in the following ways:

1. On 25 May 1967, Gromyko told Badran, 'The Soviet government fully understands the Arab point of view; it knows that the Arab countries are not the factor causing tension [in the area] and that all the steps taken by Egypt are defensive and not offensive'.[34]
2. On 26 May 1967, Kosygin told Badran, 'You have won a great

political victory, and as long as there is no war it will be possible to entrench this victory, ... What have you done so far has been done well. However, can we not envisage a juridical solution to the problem of passage through the Straits? ... In the light of the political gains you have secured, it will be easier for you to accept a juridical solution.'[35]

3. On 29 May 1967, Nasser told the Egyptian National Assembly that on the previous day Badran had brought him a letter from Kosygin, saying, 'The Soviet Union supports you in this conflict and will not allow any state to interfere until the situation is restored to what it was before 1956'.[36] This signified support for the total evacuation of the UN forces and closure of the Straits of Tiran to Israeli shipping.

On the propaganda level, the Egyptian decision to block the Straits of Tiran was presented along with the evacuation of the UN forces as a defensive necessity because of Israel's intention to attack Syria and overthrow the government there, and also as a move to restore the situation to the *status quo* before the 1956 Sinai Campaign.[37] The various commentators began to refer to the Straits as if they were Egypt's territorial waters where it had the right of passage. Immediately after the war a Soviet jurist, expert in international law, went so far as to cast doubt on Eilat being an Israeli port, since the area had been conquered by Israel after the signing of the Israel–Egypt Armistice Agreement. His argumentation was clearly aimed at turning the Gulf of Aqaba into a problem in international law and as such calling for a solution by international institutions.[38] This idea later surfaced in Soviet historiography as well,[39] which tried to present the problem not only as calling for a solution by international institutions but as a problem inseparable from the overall solution of the Arab–Israel conflict, an international problem and a function of that conflict in its widest sense.

ISRAEL AND THE WESTERN POWERS AS PERCEIVED BY THE SOVIET UNION AFTER THE DECISION ON THE BLOCKADE OF THE STRAITS

At the talks in Moscow on 28 May 1967, Grechko, Gromyko and Kosygin tried to put the following points to Badran:[40]

1. Israel would not attack Egypt alone unless impelled to do so by the United States.

2. The Western powers would not dare to start a war, given the strength of Arab countries and their unity.

3. Egypt would do better not to press the situation to the point of armed conflict. Egypt and Syria should refrain from provocative actions liable to cause local conflagrations.

4. In the event of a conflagration, the United States would be liable to intervene on the side of Israel, and the Soviet Union would then be obliged to stand at the side of Egypt. It was important to prevent such a situation from arising as it might lead to a confrontation between the powers – something which the Soviet Union was not interested in. Egypt should therefore entrench her gains by a policy of restraint and refraining from escalation.

5. The Soviet information that had been transmitted to Egypt was 'clear and accurate' and the Soviet Union was pleased that the Egyptians had acted 'properly' in accordance with the information. From now on, they must act 'to foil the Israeli plan', that is, to prevent Israel from starting a war and to refrain from starting a war against her. It was important to have world opinion on the side of Egypt.

Soviet assistance promised for the Egyptian stand

On the political level, the Soviet government announcement concerning the Middle East on 24 May 1967 included the following passage:

> Let no-one be in doubt that if somebody tried to start aggression in the Middle East, he will be faced not only with the united strength of the Arab countries but also with firm resistance to aggression on the part of the USSR and all peace-loving countries.[41]

The warning could be interpreted in the first place as support for Egypt's stand if Israel or the Western powers should attempt to restore the situation to what it had been before the Egyptian moves. Since everything Egypt had done was for defense purposes, anyone opposing these moves would be an aggressor and exposed to 'firm resistance' on the part of the Soviet Union. The aim was clear: to deter and threaten the one side and express support for the other side.

The final passage of this announcement stated, 'The USSR is doing and will continue to do everything in its power to prevent violations of the peace and security of the Middle East and to safeguard the legal rights of the peoples there'. This paragraph, too, indicated support for Egypt's legal rights and an undertaking to prevent an outbreak following Egypt's actions. This, of course, signified that the Soviet Union did not view these actions as constituting 'violations of the peace and security of the Middle East' over against the Israeli, American and British contention that closing the Straits of Tiran to Israeli shipping constituted a *casus belli*.

On the diplomatic level, the Soviet leadership was buttressing the Egyptian leadership by promising to stand beside Egypt if Israel attacked and to provide whatever assistance Egypt needed. On his return to Moscow, Badran told Nasser that Grechko had promised him that if Egypt was attacked, the Soviet Union would be found at the side of Egypt[42] (though Heikal and Nasser both said after the war that the Soviet Union had never promised it would fight).

SUMMING UP

It would appear that a chain reaction of mistaken evaluations on the part of the Soviet Union, Israel, Egypt, and Syria led to the outbreak of the Six Day War. Even though the Soviet Union may not have been *directly* involved in Nasser's decision to have the UN forces leave Sinai and the Gaza Strip and to blockade the Straits of Tiran, it was, nevertheless, the Soviet Union that gave Nasser grounds and motivation for acting as he did. This was done on the strength of the (falsified) information it fabricated for him and on the strength of the political and propaganda support it afforded him by its campaign justifying the Egyptian stand against Israel. The Soviet Union was drawn along in the wake of Nasser's decisions by its (mistaken) assumption that it would be able to entrench his gains for him, in the light of the (mistaken) evaluation that Israel would not start a war on her own, an evaluation reached in light of the

313

(mistaken) belief that if Israel were to attack Egypt, the united strength of the Arab countries could defeat her on the battlefield (if the USA did not stand beside her). Soviet support for the Egyptian decisions was therefore intended to buttress the Syrian regime by warding off the Israeli threat and to award Egypt political–military gains as compensation for her readiness to come to the aid of Syria. Thus, Soviet influence would gain ground in the Arab states and all at the expense of vital Israeli interests.

Israel believed (mistakenly) that its massive reprisal reactions would halt terrorist activity in her territory on the part of Syria and assumed (mistakenly) that Egypt would not rush to Syria's help in the event of an outburst of hostilities on the Israel–Syria border. Hence she (mistakenly) assumed that the prospect of war breaking out was unlikely, and failed to correctly evaluate Soviet interest in buttressing the pro-Soviet regime in Damascus.

Egypt saw no alternative but to request the removal of the UN forces from Sinai and Gaza and to blockade the Straits of Tiran, without her having had any previous intention of doing this, because she had an exaggerated estimate of her own strength and was inclined to accept the (mistaken) Soviet evaluation that Israel could not start a war against Egypt and Syria on her own.

Syria believed (mistakenly) that her entrenched strategic topographical situation, the Egyptian threat to Israel's security and Soviet support for her regime, taken all together, guaranteed defeat for Israel, and she therefore dared to take the lead and set out on a campaign to destroy Israel.

NOTES

1 TASS, 7 April 1966, quoted from a letter addressed to U Thant, UN General Secretary, by the Arab delegations at the UN.
2 *Pravda*, 8 April 1966, quoting from the speech of Fuad Nasser, the Secretary of the Jordanian Communist Party, given at the 23rd Congress of the CPSU, 29 March – 14 April 1966.
3 *Pravda*, 7 April 1966, quoting from a speech by Sadam, Head of the Syrian delegation to the 23rd Congress of the CPSU.
4 *Sovietskaya Rossia*, 11 April 1966, quoting an article by Samad.
5 *Izvestia*, 20 April 1966.
6 *Pravda*, 26 April 1966.
7 *Divrei Haknesset*, Vol. 45, p. 1467, 18 May 1966.
8 *Pravda*, 18 May 1966.

9   *Pravda*, 19 May 1966.
10 *Pravda*, 9 June 1966.
11 *Kol Haam*, 30 May 1966.
12 MFA Arch. File 103.1 SSR.
13 For the full text of Israel's reply, see A. Dagan, *Moscow and Jerusalem*, pp. 176–7.
14 Ibid., p. 187.
15 Ibid.
16 Ibid., p. 190.
17 In his speech in the Knesset, Prime Minister Eshkol stated that from 1965 to May 1967, 113 acts of sabotage and laying of explosives, for which Syria was responsible, had been carried out on Israeli territory. From July 1966 to May 1967, Israel had addressed 34 notes of complaint to the UN Security Council about Syrian sabotage activity. *Knesset Record*, Vol. 49, p. 2226, 22 May 1967 (Hebrew).
18 A. Dagan, *Moscow and Jerusalem* (London: Abelard-Schuman, 1970) p. 202.
19 *Ibid.*, p. 203.
20 *Izvestia*, 25 April 1966.
21 *Ha'aretz*, 11 May 1967. Presumably the information that was published in Israel after some delay was already known before that in the Soviet Union shortly before the transmission of their note to Israel of 21 April 1967.
22 M. A. Gilboa, *Six Years and Six Days* (Tel Aviv: Am Oved, 1968) p. 79 (Hebrew); and A. Tsur, *Soviet Factors and the Six-Day War* (Tel Aviv: Sifriat Hapoalim, 1975) pp. 182–6 (Hebrew).
23 *Davar*, 12 May 1967, cites Prime Minister Eshkol as saying, 'Israel takes a serious view of acts of sabotage committed on her soil in recent days and if there is no other way she will be obliged to make use of appropriate means of reacting against the nests of terrorism and those who encourage them, in accordance with the circumstances'.
    This reference to 'nests of terrorism and those who encourage them' (*Jerusalem Post*, 12 May 1967) was interpreted both by Nasser and the Soviet leadership as a direct threat aimed at the regime in Damascus. The Soviet Premier referred to this declaration of Eshkol's when he addressed the UN Emergency Assembly on 19 June 1967 as confirming Israel's warlike preparations directed against Syria.
    Parallel to this, on 12 May 1967, the UP news agency reported that guidelines had been issued by a senior Israeli officer to the effect that 'Israel would take limited military action to knock out the regime in Damascus, if Syrian terrorists kept up with acts of sabotage in Israel'.
24 Hassanein Heikal, *The Six-Day War*; extracts in *Ma'ariv*, 9 Nov. 1973.
25 In order to start a war, Israel would have had to mobilize reserves, and this was not done. Furthermore, the 1968 Cairo trial revealed that the Egyptian Chief of Staff stated on his return from a visit to Damascus that he had not seen any Israeli troop concentrations on the border with Syria (*Jerusalem Post*, 28 Feb. 1968) or any proof in the UN Secretary General's report of 18 May 1967 on his memorandum of the same day to confirm the reports of such concentrations. UN Document A/6669; S/7896.
26 H. Heikal, *op. cit.*
27 *Ibid.*
28 Speech by Nasser on the 15th anniversary of the Egyptian revolution, 23 July 1967. *International Documents on Palestine*, Beirut 1967, Doc. 393, as well as Nasser's speech when he resigned, 9 June 1967, *ibid.*, Doc. 373.

29 *Kol Haam*, 5 July 1967.
30 U Thant, UN Secretary-General, offered Egypt the possibility of total evacuation of UN forces from Sinai and the Gaza Strip. He did not want a partial withdrawal. With no other option, as far as prestige was concerned, Nasser opted for total evacuation. Hassanein Heikal in his book *The Six-Day War* (extracts in *Ma'ariv*, 9 Nov. 1973) thought that Nasser had told his guest, the Syrian foreign minister, on 17 May 1973 that he planned to leave the UN forces in Sharm a-Sheikh and Gaza 'at least for now'.
31 *Pravda*, 18 May 1967, as reported by Primakov from Cairo in 'Clouds over the Middle East'.
32 *Pravda*, 24 May 1967.
33 See note 24.
34 *Ibid.*
35 *Ibid.*
36 *International Documents on Palestine*, 1967, Doc. 329.
37 *Pravda*, 26 May 1967, commentary by A. Primakov from Cairo.
38 *Krassnaya Zvezda*, 28 June 1967, an article entitled 'Israel violates international law', signed by Y. Blishchenko, Professor of International Law and Doctor of Jurisprudence.
39 G. S. Nikitina, *The State of Israel* (Moscow: Soviet Academy of Sciences, Nauka, 1968), p. 377 (Russian).
40 See note 24 above.
41 *Pravda*, 24 May 1967.
42 Hassenein Heikal, *The Sphinx and the Commissar* (London: Collins, 1978), pp. 28, 179–80.

15 · The Six Day War and the breach of Soviet–Israeli diplomatic relations

S OVIET evaluations were mistaken, not only with respect to Israel's military capacity to confront the Arab states on the field of battle on her own but also with respect to the significance of the psychological impact of the Holocaust on the consciousness of the population of Israel when faced with declarations from Nasser and the other Arab leaders of their intention to wipe out Israel, an element which considerably heightened Israel's motivation to break out of the noose closing round her. It must nevertheless be assumed that Israel's mobilizing the reserves, Moshe Dayan's joining the government as Defense Minister, and the formation of a government of National Unity must have alerted the Soviet leadership to the imminence of a conflagration in the region as a result of the maritime blockade of Israel on the Gulf of Aqaba, the Egyptian troop concentration to the south of Israel, and Nasser's threats of extermination.

In the 1 June issue of *Pravda*, the political commentator M. Maievski stated: 'One gets the impression that someone is prepared to take dangerous steps to kindle the flames of war in the Middle East, all on account of the passage or non-passage to two to four ships a day through the Straits of Tiran'. This approach to the issue, the commentator declared, 'shows the lack of responsibility of certain circles in Israel and raises doubts about the "restraint"'. This indicates that the Soviets felt the turnabout that had taken place in the Israeli leadership and realized that the establishment of the government of National Unity could mean that Israel had no choice but to go to war. The comment cited reveals moreover a

317

certain disillusionment – the USSR had apparently believed that the line of 'restraint' among Israeli leaders would outweigh the line in favor of going to war, and now here was this turnabout.

In its note to Israel of 2 June – the last before the war broke out – the Soviet government referred to Israeli Foreign Minister Eban's declaration that Israel could wait only for a given space of time for its demands to be met, a matter of days or at most weeks. 'Israel would finally open the Straits of Tiran on her own if the great powers did not lift the blockade.' This was the first time that the Soviet government had referred to the blockade in a note to Israel. No explicit position was taken on the matter. The alarm expressed was not, however, over the blockade itself but over Eban's declaration, which the note stated could 'serve as official confirmation of information testifying to activity by adventurers on the initiative of warmongers in Israel who wish to dictate the line of action of the government and people of Israel', and in order to reassure Israel the note went on:

> The Soviet government desires to reaffirm that it will do everything in its power to prevent the possibility of military context. Its efforts are now all centered on this aim. But if the government of Israel decides to assume responsibility for the outbreak of war, it will have to pay the price for its consequences to the full.[1]

The Soviet assurance regarding efforts 'to prevent the possibility of military conflict' was not intended to refer to the aim of restoring the status quo, an idea which Soviet Premier Kosygin had absolutely repudiated in talks with the British Foreign Secretary in Moscow a few days earlier. Almost certainly, the efforts in question were concentrated on Nasser, in order to prevent him from attacking Israel as he was proclaiming he was about to do.[2]

Soviet 'efforts' to prevent the conflict were thus initiated when the Gulf of Aqaba was already blocked to Israeli shipping by the Egyptians. This meant that Israel was supposed to acquiesce in the Egyptian blockade in return for a Soviet peace, which would take the form of Nasser's refraining from attacking Israel. Neither in this Soviet note nor in the talks that followed between the Soviet Foreign Minister and the Israeli Ambassador in Moscow at the time was there the slightest indication that the USSR would act to lift the blockade of the Gulf of Aqaba and open it to Israeli shipping, nor was any readiness whatsoever displayed to recognize Israel's right of free passage there for her ships. On the contrary, the political commentators went on reiterating Egypt's unchallengeable right to navigate in the Straits of Tiran as in her own sovereign national territory. These cloudy formulations about Soviet efforts to prevent military conflict were not put forward to influence the Israeli Prime Minister not to adopt the military option. The framing of the note was guided mainly by the desire to gain time, so that the situation would gradually reach the point where the Egyptian blockade of Tiran would become a *fait accompli*.

When the war broke out on 5 June 1967, and when the first results became known, the Soviet Union had the UN Security Council convened in order to secure an immediate cease-fire and the withdrawal of the Israeli Defense Forces to their previous lines. In statements at the Security Council, in the Soviet media and in notes to Israel, the USSR adopted insulting language, expressed sharp condemnation and warned that if Israel did not immediately accept the Security Council resolution on a cease-fire, 'the Soviet government would re-assess its relations with Israel and would reach a decision on the continuation of diplomatic relations with Israel'. It would also 'consider other steps to be taken' as a result of Israel's policy. This amounted to a threat to cut off diplomatic relations accompanied by a more serious threat hinting at military intervention.[3]

At the Security Council hearings, Israel firmly rejected the Soviet accusations.[4] In its notes to the Soviet Union Israel dwelt on the background to the war – which the Soviet side had completely ignored – and placed the whole responsibility on the Arab leaders, who had pursued policies directed at the destruction of the State of Israel from the day it was established. The most striking, concrete expressions of this policy were Nasser's decisions to have the UN force removed from Sinai and the Gaza Strip and to close the Straits of Tiran to Israeli shipping, and his declarations of readiness to start a war of extermination against Israel. In these notes, Israel was careful not to place any blame on Soviet policy in the Middle East or to refer to it in terms of condemnation. The text was explanatory rather than controversial, apparently drafted with the aim of refraining from challenging the USSR openly, in order to minimize the danger of direct Soviet intervention in the fighting.

THE BREACH OF SOVIET–ISRAELI DIPLOMATIC RELATIONS

With the virtual cessation of fighting on all the fronts on 8 June 1967 it looked as if the Soviet Union was not carrying out its threats to break off relations with Israel. The decision to do so was taken on 10 June (at a gathering of the heads of all the east European parties and states, including Yugoslavia, all of which took part in the decision except for Romania), the day after Israel launched a military attack on Syria, when its forces were advancing towards Kuneitra on the way to Damascus. The opening passage of the Soviet announcement on the breach of diplomatic relations with Israel stated:

> News has just been received that Israeli forces, ignoring the Security Council resolutions on halting military actions, are continuing these actions, occupying Syrian territory and advancing in the direction of Damascus.[5]

The conclusion to be drawn from this is that the Soviet evaluation of the supposed advance of the Israeli forces towards Damascus was what turned the scales in favor of breaking off relations with Israel rather than all the reasons preceding this in the course of the war. What caused the breach?

Syria was the Soviet Union's most cherished prize in the Arab world in general and the Middle East in particular. Its geographic proximity to the Soviet Union and its pro-Soviet regime gave Syria a higher preference in Soviet strategic perception than Egypt. Israel's conquest of the Golan Heights and the advance of its troops towards Kuneitra (when Syria announced on the morning of 10 June that Israel had taken Kuneitra, the town was still in Syrian hands) were liable to endanger the pro-Soviet regime in Damascus. The Soviet Union had to take a seemingly drastic step in order to put a stop to the Israeli advance. Apparently the Soviet Union perceived this situation as more dangerous than the Israeli gains in Sinai and on the West Bank of the Jordan, which is why it had not taken the step of breaking off relations sooner. The USSR claimed afterwards that the breach of relations with Israel was what halted the Israeli advance towards Damascus. In fact, however, when the announcement was handed to Israel, an agreed cease-fire between Israel and

Syria had already come into existence, so the advance halted before the breach of relations and not the other way round.

The attack on Syria was the main cause for the breach of relations, but it appears that three additional factors contributed to the decision:

Pressure from Broz Tito, President of Yugoslavia, on the leaders of the USSR and Eastern Europe to react energetically against Israel, based on his background of personal friendship with Nasser and his fear of the establishment of a precedent of a successful invasion by foreign forces into one of the so-called non-aligned countries. He feared the use of this precedent by the USSR against Yugoslavia, and on this account it was his firm and clear intention to demonstrate solidarity with Egypt. The USSR could not act any differently from Yugoslavia towards Egypt and so was forced to follow suit.

The Soviet commitment to Syria and Egypt in encouraging them in their aggressive policy towards Israel by affording them military, political and propaganda support. Since the USSR did not intervene directly at their side in the war, it must have felt a moral obligation to compensate them to the extent of cutting off relations with Israel. The substratum of traditional anti-Semitism and hostility towards Israel in the Soviet leadership, against the background of Israel's campaign on behalf of Soviet Jewry and the national awakening of Soviet Jews themselves. Putting an end to the official Israeli presence in the heart of Moscow, thereby eradicating the physical base of Israeli activity, must certainly have appealed to the Soviet leadership as a means of damping down the national awakening among the Jews.

WAS THE ISRAELI GOVERNMENT AWARE OF THE POSSIBLE BREACH OF RELATIONS?

Moshe Dayan, the then Defense Minister, bore witness that he was the only minister in the government who feared Soviet military intervention in the war and that this was why he delayed the conquest of the Golan Heights.[6] His testimony was confirmed by the then commander of the Northern Force, David Elazar.[7] It emerges that Dayan only declared for the attack on the Golan

Heights once he saw that the Soviet Union was not intervening in the fighting and had not cut off relations with Israel after the conquest of the whole of the Sinai Peninsula and the West Bank. In the opinion of the then Director-General of the Foreign Ministry, Prime Minister Eshkol was also aware of the possibility of a breach of relations, but 'things developed at a dizzy pace' and the issue was never brought forward for discussion.[8] It seems in retrospect that even if it had been discussed, it is doubtful whether this possibility would have outweighed the consideration in favor of taking the Heights. At a later date, Abba Eban, Foreign Minister at the time in question, said that he had expected that the USSR would behave as it had done in the 1956 Sinai Campaign, that is, would recall its Ambassador but leave the framework of diplomatic relations intact.[9] This line of thought testifies to the failure to distinguish between the situation at the end of 1956 as regards Soviet involvement with the Arab states and that of mid-1967: (1) Syria's geopolitical importance for the USSR in 1967 was greater than that of Egypt in 1956; (2) the Soviet government was far more deeply involved in the events that led to the 1967 war than it had been in the events of 1956; (3) in 1956 the United States took its stand alongside the USSR and together they put pressure on Israel to withdraw from the areas taken in that campaign, while in 1967 the USSR was the only power that actually had brought pressure to bear on Israel to stop its advance on Damascus. Finally, in 1956 the Soviet Union had not yet felt the specific impact of the Israeli presence on the process of national awakening of the Jews of the Soviet Union as it had in 1967.

WAS THERE A CHANGE IN THE BASIC SOVIET ATTITUDE TOWARDS ISRAEL AFTER THE WAR?

Soviet Premier Kosygin, in his address to the UN Emergency Assembly of 19 June 1967, convened at the USSR's initiative to censure Israel and demand its immediate withdrawal to its previous border lines, stated: 'The question may be asked, "Why is the USSR so opposed to Israel?" The USSR is not opposed to Israel, but to the aggressive policy pursued by the ruling circles in that country', and he went on

For the 50 years of its history, the Soviet Union has honored all peoples, big and small. Every people has the right to its independent national state. This is one of the fundamental principles of Soviet policy. It was on this foundation that we based our attitude towards Israel when we voted in the UN in 1947 in favor of the decision to establish two independent states in the area of the former British colony of Palestine. Guided by this basic policy, the Soviet Union at a later stage established diplomatic relations with Israel.[10]

This was the first time since the leftist fraction of Ba'ath took power in Syria that a Soviet leader saw fit to proclaim publicly the right of Israel to exist as an independent state and to recall the Soviet share in its independence. It would appear that the USSR addressed this reminder to three audiences:

1. The West, in an attempt to refute the accusations directed at it by Western public opinion on account of its support for the policy of Arab leaders who wanted to destroy Israel.
2. The Arab leaders, lest they interpret Soviet military and political support for their anti-Western policies as consent to the destruction of Israel.
3. Israel, to show that there was no basis for its fears that it would be destroyed by the Arab leaders – the Soviet Union would not have supported the destruction of the State of Israel, whose independence it had itself helped to sponsor and with which it had even established diplomatic relations.

Although this was meant to improve the image of the Soviet Union, which was seen as one-sided in its support of the Arab leaders in their anti-Israel policy, it did not clarify why the Soviet Union had broken off relations with Israel. If the reason was as stated at the time, 'the aggressive policy of leading circles', why did the Soviet Union not react in the same way in her relations with other countries, in Western Europe and Asia, which had foreign anti-Soviet and anti-Communist bases on their soil?

Not that the Soviet Union was unwilling to disclose the reasons why it broke off relations with Israel. Among the political and ideological considerations there must have been the sediment of anti-Semitism deposited by history, which certainly became weightier with Israel's victory in the campaign against Egypt and Syria. It did considerable harm to the good name of Soviet weapons and military doctrine, which the Soviet Union was anxious to find takers for in the developing countries. From this point of view, there was certainly a change for the worse in the Soviet attitude to Israel. But Kosygin's main point – and it was indeed important to Israel – was that the breach of relations should not be interpreted as a denial of Israel's right to exist (an emphasis increasingly reverted to with the passage of time), and this in spite of the period immediately before the breach, when official declarations on Israel's right to exist were conspicuous by their absence. (Who knows – if the Soviet Union had intimated this right in its public declarations before the war, the leaders of Egypt and Syria might possibly have been deterred from the actions that led to the war itself.)

At the UN Emergency Assembly and in the Kosygin-Johnson talks at Glassboro, the Soviet Union apparently realized that there was no way of getting the Assembly to recommend that the Security Council call for the withdrawal of the Israeli Defense Forces to their previous positions without also calling for an end to the state of war between Israel and the Arab countries. The Soviet Union obviously wanted Israel's immediate withdrawal and knew that it would not get the decision without the offer of a tangible counterpart concession. The Arab leaders would have to agree, it seemed, to the call 'to end the state of war'. A letter sent to Nasser by the Central Committee of the CPSU at this time shows how the Soviet leaders presented their interpretation of 'an end to the state of war'. In the letter was the following passage:

> The call issued by the General Assembly to the Security Council to consider this problem will not involve a request for any political concessions at all from the Arab countries. It will not be linked to an obligation on the part of the Arab countries to recognize or negotiate with Israel. the discussions will deal with ending the state of war, nothing more, nothing less.[11]

These were the three 'no's' – no negotiations, no recognition, no peace – that were adopted at the Khartoum Conference of the Arab countries on 1 September 1967, to be or not to be, neither peace nor war. This was the Soviet strategy that influenced Arab strategy. In reality it signified that the Six Day War must not be allowed to effect any change whatsoever in the set of relations that existed, or did not exist, between Israel and the Arab states on the eve of the war.

Just as there was no change in Soviet interests in the Middle East, there was no change in the basic Soviet attitude to Israel immediately after the war. This attitude was after all part of Soviet Middle Eastern and global policy calculations (against the background of confrontation with the Western powers and mainly the United States) as well as calculations connected with the problem of the Jews in the Soviet Union and Israel's fight on their behalf.

NOTES

1 Gilboa, *Shesh Shanim ve-Shisha Yamim* (Tel Aviv: Am Hasefer, 1972) p. 196.
2 Nasser's statement to the delegation of the Council of Arab Trade Unions, according to Reuters' report from Cairo on 27 May 1967: 'Our aim will be to wipe out Israel. We now feel sufficiently strong to fight Israel and win. Seizing the straits and closing them means really facing up to Israel' (*Kol Haam*, 28 May 1967).
3 A. Dagan, *Moscow and Jerusalem*, p. 230.
4 Ibid., p. 233.
5 *Pravda*, 11 June 1967.
6 Moshe Dayan, *Avnei Derekh* (Hebrew) (Jerusalem: Idanim, 1977), pp. 474–5, 485, and in an interview with the present writer on 24 Jan. 1980.
7 'Yamim Ve-Leilot', *Maariv*, 22 Dec. 1978, p. 13, chapter from book by Hanokh Bartov, *Dado – 48 Years and 20 More Days*, 2nd edition (Tel Aviv: Sifriyat Maariv, 1979).
8 Arieh Levavi, former Director-General of the Foreign Ministry, in an interview with the present writer on 9 March 1981.
9 Abba Eban, in an address at the opening of the International Symposium on the Soviet Union and Islam, at Tel Aviv University on 28 Dec. 1980. (The symposium was initiated and organized by the Research Institute on the Soviet Union and Eastern Europe of Tel Aviv University.)
10 *Pravda*, 20 June 1967.
11 H. Heikal, *Sphinx and Commissar*.

Epilogue

A S FROM its severance of relations with Israel, until
Gorbachev's rise to power, the Soviet Union continued to
pursue a hostile policy towards Israel, characterized by an
obviously pro-Arab stand on the Arab–Israeli conflict – including
the extending of massive military and political support to Syria and
the PLO – so that it assisted in perpetuating the conflict more than
it helped resolve it. The USSR also pursued a poisonous anti-Israeli
and anti-Zionist campaign. Paradoxically, two contradictory lines
could be discerned in its policy towards Israel:

1. Despite having broken off its relations with Israel, it frequently
declared that Israel had the right to exist as an independent state
(the USSR used to do this even more often than during the period
covered by this book), which aimed at emphasizing that its one-
sided policy on the Arab–Israeli conflict was not based on the idea
of Israel's disappearance, and that the USSR did not accept the idea
of the Palestinian Covenant, negating Israel's right to existence as
an independent sovereign state with secure and recognized borders.
2. An intensive drive to isolate Israel in the international arena was
conducted by the USSR. In its propaganda campaign it presented
Israel as a servant of American imperialism, as an inciter to war
endangering peace in the Middle East and throughout the world,
who dispossessed Arabs from their lands, pursuing a cruel regime
oppressing its Arab minority. Israel was depicted as a 'devilish force'
that should be condemned constantly and should be isolated for the
sake of peace and security. Hence, its tendency to engage in its
struggle against Israel the non-aligned nations in addition to the Arab
and communist countries whom it regarded as its natural allies.

To this policy an additional source of hatred was added because of national awakening of Jews in the USSR, which swelled to large dimensions, parallel to Israel's open leading of the struggle for their sake on a world scale more forcefully than in the period when diplomatic relations existed.

In its anti-Zionist campaign the USSR stressed the following elements:

Zionism is fighting against the reduction of world tension.
It fights against the International Labor Movement, national liberation movements of oppressed people, socialism, progress, and its main psychological struggle is against communist movements and the USSR.
Zionism is striving to conquer power positions in economy and the world press.

As for immigration, there were ups and downs. In the 1970s there was mass emigration, but a drastic reduction in the 1980s. There were many thousands of refuseniks. No improvement took place in the national status of the Jews. Jewish self-organized activity, however, increased, despite the attempts by the Soviet authorities to suppress it .

As to the Arab–Israeli conflict, over the course of the 1970s and the beginning of the 1980s, the USSR presented several proposals for its settlement. The last one, in July 1987 (Gorbachev era) consisted of six principles:

1. Israel's retreat from all the territories it had conquered since 1967. The removal of all settlements it had established in these areas, and the proclamation of the frontiers between Israel and its neighboring countries as inviolable.
2. The right to self-determination for the Palestinian people, including the right to establish its own state, in the West Bank and Gaza, and the right of the Palestinian refugees to return to their homes or receive compensation.
3. To return to the Arabs East Jerusalem conquered by Israel in 1967.
4. To guarantee the right of all states in the area to independent existence in security.

5. To put an end to the state of war and establish peace between Israel and the Arab states. Israel and the Palestinian State should commit themselves to mutual respect, the political sovereignty and territorial integrity of each other, and peacefully settle the controversies between them.

6. International security guarantees to a settlement reached by the two parties. The USSR would be ready to participate in it.

As from 1989 a change was noted in the tactical stand of the Soviet Union on the question of settling the conflict. In his speech in Cairo on 23 February 1989, Foreign Minister Sheverdnadze stressed the need to respect the principle of 'balanced interests' between rights and security without rejecting the detailed Sóviet principles of the past.

The Soviets' central perception was the need to convene an international conference for the settlement of the conflict under the patronage of the permanent members of the UN Security Council without putting pressure on the participating parties, Israel, on the one hand, and the PLO 'as the sole legitimate representative of the Palestinian people and the rest of the Arab states', on the other hand.

The USSR revealed a positive stance towards Israel's peace initiative which called, among other things, for free elections in Judea, Samaria and Gaza, and favorably regarded the beginning of possible negotiations between an official Israeli representation and an elected Palestinian one, trusting that these talks would lead gradually to an international conference for the settlement of the conflict. The idea of an international conference had been present for a number of years as the single way leading to a settlement of the conflict through negotiations and by peaceful means. The military option was excluded. On different occasions the Soviet leaders stated that Israel's engagement in talks with the PLO (in January 1990 the USSR recognized the PLO's official representation in Moscow as the Embassy of the Palestinian State) leading towards an international conference would create the appropriate conditions for the renewal of Israeli–Soviet diplomatic relations. However, Israel claimed time and again that the renewal of Israeli–Soviet relations should not be made conditional upon the convening of an international conference and that it regarded the conference as an international forum for the imposition of the USSR's solutions on the sides in the dispute. Moreover, two of the five permanent members of the UN Security Council who were supposed to give their auspices to the talks – the USSR and China – did not maintain diplomatic relations with Israel. However, Israel's main reservation on an international conference was its objection to negotiating with the PLO, whose ideology was based on Israel's disappearance from the Middle East map.

There were signs, under Gorbachev's rule, that the USSR persuaded the PLO to undertake moderate positions towards Israel and as a result of this the PLO declared, in December 1988, that it recognized Security Council Resolution 242, 338, which implied that it recognized Israel's existence. The USSR also had a restraining influence on President Assad of Syria, who strived to reach a strategic military balance with Israel, even if the USSR did not stop supplying Syria with arms. There is no doubt that in this respect a positive turn occurred in Soviet policy towards Israel, since the USSR for many years had been fanning the Arab–Israeli conflict, believing that by acting in this way it would secure a strategic foothold for itself in the Middle East – but not real peace, which would have strengthened stability in the region, including the USSR's security itself, in an era of modern sophisticated weapons.

In Gorbachev's era a radical change occurred also in the national and legal status of the Jewish minority, with free organization of Jewish national and cultural associations. Encouragement was even given for the revival of Jewish religious and secular institutions in an effort to stop the emigration of Jews, which was seen by Gorbachev as a Jewish 'brain drain' of people needed for the rehabilitation of the Soviet economy and the advancement of its science, culture and technology. Yet, against the background of freedom granted to the activities of national organizations and the national awakening in the Soviet republics for more independence in the domain of cultural, educational, and self-governance, a wave of ugly anti-Semitism arose, threatening, at times, the physical existence of Jews in the USSR.

This anti-Semitism is rooted in the Russian traditional nationalism, striving at increasing its influence in Russian society and in governmental and local circles. It always saw the Jew as responsible for economic crises and a factor that stabilized the Communist regime. In the non-Russian republics the image of the Jew was depicted as the carrier of Russian culture, symbolizing an accelerated assimilation process into the Russian culture that was hated by various nationalities, and who regarded it as a means for the Soviet regime to get them to abandon their own national, cultural and social values, in favour of Russian culture.

In the domain of Israeli–Soviet relations, considerable progress was noted during the Gorbachev period. Yet the process of renewing diplomatic relations moved on slowly, comprising three stages:

(a) exchange of consular delegations (1987/88);
(b) establishment of formal relations on a consular level (1990);
(c) renewal of full diplomatic relations (October 1991) during the visit to Jerusalem of Soviet Foreign Minister Pankin, on the eve of the convening of the Madrid Peace Conference for the settlement of the Arab–Israeli dispute, under the sponsorship of the USA and the USSR.

Following the political changes in the USSR during the Gorbachev era, the end of inter-power competition, and the beginning of a new process of co-operation in the Middle East, the USSR also changed its attitude in a positive way towards Israel's peace proposals for the settlement of the Arab–Israeli dispute.

On this basis Israel accepted Soviet sponsorship together with that of the USA for the Madrid Peace Conference on 30 October 1991. At that stage the USSR's international status was in sharp decline because of its internal developments – just a few months before its dismemberment. Strangely enough it was Israel – whom the Soviet Union had pushed into a corner for the last 40 years – that accorded the USSR the same status as that of the USA, through the Madrid Peace Conference. At the opening ceremony, next to the American presentation, Gorbachev enumerated the following principles for the settlement of the Arab–Israeli conflict.

The aim of the process is to end with the achievement of a peace agreement between the conflicting parties, but without outside pressure.
Security Council Resolution 242 is to be applied to all frontiers.

The Palestinian right (the PLO was not mentioned) to self-determination is anchored in the UN Charter.

The settlement of the Arab–Israeli conflict will be implemented in stages.

Jerusalem, being a sensitive and complicated problem, will be discussed at the end of the peace-making process and not at its beginning.

Stopping the establishment of new Jewish settlements in the territories administered by Israel will be considered as a gesture by Israel towards the Arabs and will be positively appreciated by them.

Russia, as the successor to the USSR, continued its sponsorship of the Arab–Israeli peace-making process. It also continued to support the above-mentioned principles of the USSR that were expressed at the opening of the Madrid Conference, though less actively than the USA, since it was still absorbed in its immense internal problems of transition from a centralized economy to a decentralized one, in addition to its war in Chechnia, and its permanent struggle to consolidate its leadership.

After the renewal of Israeli–Soviet relations, Israel's relations with Russia developed rapidly and extensively, on the political, economic, trade, cultural, aviation, communications, scientific and tourist levels. Exchange visits increased on the ministerial and public levels. Many agreements for co-operation in almost all applied fields of activity were signed between Israel and Russia, and at the same time with the other CIS (Commonwealth of Independent States) members, to the mutual benefit of all. The list is striking, taking into consideration that these bilateral relations had to begin their development from scratch. Yet, the most striking phenomenon that has occurred since late 1989 has been the free exit of Jews from the former USSR as immigrants to Israel (about 700,000 from 1989 to the end of 1996). Simultaneously, among those who have not yet emigrated Jewish national life is also developing over a wide range of educational, cultural, social, and religious activities, whilst keeping open and direct links with Israel and the Jewish Diaspora, the world over.

The potential for further Israeli–Russian co-operation and the continuing friendly relations which are being developed between both countries is still high and not yet fully exploited. The leaders of Israel and Russia are well aware of this. The future – as seen now from Jerusalem – looks promising for Israeli–Russian relations to continue to be – what they could always have been – an example of true friendship and fruitful co-operation between the two nations.

Yosef Govrin
Jerusalem, December 1996

Bibliography

HEBREW SOURCES

Books and articles

Abramovich, M. 'Hayehudim bemifkad hasovieti 1959' ('The Jews in the 1959 Soviet Population Census'), in *Molad* 18 (144–5) (1960), pp. 320–9

Alexander, Z. 'Hamaavak al Yehudei Brit Hamoatzot' ('The Struggle for Soviet Jewry'), in *Behinot* 2–3 (1973), pp. 5–8

Altschuler, M. 'Hamiflaga Hakommunistit Hasovietit vehakiyum Hayehudi' ('The Soviet Communist Party and Jewish National Existence'), in *Molad* 1 (24), No. 3 (1967)

Azbel, M. 'Autobiografia shel Yehudi Echad' ('An Autobiography of a Jew'), in *Hainteligenzia Hayehudit Bevrith Hamoatsot* ('The Jewish Intelligentsia in the USSR'), Tel Aviv, 1976

Bartov, H. *Dado – 48 Shana veod 20 Yom* ('Dado – 48 Years and 20 More Days'), Tel Aviv: Sifriyat Maariv, 1978, 2nd edition 1979

Bar Zohar, M. *David Ben Gurion*, 3 vols., Tel Aviv: Am Oved, 1975

Ben Ami, *Bein Hapatish Vehasdan, Nissayon Ishi Bekerev Yehudei Brith Hamoatzot* ('Between the Hammer and the Sickle, Personal Experience amongst Soviet Jews'), Tel Aviv: Am Oved, 1965

Ben Tzur, A. *Gormim Sovietiim Umilchemet Sheshet Hayamim* ('Soviet Factors and the Six Day War'), Tel Aviv: Sifriyat Hapoalim, 1976

Dayan, M. *Avnei Derekh* ('Landmarks, Autobiography'), Jerusalem: Idanim, 1977

idem, *Yoman Maarekhet Sinai* ('Diary of the Sinai Campaign'), Tel Aviv: Am Hasefer, 1967

Donitz, Y. 'Ekronot Hayesod Betfisato Hapolitit-Habitchonit shel Ben Gurion Vehashkafato al Hasikhsukh Haisraeli-Arvi 1960– 1977'

('Basic principles in Ben Gurion's political and security perception and his view on the Israeli–Arab conflict in the years
1960–1977'), in *Medina u-Memshal* 1 (1971)

Eban, A. *Pirkei Haim* ('My Life'), 2 vols., Tel Aviv: Sifriyat Maariv, 1978

Erickson, G. 'Otzma Tzvayit Sovietit' ('Soviet Military Power'), Tel
Aviv: Maarakhot, Defense Ministry, 1973

Ettinger, S. 'Hahitorerut Haleumit Bekerev Yehudei Brit Hamoatzot'
('The National Awakening of the Jews in the USSR'), in *Parshiot*
33 (1972), pp. 3–17

Freigerson, Z. (A. Tsfoni) *Yoman Zikhronot 1949–1955* ('Memoirs
1949–1955'), Tel Aviv: Am Oved, 1976

Gilboa, Y. A. *Hashanim Hashekhorot shel Yahadut Brit Hamoatsot* ('The
Black Years of Soviet Jewry'), Tel Aviv: Am Hasefer, 1972

Gittelman, Z. 'Modernizatsia, Zechuyot Adam uleumi'ut Yehudit
Bivrit Hamoatsot' ('Modernization, human rights and Jewish
nationality in the USSR'), in *Shevut* 2 (1974)

Golan, G. 'Hameoravut Hasovietit Bemizrah Hatichon' ('Soviet
Involvement in the Middle East'), in *Medina u-Memshal* 1 (1974)

Goldberg, Ben Zion. *Habaya Hayehudit Bivrit Hamoatsot* ('The Jewish
Problem in the USSR'), Tel Aviv: Am Oved, 1966

Horowitz, D. 'Lokhama lelo milkhama, ofyo shel hasikhsukh
haisraeli-arvi 1949–1967' ('Beligerency withouth war: the
character of the Israeli–Arab conflict 1949–1967'), in *Molad* 4
(27), Nos. 19–20 (1971)

Katz, K. *Budapest, Warsha, Moskva: Shagrir el Medinot Mitnakrot*
('Budapest, Warsaw, Moscow: an Envoy to Unfriendly Lands'),
Tel Aviv: Sifriyat Hapoalim, 1976

Kimche, D., and D. Bavly, *Sufot Haesh, Milchemet Sheshet Hayamim,
Mekoroteha vetotsaoteha* ('The Sandstorm: the Arab–Israeli War of
1967, Prelude and Aftermath'), Tel Aviv: Am Hasefer, 1968

Kory, W. 'Mekorot Haantishemiut Hasovietit vehitpatkhuta'
('Roots of Soviet Anti-Semitism and its Development'), in *Shevut*
1 (1973)

Namir, M. *Shelikhut Bemoskva* ('Mission to Moscow'), Tel Aviv: Am
Oved, 1971

Pinkus, B. 'HaBa'ya Hale'umit Bevrit-Hamoatsot: halakha umaase'
('The National Problem in the USSR: Theory and Practice'), in
Molad 1 (24), No. 3 (1967)

idem, *Tekhiya Utekuma Leumit* ('National Rebirth and Re-establishment, Zionism and the Zionist Movement in the Soviet Union

1947–1987'), Beersheba: Ben Gurion University of the Negev Press, 1993

Rabin, Y. *Pinkas Sherut* ('Service Card'), Tel Aviv: Sifriyat Maariv, 1979

Refael, G. *Besod Leumin* ('Destination Peace: Three Decades of Israeli Foreign Policy'), Jerusalem: Idanim, 1981

Ro'i, Y. *Yahasei Israel-Brit Hamoatsot 1947–1954* ('Israeli–Soviet Relations 1947–1954'), doctoral thesis, Hebrew University of Jerusalem, 1972

idem, 'Emdat Brit Hamoatsot Legabei Haaliya Kegorem bimdiniuta klapei Hasikhsukh haisraeli-arvi 1954–1967' ('The USSR's Attitude to *aliya*, as a Factor of its Policy towards the Israeli–Arab Dispute'), in *Behinot* 5 (1974)

Safran, N. *Ha'imut Haarvi-ha'israeli 1948–1967* ('Arab–Israeli Conflict 1948–1967'), Jerusalem: Keter, 1970

Sharett, M. *Yoman Ishi* ('Private Diary'), 8 vols., Tel Aviv: Sifriyat Maariv, 1978

Silnitzky, F. 'Hatefisa haleumit shel haleninism vehabaya hayehudit' ('Leninism's Concept of Nationalism and the Jewish Problem'), in *Shevut* 2, 19 (1974)

Yodfat, A. *Brit Hamoatsot Vehamisrakh Hatikhon* ('The USSR and the Middle East'), Tel Aviv: Maarakhot, Defense Ministry, 1973

idem, 'Hayehudim hasovietiim kegorem beyakhasei Brit Hamoatsot-Israel' ('Soviet Jews as a Factor in Soviet–Israeli Relations'), in *Gesher* 1–2 (1978)

idem, 'Yakhasei Israel-Brit Hamoatsot miyemot Stalin ad Milchemet Sheshet Hayamim' ('Israel-Soviet Relations from Stalin's Death to the Six Day War'), in *Shevut* 1 (1973)

Zak, M. *40 Shnot Du-Siach im Moskva* ('Israel and the Soviet Union, a Forty-years Dialogue'), Tel Aviv: Sifriyat Maariv, 1988

Periodicals and dailies

al Hamishmar; *Bamahane*; *Behinot*; *Davar*; *Haaretz*; *Haintelligentsia Hayehudit Bivrit Hamoatsot*; *Kol Haam*; *Maariv*; *Shevut*

Documentary and archival material

Archive of the Israel Minister of Foreign Affairs
Archive of Mapai (Israeli Labor Party)
Divrei Haknesset (Israeli Parliament Verbatim)

ENGLISH SOURCES

Books and articles

Alexander, Z. 'Immigration to Israel from the USSR', *Israeli Yearbook on Human Rights* 7 (1977)

Brecher, M. *Decisions in Israel's Foreign Policy*, Oxford: Oxford University Press, 1973

Confino, M., and S. Shamir (eds.), *The USSR and the Middle East*, Tel Aviv: Israeli Universities Press, 1973

Conquest, R. *The National Killers: the Soviet Deportation of Nationalities*, London: Macmillan, 1970

idem, *Power and Policy in the USSR*, Soviet Dynamics, London: Macmillan, 1961

Dagan, A. *Moscow and Jerusalem*, London: Abelard & Schuman, 1970

Edelstein, M. 'The 1965 Split in Maki and the CPSU', in *Soviet Jewish Affairs*, 4:1 (1979), pp. 23–38

Ettinger, S. 'Historical Roots of Anti-Semitism in the USSR', in *Anti-Semitism in the USSR*, 2, The Hebrew University of Jerusalem, 1980, pp. 45–54

Hazan, B. *A Case Study of the Middle East Conflict*, Jerusalem: Keter, 1976

Heikal, H. *Sphinx and Commissar: the Rise and Fall of Soviet Influence in the Arab World*, London: Collins, 1978

Krushchev, N. *Krushchev Remembers*, London: Andre Deutsch, 1971

Lahav, V. 'The Soviet Attitude towards the Split in the Israeli Communist Party 1964–1967', Research Paper 39, The Soviet and East-European Research Centre, The Hebrew University of Jerusalem, 1980

London, I. 'Evolution of the USSR's Policy in the Middle East, 1950–1956', *Middle East Affairs*, May 1956

Raanan, U. *The USSR Arms in the Third World*, Cambridge, MA: MIT Press, 1969, pp. 13–172

Redlich, S. 'Jewish Appeals in the USSR: an Expression of National Revival', in *Soviet Jewish Affairs* 4:2 (1974), pp. 24–37

Ro'i, Y. *From Encroachment to Involvement: Documentary Study of Soviet Policy in the Middle East, 1945–1973*, Tel Aviv: Israeli Universities Press, 1979

idem. 'Soviet Policies and Attitudes towards Israel 1948–1978, an overview', in *Soviet Jewish Affairs* 8:1 (1978)

Ro'i, Y. (ed.). *The Limits to Power: Soviet Policy in the Middle East*, London: Croom Helm, 1979

Rubinstein, Z. A. (ed.). *The Foreign Policy of the Soviet Union*, New York: Random House, 1968

Voronel, A. 'The Search for Jewish Identity in Russia', in *Soviet Jewish Affairs* 5:2 (1974), pp. 69–74

Periodicals and monitoring services

BBC Monitoring Service, *Summary of the World Broadcasts, Part 1, The USSR*; *Foreign Affairs*; *Jews in Eastern Europe*; *Problems of Communism*; *Soviet Jewish Affairs*

Documentary material

Documents on International Affairs, London

International Documents on Palestine, Beirut

History of the Communist Party of the Soviet Union, Moscow

Human Rights in the Soviet Union, Parliament of the Commonwealth of Australia, Report of the Joint Committee on Foreign Affairs and Defence, Canberra, 1979

UN General Assembly, Official Records

UN Security Council, Official Records

The USSR and the Middle East, Problems of Peace and Security 1947–1971, Moscow: Novosti Press, 1972

RUSSIAN SOURCES

Books and articles

Burmistrova, T. 'Nektorie voprosy teorii natsii' ('Some questions about the theory of nation'), in *Voprosy Historii* 12 (1966)

Dzhunusov, M. 'Natsia kak sotsialno-etnicheskaya obschnost liudei' ('The nation as a socio-ethnic community of people'), in *Vosprosy Historii* 4 (1966)

Gafurov, B. *Nekotorie voprosy natsionalnoy politiki KPSS* ('Some questions on the nationality policy of the CPSU'), Moscow: 1959

idem, 'Uspekhi natsionalnoy politiki KPSS' ('The successes of the nationality policy of the CPSU'), in *Kommunist* 11 (1958)

Ivanov, K., and Z. Scheiniss, *Gosudarstvo Izrail* ('The State of Israel'), Moscow: 1958

Kozlov, V. 'Nekotorie problemy teorii natsii' ('Some problems about the theory of a nation'), in *Voprosy Historii* 1 (1967)

idem, 'O poniatii etnicheskikh obshchnostei' ('On ethnic communities'), in *Sovetskaya Etnografia* 2 (1967)

Mikunis, Sh. 'Prozrenie' ('Enlightenment'), in *Vremya i my* 48 (Jan. 1980) pp. 140–57

Nikitina, G. S. *Gosudarstvo Izrail* ('The State of Israel'), Moscow: 1968

Rogochev, P. M., and M. A. Sverdlin, 'O ponyatii natsii' ('On the Concept of Nationality'), in *Voprosy Historii* 1 (1966)

Tokarev, S. A. 'Problemy tipov etnicheskikh obshchnostey' ('Problems of Characterization of Ethnic Groups'), in *Voprosy Filosofii* 11 (1964)

Tsameryan, I. 'Actualnie voprosy Marxistko-Leninskoy theorii natsii' ('Actual questions on Marxist-Leninist theory of nation'), in *Voprosy Historii* 6 (1967)

idem, *Sovetskoye mnogonatsionalnoe gosudarstvo* ('Soviet multi-national state'), Moscow: Academy of Sciences, 1958

Zhukov, E. M. '22 s'ezd KPSS i zadachi sovetskikh istorikov' ('22nd Congress of the CPSU and the Role of Soviet Historians'), in *Voprosy Historii* 12 (1961)

Periodicals and dailies

Evreii I Evreyski Narod (Jews and the Jewish People); *Izvestia*; *Kommunist*; *Krassnaya Zvezda* (Red Star); *Mezhdunarodnaya Zhizn* (International Life); *Novoe Vremya* (New Times); *Pravda*; *Voprosy Historii* (Historical Questions)

References

Bolshaya Sovetskaya Encyclopedia ('The Great Soviet Encyclopedia') 2nd edition (1952), Vol. 15, pp. 372–8; Vol. 29, pp. 291–300; 3rd edition (1972), Vol. 9, pp. 110–14; Vol. 17, p. 375

Mezhdunarodnye Otnoshenia posle vtoroy mirovoy voiny ('International Relations after the Second World War') 1–3, Moscow: 1962

Politicheski Slovar ('Political Dictionary'), Moscow: 1958

Sovetskiy Soyuz i OON ('The USSR and the United Nations'), Moscow: 1965

I. V. Stalin, *Sochinenie* ('Works'), Vol. 2, pp. 296–7; Vol. 7, pp. 138–40; Vol. 11, pp. 333–40

Vneshnyaya Politica SSSR na novom etape ('Soviet Foreign Policy on a New Stage'), Moscow: 1964

Index

political relations, 242–8, 255–7, 276
purchase of US combat planes, 285, 286, 287
response to Soviet proposal on demilitarization, 265–7
response to Soviet reaction statement on Arab–Israeli conflict, 233–4
security needs, 37, 68, 227–8, 229, 251, 257, 258–9 n.3
seen as servant of Western interests, 16, 74
seen as spokesman of Soviet Jews, 12, 15
Sinai Campaign, 243, 244
sources of assistance, 38
Soviet description of, 74–5
struggle for Soviet Jewry, 31, 32, 39, 40, 41, 57, 58, 79, 93, 120, 179, 180–218
Israel Defense Forces, xi, 8
Israel Embassy in Moscow, xi, xii, xxiii, xxvii, 3, 57, 171–4
dissemination of information on Israel, 173, 204, 205
Israel Independence Day celebration at, 70
visits to Jewish centers, 173–4
Israel–Egypt Armistice Agreement, 311
Israel Ministry of Foreign Affairs, xviii, 6, 55–8
Israel Philharmonic Orchestra, 115, 116, 117 n.9
Israel–Soviet relations, bilateral, 33 n.5, 178, 264–5, 274, 328–30
break after Six Day War, 320–5, 326
Jewish factor in, 55–8
level of representation, 64
political dialogue, 72, 73
trade, xxxiii, 46–7, 63, 97–110, 242
Israel–Soviet relations, cultural, 53, 111–17, 201, 209, 331
Israel Independence Day celebration, 70
USSR Agricultural Exhibition (1954), 64
Davar editor visitor to USSR, 64
Soviet objectives, 113
Israel–Soviet relations, economic/trade, xxxiii, 46–7, 53, 63, 97–110, 242, 331
Israel–Soviet relations, political, xi–xviii, xx–xxi, xxxv, 3–8, 28, 37–83
ideological conflict, 12, 14, 15–16
motivation for breaking, 9–10, 12, 16, 17, 26–7
psychological factor, 16–17
renewal (1953), 28–33, 40–2
Israel–Soviet relations, scientific, 53

Israeli Communist Party, xxii, xxviii, 9, 83, 90
Israeli–Arab conflict, 39, 42, 61, 65, 76, 77, 81, 86, 90, 91, 224, 267, 276–96, 326, 331
call for settlement of, 48, 64, 68, 70, 89, 237
Soviet media description of, 89
Soviet proposal for settling, 265–75, 327–8
Soviet statement on settlement of, 231–7
status of USSR in solving, 226
Ivanov, K., 74, 91

Jerusalem, xiii, xxx, 266, 331
East, 327
Jewish Agency, 130, 204
Jewish Anti-Fascist Committee, xxiii, xxiv, 157, 169
Jewish Arab state, xx
Jewish Commissariat, 156
Jewish Council, 156
Jewish emigration from the Soviet Union, xii, xv, xviii, xxix, xxxi, xxxiii, 43, 81–2, 86, 118–48, 170, 201, 209, 210
emigration, 327, 331
call for, 9, 41, 52, 182, 189, 191, 194, 226
Jewish factor, xvi, 7
Jewish 'Kultur Gesellschaft' (Culture Society; Poland), 142
Jewish people, xix–xxii, xxiv, xxix, xxxii–xxxiv, 38
past in Middle East, 266, 267
Jewish problem, USSR, 92, 106, 139, 206
Jewish question, 76, 77, 188
solution to the, 75
Jewish Sections in the Soviet Communist Party, 156
Jewish State Theater, 157, 166, 206, 209
Jews, 266
as 'cosmopolitan', 16
in definition of nationality, 154–8
Johnson, Lyndon B., 215, 216–17 n.18, 324
Johnston's Plan, 64
Jordan, xxiv, 240, 255, 256, 257, 282, 291, 305
Jordan River, diverting water from, 63, 89, 295
Judaism, 7
Judea, 328

Kaspi, M., 89
Katz, K., xix, 87–8, 292, 296
Kennedy, Robert, 215
Khartoum Conference (1967), 324–5

Khrushchev, N., 64, 65–6, 67, 123, 146
  nn.9,25,27, 191, 195, 203, 216 n.14,
  236, 237, 246, 267–8, 269, 270, 272,
  273
  on Baghdad Pact, 231
Kisselev, K., xxvi
Kitchko, T., 209
Knesset, xix, xxviii, xxxiv, xxxv, 4–6
  Committee for Foreign and Security
    Affairs, 13, 18, 52
  debate on USSR attitude to Israel, 9,
    12
  see also Ben Gurion, Eshkol, Meir
Kol Zion Lagola broadcasts, 175, 176 n.9
Konset, 156
Korea, 24, 28
Kosygin, A., 91, 109, 115, 125, 127, 278,
  280, 310, 311, 318, 324
Kuneitra (Syria), 320
Kuznetzov, V., 107

Lapin, S., 105
Latvia, 158
Lebanon, 255, 256, 257, 288
Leibovich, S., 216 n.3
Lenin, V., 15, 91, 92
  theory on Jewish nation, 14, 151–4, 167
    n.14
Levavi, Aryeh, 325 n.8
Levavi, L., 293
Levin, A., xiii
Lithuania, 158

Madrid Peace Conference (1991), 330
MAGEN (immigration organization), 122,
  216
Maievski, M., 317
Maki (Israel Communist Party), 9, 21 n.14,
  32, 80, 81, 83, 85, 112
Malenkov, G., 27, 32, 62
Malik, J., xxx, 282, 283
Malinovskii, Marshal, 306
Mapai (Israel Labor Party), xxx, 38, 47, 50,
  61, 78, 90, 112
  criticizing USSR 11, 52
  Political Committee, 227–8
Mapam, 9, 13, 22 n.20, 93
Marshall Plan, xxvii–xxviii
  matzah, permission to bake, 162, 209
McArthur, 8
Mediterranean Sea, importance for USSR,
  221
Meir, G., xxiii–xxiv, xxvi, xxviii, xxix, 38,
  45, 47–8, 57, 82, 83, 104, 117 n.2,
  198, 259 n.10, 270, 271, 274
  ambassador to Moscow, 171

on Israel policy towards USSR, 47–8
  at UN, 19–20
Meyerson, Golda *see* Meir, Golda
Middle East Command, xxxii, xxxiii, 8,
  119, 223–7, 253
Middle East Pact, 42, 43
Mikoyan, A., 87, 146 n.24
Mikunis, Sh., xxviii, 85
military alliances, Middle East, 30, 31–2,
  68, 70, 71, 222, 227–31, 236, 237,
  253–4, 262
Ministry of Education and Culture, Israel,
  week of identification with Jews of
  USSR, 208
Moldavia, 158
Molotov, M., xxii, 27, 30, 31, 32, 42, 43, 58
  n.9, 64, 65, 66–7
Moscow Radio, 24

Namir, M., xxvi, xxix
Nasser, Gamal Abdul, 44, 134, 241, 248,
  271, 272, 306–8, 309, 311, 313, 315
  n.23, 316 n.30, 317, 319, 321, 324,
  325 n.2
National Question, 75, 151–68, 175
  'declaration of principles', 152
nationalism, 175
NATO, 24, 38, 77, 221, 224, 225, 227, 261,
  262, 265
Nazi Germany, xix
Nazi invaders, xxv, 221
Nazi-occupied areas, xx
Negev, xxiv
Nicolayev, 78
Nikitina, G. S., 73, 75
North Korea, xxxi, xxxii
nuclear weapons, 85, 265, 266

Odessa, 98
oil, 50, 109
  Soviet sales to Israel, 99–103, 242
Oren, M., 22 n.20

Pakistan, 255
Palestine, xx–xxii, xxx
Palestine Liberation Organization (PLO)
  and PLO Covenant, 84, 207, 326,
  328
'Palestine Problem', USSR approach to, 91,
  299
Palestine Question, xx, xxi
Palestinian Arabs, 277, 278, 279
  support by USSR, 94, 96 n.48
  terrorists, 309
Panyushkin, xxvii
peace, 54, 68, 226, 264, 266

For Product Safety Concerns and Information please contact our EU
representative GPSR@taylorandfrancis.com
Taylor & Francis Verlag GmbH, Kaufingerstraße 24, 80331 München, Germany

www.ingramcontent.com/pod-product-compliance
Ingram Content Group UK Ltd.
Pitfield, Milton Keynes, MK11 3LW, UK
UKHW021444080625
459435UK00011B/366